# SQL Tuning

*Dan Tow*

O'REILLY®

Beijing · Cambridge · Farnham · Köln · Paris · Sebastopol · Taipei · Tokyo

**SQL Tuning**
by Dan Tow

Copyright © 2004 O'Reilly & Associates, Inc. All rights reserved.
Printed in the United States of America.

Published by O'Reilly & Associates, Inc., 1005 Gravenstein Highway North, Sebastopol, CA 95472.

O'Reilly & Associates books may be purchased for educational, business, or sales promotional use. Online editions are also available for most titles (*safari.oreilly.com*). For more information, contact our corporate/institutional sales department: (800) 998-9938 or *corporate@oreilly.com*.

| | |
|---|---|
| **Editor:** | Jonathan Gennick |
| **Production Editor:** | Brian Sawyer |
| **Cover Designer:** | Ellie Volckhausen |
| **Interior Designer:** | Melanie Wang |

**Printing History:**

    November 2003:   First Edition.

ISBN: 0-596-00573-3
[M]

# SQL Tuning

# Other SQL resources from O'Reilly

**Related titles**
Optimizing Oracle
  Performance
Mastering Oracle SQL
SQL in a Nutshell
Oracle SQL Tuning Pocket
  Reference

MySQL Cookbook
Oracle SQL*Plus Pocket
  Reference
Oracle SQL*Plus: The
  Definitive Guide
Oracle in a Nutshell

**Database Books
Resource Center**
*db.oreilly.com* is a complete catalog of O'Reilly's books on databases and related technologies, including sample chapters and code examples.

*oreillynet.com* is the essential portal for developers interested in open and emerging technologies, including new platforms, programming languages, and operating systems.

**Conferences**
O'Reilly & Associates brings diverse innovators together to nurture the ideas that spark revolutionary industries. We specialize in documenting the latest tools and systems, translating the innovator's knowledge into useful skills for those in the trenches. Visit *conferences.oreilly.com* for our upcoming events.

Safari Bookshelf (*safari.oreilly.com*) is the premier online reference library for programmers and IT professionals. Conduct searches across more than 1,000 books. Subscribers can zero in on answers to time-critical questions in a matter of seconds. Read the books on your Bookshelf from cover to cover or simply flip to the page you need. Try it today with a free trial.

*To Parva, Tira, and Abe,*
*for a dream of more,*
*and a life surpassing the dream*

# Table of Contents

# Foreword

During my years as a developer, and later as a database administrator, the only performance tuning area in which I developed any expertise and had any level of success was that of tuning individual SQL statements. Because of that background, I was very interested when Dan Tow came to me with his idea for a book on SQL tuning.

The problem with SQL tuning, at least from my own perspective, is that it was often reasonably easy to pinpoint badly performing SQL statements that needed to be tuned, and it was reasonably easy to determine the execution plan currently being used for those badly performing statements, but then came the hard problem: finding a better execution plan, to make an offending SQL statement execute faster. Many is the time I've stared at a poorly performing SQL statement, reviewing its poorly performing execution plan, and wondered just what I should do next. For that matter, was there even any room for improvement? Perhaps the execution plan that performed so badly from a user's perspective was, in fact, the best possible execution plan. Perhaps I was wasting my time trying to guess at a better one.

There, I used that word *guess*, and that's at the heart of what sometimes made tuning SQL statements a frustrating activity. It all came down to my looking at a SQL statement and trying to guess at a better plan. Of course, I'd attempt to factor in my experience, my intuition, and my knowledge of the data being queried, and I'd pull out tips and tricks that I'd read about in books and magazine articles, but in the end I'd make a guess, try a new plan, make a guess, try a new plan, and so forth. I'd stop when one of two things happened:

- I got lucky and guessed a plan that was a good-enough improvement over the old plan to satisfy my client.
- I ran out of ideas.

It always bothered me when I ran out of ideas, because I never knew for sure whether the current plan really was optimal or whether I was just too thick-headed to intuit a better-performing execution plan than the current one. To be honest, I was always pretty hard on myself, chalking up any failure to improve a SQL statement as a personal inadequacy.

Dan doesn't guess. Let me boldface that and underline it. He doesn't execute an iterative guess-loop like I did, trying one idea after another in the hope of stumbling across an improvement. Instead, Dan uses an innovative and mathematically based diagramming method to derive the optimal, or near-optimal, execution plan for a SQL statement. Then he puts that plan into effect. And that's it. There's no guesswork, and there's no uncertainty as to whether further improvement is possible.

At first, I was skeptical of Dan's approach. But the more I read his chapters, the more I began to see the logic behind his method. Math doesn't lie, and experience is a good indicator. Dan has over 10 years of tuning experience, and he's been very successful using the method described in this book.

There are three legs that any SQL tuning effort needs to stand on. You need to know how to identify a badly performing SQL statement. You then need to be able to see the execution plan used for that statement. Finally, you need to somehow come up with an improved plan. I'm convinced that Dan's method represents a viable third leg on which your SQL tuning efforts can rest. Read his book, apply his method, and save yourself hours of wondering what to do next.

—Jonathan Gennick, author, editor, Oracle DBA

# Preface

*The seaman's story is of tempest, the plowman's of his
team of bulls; the soldier tells his wounds, the
shepherd his tail of sheep.*
—Sextus Propertius
*Elegies*

More than 10 years ago, I came to understand that the biggest factor in the performance of a business application is the speed of the SQL it runs. It took me longer to realize just how much room for improvement typically lies in that SQL. The SQL that most effects the load on a system and the productivity of its end users can usually be improved by a large factor, usually by a factor of two or more. However, I found little guidance regarding just how to tune SQL. I believe that problem persists today.

Academic journals describe detailed methods that are suitable for automated optimization, but these methods are not adapted for manual tuning. Documentation for the practitioner, so far as I've seen, is incomplete. Database vendors and independent authors document well how to review the path the database takes to reach the data. (The path to the data is known as the *execution plan*.) Armed with the execution plan, you can understand why a query runs as long as it does. With varied success, the documentation also covers what you can do to change an execution plan, if you suspect that it is not optimal. The missing part in the literature is a detailed manual process to deduce, without endless trial and error, exactly which execution plan you should *want*. Since real business-application queries can easily offer billions of alternative execution plans, tuning without a systematic method to choose your target execution plan is hopelessly inefficient. The problem is akin to finding yourself lost in a strange city without a map: working eyes and legs are not enough to take you where you need to go.

The missing piece of the problem, how to choose the best execution plan, turns out to be virtually independent of your choice of database vendor. This presents a wonderful opportunity for a single book on SQL tuning that is 80% vendor-independent, because 80% of the book has nothing to do with the uninteresting details of viewing and manipulating execution plans with vendor-specific methods. I wrote this book to fulfill that opportunity and to enable you to approach SQL tuning with this powerful, vendor-independent approach.

## Objectives of This Book

I designed this book to equip you to respond correctly to any SQL tuning problem. The narrowest and most common solution to a SQL tuning problem is a prescription for some combination of changes to the database (for example, new indexes) and, more often, changes to the SQL itself. These changes allow the formerly slow statement to run faster, with no changes in functionality and no change in the calling application, except in the SQL itself. This common solution is especially attractive, because it is usually simple and it rarely has unintended side effects.

Occasionally, when you analyze a SQL tuning problem, you discover symptoms that generally indicate a subtle functional defect that goes hand in hand with the performance defect. The method of tuning analysis I describe makes those subtle functional defects particularly easy to identify and describe, and helps you prescribe solutions that fix corner-case functional defects as a side effect of your performance analysis. This book focuses mainly on tuning, however. If you are on Oracle, you can find good advice on getting your SQL functionally correct in Sanjay Mishra's and Alan Beaulieu's book *Mastering Oracle SQL* (O'Reilly & Associates, Inc.).

Rarely, a SQL tuning problem cannot be solved just by speeding up one query; the query returns too many rows, or it runs too frequently to ever run as fast as it must, even fully optimized. For these rare problems, I describe systematic solutions in the application layer that change the problem model, creating a new problem that has ready solutions.

## Audience for This Book

I wrote this book for anyone who already knows SQL but, at least sometimes, needs to find ways to make SQL run faster. Traditionally, the same people who write the SQL in the first place, the application developers, do most SQL tuning. Certainly, I hope this book helps developers solve their own tuning problems, especially the most common types of problems. However, from my own experience as a tuning specialist, I find that it is at least equally efficient to tune other people's SQL. Fortunately, SQL provides a clear spec for which rows an application requires at a given point, and you needn't have any application-specific knowledge at all to determine a faster path to reach those same rows. Since the tuner needs no knowledge of the application, it is easy to tune SQL written by other people, and a specialist has the opportunity to learn to tune more efficiently than any nonspecialist could, especially when dealing with the hardest problems.

# Structure of This Book

For your own purposes, you might not need to read this book in order, cover to cover. The following summary should help you work out which parts of the book you can skip or skim, which parts you can reserve for occasional reference, and which parts you should read thoroughly, in which order:

Chapter 1, *Introduction*

Provides an overview of the motivation for SQL tuning and the approach this book takes to the problem, as well as some side benefits that come with following that approach. This chapter is short and easy, and I recommend you read it first.

Chapter 2, *Data-Access Basics*

Describes how databases access individual tables with full table scans and indexed reads, how databases join tables, and the tradeoffs between these alternatives. If you already know the basics of how databases execute queries, you might be able to skip or skim this chapter.

Chapter 3, *Viewing and Interpreting Execution Plans*

Covers how to read and interpret an execution plan on Oracle, Microsoft SQL Server, and DB2. If you have done any SQL tuning at all, you likely already know this for whatever database concerns you. Chapter 3 also separates the coverage of each database and even repeats material that applies to more than one database, so you need to read only the section or sections that matter to you.

Chapter 4, *Controlling Execution Plans*

Covers how to control execution plans on Oracle, Microsoft SQL Server, and DB2. This discussion includes some generic techniques that provide some control of execution plans on any relational database. If you have done significant SQL tuning, you might already know how to control execution plans for whatever database concerns you. Like Chapter 3, Chapter 4 also separates the coverage of each database and even repeats material that applies to more than one database, so you need to read only the section or sections that matter to you.

Chapter 5, *Diagramming Simple SQL Queries*

Covers the foundation for the rest of the book, which won't even make sense unless you read this chapter first. This chapter introduces a shorthand, pictorial language that greatly clarifies the core of a SQL tuning problem. Chapter 5 lays a foundation that makes the rest of the book far clearer and more concise than it could be without this pictorial language. Read the chapter and learn the pictorial language well before you read the rest of the book. (The language takes some patience to learn, but it is worth it!)

Chapter 6, *Deducing the Best Execution Plan*

Explains how to use the query diagrams you learned to make in Chapter 5 to tune 2-way, 5-way, even 115-way joins rapidly, without trial and error. This is the big payoff, so don't stop before you understand this material.

Chapter 7, *Diagramming and Tuning Complex SQL Queries*
Shows you how to tune complex queries such as queries containing subqueries that do not fit the standard, simple, *n*-way-join template. As a bonus, this chapter will also describe how to diagnose and repair logic problems with the SQL (as opposed to performance problems) that become obvious once you know how to build and interpret the query diagrams.

Chapter 8, *Why the Diagramming Method Works*
Justifies the rules of thumb I discuss in Chapters 5–7. If you don't quite trust me, or if you just think you would apply this book's method better if you had an understanding of why the method works, this chapter should help. You might even want to read this chapter early if you are losing patience with rote application of mysterious rules earlier in the book.

Chapter 9, *Special Cases*
Covers advanced material you might refer to only as problems arise, if you would rather not read so much cover-to-cover. However, I recommend at least skimming this chapter to learn what is there, so you can recognize the problems when you see them.

Chapter 10, *Outside-the-Box Solutions to Seemingly Unsolvable Problems*
Explains how to cope with even "impossible" problems, problems with no fast execution plan capable of delivering the rows required by the original SQL. This material is highly recommended, but I leave it for last because until you know how to get the best execution plan, you cannot recognize which (surprisingly few) problems require these outside-the-box solutions.

Appendix A, *Exercise Solutions*
Provides solutions to the exercises at the ends of Chapters 5, 6, and 7.

Appendix B, *The Full Process, End to End*
Follows the solution of a SQL tuning problem through the whole diagramming method, from start to finish, on Oracle, DB2, and SQL Server. If you like to work from complete, end-to-end examples, this appendix is for you.

*Glossary*
Defines key terms and phrases used in the book.

## Conventions Used in This Book

The following typographical conventions are used in this book:

*Italic*
Used for emphasis, for the first use of a technical term, for URLs, and for file and directory names.

Constant width
Used for SQL examples, file contents, and examples of output.

Hungarian_Constant_Width

Used for table and column names, whether in SQL or referring to SQL from within the body of a paragraph. Also used for alias names and *node names*, which are elements in a SQL diagram that theoretically refer to table aliases, even when a diagram sometimes shows an abstract tuning problem without referring to a specific SQL statement that corresponds to that problem. Since aliases are usually made an acronym based on a table name, such as CT for the column Code_Translations, aliases are usually pure uppercase.

(C, O, OT, OD, ODT, P, S, A)

A constant-width list of aliases, node names, or columns, bounded in parentheses. I borrow this *n-tuple* notation from mathematics to indicate an ordered list of items. In the example case, the notation describes a join order between nodes in a join diagram, representing table aliases. In another example, (Code_Type, Code) would represent a pair of indexed columns in a two-column index, with Code_Type as the first column. Alternately, Code_Translations(Code_Type, Code) represents the same index, while specifying that it is on the table Code_Translations.

<Constant_Width_Italic>

Constant-width italic text inside angle brackets describes missing portions of a SQL statement template, which you must fill in, that represents a whole class of statements. For example, SomeAlias.Leading_Indexed_Column=<Expression> represents any equality condition matching the leading column of an index with any other expression.

UPPERCASE

In SQL, uppercase indicates keywords, function names, and tables or views predefined by the database vendor (such as Oracle's PLAN_TABLE).

Pay special attention to notes set apart from the text with the following icons:

Indicates a general note, tip, or suggestion. For example, I sometimes use notes for asides specific to a particular database vendor, in the midst of an otherwise vendor-independent discussion.

Indicates a warning, used to point out special pitfalls I've seen relating to the current discussion.

# Comments and Questions

We at O'Reilly have tested and verified the information in this book to the best of our ability, but you may find that features have changed or that we have made mistakes. If so, please notify us by writing to:

O'Reilly & Associates, Inc.
1005 Gravenstein Highway North
Sebastopol, CA 95472
(800) 998-9938 (in the U.S. or Canada)
(707) 829-0515 (international or local)
(707) 829-0104 (fax)

You can also send messages electronically. To be put on the mailing list or request a catalog, send email to:

*info@oreilly.com*

To ask technical questions or comment on the book, send email to:

*bookquestions@oreilly.com*

We have an online catalog page for this book, where you can find examples and errata (previously reported errors and corrections are available for public view there). You can access this page at:

*http://www.oreilly.com/catalog/sqltuning/*

For more information about this book and others, see the O'Reilly web site:

*http://www.oreilly.com*

Readers who would like to contact the author to ask questions or discuss this book, SQL tuning, or other related topics can reach him at *dantow@singingsql.com*. You can also find the author's home page on the Web at *http://www.singingsql.com*.

# Acknowledgments

I owe my parents, Lois and Philip, scientists both, for the example they set in all aspects of their lives. My thesis advisor, Dale Rudd, showed me the highest example of keeping both eyes on the big picture, never missing an opportunity to solve the real, underlying problem for having too-narrowly defined a problem for immediate attack. My brother Bruce paved my way to relational databases and has always shared his knowledge generously.

My former manager Roy Camblin, who was CIO of Oracle at the time, pushed me to find a simple set of rules to teach SQL tuning, when I didn't know such rules myself. The rules are not so simple, but, to paraphrase Einstein, they are as simple as they *can* be. Oracle gave me the liberty to develop the rules in depth, and TenFold Corporation gave me the opportunity to see firsthand how well they applied across all relational databases. TenFold Corporation further provided generous access to test databases to verify the vendor-specific behavior that I describe in this book.

I owe a special debt of gratitude to Jonathan Gennick, the editor of this book. Jonathan lent his expert hand at all levels, catching technical glitches, correcting the organization of the material when needed, and simply making the language work. His excellent, patient, and well-explained feedback not only made this a much better book, but also made me a much better writer by the end.

Taj Johnson, David Ozenne, Dave Hunt, Alexei Chadovich, and Jeff Walker provided generous and valuable technical assistance—thank you all! For generous help to get the technical content right, I give special thanks to my two technical reviewers, both excellent and experienced practitioners, Virag Saksena and Alan Beaulieu. Any mistakes that remain are all mine, of course.

Since this book is more than just words on pages, I thank the skillful staff at O'Reilly and Associates: Brian Sawyer, the production editor and copyeditor; Robert Romano and Jessamyn Read, the very patient illustrators; Ellie Volckhausen, the cover designer; Melanie Wang, the interior designer; Julie Hawks, who converted the files; Matt Hutchinson, the proofreader; Darren Kelly and Claire Cloutier, who provided quality control, and Angela Howard, the indexer.

Finally, I owe my wife, Parva, and my children, Tira and Abe, for their endless patience and faith in me, and for giving me the best of reasons to achieve all that I can.

# CHAPTER 1

# Introduction

*Well begun is half done.*
— Aristotle
*Politics, Bk. V, Ch. 4*

This book is for readers who already know SQL and have an opportunity to tune SQL or the database where the SQL executes. It includes specific techniques for tuning on Oracle, Microsoft SQL Server, and IBM DB2. However, the main problem of SQL tuning is finding the optimum path to the data. (The path to the data is known as the *execution plan*.) This optimum path is virtually independent of the database vendor, and most of this book covers a vendor-independent solution to that problem.

The least interesting, easiest parts of the SQL tuning problem are vendor-specific techniques for viewing and controlling execution plans. For completeness, this book covers these parts of SQL tuning as well, for Oracle, Microsoft SQL Server, and IBM DB2. Even on other databases, though (and on the original databases, as new releases bring change), the vendor-independent core of this book will still apply. As such, this book is fairly universal and timeless, as computer science texts go. I have used the method at the core of this book for 10 years, on four different vendors' databases, and I expect it to apply for at least another 10 years. You can always use your own vendor's current documentation (usually available online) to review the comparatively simple, release-dependent, vendor-specific techniques for viewing and controlling execution plans.

## Why Tune SQL?

Let's begin with a basic question: should someone tune the SQL in an application, and is that someone you? Since you are reading this book, your answer is at least moderately inclined to the positive side. Since it took me several years to appreciate just how positive my own answer to this question should be, though, this chapter lays my own viewpoint on the table as an example.

Let's describe your application, sight-unseen, from an admittedly datacentric point of view: it exists to allow human beings or possibly another application to see, and possibly to enter and manipulate, in a more or less massaged form, data that your organization stores in a relational database. On the output data, it performs manipulations like addition, multiplication, counting, averaging, sorting, and formatting, operations such as those you would expect to see in a business spreadsheet. It does not solve differential equations or do any other operations in which you might perform billions of calculations even on a compact set of inputs. The work the application must do *after* it gets data out of the database, or *before* it puts data into the database, is modest by modern computing standards, because the data volumes handled outside of the database are modest, and the outside-the-database calculation load per datapoint is modest.

> Online applications and applications that produce reports for human consumption should produce data volumes fit for human consumption, which are paltry for a computer to handle. *Middleware*, moving data from one system to another without human intervention, can handle higher data volumes, but even middleware usually performs some sort of aggregation function, reducing data volumes to comparatively modest levels.

Even if the vast number of end users leads to high calculation loads outside the database, you can generally throw hardware at the application load (the load outside the database, that is), hanging as many application servers as necessary off the single central database. (This costs money, but I assume that a system to support, say, 50,000 simultaneous end users is supported by a substantial budget.)

On the other hand the database behind a business application often examines millions of rows in the database just to return the few rows that satisfy an application query, and this inefficiency can completely dominate the overall system load and performance. Furthermore, while you might easily add application servers, it is usually much harder to put multiple database servers to work on the same consistent set of business data for the same application, so throughput limits on the database server are much more critical. It is imperative to make your system fit your business volumes, not the other way around

Apart from these theoretical considerations, my own experience in over 13 years of performance and tuning, is that the database—more specifically, the SQL from the application—is the best place to look for performance and throughput improvements.

Improvements to SQL performance tend to be the safest changes you can make to an application, least likely to break the application somewhere else, and they help both performance and throughput, with no hardware cost or minimal cost at worst (in the case of added indexes, which require disk space). I hope that by the end of this book you will also be persuaded that the labor cost of tuning SQL is minimal, given expertise in the method this book describes. The benefit-to-cost ratio is so high that all significant database-based applications should have their high-load SQL tuned.

## Performance Versus Throughput

Performance and throughput are related, but not identical. For example, on a well-configured system with (on average) some idle processors (CPUs), adding CPUs might increase throughput capacity but would have little effect on performance, since most processes cannot use more than a single CPU at a time. Faster CPUs help both throughput and performance of a CPU-intensive application, but you likely already have about the fastest CPUs you can find. Getting faster SQL is much like getting faster CPUs, without additional hardware cost.

Performance problems translate to lost productivity, as end users waste time waiting for the system. You can throw money at poor performance by hiring more end users, making up for each end user's reduced productivity, rather than leave the work undone. Over short periods, end users can, unhappily, work through a performance problem by working longer hours.

You have fewer options to solve a throughput problem. You can eliminate the bottleneck (for example, add CPUs) if you are not already at the system limit, or you can tune the application, including, especially, its SQL. If you cannot do either, then the system will process less load than you want. You cannot solve the problem by throwing more end users at it or by expecting those end users to tolerate the rotten performance that results on load-saturated systems. (CPUs do not negotiate. if your business requires more CPU cycles than the CPUs deliver, they cannot be motivated to work harder.) If you cannot tune the system or eliminate nonessential load, this amounts to cutting your business off at the knees to make it fit the system and is the worst possible result, potentially costing a substantial fraction of your revenue.

# Who Should Tune SQL?

So, you are persuaded that SQL tuning is a good idea. Should you be the one to do it, on your system? Chances are that you originated at most a small fraction of the SQL on your system, since good-sized teams develop most systems. You might even—like me, in most of my own history—be looking at an application for which you wrote none of the SQL and were not even responsible for the database design. I assumed for years that the developers of an application, who wrote the SQL, would always understand far better than I how to fix it. Since I was responsible for performance, anyway, I thought the best I could do was identify which SQL statements triggered the most load, making them most deserving of the effort to tune them. Then it was (I thought) my job to nag the developers to tune their own highest-load SQL. I was horribly, embarrassingly, wrong.

As it turns out, developers who tune only their own SQL are at a serious disadvantage, especially if they have not learned a good, systematic approach to tuning (which has been lacking in the literature). It is hard to write a real-world application that works, functionally, even without worrying about performance at all. The time left over for the average developer to tune SQL is low, and the number of self-built examples that that developer will have to practice on to build tuning expertise is also low.

The method this book teaches is the best I know, a method I designed myself to meet my own needs for tuning SQL from dozens of applications other people wrote. However, if you really want to be a first-rate SQL tuner, the method is not enough. You also need practice—practice on other people's SQL, lots of other people's SQL, whole applications of SQL. But how do you cope with the sheer complexity of entire applications, even entire applications you hardly know? Here is where SQL delivered me, at least, a great surprise: you do not need to understand other people's SQL to tune it!

Treat SQL as a *spec*—a clear and unambiguous declaration of which rows of which tables the application requires at some particular point in a program. (SQL is clear because it was designed for casual use by nonprogrammers. It is necessarily unambiguous; otherwise, the database could not interpret it.) You do not need to know why the application needs those rows, or even what those rows represent. Just treat the rows and tables as abstract, even mathematical, entities. All you need to know or figure out is how to reach those rows faster, and you can learn this by just examining the SQL, tables, and indexes involved, with simple queries to the database that are completely independent of the semantic content of the data. You can then transform the SQL or the database (for example, by adding indexes) in simple ways that guarantee, almost at the level of mathematical proof, that the transformed result will return exactly the same rows in the same order, but following a much better, faster path to the data.

## How This Book Can Help

There are three basic steps to SQL tuning:

1. Figure out which execution plan (path to reach the data your SQL statement demands) you are getting.
2. Change SQL or the database to get a chosen execution plan.
3. Figure out which execution plan is best.

I deliberately show these steps out of logical order to reflect the state of most material written on the subject. Almost everything written about SQL tuning focuses almost exclusively on the first two steps, especially the second. Coverage of the third step is usually limited to a short discussion about when indexed access is preferred to full table scans. The implied SQL tuning process (lacking a systematic approach to the third step) is to repeat step 2, repeatedly tweaking the SQL, until you stumble on an execution plan that is fast enough, and, if you do not find such a plan, to keep going until you utterly lose patience.

Here is an analogy that works pretty well. Understanding the first step gives you a clear windshield; you know where you are. Understanding the second step gives you a working steering wheel; you can go somewhere else. Understanding the third step gives you a map, with marks for both where you are and where you want to be. If you can imagine being in a strange city without street signs, without a map, in a hurry to find your hotel, and without knowing the name of that hotel, you begin to appreciate the problem with the average SQL tuning education. That sounds bad enough, but without a systematic approach to step 3, the SQL tuning problem is even worse than our lost traveler's dilemma: given enough time, the traveler could explore the entire two-dimensional grid of a city's streets, but a 20-way join has about 20! (20 factorial, or $1 \times 2 \times 3 \times 4 \times ... \times 19 \times 20$) possible execution plans, which comes to 2,432,902,008,176,640,000 possibilities to explore. Even your computer cannot complete a trial-and-error search over that kind of search space. For tuning, you need a method that you can handle manually.

With this insight, we can turn the usual process on its head, and lay out a more enlightened process, now expressed in terms of questions:

1. Which execution plan is best, and how can you find it without trial and error?
2. How does the current execution plan differ from the ideal execution plan, if it does?
3. If the difference between the actual and ideal execution plans is enough to matter, how can you change some combination of the SQL and the database to get close enough to the ideal execution plan for the performance that you need?
4. Does the new execution plan deliver the SQL performance you needed and expected?

To be thorough, I cover all of these questions in this book, but by far the most important, and longest, parts of the book are dedicated to answering the first question, finding the best execution plan without trial and error. Furthermore, the range of answers to the first question heavily color my coverage of the third question. For example, since I have never seen a case, and cannot even think of a theoretical case, where the ideal execution plan on Oracle is a sort-merge join, I do not document Oracle's hint for how to force a sort-merge join. (I do explain, though, why you should always prefer a hash join on Oracle anywhere a sort-merge join looks good.)

When we look at the problem of SQL tuning in this new way, we get a surprise benefit: the only really significant part of the problem, deciding which execution plan is best, is virtually independent of our choice of relational database. The best execution plan is still the best execution plan, whether we are executing the statement on Oracle, Microsoft SQL Server, or DB2, so this knowledge is far more useful than anything we learn that is specific to a database vendor. (I even predict that the best execution plan is unlikely to change much in near-future versions of these databases.)

# A Bonus

The method this book describes reduces a query to an abstract representation that contains only the information relevant to tuning.

 I often substitute *query* for *SQL statement*. Most tuning problems, by far, are queries (SELECT statements, that is). Even for the rest, the problem usually lies in a subquery nested inside the problem update or insert.

This is akin to reducing an elaborate word problem in high-school mathematics to a simple, abstract equation, where the solution of the equation is generally almost automatic once you know the necessary math. The abstract representation of a SQL tuning problem, the query diagram, normally takes the form of an upside-down tree, with some numbers attached, as shown in Figure 1-1.

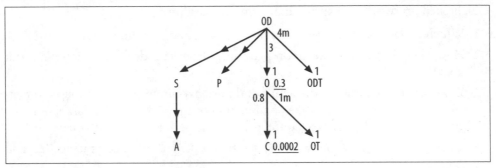

*Figure 1-1. An example of a query diagram*

As it turns out, SQL is such a flexible language that it is capable of producing queries that do not map to the usual tree form, but it turns out that such queries almost never make sense from a business perspective. This delivers an unplanned-for side benefit: in the course of tuning SQL and producing the abstract query representations that aid you in that process, certain problems with the logic of the queries become obvious, even if you have no prior knowledge of the application. Developers usually catch these problems before you see the SQL, unless the problems lie in the sort of corner cases that they might not test thoroughly, as these problems often do. These corner-case problems can be the worst kind for an application—for example, throwing accounts out of balance long after the application goes live and is assumed to be fine, in subtle ways that are hard to detect and hard to fix.

 The worst of these problems will never be found. The business will simply operate based on wrong results, under-billing, over-billing, under-paying, over-paying, or otherwise just doing the wrong thing without anyone tying these problems to a correctable application bug.

---

Sometimes, fixing a performance problem also requires you to fix a logic problem. Even when the problems are independent (when you can fix performance without fixing the logic flaw), you can perform a major added service by identifying these logic flaws and seeing that they are fixed. This book covers these logic flaws at length, including detailed descriptions of how to find each one and what to do about it. I go so far as to recommend you take any significantly complex, manually written SQL through the SQL diagramming exercise just to find these subtle logic errors, even if you already know that it performs well. Depending on the tool, some products that autogenerate SQL avoid most of these problems.

## Outside-the-Box Solutions

Finally, this book discusses outside-the-box solutions: what to do about cases in which you cannot make an individual query fast enough, when treating the query as a spec for what the application requires at that point, just tuning that single query, does not solve the problem. This brings up a class of problems where you really do need to pay some attention to what the application does, when you cannot just treat it as an abstract black box that needs a specified set of rows from some specified tables. Even so, there are some reliable rules of thumb for the kinds of application-level changes that are likely to solve these types of problems. You will likely need to work with developers who know the application details (assuming you do not) to solve these problems, but by understanding the rules you can still offer valuable suggestions without application-specific knowledge.

# CHAPTER 2
# Data-Access Basics

*Come, fill the Cup, and in the fire of Spring*
*The Winter garment of Repentance fling:*
*The bird of Time has but a little way*
*To fly—and Lo! the Bird is on the Wing.*
—Omar Khayyam, translated by Edward Fitzgerald
  *The Rubaiyat*

You need a clear understanding of the operations of arithmetic to solve an algebra problem. Similarly, you must understand how a database reaches data in individual tables and how it joins data from multiple tables before you can understand how to combine these operations for an optimized execution plan. This book focuses on access methods that are most important to real-world queries and points out which methods are rarely or never useful.

You may find this chapter to be deceptively named; some of these data-access "basics" are quite advanced and obscure, because even the most basic of database operations can be quite involved at the detail level. I urge you not to get discouraged, though. While I include lots of gory detail for those few who really want it and for the relatively rare cases for which it is useful, you can tune quite well with just a passing understanding of indexed access and nested-loops joins. Optimizing a query to make it run faster requires only a high-level understanding of the material in this chapter.

I present this chapter in all its gory detail, though, for two reasons:

- Some readers will find the later material much easier to follow and remember if they have a concrete, detailed picture in mind when I refer to specific methods of table access and table joins in later chapters. For example, such readers would have a hard time following and remembering rules of thumb about when to prefer hash joins over nested-loops joins if they knew these join methods only as black-box processes. If you are such a concrete thinker (like myself), this chapter, in all its detail, will help you understand the rest of the book.

- The same people who tune queries are often asked awkward questions, like "Why does this query take 12 times longer to return 200 rows than this other query takes to return 1,000 rows?" Another common question is "Shouldn't we be using <InsertThisYear'sFashionableObjectType> to speed up this query?" Only with a detailed understanding of the basics discussed in this chapter is it possible to answer such questions well.

A word of explanation up front: many of the specifics in this chapter come from the behavior of Oracle. I find that highly specific descriptions help intuition in performance and tuning, because you can hold a detailed, concrete picture in your head. I could have chosen another database to describe table layouts and table-access and join methods, but no single choice would please everyone. I have found that, for the most part, the differences between database brands really do not matter to SQL tuning. In the few cases in which a vendor-specific implementation matters, I do describe the differences in detail.

# Caching in the Database

All relational databases use some variant of the same general caching scheme to minimize *physical I/O*, which involves accessing disk storage, in favor of pure *logical I/O*, or memory-only data access. (Any data access is logical I/O. Memory-only I/O is pure logical I/O, while I/O from disk is both logical and physical I/O.) Figure 2-1 illustrates this basic caching approach.

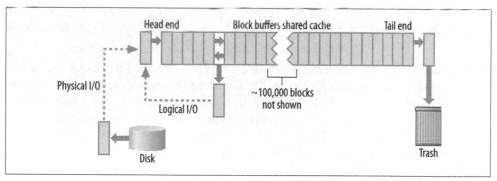

*Figure 2-1. Data caching*

The long, horizontally stretched gray rectangle (which would be *really* long if it included the 100,000 blocks excised from the middle) represents a large segment of memory available to all the database sessions at once. This memory segment, known as *block buffer cache*, contains uniform-sized (usually 2KB–16KB, depending on the database configuration) blocks of data copied from disk. The blocks contain recently accessed data from the database tables and indexes. The narrow gray rectangles represent these individual blocks.

With minor variations, the cache is populated and maintained as follows: every time the database must access a block of data not already in cache, it requests a read from disk (physical I/O) and places the newly populated block at the head end of the buffer list. Since the list length is fixed while the database runs, adding a block at the head end forces the block at the tail end of the list to fall off (i.e., to no longer be cached).

Under the covers, operations in the cache are managed by pointers in a type of linked list. The new head block is actually the same piece of memory as the old tail block, overwritten by new data and with pointers flipped to change its place on the list.

When, more commonly, the database finds a data block it needs already in the cache (requiring pure logical I/O), it removes that block from its current location and relocates it to the head of the list. Since a block involved in a logical I/O is just moved rather than added to the list, no block is pushed off the tail of the list. Again, the database handles the logical block move by pointers; it doesn't physically copy the data within memory.

Since blocks move back to the head of the list with every logical I/O, the cache ends up ordered from *most recently used* (MRU) blocks at the head end, to *least recently used* (LRU) blocks at the tail end. Frequently, touched blocks are defined to be *hot*, while rarely touched blocks are *cold*. However, how hot or cold a block is depends on whether you are talking about it being touched by logical I/O or by physical I/O. The most frequently used blocks are hot from the point of view of logical I/O, though they might be cold from the point of view of physical I/O if they never leave the cache.

The block that falls off cache as a result of a physical I/O is the LRU block on the list. For this reason, the caching algorithm I'm describing is often called an *LRU caching algorithm*, and it is a common approach to caching throughout programming, not just for relational databases. The theory is that the hottest data will cycle to the head of the list and therefore live longer on the list. Really hot data might never leave the list at all. Keeping the most frequently used data in the cache enables rapid access to that data, which in turn enables queries to run faster than they would otherwise.

When a database requests physical I/O, such a request does not necessarily cause a physical disk to move a read head and spin to the correct sector on the disk. Disk subsystems and operating systems do their own caching, and the resulting average performance of what the database sees as physical I/O is much faster, on average, than people often realize. Physical I/O is more expensive than logical I/O, so cache misses (in the database cache) matter, but they don't matter as much as you might imagine.

The LRU caching scheme has several important implications for tuning:

- The MRU blocks are the fastest to access, because they will be in the cache. It is a myth, though, that cached access is effectively free. When you count the full processing-time costs tied to logical I/O, it is from 30 to 200 times faster than physical I/O. However, this is not so fast that you can ignore logical I/O, because caching is usually so good that logical I/O happens on the order of 100 times more often than physical I/O. You can still have serious performance problems from the CPU costs of unnecessary logical I/O, even after you eliminate all physical I/O. If you work to reduce logical I/O, physical I/O will mostly take care of itself, as long as you have a reasonably sized cache.

- It takes several minutes without logical I/O for a block on a typical, well-configured system to migrate from the head of the list to the tail and fall off, so the hottest any block can be in terms of physical I/O is one I/O every few minutes. With more frequent access than that, the block becomes well cached and sees less physical I/O.

- Table rows and index entries that share a block with other data that is frequently accessed benefit from their proximity to that hot data. The more effectively you arrange for hot data to clump together within tables and indexes, the more effective the cache is

- End users benefit from recent access of hot data by other end users, since a database cache is a shared cache, usually finding most (often 99% or more) of the data they want without physical I/O.

- You will do little physical I/O on blocks that you access repeatedly within the same query, even if these blocks are normally cold, because your query itself will make them hot, and therefore cached, for most of the query.

- Small tables and indexes (tables with fewer than 10,000 rows and indexes with fewer than 90,000 entries) tend to be almost perfectly cached. Occasionally, a small table or index is touched so infrequently that it is not well cached. However, infrequent access implies that any resulting slow performance will not add up to a large problem. Even when a query against a small object requires physical I/O, not much physical I/O will be performed, because the first few physical I/Os will place the entire object in the cache for the duration of the query. I use the term *self-caching* to describe the process by which a query to normally cold blocks makes those blocks hot for the duration of the query. Self-caching lets you safely ignore potential physical I/O to small tables and indexes, even in the uncommon case in which small objects are cold.

- Even the largest indexes tend to be at least moderately well cached, because indexes are much more compact than tables, and because access plans involving these indexes tend to hit mostly the hotter parts of the indexes.

- Only large tables (tables holding over 1,000,000 rows) tend to be poorly cached, unless you systematically touch only some hot subset of a table. Minimizing the number of different blocks that you hit in the largest tables, to avoid excessive physical I/O, is particularly important to performance.

- All else being equal (i.e., given alternatives that require the same number of logical I/Os), favor the alternative that drives to hotter blocks. This is often the alternative that goes through an index, since index blocks and table blocks reached by indexed access tend to be hotter than random table blocks.

## Tables

Tables are the fundamental core of a relational database. Relational theory describes tables as abstract objects, ascribing no significance to the order of the rows or the columns that make up a table. However, tables also exist in physical form on disk in your database server, with physical ordering that affects performance. When an application queries for those physical bytes stored on disk or cached in memory, the server processes must have some way to reach them.

The physical layout of table rows affects the performance of reads of those rows, so it is important to understand the types of tables and how they affect the layout. Figure 2-2 shows four different physical tables, illustrating four basic patterns of table growth and aging, and shows how these patterns affect data layouts.

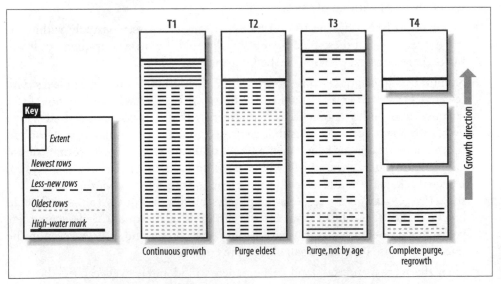

Figure 2-2. Physical table growth and aging

Tables occupy one or more contiguous areas of disk space (called *extents* on Oracle\*) that the server can read with minimal read-head movement and maximal efficiency. The database organizes table rows in blocks, which are too small to show here, usually 2KB–16KB in size. These blocks are constant-sized across most or all of the database (depending on the vendor). The blocks are the smallest units that the database reads from disk and caches, as discussed earlier. As formerly empty blocks within an extent become occupied, the *high-water mark*—the highest point of the table that the database needs to scan—rises toward the top of the extent until, reaching the top, it triggers allocation of a new extent.† Above the high-water mark is space reserved for future writes, but not space that the database will ever touch for a read. The high-water mark does not move downward unless you rebuild or truncate the table. Figure 2-2 illustrates growth patterns described in the following sections.

## Continuous Growth

The *continuous growth* pattern, shown for T1 in Figure 2-2, is the most common pattern among transaction tables, which continually acquire new rows but almost never lose old rows. It is often regrettable that old rows stay around long after they have outlived their usefulness, but deciding what is truly safe to purge is hard (and scary) work, even ignoring the effort of writing the routines to do the work. Somehow, this work always ends up at the end of the priority list for a product's features (and who needs it in the initial release of a product?), much to the delight of disk vendors.

In continuous growth tables, the level of interest in rows tends to drop with their age, making the newest rows, conveniently stored together at the top of the table and most likely to be queried, best to cache. When the newest rows are the hottest, the natural clustering of new rows makes optimum use of the cache, and even a very large table can see a good *cache-hit ratio* (the fraction of logical I/Os that avoid physical I/Os) if you use indexed access that avoids the older rows.

A query that touches all of a continuous growth table (up to the high-water mark, that is), then discards all but some of the newest rows, will look good when the table is new and tiny. However, whole-table-access runtime grows linearly, assuming a constant table-growth rate, and will likely become intolerable. An access path that touches only new rows will maintain roughly constant efficiency, given steady table growth, since you will have a roughly constant number of rows created in the last week or so.

---

\* Technically, an extent is contiguous according to virtual disk addressing, which is all the database software knows about. At a lower level, a RAID or other disk-striping/mirroring system can translate these contiguous virtual addresses to blocks on different disks, but you can safely ignore this subtlety when tuning SQL.

† This most closely describes Oracle, but the differences between vendors, in this area, are not important to SQL tuning.

## Purge Eldest

The *purge eldest* pattern, shown for T2 in Figure 2-2, I call the *Ouroboros* pattern, after the mythical snake that continually eats its own tail. In this table, the oldest rows are periodically purged (all of the oldest rows, not just some subset), completely emptying their blocks and making them available for inserts of the newest rows. The high-water mark need not move once this table reaches mature size, assuming you delete rows (once you begin deletes) at the same rate you insert them. The head of this snake (holding the newest rows) is always chasing the tail (holding the oldest rows), which retreats with every fresh delete. From the point of view of keeping the newest rows physically close together, this pattern is as good as the continuous growth pattern, with the added advantage that, since table growth halts once purging begins, the whole table has a better chance to be well cached. Note that this is an idealized case that is rarely seen, since retention of a few of the oldest rows, or a growth rate that exceeds the purge rate, will tend to gradually mix old and new rows ever more thoroughly.

## Purge, Not by Age

The *purge, not by age* pattern, shown for T3 in Figure 2-2, reflects deletes that are not age-driven. Blocks become available for fresh inserts as soon as they have empty space that exceeds some threshold (typically 60% empty on Oracle), staying eligible until empty space falls below another threshold (typically 10% empty on Oracle). This happens to blocks that are scattered fairly randomly throughout the table, so new rows scatter accordingly, and caching becomes harder with time both as a result of average blocks being emptier and as a result of interesting rows being more spread out. However, such a pattern of purging tends to imply that the level of interest in rows is not age-related, tending to make such a table hard to cache regardless of whether purging scatters new rows.

## Complete Purge and Regrowth

The *complete purge and regrowth* pattern, shown for T4 in Figure 2-2, reflects a wholesale purge with the beginnings of regrowth. In Figure 2-2, the entire table contents were recently deleted and the oldest rows shown are not that old, since the table has a long way to grow before it reaches its old high-water mark. This pattern is similar to the continuous growth pattern shown in T1, except that, since the table was formerly large and has not been rebuilt, the high-water mark has not fallen back, forcing full table scans to do just as much physical I/O as before the purge.

Oracle's TRUNCATE command, as an alternative to DELETE, can drop the high-water mark. On any database, you can also lower the high-water mark by dropping and rebuilding the table.

# Indexes

Indexes are less fundamental, functionally, than tables. Indexes are really just a means to reach table rows quickly. They are essential to performance, but not functionally necessary.

## B-Tree Indexes

The most common and most important type of index, by far, is the *B-tree index*, which reflects a tree structure that is balanced (hence the *B*) to a constant depth from the root to the leaf blocks along every branch. Figure 2-3 shows a three-deep B-tree, likely reflecting an index pointing to 90,000–27,000,000 rows in a table, the typical size range for three-deep B-trees.

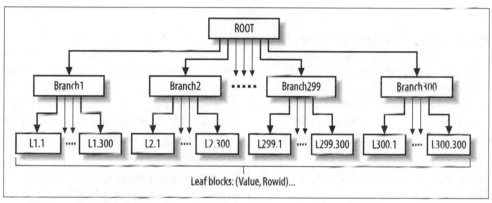

*Figure 2-3. A three-level B-tree index*

Like an index in a book, a database index helps the database quickly find references to some value or range of values that you need from a table. For example, indexing Last_Name in a Persons table allows rapid access to the list of table rows where Last_Name='SMITH' or where Last_Name>='X' AND Last_Name<'Y'. Unlike indexes in a book, however, database indexes are almost effortless to use; the database is responsible for walking through the indexes it chooses to use, to find the rows a query requires, and it usually finds the right indexes to use without being told. Databases don't always make the right choice, however, and the material in this book exists largely to address such problems.

Every index has a natural sort order, usually ascending in the order that is natural to the type of the indexed column. For example, the number 11 falls between 10 and 12, but the character string '11' falls between '1' and '2'. Indexes often cover multiple columns, but you can think of such indexes as having a single sort key made up of the concatenation of the multiple column values, with suitable padding to cause sorting on the second column to begin only after completing the sort on the first column.

Index access always begins at the single root block, which holds up to about 300 ranges of index values covered by data in the table. These ranges usually carry pointers to branch blocks for each range, when the index as a whole covers more than about 300 rows (the actual number depending on block and column sizes, mostly).* An index on a table with fewer than 300 rows typically has only the root block, which contains the pointers that lead directly to the indexed rows in the table. Each of these pointers takes the form of a block address and a row number within the block, for each indexed row. In any case, no matter how large the table, you can assume that the root block is perfectly cached, since every use of the index goes through that single block.

 A block address and row number within the block, together, are called a *rowid*. Indexes use rowids to point to rows in tables.

Assuming a table has more than about 300 indexed rows, the database follows a pointer in the root block to a branch block that covers the beginning of the range of values you requested in your query. If the table has more than about 90,000 indexed rows, the branch block, in turn, contains subranges with pointers to blocks in the next lower level. Finally (at the first branch level, with a table in the 300–90,000 indexed-row range), the database arrives at a leaf block with an exact value that matches the beginning of the range you want (assuming the range you queried has any rows at all) and a *rowid* for the first row in the range.

If the condition that drives access to the index potentially points to a range of multiple rows, the database performs an index range scan over the leaf blocks. An *index range scan* is the operation of reading (usually with logical I/O from cache) an index range over as many leaf blocks as necessary. The leaf blocks consist of value/rowid pairs in a list sorted by indexed value. The database sorts entries that repeat a value according to the order of the rowids, reflecting the natural order in which the database stores rows in the physical table. At the end of each leaf-block list, a pointer identifies the next leaf block, where the sorted list continues. If the table has multiple rows that satisfy the index range condition, the database follows a pointer from the first row to the next index entry in the range (over 99% of the time, the next index entry is within the same index leaf block), and so on, until it reaches the end of the range. Thus, each read of a range of sorted values requires one walk down the index tree, followed by one walk across the sorted leaf-block values.

---

* I speak here of indexed rows, as opposed to table rows, because not all indexes point to all rows of a table. Most notably, Oracle indexes do not contain entries that point to rows with null values on all the indexed columns, so an index on a mostly null column can be very small, even on a very large table, if few rows have non-null values for that column.

---

Usually, a range scan touches only a single leaf block, since a single leaf block holds 300 values, enough to satisfy most medium-sized range scans without leaving the block. However, a large range scan can traverse a long list of leaf blocks.

With a ballpark number of 300 entries per index block, you will find about 300 branch blocks on the first level. This is still a small enough number to cache well, so you can assume that reads of these index blocks are logical only, with no physical I/O. At the bottom, leaf level of the index, where the index uses three or more levels, there might be many more than 300 leaf blocks. However, even the leaf level of an index has a block count of roughly $n/300$, where $n$ is the number of indexed rows, and the database can cache 1,000 or more blocks of an index efficiently, if it uses the index enough to really matter.

When the entire index is too large to cache well, you will see some physical I/O when accessing it. However, keep in mind that indexes generally cover just the entity properties that define the parts of the table that are most frequently accessed. Therefore, a database rarely needs to cache all of a large index—it needs to cache only a small subset of the index blocks that point to interesting rows—so even large indexes usually see excellent cache-hit ratios. The bottom line is this: when you compare alternative execution plans, you can ignore costs of physical I/O to indexes. When physical I/O happens at all, physical I/O to tables will almost always dominate physical I/O to indexes.

## Index Costs

Having extra indexes around cannot hurt query performance, as long as you avoid using the wrong indexes. Indexes have their downsides, though. Optimizers choose the wrong indexes more often than you might think, so you might be surprised how many query performance problems are created by adding indexes to a database. Even if you have complete confidence that a new index will never take the place of a better index in a query execution plan, add indexes with caution and restraint.

In an ideal world, the only performance cost of adding indexes would come when you add, delete, or update rows. On quiet tables, the performance cost of indexes is never a problem, but on a busy, growing table, it can be a major cost. Inserts into an index are usually not a problem, especially on Oracle, which handles index-block locking for uncommitted work especially gracefully.

Deletes are more difficult than inserts, because B-trees do not behave reversibly when you add rows and then delete them. An index with heavy deletes ends up with nearly empty blocks that are less efficient to cache and read than the same index, pointing to the same rows, would otherwise be had all those deletes not occurred. Occasional, expensive index rebuilds are necessary to restore indexes that have experienced heavy deletes to full efficiency.

Updates are the most expensive index operation. When an update changes at least one indexed column, the database treats the update as both an insert (of the new value) and a delete (of the old value). This expensive two-part update, which is not necessary in tables, is necessary for indexes because updating index values actually changes where a row belongs in an index structure. Fortunately, indexes on primary keys are almost never updated, given correct database design, and updates of foreign keys are uncommon. The indexes that present the greatest danger to update performance are indexes on non-key columns that have real-world meanings that change with time, such as status columns on entities that frequently change status.

Some indexes exist for reasons that are independent of performance—for example, to enforce uniqueness. The need to enforce uniqueness is usually justification enough for a unique index, and, generally, unique indexes are also selective enough to be safe and useful. However, create nonunique indexes with caution; they are not free, and once you create them it is almost impossible to get rid of them without undue risk to performance, since it is very hard to prove that no important query requires any given index. When solving performance problems, I frequently advise creating new indexes. When I do so, though, I almost always have in mind at least one specific query, which runs often enough to matter and has proven unable to run fast enough without the new index.

# Uncommon Database Objects

Simple tables and B-tree indexes suffice for almost all database needs. However, you should at least have a passing awareness of less common database object types, if only to argue against futile attempts to solve problems with wrong and exotic tools. This section describes the more popular special object types.

## Index-Organized Tables

Index-organized tables are just indexes that don't point to tables. They are a nifty feature in Oracle, but you can approximate them in any database. Occasionally, a database will find all the columns it needs for a query in an index and will use that index without even touching the corresponding table. If you created an index that happened to have all the columns of a table, you might like to dispose of the table altogether. Index-organized tables handle just this scenario, saving space and the cost of maintaining a separate table. Since index-organized tables have no table to point to, they also avoid the need to include rowids, packing in more rows per block than ordinary indexes on the same columns. This better compactness makes index-organized tables easier to cache than ordinary indexes on the same columns. When you have an index just past the point at which it acquires an extra index level, replacing the index-table combination with a more compact, index-organized table will eliminate that extra level.

---

Consider using index-oriented organized tables under the following circumstances:

- Rows are not much longer than their index key. Tables generally store data more compactly and efficiently than an index with the same data. If rows are long, compared to their key, a much more compact key index read followed by reads of a plain table will work better, or at least as well, and more flexibly.

- You almost always reach rows through a single index, probably through all or part of the primary key index. You can create ordinary, secondary indexes on index-organized tables, but when you use those secondary indexes, you defeat the purpose of the index-organized table.

- You sometimes read rows in large ranges based on the sort order of an index. Large range reads within an index are particularly efficient compared to reading the same rows scattered randomly throughout an ordinary table. This factor in favor of index-organized tables tends to be in conflict with the previous factor, since access through a primary key is usually unique access, not access over a large range. With multipart primary keys, though, you sometimes read row ranges on partial keys, so you will occasionally see both of these factors in favor of index-organized tables.

- You add, delete, and modify rows infrequently. Ordinary tables handle frequent data changes better than index-organized tables. In Online Transaction Processing (OLTP) applications, large tables tend to have frequent data changes; otherwise, they would not grow large. This tends to argue against large, index-organized tables in the OLTP world.

If you like the idea of an index-organized table but you are not using Oracle, you can get almost the same read-time benefits by building ordinary indexes with all the columns you need in your common queries. Even on Oracle, you can follow this strategy when you prefer to leave large, rarely needed columns out of an index for greater compactness.

The biggest drawback of adding columns to ordinary indexes comes when adding columns to already-unique indexes. You can specify a leading subset of the columns in an index-organized table as the unique key, but ordinary unique indexes enforce uniqueness only over the whole combination of columns. Unique indexes usually exist both to speed performance and to enforce uniqueness over the key. However, if you add non-key columns to an ordinary unique key index, you defeat correct enforcement of key uniqueness. You can solve this problem with two indexes: a narrow one just to enforce key uniqueness and a wider one to provide index-only access to table columns. However, databases tend not to choose a wider index when a narrower one already has all the columns needed for a unique read, so you might need to put forth extra effort to force the use of the wider index.

## Single-Table Clusters

As a feature, single-table clusters have been around longer than their closely related index-organized tables. A single-table cluster physically arranges table rows in the order of some key value. When interest in rows correlates well with that sort value, such an arrangement improves the hit ratio by keeping hot rows close together. The problem, a showstopper usually, is that it is hard to keep a table organized in sorted order unless rows *arrive* in sorted order. (And if they arrive in sorted order, you do not need to cluster; natural table ordering will work fine!) If rows do not arrive in sorted order, the database must leave room to shoehorn in new rows where they belong; otherwise, it must periodically reorder rows. Reordering is expensive, and leaving space for later rows wastes space and harms cache efficiency. The bottom line on single-table clusters is that I have never needed them to get good performance, and I do not expect you will either.

## Multitable Clusters

Like single-table clusters, multitable clusters are presorted on some key, but multitable clusters have rows, in the same blocks, from multiple tables that join on that key, making the join between those tables extra fast. If you do not access the clustered tables together, having the other table's rows in the blocks you read just gets in the way, so a key question is how often you join the different tables in your application queries. If you have two or more always-joined tables that map one-to-one to each other (i.e., tables that share a unique key), multitable clusters probably work pretty well. But, in that case, why make them separate tables at all? Instead, just put the superset of all columns into a single table. More often, some master table has a one-to-many relationship with its details, such as Orders and Order_Details. Here, the problem becomes the fluidity of most one-to-many relationships. In the cluster block, you must allow for the possibility of many details and at the same time avoid wasting too much space when it turns out there is just one (or even no) detail row. As for single-table clusters, this leads to a tradeoff between wasted space and reordering costs. Just as for single-table clusters, I have never needed multitable clusters for good performance, and you probably will not either.

## Partitioned Tables

Partitioned tables are another Oracle feature, originated largely to handle maintenance on truly huge tables. Imagine you have a trade-tracking system for a major brokerage. You probably have an immense history of individual trades, but you rarely have interest in trades older than one year. You want to keep efficient, continuous access to the recent trades, while having some chance to eventually archive really old trades without disrupting your system.

Partitioned tables look like a bunch of subtables, or *partitions*, that you can maintain independently. For example, you can take one partition offline without disrupting access to the others. Query statements need to refer explicitly only to the partitioned table name that represents the whole collection. The partitions are organized according to some range condition that determines which partition owns which rows. This range condition often uses a date, such as Trade_Date in our example, for which each partition covers a substantial date range, such as a month or a year. As long as the query conditions exclude some of the partitions, the query can skip access to those partitions; it can even run if those partitions are entirely offline. Partitioned tables have some great advantages for ease of administration, but in my own experience I have never needed them just to solve a performance problem. I expect, though, that they help for some very large tables, like those in the trade-tracking example, for which the rows naturally organize along a partition condition, usually a date. From the point of view of SQL tuning, you can treat partitioned tables essentially as normal large tables.

## Bit-Mapped Indexes

Bit-mapped indexes are designed largely to address special concerns in data warehousing. The chief virtue of bit-mapped indexes is that they allow you to efficiently combine multiple, not-very-selective conditions covered by different indexes to obtain a single short list of rows that satisfy all conditions at once. However, a single, multicolumn index will allow much the same thing, but without the disadvantages that I describe in the next paragraph, so I do not expect that bit-mapped indexes are often useful; certainly, I have never needed one to tune a query. (I have done relatively little data-warehousing work, so bit-mapped indexes might be more useful to you than to me, if data warehousing is your venue.)

Each stored value of a bit-mapped index points to what amounts to a list of yes/no bits that map to the whole list of table rows, with *yes* bits mapping to table rows that have that value for the indexed column. These bit strings are easy to AND and OR together with other bit strings of other bit-mapped indexes to combine conditions across bit-mapped values on multiple indexes. The big catch is that such bit strings are expensive to maintain in sync with frequently changing table contents, especially updates in the middle of a table. Bit-mapped indexes work best for tables that are mostly read-only; however, large tables do not grow large by being read-only, and small tables do not require special indexes for efficient data access. The best scenario for success is precisely the data-warehouse scenario for which bit-mapped indexes were designed: a data-warehouse database that is read-only during the day and periodically, probably during nights or weekends, does whole-table refreshes from some transactional database in which the tables grow steadily.

# Single-Table Access Paths

The most basic query requests some subset of a single table. Such queries are rarely interesting from a tuning perspective, but even the most complex query, joining many tables, starts with a single driving table. You should choose the access path to the driving table in a multitable query, just as you would for the single-table query that would result if you stripped the multitable query down, removing the joins, the nondriving tables, and the conditions on the nondriving tables. Every query optimization problem therefore includes the choice of an optimum single-table access path to the driving table. The table implementations and table-access methods differ slightly between the database vendors. To be both accurate and concrete, in this section I will describe table access on Oracle for illustration purposes, but the differences between Oracle and other database brands are not important to SQL tuning.

## Full Table Scans

The most basic access path to a table is the *full table scan*, reading the whole table without an index. Figure 2-4 illustrates this method, as applied to a typical Oracle table.

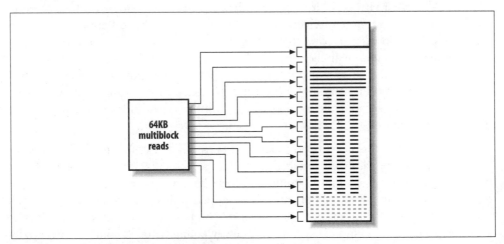

*Figure 2-4. A full table scan*

Oracle recognizes that, since it is going to read the entire table, it ought to request physical I/O in parts larger than the block size—in this case, reading 64KB at a time. This results in fewer but larger physical reads, which are faster than many small physical reads covering the same blocks. Not all database vendors follow this method, but it turns out to matter less that you might expect, because disk subsystems and operating systems usually read larger segments, even when the database requests a single block. The database might issue many small read requests, but these translate, in the lower system layers, into a few large read requests, with many smaller requests satisfied out of the disk subsystem cache. The reads continue from the first block to the high-water mark, including empty blocks along the way. Caching only allows the database to avoid a physical multiblock I/O when every block in the 64KB multiblock set of blocks is already in cache. The database reads the blocks of small to medium-sized tables into cache in the usual way, and they expire in the usual few minutes if no other query touches them. Caching entire small or medium-sized tables is often useful, and they end up remaining in cache if the database sees frequent full table scans of such tables.

Large tables present a danger to the caching strategy: the average block in a large table is unlikely to be needed often. If the database followed the usual caching strategy, a large table scan could flush most of the more interesting blocks (from indexes and other tables) out of the cache, harming the performance of most other queries. Fortunately, this is not usually a problem, because blocks from a large full table scan generally go straight to the tail of the cache, where they stay only long enough to satisfy the ongoing query, usually getting replaced by the next group of blocks from the same scan. (This behavior of large full table scans is one of the exceptions to the LRU caching behavior I described earlier.)

## Indexed Table Access

The most important costs of a full table scan usually come in the CPU: the cost of examining every block below the high-water mark and the cost of examining every row within those blocks.

Unless you are reading a tiny table (in which case, any access method is likely fine) or reading a large fraction of a larger table, you should ensure that your queries reach the rows you need through an index. Figure 2-5 illustrates an index-based table-access method.

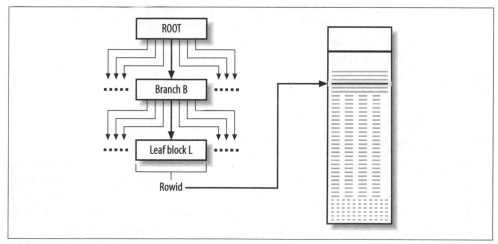

*Figure 2-5. Indexed table access*

The database begins with some indexed value that defines the beginning of a range of indexed values that meet some query criteria. Starting at the root block, it finds ranges and subranges that lead it down the index tree to the leaf block or blocks that store indexed values that satisfy the query criteria. The database finds the rowids that go with these values and follows them to the precise table blocks, and rows within those blocks, that satisfy the query.

Let's compare the indexed and full table scan access methods with a concrete example. Figure 2-6 shows two paths to read five rows, shown in black, from a 40-block table, which would typically contain around 3,200 rows.

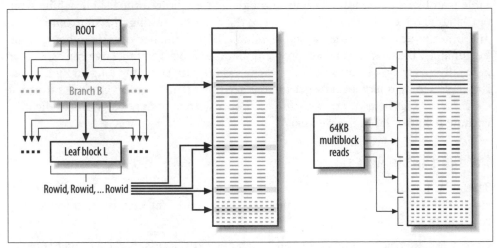

*Figure 2-6. Indexed access versus a full table scan*

In this example, the table is too small for its index to likely have more than two levels, so the database goes straight from the index root block to the leaf block that holds the start of the five-row range that the query requires. (The middle branch level, nonexistent for such a mid-sized table, is shown in gray.) Probably, the database finds all five index entries in the same leaf block, but it might need to hop to the next leaf block to complete the range if the range started right at the block boundary. Armed with the five *rowids*, the database goes to the table blocks that hold the five rows. In one case in the example, the database performs two sequential logical I/Os to the same table block, because the rows happen to be close together, but the second logical I/O will surely be cached. (This is an example of the benefit of interesting rows that happen to cluster together in a physical table.)

In the full-table-scan alternative, if the table blocks are not in cache to begin with, the database performs five 64KB reads, covering the whole table up to the high-water mark. Then, in CPU, the database steps through all 40 blocks and all 3,200 rows, discarding all but the 5 rows that match the query condition. If the database had no cache and you cared only about the time to move read heads to perform physical I/O, you would count seven physical I/O operations for the indexed plan and five for the full table scan and choose the full table scan. However, a small table and a smaller index, such as these, are likely completely cached, and 7 logical I/Os, which are to individual table blocks, are cheaper than 40 logical I/Os, even for a full table scan. Apart from logical-I/O costs, the indexed plan avoids CPU costs of looking at over 3,000 rows you do not need.

Both plans, you might suspect, would be fast enough that the difference would not matter,[*] since efficiency against small tables is not that important in single-table reads. Expanding this example to larger-sized tables, though, the questions become more interesting, mixing physical and logical I/O with runtime differences that are long enough to matter.

## Choosing Between a Full Table Scan and Indexed Access

A superficial analysis often favors full table scans. However, a more careful analysis requires you to take into account several considerations that commonly make indexed reads more favorable than they appear superficially:

- Index reads are almost always cached.
- Table blocks reached by an index tend to be hotter and are more likely to be cached, because indexed reads are specific to rows you (and others, too, probably) really want, while full table scans treat all rows equally.
- A single block is more likely to be cached than a multiblock group, so the effective cache hit ratio on a table is better for an indexed read. For example, if a randomly scattered half of the blocks in a table are cached, the hit ratio for single-block reads to the table is 50%, but the probability of finding all eight blocks of a multiblock read already cached is just 0.5 to the eighth power, or about 0.4%. To reach a 50% effective hit ratio for eight-block reads, you would need a 91.7% hit ratio on randomly cached individual blocks.
- Disk subsystems usually make single-block reads effectively multiblock, converting nearby single-block reads into virtual I/O, so the seeming advantage of multiblock reads for full table scans is less than it would seem.
- Indexed reads examine only a small part of each block, the rows you want, instead of every row in the block, saving CPU time.
- Indexed reads usually scale better as a table grows, giving stable performance, whereas a full table scan becomes steadily worse, even while it might start out a little better than the indexed plan.

---

[*] I am not trying to waste your time with an unimportant example. The difference *would* matter if I scaled the example up to larger tables and indexes, but such an example would be impossible to illustrate in the detail shown in Figure 2-6. I use this smaller example to get the general point across.

The choice to favor indexed access or a full table scan depends on the fraction of the table that the single-table query will read. The database's optimizer will make this choice for you, but not always correctly. If SQL is slow enough to merit tuning, you need to decide for yourself. Here are some general fraction-read ranges to use in choosing your best strategy:

>20% of the rows
: Favor full table scans.

<0.5% of the rows
: Favor indexed access.

0.5%–20% of the rows
: It depends.

The 0.5%–20% range is awkward to handle. Conditions should especially favor indexed access for you to prefer an index at the 20% end of this range. Likewise, don't consider a full table scan at the 0.5% end of the range unless conditions strongly favor a table scan. Here are some factors pertaining to particular queries that tend to favor indexed access toward the higher end of the 0.5%–20% range:

- The table is well-clustered on the indexed column, resulting in self-caching over the range. Multiple logical I/Os will hit the same blocks, and the later reads of those blocks will likely remain in cache after the earlier reads put them there (if necessary).

- The query accesses hotter-than-average rows, resulting in better caching over the indexed range than the full table scan will see over the whole table.

- The query goes in on one value only, reaching rows in rowid order. Where you have exact equality conditions on the fully indexed key, reading rowids for that single key value, the index scan returns those rowids in sorted order. Where the database requires physical I/O, this results in an access pattern much like the full table scan, with the read head moving smoothly from the beginning of the range to the end. Since close-together rows get read sequentially, self-caching is particularly likely, both in the database's cache and in the disk I/O subsystem's cache, when that subsystem does read-ahead.

  On the other hand, if you access a range of values, such as `Retirement_Date BETWEEN '2002/01/01' and '2003/01/01'`, you will find a whole series of sorted rowid lists for each date in that range. The read-head movement will look much more random and therefore will be less efficient. Self-caching might not even work in this case if the runtime of the query exceeds the life of the blocks in the cache. Even if you drive off an equality, you can get this less efficient alternative if you have a multicolumn index. For example, `Last_Name='Smith'` is really a range condition on an index of (`Last_Name`, `First_Name`), since this full pair has many values that satisfy the single-column condition.

The precise formulas that control the tradeoff between full table-scan performance and range-scan performance are complex and not very useful, because you'd only be able to guess at the inputs (such as the relative hit ratios between blocks reached by the range scan and other table blocks). All this sounds hideously complex, I know, if you happen to be in that awkward 0.5%–20% range, but, in practice, the problem of handling this middle range turns out to be pretty simple:

- If a table is big enough for the difference between a full table scan and indexed table access to matter, you better have a condition that is selective enough to use an index; otherwise, you are likely returning more rows than are useful! I will later describe in more detail why few well-designed queries need to return a significant fraction (even 1%) of a large table. Real-world applications exist mostly to give end users convenient access to data. When end users work with data online, they find it inconvenient to handle large data volumes. End users are somewhat more tolerant of large data volumes in reports, but even then a report that provides more data than an end user can digest is not well designed. In Chapter 10, I will discuss at length fixing queries that return far too many rows.

- If you're in doubt about whether to use a full table scan or indexed access, just time both alternatives; trial and error works fine when you have only a couple of choices. Keep in mind, though, that whichever alternative you test first will have an unfair disadvantage if you run the experiments close together, since the second experiment will find blocks cached by the first experiment. I usually run each alternative twice, in close succession, and use the second runtime for each, which generally finds perfect caching. If the runtimes come out close, I might repeat experiments 10 minutes or more apart to measure more realistic physical I/O costs, repeating the first experiment 10 minutes after the second, to observe for reproducibility.

- Do not look for small improvements. If the two alternatives are close to the same, just stick with the execution plan you already have. Changing a single statement to squeeze a few percent improvement is not likely worth the effort. You should usually look for twofold or better improvements in runtimes when tuning—these are possible surprisingly often—when the performance is slow enough for such improvements to matter.

## Calculating Selectivity

When tuning queries, you can best picture nonjoin (single-table) conditions as filters. These filters pass through the table rows that the application needs (the rows satisfying the conditions), while discarding the rows that the application does not need (the rows failing to satisfy the query conditions). The application has functional reasons to exclude unneeded rows, but from a performance point of view the job of the filter is to save the database work and time. The trick of tuning is to avoid work, as much as possible, on rows destined for the trash heap.

*Selectivity* is the power of a filter as a row-excluding tool, expressed as the fraction of table rows that the filter passes through. The database can apply filters at three points, with varying success at minimizing query cost:

*Determining the index range condition*
> Conditions that determine the limits of an index range scan require no work at all on the excluded rows.

*Determining the table rows reached from the index*
> Sometimes, conditions do not determine the index range limits but nevertheless can be evaluated in the index before reaching the table. These conditions require touching ultimately excluded row entries in the index, but not in the table.

*Determining the rows returned after table access*
> If a condition requires columns held in the table but not in an index, a database cannot evaluate that condition until it reads the table rows. Filters evaluated in the table are of no value in reducing the costs of reaching the rows of that table, though they reduce network costs because the excluded rows do not need to be returned. If the filtered table is not the last or the only table touched, any filter also reduces the costs of joins to other tables later in the execution plan.

## Filter Selectivity

In this section, I explain how to calculate the selectivity of conditions on a table. Let's begin with some definitions:

*Individual-condition filter selectivity*
> The fraction of table rows that satisfy a single condition on that table.

*Multiple-condition filter selectivity*
> The fraction of table rows that satisfy the combination of conditions referring exclusively to that table.

*Filter independence*
> The assumption, usually true, that you can calculate multiple-condition selectivity as the simple product of individual-condition selectivity fractions. For example, a condition on a person's first name and a condition on a person's Zip Code are logically independent. You can assume that the fraction of rows that have both the correct first name and the correct Zip Code will be roughly the product of the fraction of rows that have the correct name and the fraction that have the correct Zip Code. For example, if 1/100th of the rows contain the desired first name and 1/500th of the rows contain the desired Zip Code, then the multiple-condition filter selectivity is $1/100 \times 1/500 = 1/50,000$.

*Filter redundancy*
> The opposite of filter independence. The truth of one condition guarantees the truth of another. For example, a condition on the Zip Code likely guarantees a single value for telephone area code, so the selectivity of conditions on both would be no better than the selectivity of the ZIP Code alone. You can always

test for complete or partial filter redundancy by calculating the multicondition filter selectivity based on filter independence and seeing whether it equals the actual selectivity of the combination of the conditions.

When you tune a query and evaluate filter selectivity, start by asking if the query stands alone or if it represents a whole group of queries. If it represents a group of queries, ask about the distribution of values within that group. For example, consider the query:*

```
SELECT ... FROM Orders WHERE Unpaid_Flag='Y';
```

This query has (we would hope) high selectivity, being true for a small fraction of the complete history of orders. If you can count on finding a value of 'Y' for Unpaid_Flag in the query, you might want an index on that column. But if the query is part of a group that just as often searches for the unselective condition Unpaid_Flag='N', you should likely avoid the index. In this example, the meaning of the flag is likely special to the query, driving the very purpose of the query (to find bills to send out), so you can count on finding primarily queries against 'Y', which is the rare value.

 Yes, I promised earlier that you did not need to understand the application to tune the SQL. Really, you do not. You can always ask the developers if the application SQL will consistently point to the rare indexed value. However, you might be surprised how much you can deduce about an application with just a little thought about what makes sense, given the names of the tables and columns.

To calculate the selectivity of the condition Unpaid_Flag='Y', begin by executing the following two queries:

```
SELECT COUNT(*) FROM Orders WHERE Unpaid_Flag='Y';
SELECT COUNT(*) FROM Orders;
```

The selectivity of the condition is the first count divided by the second.

On the other hand, consider the query:

```
SELECT ... FROM Order_Details WHERE Order_ID=:id;
```

End users would query for details of orders roughly at random. You could assume this even if the application replaced the bind variable :id with an actual value, since an application would have no reason to always query the same order. The query against any particular ID does not stand alone, but represents a whole family of queries that you should tune as a unit. End users are as likely to query one order as another, so you could estimate the filter selectivity with:

```
SELECT 1/COUNT(DISTINCT Order_ID) FROM Order_Details;
```

---

* Note that I usually replace the SELECT list with ... in my examples. It turns out that the list of columns and expressions that you select has little impact on query performance, which is dominated by the list of tables in the FROM clause and the conditions in the WHERE clause.

A more subtle case arises when the end user might query on any value, but the end user is more likely to query on common values than uncommon values. For example, if operators bring up customers by finding all customers that have the last name of the calling customer, they will bring up common last names more often than uncommon ones with a query such as:

```
SELECT ... FROM Customers WHERE Last_Name = 'SMITH';
```

Here, if you just counted distinct names, as you counted order IDs earlier, you would see an over-optimistic selectivity that assumed you were just as likely to search for Last_Name='KMETEC' as for Last_Name='SMITH'. Each last name has a selectivity of $n(i)/C$, where $n(i)$ is the count of rows with the $i$th nonnull last name and $C$ is the count of all rows in the table. If choosing any last name were equally probable, you could just average $n(i)/C$ over all the last names. That average would equal one over the number of distinct names. However, the probability of searching on a last name in this scenario is $n(i)/C'$, where $C'$ is the count of rows having nonnull last names. Therefore, you really need the sum of the selectivities times the probability of seeing each selectivity—i.e., the sum of $(n(i)/C') \times (n(i)/C)$—over all last names. Since $C'$ is also the sum of the individual $n(i)$ values, you can compute the filter selectivity in SQL as follows:

```
SELECT SUM(COUNT(LastName)*COUNT(Last_Name))/
       (SUM(COUNT(Last_Name))*SUM(COUNT(*)))
FROM Customers GROUP BY Last_Name;
```

## Index Range-Condition Selectivity

Index range-condition selectivity is the fraction of table rows the database examines in an index while scanning the index. Every index range scan must have two endpoints that define the beginning and end of the range. These endpoints can be equivalent to positive or negative infinity, meaning that the range can be unbounded on either end, though not generally on both ends. The range can exclude either or both of the range endpoints, depending on the nature of the bounding condition. For example, the range condition (Salary > 4000 AND Salary < 8000) excludes both endpoints with > and < bounding conditions.

There are common problems that prevent a database from finding a concrete beginning and end for a range scan, even given a very selective condition on the indexed column, generally preventing effective use of the index. It is hard or even impossible (depending on the function) to translate a condition on SomeFunction(Some_Column) into a single range condition on a simple index leading with Some_Column. Generally, a database does not even try to do so.

 Function-based indexes, supported on Oracle, are the main exception to this rule. They allow you to specifically index the result of some expression on a table's columns—for example, UPPER(Last_Name)—to drive indexed access to conditions on that expression—for example, UPPER(Last_Name) LIKE 'SMITH%'.

Therefore, expressions that do more than simply name a column do not usually enable indexed access to ranges defined on that column, often making indexes useless for queries using those expressions. This is a double-edged sword: it forces you to rewrite some queries to enable the index that you want to use, but it is also a useful tool, allowing to you rewrite other queries to prevent the database from using indexes that you do not want to use.

A subtle example of a function that disables use of an index is when you compare expressions of different types and the database applies a type-conversion function implicitly. For example, the type-inconsistent condition CharacterColumn=94303 implicitly becomes, in Oracle, TO_NUMBER(CharacterColumn)=94303. To resolve this problem and enable use of an index on the character column, perform the conversion explicitly on the other side. For example:

| Replace | With |
|---------|------|
| CharacterColumn=94303 | CharacterColumn='94303' |
| CharacterColumn=TRUNC(SYSDATE) | CharacterColumn=TO_CHAR(SYSDATE,'DD-MON-YYYY') |

Comparing a character expression to anything else in Oracle results in the character value converting to the other type, unless you convert the other side of the comparison explicitly. This is a bit surprising, since numbers and dates can always convert without error to character strings, but character strings frequently fail to convert to numbers and dates.

Even when comparing numbers to numbers, type conversion can lead to difficulties when a database vendor supports different number types, such as integer and decimal types. Type conversions also interfere with efficient, indexed join paths for which a foreign key of one type points to a primary key of another type.

To avoid the problem of implicit type conversion preventing the use of indexes, your database design should always use foreign keys with the same type as the primary keys they reference.

Several rules apply when you figure out how large an index range scan will be:

- Conditions on the leading column of the index under consideration are suited to provide a range start or endpoint. Conditions on later columns of the same index are not suited to provide a range start or endpoint, unless you also have exact equality conditions on all preceding columns of that index. For example, an index on (Date_Column, ID_Number) applied to the condition Date_Column >= TO_DATE('2003/01/01', 'YYYY/MM/DD') delivers a range scan fully determined by the date condition. Further conditions on the second column, such as ID_Number=137, do not further narrow the index range scan. To further narrow the range based on the second condition, you have to look at a long list of ranges, one for each possible value of

`Date_Column` that satisfies the first condition, but databases do not do this. However, if you flip the index column order to (`ID_Number, Date_Column`), then the same two conditions *together* define the range endpoints and you get a much shorter, faster index range scan.

> Since query conditions on dates (and even more so on *date-times*, which are dates that include a time component) tend not to be equality conditions, multicolumn indexes usually should not lead with a date-type column.

- Depending on the database, the database usually assumes that `Indexed_Col IS NULL` denotes too large a range to be useful, and the database ignores such conditions for establishing range endpoints.

> DB2 is the exception to this rule. Oracle does not include references to rows that have only null values for all columns in an index. DB2 does, though, and it appears to treat nulls as just another value, having the same likelihood of appearing as other values. This tends to make DB2 all too likely to choose a plan driving from an is-null condition, since nulls, where allowed, tend to be much more common than individual nonnull values.

- The database assumes that `Indexed_Col IS NOT NULL` covers too large a range to be useful, so the database will not drive to an index from this condition. In rare cases, having any nonnull value is so rare that an index range scan over all possible nonnull values is beneficial. In such cases, if you can figure out a safe lower or upper limit to the range of all possible values, you can enable a range scan with a condition such as `Positive_ID_Column > -1` or `Date_Column > TO_DATE('0001/01/01','YYYY/MM/DD')`.

- `Indexed_Char_Col LIKE 'ABC%'` establishes the start and end of a legal range for an index, with `Indexed_Char_Col` as the leading column of the index. (`LIKE` is SQL's pattern-matching comparator, and % is the pattern-matching wildcard.)

- `Indexed_Char_Col LIKE 'ABC%DEF'` also establishes the start and end of a legal range, but in this case only the `'ABC%'` part of the comparison string contributes to narrowing the index range scan.

- `Indexed_Number_Column LIKE '123%'` does not establish the start and end of a legal range, because the `LIKE` comparison is meaningful only when applied to character strings and the database must implicitly convert `Indexed_Number_Column` to a character string to check this condition, disabling any index leading with `Indexed_Number_Column`. In terms native to numbers, this condition would point to a whole series of ranges:

```
(Indexed_Number_Column >= 123 AND Indexed_Number_Column < 124) OR
(Indexed_Number_Column >= 1230 AND Indexed_Number_Column < 1240) OR
(Indexed_Number_Column >= 12300 AND Indexed_Number_Column < 12400) OR...
```

- `Indexed_Char_Col LIKE '%ABC%'` does not establish the start and end of a legal range, because the leading wildcard implies this pattern might be matched anywhere in the entire range of the index.

- Equality (=), `BETWEEN`, and most inequality (<, <=, >, >=) conditions on first columns of indexes establish legitimate index range endpoints.

- The not-equal-to inequality condition, usually expressed as `!=` or `<>`, does not establish an index range, because the database assumes this condition to be too unselective to be worth indexed access. If the excluded value covers almost all the rows, with other values being rare, you can usefully enable indexed access by replacing the negative condition `Column!='DominantValue'` with `Column IN (<List of all other values, all of which are rare>)`, although it could prove inconvenient to keep this list up-to-date as the application evolves.

- Series of conditions combined by `OR` or by an `IN` list can lead to a series of range scans, but only if every such condition points to a legal range. For example, `IDColumn IN (123,124,125)` yields three legal equality conditions that deliver three range scans, and `(Name='Smith' OR Name='Jones')` yields a pair of range scans, but `(Name='Smith' OR Name IS NULL)` does not enable use of an index (except on DB2), since `IS NULL` does not mark a legal range.

If you have conditions that do not specify a restricted range on at least the first column of an index, the only way to use an index at all is to perform a *full index scan*, a scan of every index entry, across all leaf blocks. Databases will not usually choose full index scans, because to read an entire index is expensive and full index scans usually end up pointing to much of the table as well, with a net cost greater than the competing full table scan. You can force full index scans (often without meaning to) by adding a query hint (more on these later) that instructs the database to use an index even though it would not choose to use that index on its own. More often than not, adding such a hint is a mistake, a desperate attempt to get something better than a full table scan. Usually, this happens when a developer values an index too much, actually leading to a worse plan than the plan the database would choose without help.

Even in cases for which a full index scan is better than the competing full table scan, it is almost surely worse than a third alternative: usually driving from a different, sometimes new index or changing a condition on a function to enable a narrow range scan.

## Selectivity on Table Rows Reached from the Index

Since indexes are compact and better cached objects, compared to tables, selectivity of an index range scan matters less than efficient table access. Even when an index and table are perfectly cached, the selectivity on the table matters more than on the index, because you read about 300 index rows in a single logical I/O to a leaf block but you must do a separate logical I/O for every table row. This brings us to the second part of evaluating the usefulness of an index: how narrowly will the index restrict access to the table? Fortunately, database implementations are smart enough to check all conditions as early in the execution plan as possible, before touching a table, when the index allows. This reduces table reads whenever an index includes columns required to evaluate a condition, even if the database cannot use that condition to determine the range scan endpoints. For example, consider a Persons table with one index that includes the Area_Code, Phone_Number, Last_Name, and First_Name columns. Consider a query against this table with the conditions:

```
WHERE Area_Code=916 AND UPPER(First_Name)='IVA'
```

Only the first condition contributes to the endpoints of the index range scan. The second condition, on the fourth indexed column, fails to narrow that index range scan for three reasons:

- The second index column, Phone_Number, has no equality condition specified (no condition at all, for that matter).
- The third column, Last_Name, also has no equality condition specified.
- The condition on First_Name is disabled as range-limiting by the UPPER function.

Fortunately, none of these reasons prevents the database from checking the second condition before accessing the table. Because the index contains the First_Name column, the database can test conditions against that column using data from the index. In this case, the database uses the Area_Code condition to define an index range scan. Then, as it looks at each index entry in the range, the database discards entries with first names other than Iva. The likely result is just one or two table-row reads on this selective combination of conditions.

Let's examine this situation more closely to decide whether it would be worthwhile to create a better index for this combination of conditions. Both Area_Code and First_Name will see skewed distributions. You will query the common area codes and common first names more often than the uncommon ones, so follow the approach for skewed distributions and find the individual selectivity factors:

```
SELECT SUM(COUNT(Area_Code)*COUNT(Area_Code))/
       (SUM(COUNT(Area_Code))*SUM(COUNT(*)))
FROM Customers GROUP BY Area_Code;

SELECT SUM(COUNT(First_Name)*COUNT(First_Name))/
       (SUM(COUNT(First_Name))*SUM(COUNT(*)))
FROM Customers GROUP BY First_Name;
```

Let's say that the first calculation yields a selectivity of 0.0086, and the second yields a selectivity of 0.018. Let's further assume that you have a 1,000,000-row table and the index references 200 rows per leaf block (less than usual, because this is an unusually wide index key). The condition on Area_Code alone determines the number of index blocks scanned, so first find the number of rows that condition references.

The calculation is $0.0086 \times 1,000,000 = 8,600$, indicating that the database scans 43 (8600/20) leaf blocks. (You can always neglect root and branch block reads in single-table queries.) These 43 leaf blocks are likely well cached and require about a millisecond to read.

> Databases can perform about 60,000 logical I/Os per second on typical CPUs. However, your mileage will vary considerably. Throughout this book, I include figures like 300 index row entries per leaf block and 60,000 logical I/Os per second because I have found them to be roughly correct and useful for an intuitive understanding of tuning priorities. Across a wide range of database and CPU vendors and a wide range of block and column sizes, these numbers can easily be off by a factor of four or more, and performance will no doubt improve greatly in the years after this book is published. Your intuitive understanding from knowing at least the order-of-magnitude ballpark for these numbers will still help, though, and I hope you find remembering a number easier than remembering a complex, conditional range.

Going to the table with 8,600 reads could be a problem, but, fortunately, you pick up the additional selectivity of the condition on First_Name before reaching the table, reducing the row count to about 155 ($8,600 \times 0.018$) rows. You will see about 155 logical I/Os to the table, with a few physical I/Os, since you will see a less favorable hit ratio on the table, compared to the more compact index.

The multicolumn filter selectivity, $0.0086 \times 0.018 \approx 0.000155$, is well into the range that favors indexed access, even though the individual selectivity of the first column alone is in the gray area. Notice that even if you modify the query or the data model to pick up the full selectivity in the index range conditions, the cost will go down only marginally, eliminating most of the 43 well-cached index leaf-block reads and speeding the query by about a millisecond. This will have no effect on the 155 more expensive table-block reads. (You could modify the application to do a case-sensitive match on the first name, and create a new index to cover just these two columns. Alternatively, you could modify the table to store the uppercase first names and index the new column together with area code.) Therefore, even though this query and index are not perfectly suited to one another, the index is good enough to use. It is not worthwhile to add a new index and change the query for the small potential gain.

## Combining Indexes

Occasionally, the database finds equality-condition filters that point to different single-column indexes. By combining index range scans on these indexes, the database can pick up the multicolumn filter selectivity before reaching the table. Let's reuse the earlier example of a query that specifies area code and customer first name, but replace the multicolumn index with single-column indexes on the two columns. Further, replace the condition on UPPER(First_Name) with a simple match on the column, assuming the column already stores uppercase values. Typical conditions are then:

```
WHERE Area_Code=415 AND First_Name='BRUCE';
```

You can now assume that you have closer to the typical 300 rows or more per index leaf block, since these are single-column indexes on short columns. Using the same single-column filter selectivity factors and assuming as before that the table holds 1,000,000 rows, you can again predict that the Area_Code condition will yield 8,600 (0.0086×1,000,000) rows, requiring 29 (8,600/300) index leaf blocks. The second index range scan, for First_Name, will yield 18,000 (0.018×1,000,000) rows, requiring 60 (18,000/300) index leaf blocks. Since these are both equality conditions, the database finds the two rowid lists for these two conditions presorted, and it can easily merge these two sorted lists to find the same 155 table rowids found with the earlier multicolumn index.

The operation just described, merging lists of rowids from two indexes, is called the index *AND-EQUAL MERGE operation*, and the database can do this between any number of equality conditions on single-column indexes. The cost of the table access is the same as finding the rows with one multicolumn index, but you must read more index leaf blocks—in this case, 89 (29+60) instead of the earlier example of 43.

As you can see, the AND-EQUAL MERGE is more expensive than a multicolumn index, but it might be better than using just one single-column index. But this case, in which the AND-EQUAL MERGE is reasonably attractive, is rare. Almost always, the most selective single-column condition is fine by itself and the cost of the less selective index range scan exceeds the savings in table access, or the added cost of the AND-EQUAL MERGE justifies creating a multicolumn index. When you see an AND-EQUAL MERGE in an execution plan, you should almost always either suppress use of the less selective index or create a multicolumn index to use instead. The new multicolumn index should start with the more selective column—in this case, Area_Code—and should usually take the place of any index on that column alone. Such an index sometimes enables you to drop the index on the other column as well.

# Joins

Single-table queries quickly pale as interesting tuning problems. Choices are few enough that even trial and error will quickly lead you to the best execution plan. Multitable queries yield much more interesting problems. To tune multitable queries, you need to understand the different join types and the tradeoffs between the different join execution methods.

# Join Types

Let's begin by trying to understand clearly what a multitable query means. First, consider how databases interpret *joins*, the operations that combine rows from multiple tables into the result a query demands. Let's begin with the simplest imaginable multitable query:

```
SELECT ... FROM Orders, Order_Details;
```

With no WHERE clause at all, the database has no instructions on how to combine rows from these two large tables, and it does the logically simplest thing: it returns every possible combination of rows from the tables. If you had 1,000,000 orders and 5,000,000 order details, you would get (if you could wait long enough) 5,000,000,000,000 rows back from the query! This is the rarely used and even more rarely useful *Cartesian join*. The result, every combination of elements from two or more sets, is known as the *Cartesian product*. From a business perspective, you would have no interest in combining data from orders and order details that had no relationship to each other. When you find Cartesian joins, they are almost always a mistake.

 The most common, but still very rare, exception to this rule is when one of the tables returns only a single row. In that case, you can view a Cartesian join query as a more sensible combination of results from a single-row query appended, for convenience, to results of a logically independent multirow query.

## Inner joins

Any given order-processing application would surely need details pertaining to given orders, so you aren't too likely to see a Cartesian join. Instead, you would more likely see a join condition that tells the database how the tables relate:

```
SELECT ... FROM Orders O, Order_Details D WHERE O.Order_ID=D.Order_ID;
```

Or, shown in the newer-style notation:

```
SELECT ... FROM Orders O
       INNER JOIN Order_Details D ON O.Order_ID=D.Order_ID;
```

Logically, you can still think of this as a Cartesian product with a filtered result: "Give me all the combinations of orders and order details, but discard those combinations that fail to share the same order ID." Such a join is referred to as an *inner join*. Even in the worst cases, databases virtually always come up with a better way to find the requested rows than this brute-force method of Cartesian product first, followed by discards based on unmet join conditions. This is fortunate indeed, since a many-way Cartesian join between several large tables could take years or even eons to complete. Most joins, like the one shown, consist of an equality between a foreign key in some detail table matched to a primary (unique) key in some master table, but any condition at all that mentions two or (rarely) more tables is a join condition.

From a procedural perspective, the database has several choices for how best to join the tables in the preceding queries:

- Start with the master table and find the matching details.
- Start with the detail table and look up the matching master rows.
- Go to both sets of rows independently (but not with a Cartesian product) and somehow merge those rows that match up on the joined column values.

While they yield identical functional results, these alternatives often yield radically different performance, so this book will explain at length how to choose the best alternative.

### Outer joins

A common alternative to the inner join is the *outer join*. An outer join is easiest to describe in procedural terms: start with rows from a driving table and find matching rows, where possible, from an outer-joined table, but create an artificial all-nulls matching row from the outer-joined table whenever the database finds no physical matching row. For example, consider the old-style Oracle query:

```
SELECT ..., D.Department_Name FROM Employees E, Departments D
        WHERE E.Department_ID=D.Department_ID(+);
```

In the newer style notation, on any database, you query the same result with:

```
SELECT ..., D.Department_Name
        FROM Employees E
            LEFT OUTER JOIN Departments D
                        ON E.Department_ID=D.Department_ID;
```

These queries return data about all employees, including data about their departments. However, when employees have no matching department, the query returns the employee data anyway, filling in inapplicable selected fields, such as D.Department_Name, with nulls in the returned result. From the perspective of tuning, the main implication of an outer join is that it eliminates a path to the data that drives from the outer-joined table to the other table. For the example, the database cannot start from the Departments table and find the matching rows in the Employees table, since the database needs data for all employees, not just the ones with matching departments. Later, I will show that this restriction on outer joins, limiting the join order, is not normally important, because you would not normally want to join in the forbidden order.

## Join Execution Methods

The join types determine which results a query requires but do not specify how a database should execute those queries. When tuning SQL, you usually take as a given which results a query requires, but you should control the execution method to force good performance. To choose execution methods well, you need to understand how they work.

## Nested-loops joins

The simplest method of performing an efficient join between two or more tables is the *nested-loops join*, illustrated in Figure 2-7.

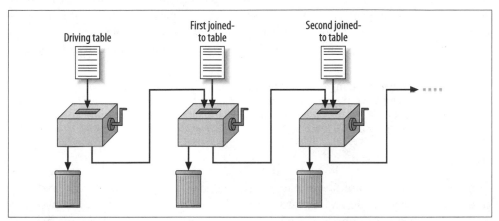

*Figure 2-7. Nested-loops joins*

The query execution begins with what amounts to a single-table query of the *driving table* (the first table the database reads), using only the conditions that refer solely to that table. Think of the leftmost box in Figure 2-7, with the attached crank, as a machine to perform this single-table query. It separates uninteresting rows (destined for the wastebasket at lower left) from interesting rows (rows that satisfy the single-table query conditions) from the driving table. Since the query is a join, the database does not stop here. Instead, it passes the result rows from that first box to the next box. The job of the second box is to take rows from the first box, one at a time, find matching rows from the first joined-to table, then again discard rows that do not meet query conditions on tables so far touched, while passing on rows that meet these conditions. The database usually performs this matching step in a nested-loops join by indexed lookups on the join key, repeated for each row from the driving table.

When the join is an inner join, the database discards rows from the earlier step that fail to find matches in the joined-to table. When the join is an outer join, the database fills in joined-to table values with nulls when it fails to find a match, retaining all rows from the earlier step. This process continues with further boxes to join each of the rest of the tables in the same way until the query is finished, leaving a fully joined result that satisfies all query conditions and joins.

Internally, the database implements this execution plan as a nested series of loops—the outermost loop reads rows off the driving table, the next loop finds matching rows in the first joined table, and so on—which is why these are called *nested-loops* joins. Each point in the process needs to know only where it is at that moment and the contents of the single result row it is building, so this process requires little memory to execute and no scratch space on disk. This is one of the reasons that nested-loops plans are *robust*: they can deliver huge result sets from huge tables without ever running out of memory or disk scratch space, as long as you can wait long enough for the result. As long as you choose the right join order, nested loops work well for most sensible business queries. They either deliver the best performance of all join methods, or they are close enough to the best performance that the robustness advantage of this join method weighs in its favor, in spite of a minor performance disadvantage.

 When speaking of robustness, I speak only of the join method. Independent of the join, the query might call for a large sorted result (for example, with an ORDER BY clause) that requires a large combination of memory and disk scratch space, regardless of the join method.

### Hash joins

Sometimes, the database should access the joined tables independently and then match rows where it can and discard unmatchable rows. The database has two ways to do this: *hash joins*, which I discuss in this section, and *sort-merge joins*, which I discuss next. Figure 2-8 illustrates a hash join.

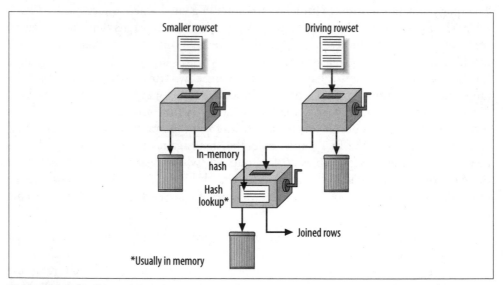

*Figure 2-8. A hash join*

In Figure 2-8, each of the top two boxes with cranks acts like an independently optimized single-table query. Based on table and index statistics, the cost-based optimizer[*] estimates which of these two independent tables will return fewer rows after

---

[*] Oracle's rule-based optimizer will never choose a hash join, but its cost-based optimizer often will. The other database vendors do not offer rule-based optimizers.

discarding filtered rows. It chooses to hash the complete result from that single-table query. In other words, it performs some randomizing mathematical function on the join key and uses the result of that function to assign each row to a *hash bucket*. The ideal hash algorithm spreads the rows fairly evenly between a number of buckets approximating the number of rows.

Since the hash buckets are based on the smaller result set, you can hope those hash buckets fit entirely in memory, but, if necessary, the database temporarily dedicates scratch disk space to hold the buckets. It then executes the larger query (as shown in the upper-right box in Figure 2-8), returning the driving rowset. As each row exits this step, the database executes the same hash function in its join key and uses the hash-function result to go directly to the corresponding hash bucket for the other rowset. When it reaches the right hash bucket, the database searches the tiny list of rows in that bucket to find matches.

Note that there may not be any matches. When the database finds a match (illustrated in the lower-middle box with a crank), it returns the result immediately or sends the result on to the next join, if any. When the database fails to find a match, the database discards that driving row.

For the driving rowset, a hash join looks much like a nested-loops join, both require that the database hold just the current row in memory as it makes a single pass through the rowset. For the smaller, prehashed rowset, however, the hash join approach is less robust if the prehashed rowset turns out to be much larger than expected. A large prehashed rowset could require unexpected disk scratch space, performing poorly and possibly even running out of space. When you are fully confident that the smaller rowset is and always will be small enough to fit in memory, you should sometimes favor the hash join over a nested-loops join.

### Sort-merge joins

The sort-merge join, shown in Figure 2-9, also reads the two tables independently, but, instead of matching rows by hashing, it presorts both rowsets on the join key and merges the sorted lists. In the simplest implementation, you can imagine listing the rowsets side-by-side, sorted by the join keys. The database alternately walks down the two lists, in a single pass down each list, comparing top rows, discarding rows that fall earlier in the sort order than the top of the other list, and returning matching rows. Once the two lists are sorted, the matching process is fast, but presorting both lists is expensive and nonrobust, unless you can guarantee that both rowsets are small enough to fit well within memory.

When you compare a sort-merge join with a nested-loops alternative, the sort-merge join has roughly the same potential advantages that hash joins sometimes have. However, when you compare a sort-merge join with a hash join, the hash join has all

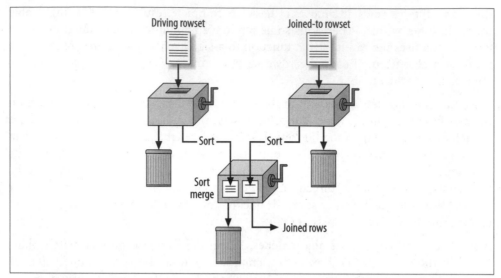

*Figure 2-9. A sort-merge join*

the advantages: it avoids placing the larger rowset into memory or scratch disk space, with essentially no downside cost. Therefore, when you have a choice between a sort-merge join and a hash join, never choose a sort-merge join.

## Join methods summary

In summary, you should usually choose nested loops for both performance and robustness. You will occasionally benefit by choosing hash joins, when independent access of the two tables saves significantly on performance while carrying a small enough robustness risk. Never choose sort-merge joins, unless you would prefer a hash join but find that method unavailable (for example, as with Oracle's rule-based optimizer). In later chapters, I will treat nested-loops joins as the default choice. The rules that cover when you can benefit by overriding that default are complex and depend on the material in the later chapters. The main purpose of this section was to explain the internal database operations behind that later discussion.

# CHAPTER 3

# Viewing and Interpreting Execution Plans

*Set the cart before the horse.*
—John Heywood
*Proverbs [1546], Pt. I, Ch. 7*

This chapter covers basic material about generating and reading execution plans. It's optional, in terms of both when and whether you need to read it for the rest of the book to make sense. The database vendors all provide specialized, often graphical tools to generate and view execution plans. There are also popular third-party tools, such as TOAD, for this purpose. If you have access to these well-documented tools and already know how to use them, you can probably skip or skim this chapter. Otherwise, this chapter is not intended to replace or compete with specialized tools or their documentation. Instead, I describe the most basic methods of generating and reading execution plans, methods that are guaranteed to be available to you regardless of the available tools in your environment. These basic methods are especially useful to know if you work in diverse environments, where you cannot count on having the specialized tools readily available. If you already have and use more elaborate tools, you won't need (and might not even like) my methods. In my own work, across diverse environments, I never bother with the more elaborate tools. I have found that when you know which execution plan you want and how to get it, simple tools, native to the database, will suffice. Reading an execution plan is just a quick check for whether the database is using the desired plan.

If you choose to read this chapter, you can probably skip straight to the section on reading execution plans for your choice of vendor database, unless you want to tune on multiple vendor databases. Each of those sections stands alone, even repeating material from the other sections, when applicable. However, as you read this chapter, please keep in mind that the execution plans you see will not really be useful to you until you have learned the material of Chapters 5–7. These later chapters will teach you how to decide which execution plan you even want, and viewing execution plans is of little use unless you know which plan you want.

# Reading Oracle Execution Plans

Oracle uses a SQL-centric approach to generating and displaying execution plans. You use SQL to place plan data into a table, after which you can view the data with a normal SQL query. The process can seem awkward at first, especially if you perform it manually. SQL Server sends execution-plan descriptions directly to your screen upon request, but Oracle's SQL-centric approach, writing to a plan table, is much more flexible when you wish to automate the process or analyze whole sets of execution plans at once.

## Prerequisites

Oracle places execution-plan data into a table, which is normally called PLAN_TABLE. If you do not already have a PLAN_TABLE in the schema you are using to investigate execution plans, create one. You can create an up-to-date PLAN_TABLE with the *utlxplan.sql* script in the *rdbms/admin* directory under *ORACLE_HOME*. If you cannot reach *ORACLE_HOME*, you can create a serviceable PLAN_TABLE with this script:

```
CREATE TABLE PLAN_TABLE(
    STATEMENT_ID              VARCHAR2(30),
    TIMESTAMP                 DATE,
    REMARKS                   VARCHAR2(80),
    OPERATION                 VARCHAR2(30),
    OPTIONS                   VARCHAR2(30),
    OBJECT_NODE               VARCHAR2(128),
    OBJECT_OWNER              VARCHAR2(30),
    OBJECT_NAME               VARCHAR2(30),
    OBJECT_INSTANCE           NUMBER(38),
    OBJECT_TYPE               VARCHAR2(30),
    OPTIMIZER                 VARCHAR2(255),
    SEARCH_COLUMNS            NUMBER(38),
    ID                        NUMBER(38),
    PARENT_ID                 NUMBER(38),
    POSITION                  NUMBER(38),
    COST                      NUMBER(38),
    CARDINALITY               NUMBER(38),
    BYTES                     NUMBER(38),
    OTHER_TAG                 VARCHAR2(255),
    OTHER                     LONG);
```

## The Underlying Process of Displaying Execution Plans

You use a four-step process from SQL*Plus to generate and display execution plans on Oracle with the least interference to other end users, who may also be using the plan table:

1. Delete all rows from Oracle's special execution-plan table PLAN_TABLE in the schema you are using to generate the execution plans. You can generate an execution plan for a SQL statement only from a database user that has the privilege

to run that SQL statement. Therefore, you usually generate execution plans while connected to the same schema in which the SQL to be tuned runs.

 It is sometimes tempting to set up special analysis-only database users and schemas for purposes such as generating execution plans, and to grant the users enough privilege to execute the SQL to be tuned. This approach must be used with caution, because the special schemas will operate from their own namespace (potentially seeing different versions of a view, for example). When you connect to these special users, the database will potentially interpret a given query differently than it is interpreted within the business application, yielding a different execution plan.

2. Generate the execution-plan records in PLAN_TABLE with the SQL statement EXPLAIN PLAN FOR <Statement_To_Be_Tuned>;.

3. Display the execution plan with a statement like this:

```
SELECT LPAD(' ',2*(LEVEL-1))||OPERATION||' '||OPTIONS||' '||
       DECODE(OBJECT_INSTANCE, NULL, OBJECT_NAME,
              TO_CHAR(OBJECT_INSTANCE)||'*'|| OBJECT_NAME) PLAN
FROM PLAN_TABLE
START WITH ID=0
CONNECT BY PRIOR ID = PARENT_ID
ORDER BY ID;
```

4. Clean up your work with ROLLBACK;.

Let's follow this process to analyze the execution plan for a simple query:

```
SELECT Last_Name, First_Name, Salary FROM Employees
WHERE Manager_ID=137
ORDER BY Last_Name, First_Name;
```

Following is the actual content of a SQL*Plus session to manually determine the execution plan of this query:

```
SQL> delete from plan_table;

0 rows deleted.

SQL> EXPLAIN PLAN FOR SELECT Last_Name, First_Name, Salary FROM Employees
  2  WHERE Manager_ID=137
  3  ORDER BY Last_Name, First_Name;

Explained.

SQL> SELECT LPAD(' ',2*(LEVEL-1))||OPERATION||' '||OPTIONS||' '||
  2          DECODE(OBJECT_INSTANCE, NULL, OBJECT_NAME,
  3                 TO_CHAR(OBJECT_INSTANCE)||'*'|| OBJECT_NAME) PLAN
  4  FROM PLAN_TABLE
  5  START WITH ID=0
  6  CONNECT BY PRIOR ID = PARENT_ID
  7  ORDER BY ID;
```

```
PLAN
------------------------------------------------------------------------------------------
SELECT STATEMENT
  SORT ORDER BY
    TABLE ACCESS BY INDEX ROWID 1*EMPLOYEES
      INDEX RANGE SCAN EMPLOYEES_MANAGER_ID

4 rows selected.

SQL> rollback;

Rollback complete.
```

This shows an execution plan that finds the index range (on the index Employees_
Manager_ID) that covers employees who report to the manager with ID 137. That
index range scan (as shown in the last row of output above the feedback 4 rows
selected) delivers a list of rowids that point to specific rows in specific blocks of the
Employees table. For each of those rowids, Oracle performs logical I/O and, if necessary, physical I/O to the necessary table block, where it finds the specific row indicated. Following the table reads, Oracle sorts the rows in ascending order, based on
the indicated ORDER BY columns.

## The Practical Process of Displaying Execution Plans

To a beginner, Oracle's process for displaying execution plans looks clumsy, I know,
but you can automate the underlying steps with a little simple scripting. If you are
working from Unix, create the following files:

```
-- File called head.sql:
set pagesize 999
set feedback off
DELETE FROM PLAN_TABLE WHERE STATEMENT_ID = '<Your name>';
EXPLAIN PLAN SET STATEMENT_ID = '<Your name>' FOR

-- File called tail.sql:
SELECT LPAD(' ',2*(LEVEL-1))||OPERATION||' '||OPTIONS||' '||
DECODE(OBJECT_INSTANCE, NULL, OBJECT_NAME,
                    TO_CHAR(OBJECT_INSTANCE)||'*'|| OBJECT_NAME) PLAN
FROM PLAN_TABLE
START WITH ID=0 AND STATEMENT_ID = '<Your name>'
CONNECT BY PRIOR ID = PARENT_ID AND STATEMENT_ID = '<Your name>'
ORDER BY ID;
ROLLBACK;

-- File called ex.sql:
!cat head.sql tmp.sql tail.sql > tmp2.sql
spool tmp.out
@tmp2
spool off
```

You then can iterate execution plans rapidly by editing a copy of the SQL in question (complete with terminating ;) in *tmp.sql*, using the editor of your choice, in one

window. In another window, start a SQL*Plus session from the directory that holds *head.sql*, *tail.sql*, *ex.sql*, and *tmp.sql*. Generate new execution plans for the current version of *tmp.sql* (after you save it!) by issuing the command @ex from the SQL> prompt in the window that is running SQL*Plus. The process for analyzing and displaying execution plans then becomes:

1. Place the bare SQL to be analyzed into *tmp.sql*, in the same directory as *ex.sql*, *head.sql*, and *tail.sql*.

2. From a SQL*Plus session started in that same directory, run @ex from the SQL> prompt.

3. View the execution plan.

4. Tweak the database (for example, with index changes) and the SQL to be tuned in *tmp.sql* (following the methods of Chapter 4).

5. Save *tmp.sql* and loop back to Step 2. Repeat until you have the execution plan you want, and then save the corrected result someplace permanent.

With this process, it takes just seconds to make a change and see the results. If you need to print the execution plan or to view it with an editor (especially if it is large), it is already available, spooled to the file *tmp.out*.

In operating systems other than Unix, you can try similar tricks or you can always just add the contents of *head.sql* to the top of *tmp.sql*, add the contents of *tail.sql* to the bottom, and run @tmp from the SQL> prompt, an approach that works in any operating system.

In practice, about half the changes you will make to force the execution plan you want will be to *tmp.sql*, and the other half will be to the database environment, through SQL*Plus, with operations such as creating and dropping indexes, generating table and index statistics, or modifying session optimization parameters.

## Robust Execution Plans

When tuning SQL, you'll usually want to verify that you are getting simple execution plans that drive through nested loops in the correct join order. I refer to these execution plans as *robust*, because they tend to scale well to high data volumes. Here's an example that returns a robust plan, to make the process clear, with the following SQL statement to be tuned, placed in *tmp.sql*:

```
-- File called tmp.sql
SELECT /*+ RULE */ E.First_Name, E.Last_Name, E.Salary,
       LE.Description, M.First_Name, M.Last_Name, LM.Description
FROM Locations LE, Locations LM, Employees M, Employees E
WHERE E.Last_Name = :1
  AND E.Manager_ID=M.Employee_ID
  AND E.Location_ID=LE.Location_ID
  AND M.Location_ID=LM.Location_ID
  AND UPPER(LE.Description)=:2;
```

From SQL*Plus, in the directory with *tmp.sql*, *head.sql*, *tail.sql*, and *ex.sql*, the command @ex from the SQL> prompt produces the following output, with indexes only on the primary keys and on Employees(Last_Name):

```
SQL> @ex

PLAN
-----------------------------------------------------------------------
SELECT STATEMENT
  NESTED LOOPS
    NESTED LOOPS
      NESTED LOOPS
        TABLE ACCESS BY INDEX ROWID 4*EMPLOYEES
          INDEX RANGE SCAN EMPLOYEE_LAST_NAME
        TABLE ACCESS BY INDEX ROWID 3*EMPLOYEES
          INDEX UNIQUE SCAN EMPLOYEE_PKEY
      TABLE ACCESS BY INDEX ROWID 2*LOCATIONS
        INDEX UNIQUE SCAN LOCATION_PKEY
    TABLE ACCESS BY INDEX ROWID 1*LOCATIONS
      INDEX UNIQUE SCAN LOCATION_PKEY
SQL>
```

 The preceding example uses a RULE hint for convenience only, not to imply that you should prefer the rule-based optimizer. A RULE hint is just a convenient way to get a reproducible, nested-loops plan on empty tables, such as I wished to demonstrate.

## How to interpret the plan

Here is how you read the execution-plan output:

• All joins are nested loops, based on the nested series of rows stating NESTED LOOPS. If you have a mix of join methods, the first join executed will be the innermost (most highly indented) one, the last one listed. You'll read the order of join methods executed from the inside out, or from the bottom up.

 This standard way of displaying Oracle execution plans is confusing, if you think about it. If you were to implement comparable nested loops as your own procedural program, the first join, shown as the innermost loop, would actually be the *outermost* loop in the true nested-loops structure! When I first drafted Chapter 2, I even erroneously described the first-executed nested-loops join as the innermost loop, since I was so used to the way Oracle displays execution plans. An alternative method of display would be useful, if everyone could start from scratch. Unfortunately, by now, so many tools and so much practice and education have trained Oracle developers to expect this form of output that changing it would only add to the confusion. If you are new to this, take heart: it will feel natural soon enough.

- The order of table access is Employees, twice, followed by Locations, twice—the same order they appear in the execution-plan output. When SQL references the same tables multiple times, aliases for those tables are mandatory. As you can see in the example FROM clause, the Employees table is aliased to both E and M. You might guess from the index choices that alias E, rather than alias M, represents the driving table, even though both aliases map to the same Employees table. It is less obvious which alias mapping to Locations the database reaches first. This is where the numbers in front of the table names come in: they indicate the order of the alias reference in the FROM clause, so you know that the first Locations alias, LE, is actually the last one the execution plan reaches.

 This addition of the number in front of the table name is the only real change I have made from the standard form that Oracle developers use to view execution plans. My addition of TO_CHAR(OBJECT_INSTANCE)||'*' in the plan-display SQL adds this ambiguity-resolving feature. The number helps in cases when the same table appears multiple times in a FROM clause but one join order to those aliases is superior to another.

- All four table reads are through some index, as shown by the phrase TABLE ACCESS BY INDEX ROWID in front of each table name. The indexes used, and indication of whether the index use is guaranteed to be unique, come in the indented entries just below each table access. Thus, you know that the driving table E is reached through an index range scan (a read that at least potentially touches multiple rows at a time) on the index EMPLOYEE_LAST_NAME. The rest of the table accesses are unique reads through the tables' primary keys. Since all reads after the driving table are for unique joins, you know that the query will read at most the same number of rows for each of these other tables as it reads for the driving table.

 For this example, I contrived index names that make clear which indexed column provides the table access, but indexes are often much more cryptically named than this. If it is not completely clear which column or columns are included in the index used, *do not guess—check*! One of the most common pitfalls in tuning on Oracle is to assume that the index range scan you wanted is the index range scan you got!

When you find unique scans on an index, you can safely assume they serve an equality condition on a unique key. There is usually only one column or combination of columns the index could cover to provide that unique scan, but even if there is a choice, it does not especially matter which unique condition the database uses, so you can safely guess. Index range scans are another matter. If you do not already know the indexes for a table and how they are named for each combination of columns, and if the index names do not resolve the question, always check in case the index range scan is not the one you expected. The simplest script to provide this check is as follows:

```
-- File called index.sql
column column_name format a40
set pagesize 999
SELECT INDEX_NAME, COLUMN_NAME
FROM USER_IND_COLUMNS
WHERE TABLE_NAME = UPPER('&&1')
ORDER BY INDEX_NAME, COLUMN_POSITION;
```

From SQL*Plus, logged into the schema that holds the table you need to check, run @index *<NameOfTable>* from the SQL> prompt. The script lists multicolumn indexes in order, first column first. Here is an example use of this script:

```
SQL> @index Locations

INDEX_NAME                         COLUMN_NAME
-----------------------------      ----------------------------------------
LOCATION_PKEY                      LOCATION_ID
SQL>
```

To see functional indexes, where those would apply (usually where you are matching UPPER(*<Some_Column>*) or LOWER(<Some_Column>), or a type conversion on a column), use the *findex.sql* script:

```
-- File called findex.sql
set long 40
set pagesize 999
SELECT INDEX_NAME, COLUMN_EXPRESSION
FROM USER_IND_EXPRESSIONS
WHERE TABLE_NAME = UPPER('&&1')
ORDER BY INDEX_NAME, COLUMN_POSITION;
```

### Narrative interpretation of the execution plan

I just explained how to find the join order, the join methods, and the table-access methods for the robust execution plan I showed earlier. If you combine that with the basics covered in Chapter 2, you should understand how Oracle will reach the data, from end to end. To test your understanding, try constructing a narrative that explains the full execution plan in English, as a set of instructions to the database. Compare your result with what follows. If it does not match well, try again later, after you have read a few more execution plans, to see if your understanding has improved. Here is the execution plan expressed in narrative form, as instructions to the database:

1. Using the condition E.Last_Name = :1, go to the index EMPLOYEE_LAST_NAME and find the list of rowids that correspond to employees with the requested last name.

2. For each of these rowids, go to the table Employees (E) with a single-block read (logical read, physical when necessary) according to each rowid from the previous step, using the block-address part of the rowid. Using the row-address part of the rowid, find the specific row that the rowid points to and read all necessary data (requested data for alias E) from that row.

3. For each such row, using the join condition E.Manager_ID=M.Employee_ID, go to the primary-key index EMPLOYEE_PKEY to find a single matching rowid that corresponds to the employee record of the manager for the employee whose record you already read. If no matching row is found, discard the result row being built.

4. Otherwise, for the matching rowid, go to the table Employees (M) with a single-block read (logical read, physical when necessary) according to the rowid from the previous step, using the block-address part of the rowid. Using the row-address part of the rowid, find the specific row that the rowid points to and read all necessary data (requested data for alias M) from that row. Append the applicable data to the incoming row from the earlier table read to build a partial result row.

5. For each such row, using the join condition M.Location_ID=LM.Location_ID, go to the primary-key index LOCATION_PKEY to find a single matching rowid that corresponds to the location record that matches the manager for the employee whose record you already read. If no matching row is found, discard the result row being built.

6. Otherwise, for the matching rowid, go to the table Locations (LM) with a single-block read (logical read, physical when necessary) according to the rowid from the previous step, using the block-address part of the rowid. Using the row-address part of the rowid, find the specific row that the rowid points to and read all necessary data (requested data for alias LM) from that row. Append the applicable data to the incoming row from the earlier table reads to build a partial result row.

7. For each such row, using the join condition E.Location_ID=LE.Location_ID, go to the primary-key index LOCATION_PKEY to find a single matching rowid that corresponds to the location record that matches the employee whose record you already read. If no matching row is found, discard the result row being built.

8. Otherwise, for the matching rowid, go to the table Locations (LE) with a single-block read (logical read, physical when necessary) according to the rowid from the previous step, using the block-address part of the rowid. Using the row-address part of the rowid, find the specific row that the rowid points to and read all necessary data (requested data for alias LE) from that row. Append the applicable data to the incoming row from the earlier table reads to complete the result row. Discard the whole result row if it contains data that fails to meet the condition UPPER(LE.Description)=:2. Otherwise, immediately return the fully built result row.

You will find no explicit step in the execution plan for this last filter, which discards rows that fail to meet the condition on the location description. I call this filter a *post-read filter*, since it does not contribute to the method of reaching a table row but instead is used to discard some rows after they are read. Oracle does not make the discard actions on post-read filters explicit in the execution plan, but you can always count on Oracle to apply them at the first opportunity, as soon as it has reached the data necessary to evaluate the truth of their conditions. If the execution plan included further joins after this last join, Oracle would only perform those joins on rows that passed this post-read filter, discarding the rest.

## Nonrobust Execution Plans

Execution plans for the SQL you tune will often be nonrobust in the beginning, often as a part of the performance problem you must resolve. These nonrobust execution plans use join methods other than nested loops. You often do not need to understand the nonoptimal execution plans you start with in detail, as long as you can recognize that they are not the plans you want. However, it is useful to have at least a rough idea of why the starting execution plans are as slow as they are, to guess how much better your optimal plans will be. Now, I'll show how alternative execution plans appear for the query you've been looking at for the past couple sections. If I drop all the indexes, the rule-based optimizer delivers a new execution plan:

```
PLAN
--------------------------------------------------------------------------------
SELECT STATEMENT
  MERGE JOIN
    SORT JOIN
      MERGE JOIN
        SORT JOIN
          MERGE JOIN
            SORT JOIN
              TABLE ACCESS FULL 4*EMPLOYEES
            SORT JOIN
              TABLE ACCESS FULL 3*EMPLOYEES
          SORT JOIN
            TABLE ACCESS FULL 2*LOCATIONS
      SORT JOIN
        TABLE ACCESS FULL 1*LOCATIONS
```

This shows the same join order, but now the database performs sort-merge joins and finds the rows for each table through full table scans.

Hash joins are more common than merge joins in cost-based execution plans, and you will occasionally even prefer them over nested-loops joins, so I next show an example that produces this style of join. Note that the original SQL that produced the previous plan has a hint (/*+ RULE */) immediately following the SELECT keyword. If I replace the hint /*+ RULE */ with /*+ORDERED USE_HASH(M LE LM) */ and reverse the order of the FROM clause—with empty tables, no indexes, and complete statistics—the cost-based optimizer delivers a new execution plan:

```
PLAN
------------------------------------------------------------------------
SELECT STATEMENT
  HASH JOIN
    HASH JOIN
      HASH JOIN
        TABLE ACCESS FULL 1*EMPLOYEES
        TABLE ACCESS FULL 2*EMPLOYEES
      TABLE ACCESS FULL 3*LOCATIONS
    TABLE ACCESS FULL 4*LOCATIONS
```

This is identical to the previous execution plan, except that it replaces the merge joins with hash joins.

## Complex Execution Plans

There are other execution-plan features, such as indicators of which joins are outer joins and steps for sorts and sort-unique operations that discard duplicates that you will see regularly, but these are fairly self explanatory and are not usually important to performance. The only remaining important subtleties that you will often see deal with subqueries and multipart execution plans. I'll cover both of these at once with one final example:

```
SELECT /*+ RULE */ E.First_Name, E.Nickname, E.Last_Name,
       F.Phone_Number, L.Description
FROM Employees E, Locations L
WHERE (E.First_Name='Kathy' OR E.Nickname='Kathy')
  AND E.Location_ID=L.Location_ID
  AND EXISTS (SELECT null
                FROM Wage_Payments P
                WHERE P.Employee_ID=E.Employee_ID
                  AND P.Payment_Date > sysdate-31);
```

Place indexes on:

- Employees(First_Name)
- Employees(Nickname)
- Locations(Location_ID)
- Wage_Payments(Employee_ID)

You then find the following execution plan:

```
PLAN
------------------------------------------------------------------------
SELECT STATEMENT
CONCATENATION
    FILTER
      NESTED LOOPS
        TABLE ACCESS BY INDEX ROWID 1*EMPLOYEES
```

```
        INDEX RANGE SCAN EMPLOYEE_NICKNAME
      TABLE ACCESS BY INDEX ROWID 2*LOCATIONS
        INDEX UNIQUE SCAN LOCATION_PKEY
    TABLE ACCESS BY INDEX ROWID 3*WAGE_PAYMENTS
      INDEX RANGE SCAN WAGE_PAYMENT_EMPLOYEE_ID
  FILTER
    NESTED LOOPS
      TABLE ACCESS BY INDEX ROWID 1*EMPLOYEES
        INDEX RANGE SCAN EMPLOYEE_FIRST_NAME
      TABLE ACCESS BY INDEX ROWID 2*LOCATIONS
        INDEX UNIQUE SCAN LOCATION_PKEY
```

The CONCATENATION step indicates that the optimizer has implemented this as the implicit UNION of essentially two distinct queries, one driving from the index on First_Name and the other driving from the index on Nickname. Following the completion of the outer query, the FILTER step implements the correlation join on P.Employee_ID=E.Employee_ID, following the index on the foreign key from Wage_Payments to Employees. This FILTER step is really no different than a nested-loops join, except that it halts after finding the first matching row, if there is one. Note that the second FILTER step refers back to the same correlation join to Wage_Payments as the first FILTER step. This is an artifact of the concatenated execution plan, which repeats the steps for the joins in the outer query, but not the steps for the correlated join.

# Reading DB2 Execution Plans

DB2 uses multiple approaches to generate and display execution plans. You use SQL to place plan data into a table, after which you can view the data by several means. These are the primary methods that IBM itself describes in its documentation:

*Visual Explain*
> Visual Explain requires a client installation on your workstation and is not available on all supported platforms. For that reason, I've never used it; I prefer a tool that I can always count on being readily accessible.

*The db2exfmt tool*
> This tool runs from the command line in any environment, including nongraphical environments, so you can count on it being available. However, I find that it tells me far more than I want to know, making it hard to find the forest for the trees, so to speak. For example, it produced a 1,216-line report for an execution plan of a simple four-way join. Even the portion of the report that shows the big picture is hard to use. It displays the execution plan tree in an ASCII text layout that mimics a graphical picture of the tree structure, but it requires far more line-width than you can easily view for all but the simplest execution plans.

*Handwritten queries against the plan-data tables*
This approach works best for me, so I describe it in this section in detail. If you already know how to answer the basic questions about an execution plan (e.g., the join order, the join methods, and the table-access methods) using the other tools, you probably don't need this section and can function well with the method you already know.

## Prerequisites

DB2 places execution-plan data into the following seven tables:

- EXPLAIN_INSTANCE
- EXPLAIN_STREAM
- EXPLAIN_OBJECT
- EXPLAIN_ARGUMENT
- EXPLAIN_OPERATOR
- EXPLAIN_PREDICATE
- EXPLAIN_STATEMENT

To create these tables, run the *EXPLAIN.DDL* script located in the *misc* subdirectory under the *sqllib* directory, while connected to the schema in which you need these tables. From the *misc* directory, connect and change to the schema that belongs to the user you will use when generating execution plans. From the Unix prompt, you then execute the command:

```
db2 -tf EXPLAIN.DDL
```

DB2's plan tables contain a hierarchy of data about each execution plan stored, with EXPLAIN_INSTANCE at the top of the hierarchy with one row per execution plan. When you delete an EXPLAIN_INSTANCE row, the delete cascades to remove details for that execution plan from the other tables as well. Normally, your execution plans end up in these tables in the schema that belongs to the end user you logged on as. For example, you might have connected with this command:

```
CONNECT TO Server_Name USER User_Name USING SomePassword;
```

In this case, you likely set your schema to the schema that contains the application data, so you could run and explain queries against that data:

```
SET SCHEMA Appl_Schema;
```

However, this latter step has no effect on where execution plans you generate will end up; they still go to EXPLAIN_ tables in the User_Name schema.

## The Underlying Process of Displaying Execution Plans

You use a four-step process from the DB2 command-line interpreter to generate and display execution plans with the least interference to other end users who might also be using the plan table:

1. Delete all rows from the top-level execution-plan table EXPLAIN_INSTANCE in the schema you are using to store the execution plans, usually the schema belonging to the user you logged in as. The DELETE from the EXPLAIN_INSTANCE table automatically cascades to clean up the execution plan data in the other six tables as well.

2. Generate the execution-plan records with the SQL statement EXPLAIN PLAN FOR *<Statement_To_Be_Tuned>*;.

3. Display the execution plan with a statement by any of several means that DB2 provides, as I described in the earlier, just under the heading "Reading DB2 Execution Plans."

4. Clean up your work with ROLLBACK;.

I'll demonstrate this process to show the execution plan for a simple query:

```
SELECT Last_Name, First_Name, Salary FROM Employees
WHERE Manager_ID=137
ORDER BY Last_Name, First_Name;
```

Here is the actual content of a DB2 session to manually determine the execution plan of this query, with generic passwords and names:

```
$ db2 +c -t
(c) Copyright IBM Corporation 1993,1997
Command Line Processor for DB2 SDK 5.2.0

You can issue database manager commands and SQL statements from the command
prompt. For example:
    db2 => connect to sample
    db2 => bind sample.bnd

For general help, type: ?.
For command help, type: ? command, where command can be
the first few keywords of a database manager command. For example:
 ? CATALOG DATABASE for help on the CATALOG DATABASE command
 ? CATALOG        for help on all of the CATALOG commands.

To exit db2 interactive mode, type QUIT at the command prompt. Outside
interactive mode, all commands must be prefixed with 'db2'.
To list the current command option settings, type LIST COMMAND OPTIONS.

For more detailed help, refer to the Online Reference Manual.

db2 => CONNECT TO Server_Name USER User_Name USING SomePassword;
```

```
Database Connection Information

 Database server       = DB2/SUN 5.2.0
 SQL authorization ID  = USER_NAME
 Local database alias  = SERVER_NAME

db2 => SET SCHEMA Appl_Schema;
DB20000I  The SQL command completed successfully.
db2 => DELETE FROM USER_NAME.EXPLAIN_INSTANCE;
DB20000I  The SQL command completed successfully.
db2 => EXPLAIN PLAN FOR SELECT Last_Name, First_Name, Salary FROM Employees
db2 (cont.) => WHERE Manager_ID=137
db2 (cont.) => ORDER BY Last_Name, First_Name;
DB20000I  The SQL command completed successfully.
db2 => SELECT O.Operator_ID, S2.Target_ID, O.Operator_Type,
db2 (cont.) =>        S.Object_Name, CAST(O.Total_Cost AS INTEGER) Cost
db2 (cont.) => FROM USER_NAME.EXPLAIN_OPERATOR O
db2 (cont.) =>      LEFT OUTER JOIN USER_NAME.EXPLAIN_STREAM S2
db2 (cont.) =>                  ON O.Operator_ID=S2.Source_ID
db2 (cont.) =>      LEFT OUTER JOIN USER_NAME.EXPLAIN_STREAM S
db2 (cont.) =>                  ON O.Operator_ID = S.Target_ID
db2 (cont.) =>                  AND O.Explain_Time = S.Explain_Time
db2 (cont.) =>                  AND S.Object_Name IS NOT NULL
db2 (cont.) => ORDER BY O.Explain_Time ASC, Operator_ID ASC;


OPERATOR_ID TARGET_ID OPERATOR_TYPE OBJECT_NAME       COST
----------- --------- ------------- ----------------- -----------
          1         - RETURN        -                         186
          2         1 TBSCAN        -                         186
          3         2 SORT          -                         186
          4         3 FETCH         EMPLOYEES                 186
          5         4 IXSCAN        EMP_MGR_ID                 25

  5 record(s) selected.

db2 => ROLLBACK;
DB20000I  The SQL command completed successfully.
db2 =>
```

This shows an execution plan that finds the index range (on the index Emp_Mgr_ID) that covers employees who report to the manager with ID 137. That index range scan delivers a list of rowids that point to specific rows in specific blocks of the Employees table. For each of those rowids, DB2 performs logical I/O and, if necessary, physical I/O to the necessary table block, where it finds the specific row indicated. Following the table reads, DB2 sorts the rows in ascending order into a temporary table, based on the indicated ORDER BY columns. Finally, it scans the temporary table that contains the sorted result.

This form of query shows steps labeled by OPERATOR_ID and allows tracing of a tree-like plan through the column TARGET_ID. TARGET_ID points to the step that is a parent of the step shown. In the example, each parent has a single child, but many potential steps, such as nested-loops steps, are parents to a pair of later steps. You can use `TARGET_ID` to lay the steps out in a tree structure that corresponds to the execution plan. DB2's other methods for showing execution plans show this same tree structure directly, though it is hard to see all at once on your screen.

The same sort of tree structure is reflected in the indentation of the execution plans from the earlier query I showed to illustrate Oracle execution plans, but that query uses `CONNECT BY`, a feature lacking in DB2. SQL Server also uses indentation to show the tree structure of the underlying execution plan, in plans shown with `SHOWPLAN_TEXT`, described later.

## The Practical Process of Displaying Execution Plans

To a beginner, the process for displaying DB2 execution plans looks clumsy, I know, but you can automate the underlying steps with a little simple scripting. If you are working from Unix, create the following files:

```
-- File called head.sql
DELETE FROM User_Name.EXPLAIN_INSTANCE;
EXPLAIN PLAN FOR

-- File called tail.sql
SELECT O.Operator_ID, S2.Target_ID, O.Operator_Type,
       S.Object_Name, CAST(O.Total_Cost AS INTEGER) Cost
FROM User_Name.EXPLAIN_OPERATOR O
     LEFT OUTER JOIN User_Name.EXPLAIN_STREAM S2
                ON O.Operator_ID=S2.Source_ID
     LEFT OUTER JOIN User_Name.EXPLAIN_STREAM S
                ON O.Operator_ID = S.Target_ID
                AND O.Explain_Time = S.Explain_Time
                AND S.Object_Name IS NOT NULL
ORDER BY O.Explain_Time ASC, Operator_ID ASC;
ROLLBACK;
```

With the aid of *head.sql* and *tail.sql*, the practical process of displaying execution plans, after you have chosen the execution plan you want (see Chapters 5–7), becomes:

1. Place the bare SQL to be analyzed into *tmp.sql*, in the same directory as *head.sql* and *tail.sql*.

2. From a DB2 session started in that same directory, after running `quit;` to reach the shell prompt, run `cat head.sql tmp.sql tail.sql | db2 +c +p -t` from the shell prompt.

3. Tweak the database (for example, with index changes) and the SQL to be tuned in *tmp.sql* (following the methods of Chapter 4) and repeat the previous step from the shell prompt until you have the execution plan you want. Then, save the corrected result in a permanent location.

Begin by editing a copy of the SQL in question (complete with terminating semi-colon) in *tmp.sql*, using the editor of your choice, in one window. In another window, start a DB2 session from the directory that holds *head.sql*, *tail.sql*, and *tmp.sql*. Next, exit the *db2* command-line processor with quit, but stay at the shell prompt. Generate and view new execution plans for the current version of *tmp.sql* (after you save it!) with the following command:

```
cat head.sql tmp.sql tail.sql | db2 +c +p -t
```

Use your favorite shell shortcut to repeat this command as needed. With this process, it takes just seconds to make a change and see the results. If you need to print the execution plan or to view it with an editor, you can redirect the output:

```
cat head.sql tmp.sql tail.sql | db2 +c +p -t > tmp.out
```

In operating systems other than Unix, you can try similar tricks or you can always just add the contents of *head.sql* to the top of *tmp.sql*, add the contents of *tail.sql* to the bottom, and run the whole script at one time, an approach that works in any operating system. Here is an example of the process in action, with the same query I explained earlier, beginning with the quit command to reach the shell prompt:

```
db2 => quit;
DB20000I  The QUIT command completed successfully.
$ cat head.sql tmp.sql tail.sql | db2 +c +p -t
DB20000I  The SQL command completed successfully.
DB20000I  The SQL command completed successfully.


OPERATOR_ID TARGET_ID OPERATOR_TYPE OBJECT_NAME          COST
----------- --------- ------------- -------------------- -----------
          1         - RETURN        -                            186
          2         1 TBSCAN        -                            186
          3         2 SORT          -                            186
          4         3 FETCH         EMPLOYEES                    186
          5         4 IXSCAN        EMP_MGR_ID                    25

  5 record(s) selected.

DB20000I  The SQL command completed successfully.
$
```

In practice, about half the changes you will make to force the execution plan you want will be to *tmp.sql*, and the other half will be to the environment, through the *db2* command-line interface, with operations such as creating and dropping indexes, generating table and index statistics, or modifying session optimization parameters.

# Robust Execution Plans

When tuning SQL, you'll usually want to verify that you are getting simple execution plans that drive through nested loops in the correct join order. I refer to these execution plans as *robust*, because they tend to scale well to high data volumes.

Here's an example that generates a robust plan, to better understand the process, with the following SQL statement to be tuned, placed in *tmp.sql*:

```
-- File called tmp.sql
SELECT E.First_Name, E.Last_Name, E.Salary, LE.Description,
       M.First_Name, M.Last_Name, LM.Description
FROM Employees E
    INNER JOIN Locations LE ON E.Location_ID=LE.Location_ID
    INNER JOIN Employees M ON E.Manager_ID=M.Employee_ID
    INNER JOIN Locations LM ON M.Location_ID=LM.Location_ID
WHERE E.Last_Name = ?
  AND UCASE(LE.Description) = ? ;
```

To demonstrate this SQL on a realistic case, I populated the Employees table with 100,000 rows, having 10,000 different values for Last_Name. I populated the Locations table with 1,000 rows. I quit to the shell prompt after connecting to DB2 in the directory with *tmp.sql*, *head.sql*, and *tail.sql*. I executed cat head.sql tmp.sql tail.sql | db2 +c +p -t from the shell prompt and produced the following output, with indexes only on the primary keys and on Employees(Last_Name):

```
$ cat head.sql tmp.sql tail.sql | db2 +c +p -t
DB20000I  The SQL command completed successfully.
DB20000I  The SQL command completed successfully.

OPERATOR_ID TARGET_ID OPERATOR_TYPE OBJECT_NAME          COST
----------- --------- ------------- ------------------- -----------
          1         - RETURN        -                    305
          2         1 NLJOIN        -                    305
          3         2 NLJOIN        -                    285
          4         3 NLJOIN        -                    260
          5         4 FETCH         EMPLOYEES             80
          6         5 IXSCAN        EMP_LAST_NAME         50
          7         4 FETCH         LOCATIONS             50
          8         7 IXSCAN        LOCATION_PKEY         25
          9         3 FETCH         EMPLOYEES             75
         10         9 IXSCAN        EMPLOYEE_PKEY         50
         11         2 FETCH         LOCATIONS             50
         12        11 IXSCAN        LOCATION_PKEY         25

  12 record(s) selected.

DB20000I  The SQL command completed successfully.
$
```

### How to interpret the plan

Here is how you read the execution plan output:

- All joins are nested loops, based on the series of rows that state NLJOIN. If you have a mix of join methods, the first join executed will be the last one listed. You read the order of join methods executed from the bottom up.

- The order of table access is Employees, Locations, Employees, Locations—the same order they appear in the execution plan output. When SQL references the same tables multiple times, aliases for those tables are mandatory. As you can see in the example FROM clause, the Employees table is aliased to both E and M. You can tell from the index choices that alias E, rather than alias M, represents the driving table, even though both aliases map to the same Employees table. It is less obvious which alias that maps to Locations the database reaches first, but it must be LE, since only that alias is reachable second in the join order.

- All four table reads are through some index, as shown by the OPERATOR_TYPE FETCH in front of each table name. The indexes used come in the OPERATOR_TYPE IXSCAN entries just below each table access. Thus, you know that the driving table E is reached through an index scan (a read that potentially touches multiple rows at a time) on the index EMP_LAST_NAME. The rest of the table accesses are unique reads since they use equality conditions on the tables' primary keys. Since all reads after the driving table are for unique joins, you know that the query will read at most the same number of rows for each of these other tables as it reads for the driving table.

 For this example, I contrived index names that make clear which indexed column provides the table access, but indexes are often much more cryptically named than this. If it is not completely clear which column or columns are included in the index used, *do not guess—check*! One of the most common pitfalls in tuning is to assume that the index range scan you wanted is the index range scan you got!

If you do not already know the indexes for a table, you don't know how they are named for each combination of columns, and the index names do not resolve the question. Always check in case the index range scan is not the one you expected. The simplest script to provide this check is as follows:

```
-- File called inddb2.sql
SELECT IndName, ColNames
FROM SYSCAT.INDEXES
WHERE TabName = UCASE('EMPLOYEES');
```

From DB2, logged into the schema that holds the table you need to check, edit the script to reference the table you want to investigate and run db2 -tf inddb2.sql from the shell prompt. The script lists multicolumn indexes in order, first column first, on a single line, separated by + signs. Here is an example of the use of this script:

```
$ db2 -tf inddb2.sql

INDNAME                COLNAMES
------------------     ---------------------
EMP_MGR_ID             +MANAGER_ID
EMPLOYEE_PKEY          +EMPLOYEE_ID
EMP_LOCATION_ID        +LOCATION_ID
EMP_DEPARTMENT_ID      +DEPARTMENT_ID
EMP_HIRE_DATE          +HIRE_DATE
EMP_LAST_NAME          +LAST_NAME
EMP_NICKNAME           +NICKNAME
```

```
EMP_FIRST_NAME       +FIRST_NAME
```

    8 record(s) selected.

### Narrative interpretation of the execution plan

I just explained how to find the join order, the join methods, and the table-access methods for the robust execution plan I showed earlier. If you combine that with the basics covered in Chapter 2, you should understand how DB2 will reach the data, from end to end. To test your understanding, try constructing a narrative that explains the full execution plan in English, as a set of instructions to the database. Compare your result with what follows. If it does not match well, try again later, after you have read a few more execution plans, to see if your understanding has improved. Here is the execution plan expressed in narrative form, as instructions to the database:

1. Using the condition E.Last_Name = ?, go to the index EMP_LAST_NAME and find the list of rowids that correspond to employees with the requested last name.

2. For each of these rowids, go to the table Employees (E) with a single-block read (logical read, physical when necessary) according to each rowid from the previous step, using the block-address part of the rowid. Using the row-address part of the rowid, find the specific row that the rowid points to and read all necessary data (requested data for alias E) from that row.

3. For each such row, using the join condition E.Location_ID=LE.Location_ID, go to the primary-key index LOCATION_PKEY to find a single matching rowid that corresponds to the location record that matches the employee whose record you already read. If no matching row is found, discard the result row being built.

4. Otherwise, for the matching rowid, go to the table Locations (LE) with a single-block read (logical read, physical when necessary) according to the rowid from the previous step, using the block-address part of the rowid. Using the row-address part of the rowid, find the specific row that the rowid points to and read all necessary data (requested data for alias LE) from that row. Append the applicable data to the incoming row from the earlier table read to complete the result row. Discard the whole result row if it contains data that fails to meet the condition UCASE(LE.Description) = ?.

 Note that you will find no explicit step in the execution plan for this last filter, which discards rows that fail to meet the condition on the location description. I call this filter a *post-read filter*, since it does not contribute to the method of reaching this table row but instead is used to discard some rows after they are read. DB2 does not make the discard actions on post-read filters explicit in the tables I queried, but you can always count on DB2 to apply them at the first opportunity, as soon as it has reached the data necessary to evaluate the truth of their conditions. Since the execution plan includes further joins after this join, DB2 performs those joins only on rows that passed this post-read filter, discarding the rest.

For each row returned that combines E and LE:

5. Using the join condition E.Manager_ID=M.Employee_ID, go to the primary-key index EMPLOYEE_PKEY to find a single matching rowid that corresponds to the employee record of the manager for the employee whose record you already read. If no matching row is found, discard the result row being built.

6. Otherwise, for the matching rowid, go to the table Employees (M) with a single-block read (logical read, physical when necessary) according to the rowid from the previous step, using the block-address part of the rowid. Using the row-address part of the rowid, find the specific row that the rowid points to and read all necessary data (requested data for alias M) from that row. Append the applicable data to the incoming row from the earlier table reads to build a partial result row.

7. For each such row, using the join condition M.Location_ID=LM.Location_ID, go to the primary-key index LOCATION_PKEY to find a single matching rowid that corresponds to the location record that matches the manager for the employee whose record you already read. If no matching row is found, discard the result row being built.

8. Otherwise, for the matching rowid, go to the table Locations (LM) with a single-block read (logical read, physical when necessary) according to the rowid from the previous step, using the block-address part of the rowid. Using the row-address part of the rowid, find the specific row that the rowid points to and read all necessary data (requested data for alias LM) from that row. Append the applicable data to the incoming row from the earlier table reads to complete each result row. Immediately return the fully built result row.

## Nonrobust Execution Plans

Execution plans often use join methods other than nested loops, especially the starting plans you will need to tune, so I next show an example that performs one of the joins by the less robust sort-merge method. If I drop all the indexes, DB2 delivers a new execution plan:

```
$ cat head.sql tmp.sql tail.sql | db2 +c +p -t
DB20000I  The SQL command completed successfully.
DB20000I  The SQL command completed successfully.
```

| OPERATOR_ID | TARGET_ID | OPERATOR_TYPE | OBJECT_NAME | COST |
|---|---|---|---|---|
| 1 | - | RETURN | - | 21033 |
| 2 | 1 | NLJOIN | - | 21033 |
| 3 | 2 | NLJOIN | - | 20830 |
| 4 | 3 | MSJOIN | - | 10517 |
| 5 | 4 | TBSCAN | - | 204 |
| 6 | 5 | SORT | - | 204 |
| 7 | 6 | TBSCAN | LOCATIONS | 204 |

```
    8         4 FILTER         -                 10313
    9         8 TBSCAN         -                 10313
   10         9 SORT           -                 10313
   11        10 TBSCAN         EMPLOYEES         10313
   12         3 TBSCAN         EMPLOYEES         10313
   13         2 TBSCAN         LOCATIONS           202

  13 record(s) selected.

  DB20000I  The SQL command completed successfully.
  $
```

In steps shown with OPERATOR_ID 5 through 11, DB2 sorts full table scans of Locations and Employees (aliases LE and E) on the join key Location_ID, discarding rows that fail to meet the filter conditions on these tables. In the step shown with OPERATOR_ID=4, DB2 performs a sort-merge join between E and LE. Interestingly, since it sees such good filters on both these tables, it estimates it will likely have at most a single row left at that step, and it chooses to do nested loops to full table scans to join to aliases M and LM, as the last two steps. Nested loops to full table scans such as this would scale badly if the data caused DB2 to loop many times. The cost of merge or hash joins would be slightly higher than nested loops to a single full table scan, but such joins would scale much better.

## Complex Execution Plans

There are other execution-plan features, such as indicators of which joins are outer joins and steps for sorts and sort-unique operations that discard duplicates that you will see regularly, but these are fairly self-explanatory and are not usually important to performance. The only remaining important subtleties that you will often see deal with subqueries and multipart execution plans. I'll cover both of these at once with one final example:

```
SELECT E.First_Name, E.Nickname, E.Last_Name,
E.Phone_Number, L.Description
FROM Employees E
    INNER JOIN Locations L ON E.Location_ID=L.Location_ID
WHERE (E.First_Name= ? OR E.Nickname= ?)
AND EXISTS (SELECT 1 FROM Wage_Payments P
           WHERE P.Employee_ID=E.Employee_ID
           AND P.Payment_Date > CURRENT DATE - 31 DAYS);
```

Populate Wage_Payments with 500,000 rows. Place indexes on:

- Employees(First_Name)
- Employees(Nickname)
- Locations(Location_ID)
- Wage_Payments(Employee_ID)

You then find the following execution plan:

```
$ cat head.sql tmp.sql tail.sql | db2 +c +p -t
DB20000I  The SQL command completed successfully.
DB20000I  The SQL command completed successfully.

OPERATOR_ID TARGET_ID OPERATOR_TYPE OBJECT_NAME        COST
----------- --------- ------------- ------------------ -----------
          1         - RETURN        -                         2014
          2         1 MSJOIN        -                         2014
          3         2 TBSCAN        -                          203
          4         3 SORT          -                          203
          5         4 TBSCAN        LOCATIONS                  202
          6         2 FILTER        -                         1810
          7         6 TBSCAN        -                         1810
          8         7 SORT          -                         1810
          9         8 NLJOIN        -                         1810
         10         9 FETCH         EMPLOYEES                  422
         11        10 RIDSCN        -                          100
         12        11 SORT          -                           50
         13        12 IXSCAN        EMP_FIRST_NAME              50
         14        11 SORT                                      50
         15        14 IXSCAN        EMP_NICKNAME                50
         16         9 FETCH         WAGE_PAYMENTS              134
         17        16 IXSCAN        WAGE_PYMNT_EMP_ID           50

  17 record(s) selected.

$
```

Steps shown with OPERATOR_ID 11 through 15 show the collection of a union of the
sets of rowids from the name conditions joined by OR on E. The resulting new set of
rowids feeds into the step labeled OPERATOR_ID=10 to get just the set of employees that
have the chosen name or nickname. From that list, DB2 chooses nested loops
(NLJOIN) to Wage_Payments. The loops halt as soon as the first match is found, since
this is an EXISTS correlated join. This nested-loops join is labeled OPERATOR_ID=9. It
discards any Employees records that fail to find a matching Wage_Payment in the subquery. Since DB2 calculates that it still has a fairly long list of Employees by that
point, it chooses to read the Locations table once and perform a merge join (MSJOIN)
with the Employees records, sorting both rowsets on the join keys.

# Reading SQL Server Execution Plans

Microsoft SQL Server uses multiple approaches to generate and display execution
plans. These approaches create execution plans sent to your screen, in either graphical or text form, rather than place execution-plan data into tables, as DB2 and Oracle do.

If you bought this book hoping to tune Sybase Adaptive Server, take heart. The two databases share a common heritage, and almost all of what I will say about Microsoft SQL Server applies to Sybase as well, except for the SQL Server Query Analyzer graphical plan facility, which Microsoft added after the two versions split.

## Displaying Execution Plans

SQL Server has two approaches to displaying execution plans: a graphical approach, built into the SQL Server Query Analyzer, and a text-based approach, driven by the underlying database. The graphical display does not fit a whole execution plan of even a modest-sized multitable query onto a single screen. Therefore, I find it difficult to use the graphical display to answer the key questions about a long execution plan:

- What is the join order?
- What method is used for each join?
- What method is used for each table access?

The text-based execution-plan display provides the answers to all three of these questions easily and fairly compactly.

### Displaying execution plans graphically

To see execution plans graphically, you click on the Display Estimated Execution Plan button in SQL Server Query Analyzer. In the window where you usually see query results, you see a diagram of arrows connecting a series of icons that indicate the type of action (nested loops, indexed read, table access, etc.). Text goes with each icon, but the text is generally truncated so that it contains nothing useful until you point to it with your mouse, at which point you get a window that shows the missing details. Furthermore, for even a simple four-way join, the whole diagram doesn't fit on the screen, even with Query Analyzer maximized to fill the screen. I find the graphical approach less useful than the text-based approach, which tells me everything I need to know at a glance.

### Displaying execution plans textually

In the alternative to graphical execution-plan display, you place the query in the Query window of the SQL Server Query Analyzer, preceded by SET SHOWPLAN_TEXT ON, then click on Query Analyzer's Execute Query button:

```
SET SHOWPLAN_TEXT ON
GO
SELECT E.First_Name, E.Last_Name, E.Salary, LE.Description,
       M.First_Name, M.Last_Name, LM.Description
FROM Locations LE, Locations LM, Employees M, Employees E
WHERE E.Last_Name = 'Stevenson'
  AND E.Manager_ID=M.Employee_ID
```

```
   AND E.Location_ID=LE.Location_ID
   AND M.Location_ID=LM.Location_ID
   AND UPPER(LE.Description) = 'SAN FRANCISCO'
```

 If you're on Sybase, just replace SHOWPLAN_TEXT with SHOWPLAN. If you want an even more detailed execution plan, you can also use SHOWPLAN_ALL on Microsoft SQL Server.

When I run the preceding commands with empty tables having statistics, I find the following output in my results window (insignificant text is replaced with ..., and, to fit the output on the page, I've added **(wrapped line)** to show continued lines):

```
StmtText
----------------------------------------------------------------
SELECT E.First_Name, E.Last_Name, E.Salary, LE.Description,
       M.First_Name, M.Last_Name, LM.Description
FROM Locations LE, Locations LM, Employees M, Employees E
WHERE E.Last_Name = 'Stevenson'
  AND E.Manager_ID=M.Employee_ID
  AND E.Location_ID=LE.Location_ID
  AND M.Location_ID=LM.Location_ID
  AND UPPER(LE.Description) = 'SAN FRANCISCO'


(1 row(s) affected)

StmtText
----------------------------------------------------------------
  |--Bookmark Lookup(BOOKMARK:([Bmk1001]), OBJECT:([my_acct].[dbo].[Locations] AS
[LM]))
       |--Nested Loops(Inner Join)
            |--Bookmark Lookup(...(...[Employees] AS [M]))
            |    |--Nested Loops(Inner Join)
            |        |--Filter(WHERE:(upper([LE].[Description])='SAN FRANCISCO'))
            |        |    |--Bookmark Lookup(...(...[Locations] AS [LE]))
            |        |        |--Nested Loops(Inner Join)
            |        |            |--Bookmark Lookup(...(...[Employees] AS [E]))
            |        |            |    |--Index Seek(...(...[Employees].
(wrapped line) [Emp_Last_Name] AS [E]), SEEK:([E].[Last_Name]='Stevenson') ORDERED)
            |        |            |--Index Seek(...(...[Locations].[Location_PKey]
(wrapped line) AS [LE]), SEEK:([LE].[Location_ID]=[E].[Location_ID]) ORDERED)
            |        |--Index Seek(...(...[Employees].[Employee_PKey]
(wrapped line) AS [M]), SEEK:([M].[Employee_ID]=[E].[Manager_ID]) ORDERED)
            |--Index Seek(...(...[Locations].[Location_PKey]
(wrapped line) AS [LM]), SEEK:([LM].[Location_ID]=[M].[Location_ID]) ORDERED)

(12 row(s) affected)
```

After you have executed the query analysis once, you no longer need the top two lines activating SHOWPLAN_TEXT. All future queries will show plans only, until you click on Query Analyzer's Execute Query button for:

```
SET SHOWPLAN_TEXT OFF
GO
```

## How to Interpret the Plan

Here is how you read the execution-plan output:

- All joins are nested loops, based on the series of rows that state Nested Loops(Inner Join). If you have a mix of join methods, the first join executed will be the innermost one, the last one listed. You read the order of join methods executed from the bottom up.

- The order of table access is Employees (E), Locations (LE), Employees (M), Locations (LM)—the reverse order that the tables appear in the execution plan output, from the innermost nesting out. When SQL references the same tables multiple times, aliases for those tables are mandatory. Since the execution plan explicitly references the aliases, there is no ambiguity regarding which alias each step refers to.

- All four table reads are through some index, as shown by the phrase Bookmark Lookup in front of each table name. The indexes used come in the lower entries with matched indentation for each Bookmark Lookup. Thus, you know that the driving table E is reached through an index range scan (a read that at least potentially touches multiple rows at a time) on the index EMPLOYEE_LAST_NAME. The rest of the table accesses are unique reads through the tables' primary keys. Since all reads after the driving table are for unique joins, you know that the query will read at most the same number of rows for each of these other tables as it reads for the driving table.

When you find scans on an index, the condition following the index name makes clear how much of a range the scan will cover. If you need to see other indexes available on a table, the simplest way is to use the sp_helpindex stored procedure. Here are the command and its result:

**sp_helpindex Employees**

| index_name | index_description | index_keys |
| --- | --- | --- |
| Employee_Manager_ID | nonclustered located on PRIMARY | Manager_ID |
| Employee_Last_Name | nonclustered located on PRIMARY | Last_Name |
| Employee_Location_ID | nonclustered located on PRIMARY | Location_ID |
| Employee_Department_ID | nonclustered located on PRIMARY | Department_ID |
| Employee_Hire_Date | nonclustered located on PRIMARY | Hire_Date |
| Employee_PKey | nonclustered, unique located on PRIMARY | Employee_ID |
| Employee_First_Name | nonclustered located on PRIMARY | First_Name |
| Employee_Nickname | nonclustered located on PRIMARY | Nickname |

When an index covers multiple columns, they are listed in order in the index_keys column. You can also use sp_help to see a complete description of a table, which includes a list of the table's indexes.

# Narrative Interpretation of the Execution Plan

I just explained how to find the join order, the join methods, and the table-access methods for the robust execution plan I showed earlier. If you combine that with the basics covered in Chapter 2, you should understand how SQL Server will reach the data, from end to end. To test your understanding, try constructing a narrative that explains the full execution plan in English, as a set of instructions to the database. Compare your result with what follows. If it does not match well, try again later, after you have read a few more execution plans, to see if your understanding has improved. Here is the execution plan expressed in narrative form, as instructions to the database:

1. Using the condition E.Last_Name = 'Stevenson', go to the index EMPLOYEE_LAST_NAME and find the list of rowids that correspond to employees with the requested last name.

2. For each of these rowids, go to the table Employees (E) with a single-block read (logical read, physical when necessary) according to each rowid from the previous step, using the block-address part of the rowid. Using the row-address part of the rowid, find the specific row that the rowid points to and read all necessary data (requested data for alias E) from that row.

3. For each such row, using the join condition E.Location_ID=LE.Location_ID, go to the primary-key index LOCATION_PKEY to find a single matching rowid that corresponds to the location record that matches the employee whose record you already read. If no matching row is found, discard the result row being built.

4. Otherwise, for the matching rowid, go to the table Locations (LE) with a single-block read (logical read, physical when necessary) according to the rowid from the previous step, using the block-address part of the rowid. Using the row-address part of the rowid, find the specific row that the rowid points to and read all necessary data (requested data for alias LE) from that row. Append the applicable data to the incoming row from the earlier table read to build a partial result row.

5. For each such row, discard the whole result row if it contains data that fails to meet the condition UPPER(LE.Description)= 'SAN FRANCISCO'.

6. For each remaining row, using the join condition E.Manager_ID=M.Employee_ID, go to the primary-key index EMPLOYEE_PKEY to find a single matching rowid that corresponds to the employee record of the manager for the employee whose record you already read. If no matching row is found, discard the result row being built.

7. Otherwise, for the matching rowid, go to the table Employees (M) with a single-block read (logical read, physical when necessary) according to the rowid from

the previous step, using the block-address part of the rowid. Using the row-address part of the rowid, find the specific row that the rowid points to and read all necessary data (requested data for alias M) from that row. Append the applicable data to the incoming row from the earlier table reads to build a partial result row.

8. For each such row, using the join condition M.Location_ID=LM.Location_ID, go to the primary-key index LOCATION_PKEY to find a single matching rowid that corresponds to the location record that matches the manager for the employee whose record you already read. If no matching row is found, discard the result row being built.

9. Otherwise, for the matching rowid, go to the table Locations (LM) with a single-block read (logical read, physical when necessary) according to the rowid from the previous step, using the block-address part of the rowid. Using the row-address part of the rowid, find the specific row that the rowid points to and read all necessary data (requested data for alias LM) from that row. Append the applicable data to the incoming row from the earlier table reads to complete and immediately return the fully built result row.

## Interpreting Nonrobust Execution Plans

Execution plans often use join methods other than nested loops, especially as the starting plans you will need to tune, so I next show an example that performs hash joins in place of robust nested-loops joins. If I drop all the indexes and add an OPTION(HASH JOIN) hint at the end of the query, SQL Server delivers a new execution plan:

```
StmtText
-----------------------------------------------------------------------
SELECT E.First_Name, E.Last_Name, E.Salary, LE.Description,
       M.First_Name, M.Last_Name, LM.Description
FROM Locations LE, Locations LM, Employees M, Employees E
WHERE E.Last_Name = 'Stevenson'
  AND E.Manager_ID=M.Employee_ID
  AND E.Location_ID=LE.Location_ID
  AND M.Location_ID=LM.Location_ID
  AND UPPER(LE.Description) = 'SAN FRANCISCO'
  OPTION(HASH JOIN)

(1 row(s) affected)

StmtText
------------------------------------------------------------------------
  |--Hash Match(Inner Join, ...([LM].[Location_ID])=([M].[Location_ID]),...)
      |--Table Scan(...(...[Locations] AS [LM]))
      |--Hash Match(Inner Join, ...([M].[Employee_ID])=([E].[Manager_ID]),...)
          |--Table Scan(...(...[Employees] AS [M]))
          |--Hash Match(Inner ...([E].[Location_ID])=([LE].[Location_ID]),...)
              |--Table Scan(...(...[Employees] AS [E]),
```

```
(wrapped line) WHERE:([E].[Last_Name]='Stevenson'))
                   |--Filter(WHERE:(upper([LE].[Description])='SAN FRANCISCO'))
                      |--Table Scan(...(...[Locations] AS [LE]))
```

(8 row(s) affected)

This shows table scans for every table access. The query drives from LE and filters for locations with the correct description. The second table accessed is E, which is filtered for employees with the correct last name. The remaining rows from these two tables are hashed and joined. This result is next hash-joined to a full scan of M and, finally, to a full scan of LM.

## Complex Execution Plans

There are other execution-plan features that you will see regularly, such as indicators of which joins are outer joins and steps for sorts and sort-unique operations that discard duplicates, but these are fairly self-explanatory and are not usually important to performance. The main remaining important subtlety that you will often see deals with subqueries. I'll cover this with one final example:

```
SELECT E.First_Name, E.Nickname, E.Last_Name,
E.Phone_Number, L.Description
FROM Employees E
     INNER JOIN Locations L ON E.Location_ID=L.Location_ID
WHERE (E.First_Name= ? OR E.Nickname= ?)
AND EXISTS (SELECT 1 FROM Wage_Payments P
            WHERE P.Employee_ID=E.Employee_ID
            AND P.Payment_Date > CURRENT DATE - 31 DAYS);
```

Leave all tables empty. Place indexes on:

- Employees(First_Name)
- Employees(Nickname)
- Locations(Location_ID)
- Wage_Payments(Employee_ID)

You then find the following execution plan:

```
StmtText
-----------------------------------------------------------------------------
SELECT E.First_Name, E.Nickname, E.Last_Name,
       E.Phone_Number, L.Description
FROM Employees E, Locations L
WHERE (E.First_Name='Kathy' OR E.Nickname='Kathy')
  AND E.Location_ID=L.Location_ID
  AND EXISTS (SELECT null
              FROM Wage_Payments P
              WHERE P.Employee_ID=E.Employee_ID
              AND P.Payment_Date > DATEADD(DAY,-31,GETDATE( )));
```

(1 row(s) affected)

```
StmtText
--------------------------------------------------------------------------------
  |--Nested Loops(Left Semi Join)
       |--Filter(WHERE:([E].[First_Name]='Kathy' OR [E].[Nickname]='Kathy'))
       |    |--Bookmark Lookup(...(...[Employees] AS [E]))
       |         |--Nested Loops(Inner Join)
       |              |--Table Scan(...(...[Locations] AS [L]))
       |              |--Index Seek(...[Employees].[Employee_Location_ID]
(wrapped line) AS [E]), SEEK:([E].[Location_ID]=[L].[Location_ID]) ORDERED)
       |--Filter(WHERE:([P].[Payment_Date]>dateadd(4, -31, getdate())))
            |--Bookmark Lookup(...(...[Wage_Payments] AS [P]))
                 |--Index Seek(...(...[Wage_Payments].[Wage_Payment_Employee_ID]
(wrapped line) AS [P]), SEEK:([P].[Employee_ID]=[E].[Employee_ID]) ORDERED)

(9 row(s) affected)
```

The execution plan shows a full table scan on Locations as the driving table, since it
is the first data-access step at the innermost level of nesting. SQL Server then follows nested loops into the foreign-key index Employee_Location_ID to join to
Employees. Once SQL Server reaches Employees, it discards rows that fail to meet the
conditions on First_Name and Nickname. SQL Server then performs a special join
called a *semi-join* to reach the correlated subquery on the join on matching
Employee_IDs, with the index Wage_Payment_Employee_ID. That index provides rowids
to reach Wage_Payments, following which the final filter condition on Payment_Date
discards nonrecent rows that do not satisfy the EXISTS subquery. The join to the correlated EXISTS subquery is shown as the top step, which is described as a Left Semi
Join. This result is not the optimum execution plan for fully populated tables, but
since the test was with empty tables, I would not usually expect an execution plan
that scales well to high data volumes.

# CHAPTER 4

# Controlling Execution Plans

*Saying is one thing and doing is another.*
—Michel Eyquem de Montaigne
*Essays, Bk. II, Ch. 31*

This chapter covers two classes of tuning techniques for controlling execution plans: universal techniques that work independently of your choice of database vendor, and techniques that are database specific. Database-specific techniques are covered well by your own vendor's documentation, so you might know them well already. In general, you need both types of techniques to get precisely the execution plan you want. Each of the vendor-specific sections stands alone, even repeating material from the other sections when applicable. Therefore, you can skip the vendor sections that you don't need.

Much ado has been made over controlling execution plans, sometimes with elaborate tools. This chapter focuses on the simplest ways to control plans, with a strong emphasis on getting the types of plans you will need to optimize real-world SQL. I have found that when you know which execution plan you want in advance, getting it is easy and requires only simple tools.

## Universal Techniques for Controlling Plans

This section describes a number of database-independent techniques you can use to control execution plans. The techniques are good for the following purposes:

- Enabling use of the index you want
- Preventing use of the wrong indexes
- Enabling the join order you want
- Preventing join orders you do not want
- Choosing the order to execute outer queries and subqueries
- Providing the cost-based optimizer with good data
- Fooling the cost-based optimizer with bad data

These vendor-independent techniques often offer an alternative method to achieve ends you could also achieve with vendor-specific methods. When you have a choice, the vendor-specific methods are usually cleaner. However, some problems are solvable only by these universal techniques, which offer solutions that can sometimes work on SQL that is intended to run on multiple vendor databases.

## Enabling Use of the Index You Want

To enable efficient use of an index, you need a reasonably selective condition on the leading column (or only column) of that index. The condition must also be expressed in a way that enables the database to establish a reasonably narrow index range for the index values. The ideal form this takes is:

```
SomeAlias.Leading_Indexed_Column=<Expression>
```

In less ideal cases, the comparison is with some range of values, using BETWEEN, LIKE, <, >, <=, or >=. These range comparisons also potentially enable use of the index, but the index range is likely to be larger and the resulting query therefore slower. If the index range is too large, the optimizer might conclude that the index is not worth using and choose another path to the data. When you combine equalities and range conditions for multicolumn indexes, you should prefer indexes that lead with the columns that have equality conditions and finish with columns that have range conditions. Note that the left side of the comparison simply names the column, with no function around the column, and no expression (such as addition) using the column. Use of a function, a type conversion, or an arithmetic expression on the side with the indexed column will generally disable use of that index.

Type conversions are a particularly subtle way that SQL sometimes disables use of an index. DB2 returns an error if you compare two expressions with incompatible types. SQL Server prefers to perform the implicit conversion on the side of the comparison that does not disable the index. Oracle implicitly converts character-type expressions to the type of the other side, even when this disables index use. For example, consider this expression:

```
P.Phone_Number=5551212
```

If Phone_Number were a character-type column, this would likely evaluate internally on Oracle and SQL Server as:

```
On Oracle:     TO_NUMBER(P.Phone_Number)=5551212
On SQL Server: P.Phone_Number=CAST(5551212 AS VARCHAR)
```

SQL Server preserves indexed access to the column. On Oracle, the implicit use of TO_NUMBER( ) disables use of the index just as surely as if you made the expression explicit. (The only real difference is that the problem is harder to find in the implicit form.) The same problem can plague index use for joins, as well as for single-table conditions. For example, consider the join:

```
P.Phone_Number=C.Contact_Number
```

If `Contact_Number` were a number type and `Phone_Number` were a character type, the implicit conversion on Oracle would prevent an index-driven nested-loops join from C to P. A join in the other direction would be unhindered.

The expression opposite the indexed column reference can be arbitrarily complex. However, it must not reference columns in the same alias with the indexed column. For example, consider the condition:

```
P.Phone_Number=P.Area_Code||'5551212'
```

The database cannot drive into the index on `P.Phone_Number` with this condition, because the database must reach alias P before it can evaluate the expression on the right side. This chicken-and-egg problem prevents identifying (with the index) the subset of the table that meets this condition until after the database examines the whole table.

The final way that SQL often disables index use is with conditions combined with OR. For example, consider the query:

```
SELECT ...
FROM Order_Details D, ...
WHERE ...
   AND (D.Order_ID=:1 or :1 IS NULL)
   AND ...
```

In this example, the database can reach `Order_Details` through an index on `Order_ID` if the bind variable :1 happens to be nonnull. But if :1 is bound to a null value, there is no restriction at all on `Order_ID` and thus no use for that index. Since the database cannot tell what :1 will be bound to when it parses the SQL and prepares the plan, it will find no good opportunity to use the index. In this case, the solution is to create a two-part plan, with each part optimized for one of the cases:

```
SELECT ...
FROM Order_Details D, ...
WHERE ...
   AND D.Order_ID=:1
   AND :1 IS NOT NULL
   AND ...
UNION ALL
SELECT ...
FROM Order_Details D, ...
WHERE ...
   AND :1 IS NULL
   AND ...
```

When you view the execution plan for this query, it shows both indexed access through the index on `Order_Details(Order_ID)` and full-table-scan access to `Order_Details`. This might appear to be the worst of both worlds, but you are saved by the conditions:

```
AND :1 IS NOT NULL
...
AND :1 IS NULL
```

These conditions make no reference at all to any data in the database, so the database can and does evaluate them before it even begins reading data for that half of the combined statement. Therefore, it never actually executes the full table scan when :1 is not null, and it never actually executes an indexed read (or any other part of the execution plan for the first half of the query) when :1 is null. This amounts to a method to branch your execution plan depending on conditions on the bind variables, the variables that determine which data is available to drive the query. The only catch is that you must ensure that the conditions on the bind variables are mutually exclusive, so that exactly one of the branches actually returns data. For example, if you have another bind variable to provide Customer_Name, you might put together a query like this:

```
SELECT ...
FROM Order_Details D, Customers C, ...
WHERE ...
  AND D.Order_ID=:1
  AND :1 IS NOT NULL
  AND (C.Customer_Name=:2 OR :2 IS NULL)
  AND ...
UNION ALL
SELECT ...
FROM Order_Details D, Customers C, ...
WHERE ...
  AND :1 IS NULL
  AND :2 IS NOT NULL
  AND C.Customer_Name=:2
  AND ...
UNION ALL
SELECT ...
FROM Order_Details D, Customers C, ...
WHERE ...
  AND :1 IS NULL
  AND :2 IS NULL
  AND ...
```

This could support a three-part plan, in which the database would:

1. Drive into Orders on the index on Order_ID (your first choice), when possible.

2. Otherwise, drive into Customers on the index on Customer_Name (your second choice) when it has no Order_ID specified but has a customer name.

3. Otherwise, just get all the rows, probably beginning with a full table scan, when it has no selective conditions at all.

In any case, the conditions on the bind variables in the three parts are contrived to be mutually exclusive:

```
AND :1 IS NOT NULL
...
AND :1 IS NULL
AND :2 IS NOT NULL
...
AND :1 IS NULL
AND :2 IS NULL
```

# Preventing Use of the Wrong Indexes

Join expressions are usually simple, usually between consistent types, and usually between numerical IDs. Conditions on the driving table are usually simple and compatible with index use. A more frequent problem than enabling use of the right index is preventing use of the wrong indexes. In many queries, there are multiple single-table conditions that are capable of reaching multiple indexes, but you want to use only a specific one of those indexes. Join conditions are usually expressed to allow index-driven joins in either direction, although only one of the possible join directions turns out to be optimal. Occasionally, you'll prefer to disable use of an index on a join altogether, to force a hash or sort-merge join.

To disable use of an index, create the simplest possible expression around the indexed column reference. For example, you should prevent use of an index on Status_Code for the unselective condition on closed orders, as the number of closed orders will eclipse open orders as you do more and more business:

```
O.Status_Code='CL'
```

Since Status_Code is a character-type column, a simple expression to disable index use without changing the results would simply concatenate an empty string to the end of Status_Code:

```
On Oracle and DB2: O.Status_Code||''='CL'
On SQL Server:     O.Status_Code+''='CL'
```

For number-type columns, you can add 0:

```
O.Region_ID+0=137
```

All databases have some sort of function that evaluates to the first argument when the argument is null and otherwise returns the second argument. On Oracle, the function is NVL( ). On SQL Server and DB2, it is COALESCE( ). If both arguments are the same column, the function always returns the same result as the bare column, regardless of the column type. Therefore, this makes a handy recipe to deactivate index use regardless of column type:

```
On Oracle:             NVL(O.Order_Date,O.Order_Date)=<Value>
On DB2 and SQL Server: COALESCE(O.Order_Date,O.Order_Date)=<Value>
```

In a join condition, a join that disables an indexed path to O.Region_ID (but not to R.Region_ID) could look like this:

```
O.Region_ID+0=R.Region_ID
```

Using the type-independent approach, this same join would look like this:

```
NVL(O.Region_ID,O.Region_ID)=R.Region_ID
```

## Enabling the Join Order You Want

Apart from unintentionally disabled indexes, there are two issues that sometimes disable desired join orders:

- Outer joins
- Missing redundant join conditions

### Outer joins

Consider an outer join query, in Oracle-style notation:

```
SELECT ...
FROM Employees E, Locations L
WHERE E.Location_ID=L.Location_ID(+)
```

or in the newer, universal notation:

```
SELECT ...
FROM Employees E LEFT OUTER JOIN Locations L
    ON E.Location_ID=L.Location_ID
```

This query requests employee records with their matching locations, when employees have locations; otherwise, null location data is used for employees that have no matching locations. Based on the request, it is clear that the query cannot effectively drive from `Locations` to `Employees`, since even employees without locations are needed. Consider a case in which this query is just a template to which an application adds conditions that depend on search criteria provided by an end user. If the end user wants to see employees for a particular location, the application might create this query:

```
SELECT ...
FROM Employees E LEFT OUTER JOIN Locations L
    ON E.Location_ID=L.Location_ID
WHERE L.Description='Headquarters'
```

In the outer case of the join from `Employees` to `Locations`, `L.Description` will be assigned a generated value of `null`, and the condition on `L.Description` will be false. Only the inner case of the join will return rows that might meet the restriction on `L.Description`, so now it makes perfect sense to drive the query in the other join order, from `Locations` to `Employees`. However, the existence of the outer join often prevents automated optimizers from allowing this reversed order on the outer joins, so you need to make the join explicitly an inner join to get the reversed join direction:

```
SELECT ...
FROM Employees E INNER JOIN Locations L
    ON E.Location_ID=L.Location_ID WHERE L.Description='Headquarters'
```

### Missing redundant join conditions

Normally, between any number of tables, the join count is the number of tables minus one. For example, between three tables, you expect to find two joins. Occasionally, a query permits an extra, redundant join. For example, if you have an `Addresses` table that contains all addresses significant to the company, it might have a one-to-zero or one-to-one relationship with the earlier `Locations` table, which contains only locations owned by the company and which references `Addresses` through a matching primary key. In this case, you might find a query like the following:

```
SELECT ...
FROM Employees E, Locations L, Addresses A
WHERE E.Location_ID=L.Location_ID
  AND E.Location_ID=A.Address_ID
  AND A.ZIP_Code=95628
```

By *transitivity* (if *a=b* and *b=c*, then *a=c*), you can deduce that the condition `L.Location_ID=A.Address_ID` must be true for all rows this query would return. However, that condition is not explicit in the query, and not all databases will deduce it and fill it in if it is left out. The best plan, in this case, will likely begin with all addresses within that ZIP Code and immediately join to `Locations` to discard all addresses except the one or two that correspond to company locations, before joining to `Employees`. Since that join order requires the missing join condition to support an indexed path from `Addresses` to `Locations`, you should make the missing join condition explicit:

```
SELECT ...
FROM Employees E, Locations L, Addresses A
WHERE E.Location_ID=L.Location_ID
  AND E.Location_ID=A.Address_ID
  AND L.Location_ID=A.Address_ID
  AND A.ZIP_Code=95628
```

Since you do not want to follow the join from `Addresses` to `Employees` directly, you could also remove, if necessary, the redundant join condition `E.Location_ID=A. Address_ID`, to discourage that unwanted join operation.

## Preventing Join Orders You Do Not Want

Forcing joins in the direction you want, using the earlier techniques for preventing use of the wrong indexes, will prevent many undesired join orders. What do you do when you want the database to follow a particular join direction eventually, but not too early in the execution plan? You cannot afford to disable an index, because you must use that index eventually, just not too early. Consider the following two joins, in which you want to start the query with reads of T1 and then join to T2 before joining to T3:

```
... AND T1.Key2_ID=T2.Key2_ID
AND T1.Key3_ID=T3.Key3_ID ...
```

Here, you want to follow nested loops into both T2 and T3, following indexes in the keys mentioned and reaching T2 before reaching T3. To postpone the join you want to happen later, make it depend (or at least to appear to depend) on data from the join that must happen earlier. Here is a solution:

```
... AND T1.Key2_ID=T2.Key2_ID
AND T1.Key3_ID+0*T2.Key2_ID=T3.Key3_ID ...
```

You and I know that the second version is logically equivalent to the first. However, the database just finds an expression on the left side of the second join that depends on both T1 and T2 (not recognizing that no value from T2 can change the result), so it won't try to perform the join to T3 until after T2.

If necessary, you can string together joins like this to completely constrain a join order. For each join after the first, add a logically irrelevant component referencing one of the columns added in the preceding join to the join expression. For example, if you want to reach tables T1 through T5 in numerical order, you can use the following. Notice that the join condition for the T3 table uses the expression 0*T2.Key2_ID to force the join to T2 to occur first. Likewise, the join condition for the T4 table uses 0*T3.Key3_ID to force T3 to be joined first.

```
... AND T1.Key2_ID=T2.Key2_ID
AND T1.Key3_ID+0*T2.Key2_ID=T3.Key3_ID
AND T1.Key4_ID+0*T3.Key3_ID=T4.Key4_ID
AND T1.Key4_ID+0*T4.Key4_ID=T5.Key5_ID ...
```

I'll apply this method to a concrete example. Consider the following SQL, adapted from Chapter 3:

```
SELECT E.First_Name, E.Last_Name, E.Salary, LE.Description,
       M.First_Name, M.Last_Name, LM.Description
FROM Locations LE, Locations LM, Employees M, Employees E
WHERE E.Last_Name = 'Johnson'
  AND E.Manager_ID=M.Employee_ID
  AND E.Location_ID=LE.Location_ID
  AND M.Location_ID=LM.Location_ID
  AND LE.Description='Dallas'
```

Assume that you have an execution plan that drives from the index on the employee's last name, but you find that the join to the employee's location (alias LE) to discard employees at locations other than Dallas is unfortunately happening last, after the other joins (to M and LM). You should join to LE immediately from E, to minimize the number of rows you need to join to the other two tables. Starting from E, the join to LM is not immediately possible, so if you prevent the join to M before LE, you should get the join order you want. Here's how:

```
SELECT E.First_Name, E.Last_Name, E.Salary, LE.Description,
       M.First_Name, M.Last_Name, LM.Description
FROM Locations LE, Locations LM, Employees M, Employees E
WHERE E.Last_Name = 'Johnson'
  AND E.Manager_ID+0*LE.Location_ID=M.Employee_ID
  AND E.Location_ID=LE.Location_ID
  AND M.Location_ID=LM.Location_ID
  AND LE.Description='Dallas'
```

The key here is that I've made the join to M dependent on the value from LE. The expression O*LE.Location_ID forces the optimizer to join to LE before M. Because of the multiply-by-zero, the added expression has no effect on the results returned by the query.

## Forcing Execution Order for Outer Queries and Subqueries

Most queries with subqueries can logically drive from either the outer query or the subquery. Depending on the selectivity of the subquery condition, either choice can be best. The choice generally arises for queries with EXISTS or IN conditions. You can always convert between an EXISTS condition on a correlated subquery and the equivalent IN condition on a noncorrelated subquery. For example, you can convert this:

```
SELECT ...
FROM Departments D
WHERE EXISTS (SELECT NULL FROM Employees E
                        WHERE E.Department_ID=D.Department_ID)
```

to this:

```
SELECT ...
FROM Departments D
WHERE D.Department_ID IN (SELECT E.Department_ID FROM Employees E)
```

The first form implies that the database drives from the outer query to the subquery. For each row returned by the outer query, the database executes the join in the subquery. The second form implies that you begin with the list of distinct departments that have employees, as found in the noncorrelated subquery, and drive from that list into the matching list of such departments in the outer query. Sometimes, the database itself follows this implied join order, although some databases can make the conversion internally if their optimizer finds that the alternate order is better. To make your own SQL more readable and to make it work well regardless of whether your database can convert the forms internally, use the form that implies the order you want. To force that order even when the database could make the conversion, use the same join-direction-forcing technique used in the earlier section "Preventing Join Orders You Do Not Want." Thus, an EXISTS condition that forces the outer query to execute first would look like this:

```
SELECT ...
FROM Departments D
WHERE EXISTS (SELECT NULL FROM Employees E
                        WHERE E.Department_ID=D.Department_ID+0)
```

For the contrary order, an IN condition that forces the implied driving order from the subquery to the outer query would look like this:

```
SELECT ...
FROM Departments D
WHERE D.Department_ID IN (SELECT E.Department_ID+0 FROM Employees E)
```

This latter order would be a bad idea, unless you found a strange case in which you had more departments than employees!

You can have several subqueries in which the database either must drive from the outer query to the subquery (such as NOT EXISTS subqueries) or should drive in that order. Such a case implies a choice of the order of execution of the subqueries. You can also have choices about whether to execute subqueries after completing the outer query, or at the first opportunity, as soon as the correlation join is possible, or at some point between these extremes.

The first tactic for controlling the order of subquery execution is simply to list the subqueries in order in the WHERE clause (i.e., the top subquery to be executed should be listed first). This is one of the few times when WHERE-clause order seems to matter.

Rarely, the database will execute a subquery sooner than you would like. The same tactic for postponing joins (described in the section "Preventing Join Orders You Do Not Want") works for *correlation joins*, the joins in subqueries that correlate the subqueries to the outer queries. For example, consider this query:

```
SELECT ...
FROM Orders O, Customers C, Regions R
WHERE O.Status_Code='OP'
  AND O.Customer_ID=C.Customer_ID
  AND C.Customer_Type_Code='GOV'
  AND C.Region_ID=R.Region_ID
  AND EXISTS (SELECT NULL
                FROM Order_Details OD
                WHERE O.Order_ID=OD.Order_ID
                  AND OD.Shipped_Flag='Y')
```

For this query you might find that the subquery runs as soon as you reach the driving Orders table, but you might wish to perform the join to Customers first, to discard nongovernmental orders, before you take the expense of the subquery execution. In this case, this would be the transformation to postpone the correlation join:

```
SELECT ...
FROM Orders O, Customers C, Regions R
WHERE O.Status_Code='OP'
  AND O.Customer_ID=C.Customer_ID
  AND C.Customer_Type_Code='GOV'
  AND C.Region_ID=R.Region_ID
  AND EXISTS (SELECT NULL
                FROM Order_Details OD
                WHERE O.Order_ID+0*C.Customer_ID=OD.Order_ID
                  AND OD.Shipped_Flag='Y')
```

Notice the addition of +0*C.Customer_ID to the subquery's WHERE clause. This ensures the join to Customers occurs first, before the subquery executes.

## Providing the Cost-Based Optimizer with Good Data

On any cost-based optimizer (that is, for any query except one running on the Oracle rule-based optimizer, since only Oracle has a rule-based optimizer), the second most common source of poor execution plans (after missing indexes) is missing statistics on the tables, columns, and indexes involved in the query. In all, cost-based optimizers do a fairly good job of finding the best plan without help when they have good information to begin with. However, when they are missing information—for example, because a table or index has been rebuilt without regenerating statistics for that object—they tend to make terrible assumptions.

If you are running on any database except Oracle, or if you are on Oracle's cost-based optimizer (as is most common and as Oracle recommends) and not forcing the rule-based optimizer, the first thing you should try if you are not getting the execution plan you want is to regenerate statistics on every table and index relevant to the query. Standard statistics will usually suffice to get reasonable execution plans.

Cost-based optimizers usually assume that data is uniformly distributed. For example, if the optimizer statistics show a table of 1,000,000 rows with 50,000 distinct values for some indexed foreign key, the database will optimize on the assumption that every value of that key will match exactly 20 rows. For most indexed columns, like foreign keys, this assumption of a uniform data distribution works well. However, some columns have highly skewed distributions, such as status, code, or type columns, or foreign keys to status or type tables. For example, consider this query:

```
SELECT ... FROM Orders WHERE Status_Code = 'OP'
```

There might only be three or four values of Status_Code across a 1,000,000-row Orders table, but if 'OP' means this is an open order, not yet fulfilled or cancelled, this condition is far more selective than the optimizer would expect based solely on the number of distinct values. If the column had an index, the optimizer might never use that index if it knew only the small number of distinct indexed values. However, on some databases, you can generate added statistics that let the database know not only the number of distinct values but also the distribution of those values, a necessary step when you have such highly skewed distributions.

## Fooling the Cost-Based Optimizer with Incorrect Data

This last technique is dangerous, and I recommend it only as a last resort. Sometimes, you want to simulate a large database on a small, development database. If you can extrapolate (or, better, measure from an actual database) statistics that apply to a large database, you can manually modify the data-dictionary tables that store those statistics for the optimizer, to fool the optimizer into thinking it is working with a large database. The small database will have statistics that show large tables with many distinct values on most indexes. This is a handy way to see execution plans that will apply to production volumes when you have only a test database with toy data volumes. For such toy-sized databases, there is no great risk to this approach. On production databases, the optimizer will occasionally make better choices if it has the wrong data, usually if it has data that exaggerates the selectivity of desired indexes or that exaggerates the size of a table when a full table scan is undesirable.

Imagine reversing the logic the optimizer follows: ask "What would I need to believe about the tables and indexes of this query to find an alternative plan (the alternative that you, the human optimizer, want) much more attractive?" It is not hard to fool the optimizer into doing what you want rather than what it would choose on its own, if you lie to it about the statistics. However, on production systems, this is dangerous in several ways:

- As soon as anyone regenerates statistics for the tables or indexes, the optimizer will revert to the original error, unless the manual statistics-tweak is reapplied. You will have to rigorously control statistics generation to prevent this.

- As soon as the database optimizer improves—with the next release, perhaps—it is denied the chance to exploit those improvements with correct data.

- Most importantly, every other query against the tables and indexes with false statistics is at risk and will potentially be harmed, just to help the one query you wanted to tune when you fudged the statistics.

I have never needed to play this card to get an adequately optimized plan on Oracle, SQL Server, or DB2, and I recommend you avoid it if possible.

## Controlling Plans on Oracle

Oracle currently offers two completely different optimizers, the rule-based optimizer (RBO) and the cost-based optimizer (CBO), and the methods for tuning on each differ.

The RBO is Oracle's original automated optimizer, back from the days of Oracle Version 6 and earlier. By *rule-based*, Oracle means that the optimizer uses only fixed properties of the tables, indexes, and SQL to guess an optimum execution plan from a set of simple rules of thumb (or *heuristics*) built into the automated optimizer. The RBO uses no data about the sizes of the tables or indexes, or about the distribution of data within those objects. It does use data on the fixed properties of the indexes: whether they are unique, which columns they cover, in which order, and how well those match up with the most selective-looking filter conditions and joins in the SQL. As tables grow and data distributions change, the RBO should go right on delivering the same plan indefinitely, as long as you don't alter the indexes (for example, from unique to nonunique) or change the table structure (for example, from an ordinary table to a partitioned table). However, at some future time, perhaps even in Oracle Database 10*g*, Oracle will drop all support for the rule-based optimizer, and cost-based optimization will become your only choice.

Since Oracle7, the RBO has been even more stable than before, because Oracle chose to freeze the RBO code beginning with Oracle7, except for rare, slight changes necessary to deliver functionally correct (as opposed to necessarily optimum) results. Therefore, an execution plan that is correct on the RBO today will likely stay unchanged until Oracle drops the RBO altogether. This is appealing from the perspective of stability, although the dark side of this stability is that the execution plans never get any better either.

Execution plans on the RBO never change to adapt to changing data distributions, and this is often cited as an argument to switch to the CBO. However, in my own experience, data-distribution change is the least of the reasons for cost-based optimization. In over 10 years, I have yet to find a single case in which it was important to use different execution plans for different real-world data distributions with the same SQL.

I have seen many cases in which one plan is not perfectly optimal for all real-world data distributions, but in all these cases, one robust plan exists that is at least nearly optimal across the board.

Another argument cited in favor of the CBO is that it can deliver *parallel execution plans*, plans that can bring multiple processors to bear on the SQL statement at once. I have not found this to be a compelling argument, since I have yet to find a real-world case in which the optimum SQL, with the optimum database design, required parallel execution for adequate performance. I expect some such cases exist in data-warehousing environments, which are not where most of my experience lies, I admit, but almost all cases in which parallel execution plans appear to shine are really covering up some mistake in database design, indexing, or application design, compensating for design deficiencies with horsepower. That, by itself, would not be such a bad thing; extra horsepower might be cheaper than fixing the application. However, parallel plans are usually in service of large batch processes, competing heavily for resources with online processes that are more critical to end users. Therefore, parallel plans often rob needed resources from other processes that are more critical.

These are the strongest arguments against using the RBO:

- It will become unavailable in some future release, perhaps during Oracle Database 10g, and you will not be able to use an older release forever.

- The CBO keeps getting better, while the RBO is stuck with all the old problems it has ever had.

- The CBO has a huge inherent advantage in the information available to it to calculate the best plan.

- The RBO cannot take advantage of features created since the CBO appeared in Oracle7, and in most cases the RBO will simply push queries that involve newer object types, such as bit-mapped indexes, off to the CBO. (See the following section, "Controlling the Choice of Oracle Optimizer," for details about which features the RBO cannot handle.)

That said, the RBO does a surprisingly good job; its heuristics are well designed to get along with the tiny amount of information that the RBO uses to guess the best plan. In Chapter 6, I will describe properties of what I call a *robust* execution plan, one that behaves well across a wide range of data distributions. The RBO almost always delivers a robust plan when the necessary indexes are available and when the developer has not prevented use of an index with some index-disabling expression, as discussed earlier in this chapter. Given the right indexes, you can almost always get the best robust plan on either optimizer, with manual tuning. With automated tuning, the biggest advantage of the CBO is that it is more resourceful when dealing with imperfect indexing and nonoptimally written SQL; more often, it delivers at least an adequate plan in these cases, without manual tuning. When more than one robust plan is possible, the CBO is also more likely to find the best robust plan, while the RBO will pick one without knowing relative costs, unless you manually tune the SQL.

## Controlling the Choice of Oracle Optimizer

It is unrealistic to optimize Oracle queries simultaneously for both the rule-based and the cost-based optimizers. Therefore, you should understand the factors that lead Oracle to choose which optimizer it applies, so that you can control those factors and get the optimizer you choose.

The RBO cannot handle certain object types and object properties that did not yet exist when Oracle froze the RBO code. However, rather than simply have its code error out, Oracle modified the RBO code just enough to let it recognize the cases it cannot handle and to have it pass those cases on to the CBO. Thus, even if you think you have set up your system for rule-based optimization, the following circumstances will absolutely force cost-based optimization:

- Bit-mapped indexes on any column of a table referenced in the SQL, even if those indexes are on columns the SQL does not touch.
- Function-based indexes in a table referenced in the SQL, if such and index is on an expression the SQL references.
- Partitioned tables touched by the SQL.
- Tables or indexes configured with parallel degree. The optimizer interprets these as a command to find parallel execution plans, which the RBO does not know how to do. As for bit-mapped indexes, indexes configured with parallel degree will disable use of the RBO on a table referenced by your SQL, even if the parallel-degree index is on columns the SQL does not touch.

## Unintentionally Disabling Use of the RBO

Here's a real-world scenario I have seen more than once: you have a stable production application performing nicely on the RBO when, without warning, large portions of the application suddenly slow to a crawl. Panic and finger-pointing ensue. After much investigation, it turns out that the night before, a database administrator (DBA) innocently dropped and recreated some large, central-table index, perhaps to move it to a new filesystem that had more space available. Your DBA cleverly recognized that this was such a large index that it might take prohibitively long to create the old-fashioned way, so he chose to create it in parallel, using something like this:

```
CREATE INDEX Order_Ship_Date
ON Orders(Ship_Date)
PARALLEL 10;
```

This brought 10 simultaneous threads to bear on the index creation and greatly sped up that process, meeting the time window available for the work. So far, this is well and good. What no one realized was that it also left behind an index property that instructed Oracle to use cost-based optimization, regardless of the database configuration, to attempt to find plans using this index in parallel threads for all SQL that referenced this table. Since no one expected the CBO to apply to this application, no one bothered to create statistics on the tables and indexes, so the CBO operated in ignorance of correct statistics and suddenly delivered horrible plans on most SQL to this central table. Once recognized, the problem is solvable with this command:

```
ALTER INDEX Order_Ship_Date PARALLEL 1;
```

Because this statement only tweaks a value in the data dictionary, rather than rebuild the index, it runs almost instantly, and the application immediately reverts to its old performance. You can find indexes with this problem with this query:

```
SELECT Index_Name
FROM ALL_INDEXES
WHERE Degree!=1;
```

If the tables and indexes involved in your SQL do not prevent using the RBO, Oracle chooses between the RBO and the CBO as follows:

1. If any SELECT keyword in the SQL (even in a subquery or a view definition) is followed by any valid hint other than /*+ RULE */ or /*+ CHOOSE */, Oracle will use the CBO.

2. Otherwise, if any SELECT keyword in the SQL (even in a subquery or a view definition) is followed by /*+ CHOOSE */ and there are any statistics on any table or index referenced by the SQL, Oracle will choose the CBO.

3. Otherwise, if any SELECT keyword in the SQL (even in a subquery or a view definition) is followed by /*+ RULE */, Oracle will choose the RBO.

4. Otherwise, if the session optimizer_mode parameter is set at the session level (by ALTER SESSION SET OPTIMIZER_MODE=<Your_Choice>;), Oracle will choose according to that session-level parameter.

5. Otherwise, if the `optimizer_mode` parameter is set for the database instance, in the *init.ora* file, Oracle will choose according to that instance-level parameter.

6. Otherwise, Oracle will choose according to the ultimate default `optimizer_mode` parameter, `CHOOSE`.

In the last three steps of this decision cascade, Oracle chooses according to an `optimizer_mode` parameter, which you or your DBA sets. These are the four possible parameter values and how they affect the choice:

RULE
Oracle uses rule-based optimization.

ALL_ROWS
Oracle uses cost-based optimization with the goal of minimizing the cost of the whole query. This default version of cost-based optimization sometimes results in nonrobust plans (plans that use join methods other than nested-loops), with risks described in Chapter 6. However, the optimizer chooses these plans only when it calculates that they are faster than the best robust plans.

FIRST_ROWS
Oracle uses cost-based optimization with the goal of minimizing the cost of reaching the first rows from the query. In practice, this tends to favor robust, nested-loops plans similar to those plans the rule-based optimizer favors but built with much more knowledge of the data distributions and probable execution costs. The `FIRST_ROWS` optimization level creates the same effect as the `OPTIMIZE FOR 1 ROW` hint on DB2 and the `OPTION(FAST 1)` hint on SQL Server.

CHOOSE
Oracle uses cost-based optimization, as for the `ALL_ROWS` goal, unless no table or index involved in the query has optimization statistics available, in which case Oracle uses rule-based optimization.

Here's a quick way to check the instance-level parameter for `optimizer_mode`:

```
SELECT VALUE FROM V$PARAMETER WHERE NAME = 'optimizer_mode';
```

When you have an execution plan in `PLAN_TABLE`, a quick way to see whether it is cost-based is to run the following query:

```
SELECT POSITION FROM PLAN_TABLE WHERE ID=0;
```

This returns the cost of the entire execution plan, in arbitrary units, when the plan is cost-based. When cost is not null, you have a cost-based plan.

## Controlling Oracle Rule-Based Execution Plans

Most of the methods for controlling rule-based execution plans are the universal techniques of controlling plans, covered in the first section of this chapter. The primary Oracle-specific method of tuning under a rule-based default `optimizer_mode` is

## Mixing Cost and Rule

The CHOOSE option offers the potential to mix your optimization styles on a database instance. For example, you might use CHOOSE if you wish to run two distinct applications: one that has SQL certified and optimized for rule-based optimization and one that expects cost-based optimization. You would then avoid generating statistics for the tables referenced by the first application, so its SQL would be optimized by the RBO.

Although this sounds good, I do not recommend it. Chances are, you will have overlap between the tables the two applications use; otherwise, you would not have bothered to put them on the same database instance. In that case, you will end up with some SQL optimized under the worst possible arrangement—using the CBO, but lacking statistics on one or more tables.

Even if you have completely disjoint sets of tables for the two applications, it is always much too likely that someone, some time, will generate statistics on some of the tables for the application that expects to use the RBO. Again, this results in the worst arrangement—cost-based plans against SQL that mixes tables with and without statistics. It is far safer to use separate instances, with the setting optimizer_mode=rule set instance-wide on the application that needs it. Alternatively, have one of the applications explicitly set the optimizer_mode when it connects to the database, overriding the instance optimizer_mode setting, and use the instance-wide setting to choose the optimizer the other application uses.

---

simply to switch modes to cost-based optimization, usually with a hint such as /*+ FIRST_ROWS */. In other words, you can always control a plan via hints, and hints (with the exception of the /*+ RULE */ hint) in a statement cause Oracle to use the CBO for that statement.

However, if you prefer not to use cost-based optimization, thus precluding the use of hints, one RBO-specific technique remains: in the FROM clause, list tables and their aliases in exactly the reverse order from the join order you want. This usually gives enough control of the join order, without using the techniques described earlier in the section "Preventing Join Orders You Do Not Want." In particular, eligible, unique joins toward primary keys happen in the reverse order they are listed in the FROM clause, without changing the join conditions. For example, consider this query:

```
SELECT /*+ RULE */ E.First_Name, E.Last_Name, E.Salary, LE.Description,
       M.First_Name, M.Last_Name, LM.Description
FROM Locations LM, Employees M, Locations LE, Employees E
WHERE E.Last_Name = 'Johnson'
  AND E.Manager_ID=M.Employee_ID
  AND E.Location_ID=LE.Location_ID
  AND M.Location_ID=LM.Location_ID
  AND LE.Description='Dallas';
```

Unlike the earlier version of this query in Chapter 3, which had the wrong order in the FROM clause, you now get the correct join order. In this correct execution plan, E joins to LE before joining to M or LM, as shown by the plan output:

```
SQL> @ex

PLAN
---------------------------------------------------------------------
SELECT STATEMENT
  NESTED LOOPS
    NESTED LOOPS
      NESTED LOOPS
        TABLE ACCESS BY INDEX ROWID 4*EMPLOYEES
          INDEX RANGE SCAN EMPLOYEE_LAST_NAME
        TABLE ACCESS BY INDEX ROWID 3*LOCATIONS
          INDEX UNIQUE SCAN LOCATION_PKEY
      TABLE ACCESS BY INDEX ROWID 2*EMPLOYEES
        INDEX UNIQUE SCAN EMPLOYEE_PKEY
    TABLE ACCESS BY INDEX ROWID 1*LOCATIONS
      INDEX UNIQUE SCAN LOCATION_PKEY
```

When the RBO otherwise has no preference based on the conditions and indexes, the RBO joins tables by working from right to left in the FROM clause. However, this method offers only limited control by itself, because the RBO follows its other rules of thumb before considering the join order in the FROM clause. For example, the RBO always chooses to perform unique indexed reads and joins before doing indexed range scans, when it can.

## Controlling Oracle Cost-Based Execution Plans

There are two main parts involved in tuning on the Oracle CBO:

- Providing the optimizer with good statistics about the tables and indexes, so it can calculate the costs of alternatives accurately. This is effectively a prerequisite to any manual tuning on a CBO.

- Adding hints to queries that the CBO fails to optimize well even with complete statistics about the tables and indexes that the queries reference.

### Oracle cost-based optimizer prerequisites

Proving that a little knowledge is a dangerous thing, cost-based optimizers often do a terrible job if they do not have statistics on all the tables and indexes involved in the query. It is therefore imperative to maintain statistics on tables and indexes reliably, including regenerating statistics whenever table volumes change much or tables or indexes are rebuilt. It is safest to regenerate statistics periodically, during times that load is relatively quiet, such as nightly or at least weekly. The best way to generate and update statistics is with Oracle's DBMS_STATS package, documented at length in *Oracle8i Supplied PL/SQL Packages Reference* and *Oracle9i Supplied PL/SQL Packages and Types Reference*. Here is a simple example of using DBMS_STATS to generate statistics for a whole schema, Appl_Prod, sampling 10% of the data in the larger tables and cascading statistics collection to the indexes:

```
BEGIN
    DBMS_STATS.GATHER_SCHEMA_STATS ('Appl_Prod',10,
        CASCADE => TRUE);
END;
/
```

Often, queries include conditions on highly skewed distributions, such as conditions on special types, codes, or flags, when these columns have only a few values. Normally, the CBO evaluates selectivity of a condition based on the assumption that all nonnull values of a column are equally selective. This assumption generally works well for foreign and primary keys that join business entities, but it is inaccurate when the columns have permanent special meanings and certain meanings apply much more rarely than others.

For example, in an Orders table, you might have a Status_Code column with three possible values: 'CL' for *closed* (i.e., fulfilled) orders, 'CA' for *cancelled* orders, and 'OP' for *open* orders. Most orders, by far, would be fulfilled, once the application has been running for a few months. A steady, significant fraction of orders would end up cancelled, so that value would also eventually point to a large list of orders. However, as long as the business keeps up with incoming orders, the number of open orders would remain moderate and steady, even as data accumulates for years. Quite early, a condition specifying Status_Code='OP' would be selective enough to justify indexed access, if you had an index with that leading column, and it is important to enable the optimizer to realize this fact, preferably without a lot of manual tuning. Enabling the CBO to recognize when a column is selective requires two things:

- The SQL must mention the specific selective value, rather than use a bind variable, prior to Oracle 9*i* Database. Use of bind variables is commonly attractive, since it makes SQL more general and easier to share between processes. However, this need to hardcode especially selective values is the exception to that rule. If you use Status_Code=:1 instead of Status_Code='OP', prior to Oracle 9*i*, you will deny the CBO potential knowledge of the selectivity of the condition at parse time, when it does not yet know whether the bind variable :1 will be assigned a common or a rare Status_Code. Fortunately, in these cases, the usual reason to prefer using bind variables does not generally apply; since these special codes have special business meanings, it is unlikely that the SQL ever requires substituting a different value than the single selective value.

 In Oracle 9*i*, Oracle introduced *bind variable peeking*, wherein Oracle checks the first value assigned to each bind variable (when a query sees its first hard parse) when choosing an execution plan. This eliminates the need to specify fixed values in place of bind variables, as long as all the values to be bound are of similar selectivity. However, if the bind variable will be bound sometimes to selective values and sometimes to nonselective values, you still must hardcode the values to obtain different plans in the two cases.

- You need to provide the CBO with special statistics that quantify how rare the uncommon code, type, or status values are, so it can know which values are highly selective.

Oracle stores special statistics on distribution when you request them, based on sorting the rows for a column and arranging the sorted list into a specified number of buckets that each contain the same number of rows. Since Oracle already knows that the range each bucket holds has the same number of rows, Oracle needs to know only the value-range endpoints in each bucket. In the current example, with 20 buckets, the first bucket might hold the range 'CA' to 'CA', and the second bucket might hold the range 'CA' to 'CL'. The next 17 buckets would hold the most common range, 'CL' to 'CL'. The last bucket would hold the range 'CL' to 'OP', which includes the rarest value. From this, Oracle can deduce that the selectivity of the column is 5–10% for the value 'CA', 85–95% for the value 'CL', and 0–5% for the value 'OP'. Since you want the optimizer to know more closely how selective the 'OP' value is, you would choose more buckets than this, perhaps the maximum of 254. (Oracle compresses the bucket information when so few values apply, so the large number of buckets should be inexpensive.) To create 254 buckets for the example case, in the schema owned by Appl_Prod, use this:

```
BEGIN
    DBMS_STATS.GATHER_TABLE_STATS ('Appl_Prod','Orders',
        METHOD_OPT => 'FOR COLUMNS SIZE 254 Status_Code');
END;
/
```

Generate the histogram statistics after you generate the general table statistics, because table-statistics generation deletes earlier histogram statistics.

## General hint syntax

Oracle uses hints for manual control of cost-based optimization. Syntactically, these hints take the form of comments, like /*+ <Hint_String> */, immediately following the SELECT keyword. Oracle recognizes that this syntax encloses a hint, not a comment, by the + at the beginning and by the location of the hint, which must immediately follow SELECT. However, since these are comments from the point of view of standard SQL syntax, they do not interfere with parsing the SQL if the SQL is also to be executed on non-Oracle databases.

 Oracle hints don't help get a fast execution plan on non-Oracle databases either, but unfortunately, it is not currently possible to share manually tuned SQL on multiple vendor databases and have the manual tuning work uniformly well on them all.

Each hint directly affects only the SELECT block that has the comment. Thus, to control the order of joins and index choices within a subquery, place the hint after the

SELECT keyword that begins the subquery. But to affect the outer-query order of joins and index choices, place a hint immediately after the outer-query SELECT.

### Approaches to tuning with hints

There are two basic extremes involved in tuning with hints:

- Use as little direction as possible to get the execution plan you want, or at least to get close enough to the plan you want for reasonable performance. This approach reasons that the CBO has more information than you have and should be left free to adapt to changing data distributions and to take advantage of improvements in Oracle with future releases. By leaving the CBO the maximum degrees of freedom, you maximize its power to optimize well for you in the future. However, until you try, you won't know how much direction the CBO will need if it did not get the plan right in the first place, so this approach is likely to be iterative, involving the addition of one hint at a time until the CBO delivers a good plan.

- If you did not get the plan you wanted from the CBO automatically, assume the CBO has made bad assumptions that will propagate to distort all of its calculations. Therefore, leave it with little freedom, specifying essentially the whole plan you want.

If you are confident in your chosen execution plan, as you should be if you apply the methods I describe later in this book, there is little reason to hold back from fully specifying that plan. I have yet to find a case where a well-chosen, robust execution plan needed to evolve to handle new data distributions or new database features. On the other hand, it is easy for SQL with a partially restricting set of hints to go wrong, especially if some table or index loses its statistics. When the CBO chooses incorrectly, the error that made the CBO choose incorrectly will likely propagate over the entire plan. For example, consider this query:

```
SELECT E.First_Name, E.Last_Name, E.Salary, LE.Description,
       M.First_Name, M.Last_Name, LM.Description
FROM Locations LM, Employees M, Locations LE, Employees E
WHERE E.Hire_Date > :1
  AND E.Manager_ID=M.Employee_ID
  AND E.Location_ID=LE.Location_ID
  AND M.Location_ID=LM.Location_ID
```

At parse time, when the optimizer does its work, it cannot know that the bind variable :1 will likely be set to a value in the current week, so it makes a conservative assumption about the selectivity of that condition on Hire_Date. Having made that assumption, it might not only forego using an index on Hire_Date (depending on the data distribution), but it might also further calculate that it will hit most of the rows of all the joined tables as well, and the CBO might choose full table scans with hash joins on them. Even if you instruct the CBO to use the index on Hire_Date, it still retains its initial assumption that the driving condition is unselective, and will likely retain its poor choices for the other joins and table-access methods. This is really no flaw in the optimizer; it cannot know what the application developer knows about the likely values to be assigned to the bind variable. However, the consequence is that, if you need to be any more specific than just specifying ALL_ROWS or FIRST_ROWS, chances are relatively high that the optimizer will need help across the board, to correct for some incorrect assumption somewhere.

 ALL_ROWS and FIRST_ROWS hints are a safe way to begin optimization. If you are using the rule-based optimizer, you can safely try out these cost-based approaches with a hint, even before you do the work of finding the best execution plan. If the result is already fast enough, you might save yourself any further work. If your optimization is already cost-based, under either the ALL_ROWS or FIRST_ROWS mode, try the other one. If an optimizer_mode hint alone solves your problem, the optimizer is making reasonable assumptions and you can trust it.

### Table-access hints

These are the main hints to control table-access methods:

INDEX(<*Alias_Name*> <*Index_Name*>)
> This directs Oracle, when possible, to access the alias <*Alias_Name*> using the index named <*Index_Name*>. Repeat this hint for each index/alias combination you need to control.

FULL(<*Alias_Name*>)
> This directs Oracle, when possible, to access the alias <*Alias_Name*> using a full table scan. Repeat this hint for each full table scan you require.

INDEX_DESC(<*Alias_Name*> <*Index_Name*>)
> This directs Oracle, when possible, to access the alias <*Alias_Name*> using the index named <*Index_Name*>, reaching the rows in descending order (the reverse of the normal index-sorted order). Repeat this hint for each index/alias combination you need to control, although it is unlikely you will need it more than once in a query.

The INDEX and FULL hints are common and easy to use. The INDEX_DESC hint is useful only rarely, but it is occasionally vital to use. For example, if you want to know all about the last employee hired in April, you might use this query:

```
SELECT *
FROM Employees E
WHERE Hire_Date>=TO_DATE('2003-04-01','YYYY-MM-DD')
  AND Hire_Date< TO_DATE('2003-05-01','YYYY-MM-DD')
ORDER BY Hire_Date DESC
```

You'll find the most recently hired employee you want at the top of the list of rows returned by this query. To avoid reading all the data for other employees hired in April, you might think to add a condition AND ROWNUM=1 to the query. However, this sometimes will not yield the desired result, because (depending on the data) Oracle will sometimes apply that condition before performing the descending sort. If Oracle uses a full table scan, it will return the first employee hired in April it finds in the table, likely the least recently hired. If it uses a simple index range scan on an index on Hire_Date, it will begin, as range scans generally do by default, at the low end of the index range, returning the first employee hired in April. However, the INDEX_DESC hint, with the index Employee_Hire_Date on the Hire_Date column, neatly solves the problem, returning the desired row with just a single logical I/O to the table:

```
SELECT /*+ INDEX_DESC(E Employee_Hire_Date) */ *
FROM Employees E
WHERE Hire_Date>=TO_DATE('2003-04-01','YYYY-MM-DD')
   AND Hire_Date< TO_DATE('2003-05-01','YYYY-MM-DD')
   AND ROWNUM=1
```

Note that I removed the explicit ORDER BY clause, since it gives the false impression that it has effect, given the condition on ROWNUM.

> The preceding example might strike you as risky code, apt to break functionally, for example, if someone drops or renames the index used. It is risky, and I recommend it only if the value of the performance improvement exceeds the cost of the risk of incorrect results. This is a clear case for SQL syntax that allows such top-*n* queries that take full advantage of the best indexed path. With current syntax, I haven't found a solution that is both optimal and functionally safe.

There are several other table-access hints that I have not described in this section, but I have never found them necessary.

### Execution-order hints

These are the main hints to control the order of execution for joins and subqueries:

ORDERED

This directs Oracle, when possible, to join the tables in the FROM clause in the same order that they are listed.

> This hint, unlike the others, usually requires that you alter the body of the SQL (or at least the FROM clause) to get the plan you want, since the hint refers to the FROM-clause order. Notice that the desired FROM-clause order will be precisely the opposite of the best FROM-clause order you would choose for rule-based optimization. That's because the RBO works from right to left, whereas this hint causes the CBO to work through the FROM clause from left to right.

LEADING(<*Alias_Name*>)

In the absence of an ORDERED hint, this selects the driving table, the first table in the join order. Although this gives less control over the join order than the ORDERED hint, it does not require modifying the FROM clause. Often, getting just the driving table correct is all you need to get at least close to the performance of the optimal plan. Later choices in the join order tend to matter less and will likely be well chosen by the optimizer, without your help.

PUSH_SUBQ

This hint instructs the optimizer to perform correlated subqueries at the first opportunity, as soon as the outer query reaches the join columns needed to evaluate them. Oracle's CBO normally performs correlated subqueries only after completing all the joins in the outer query.

The ORDERED and LEADING hints are common and straightforward to use. The PUSH_SUBQ hint is occasionally useful.

When it comes to subqueries, Oracle offers hint-based control only at the two extremes: executing subqueries as early or as late as possible. However, you can gain full control of when subqueries execute if you combine the PUSH_SUBQ hint with the earlier methods of postponing correlated joins. For example, consider the earlier query:

```
SELECT ...
FROM Orders O, Customers C, Regions R
WHERE O.Status_Code='OP'
  AND O.Customer_ID=C.Customer_ID
  AND C.Customer_Type_Code='GOV'
  AND C.Region_ID=R.Region_ID
AND EXISTS (SELECT NULL
            FROM Order_Details OD
            WHERE O.Order_ID+0*C.Customer_ID=OD.Order_ID
              AND OD.Shipped_Flag='Y')
```

Without a hint, Oracle would execute the EXISTS check after joining all three outer-query tables. The point of the expression O.Order_ID+0*C.Customer_ID was to delay the EXISTS check until after the join to C, but not after the join to R. However, without any hint, all EXISTS conditions are automatically delayed until after all outer-query joins. To force the EXISTS condition to execute between the joins to C and R, use both the hint and the correlating-join-postponing expression:

```
SELECT /*+ PUSH_SUBQ */ ...
FROM Orders O, Customers C, Regions R
WHERE O.Status_Code='OP'
  AND O.Customer_ID=C.Customer_ID
  AND C.Customer_Type_Code='GOV'
  AND C.Region_ID=R.Region_ID
  AND EXISTS (SELECT NULL
              FROM Order_Details OD
              WHERE O.Order_ID+0*C.Customer_ID=OD.Order_ID
                AND OD.Shipped_Flag='Y')
```

Now, the PUSH_SUBQ hint causes Oracle to execute the EXISTS condition as early as possible, and the expression O.Order_ID+0*C.Customer_ID ensures that "as early as possible" doesn't come until after the join to C.

## Join-method hints

These are the main hints to control the join methods:

USE_NL(<List_Of_Aliases>)
> This directs Oracle, when possible, to join the tables indicated in the alias list by using nested loops. The alias list is without commas—for example, USE_NL(T1 T2 T3).

USE_HASH(<List_Of_Aliases>)
> This directs Oracle, when possible, to join to the tables indicated in the alias list by using hash joins. The alias list is without commas— for example, USE_HASH(T1 T2 T3).

## Example

Here's an example to illustrate the most frequently useful hints to yield complete control of an execution plan. I'll force the join order, the access method to every table, and the join method to every table. Consider the earlier example tuned for the RBO, shown at the end of "Controlling Oracle Rule-Based Execution Plans." To fully force the same plan, but substitute a hash join for the first nested-loops join, with the employee locations read through the index on Description, use this query:

```
SELECT /*+ ORDERED USE_NL(M LM) USE_HASH(LE) INDEX(E Employee_Last_Name)
           INDEX(LE Location_Description) INDEX(M Employee_Pkey)
           INDEX(LM Location_Pkey) */
       E.First_Name, E.Last_Name, E.Salary, LE.Description,
       M.First_Name, M.Last_Name, LM.Description
FROM Employees E, Locations LE, Employees M, Locations LM
WHERE E.Last_Name = 'Johnson'
  AND E.Manager_ID=M.Employee_ID
  AND E.Location_ID=LE.Location_ID
  AND M.Location_ID=LM.Location_ID
  AND LE.Description='Dallas'
```

This results in the execution plan, as shown here:

```
SQL> @ex

PLAN
-------------------------------------------------------------------------
SELECT STATEMENT
  NESTED LOOPS
    NESTED LOOPS
      HASH JOIN
        TABLE ACCESS BY INDEX ROWID 1*EMPLOYEES
          INDEX RANGE SCAN EMPLOYEE_LAST_NAME
        TABLE ACCESS BY INDEX ROWID 2*LOCATIONS
          INDEX RANGE SCAN LOCATION_DESCRIPTION
      TABLE ACCESS BY INDEX ROWID 3*EMPLOYEES
        INDEX UNIQUE SCAN EMPLOYEE_PKEY
    TABLE ACCESS BY INDEX ROWID 4*LOCATIONS
      INDEX UNIQUE SCAN LOCATION_PKEY
```

# Controlling Plans on DB2

DB2 offers relatively sparse vendor-specific tools to control execution plans, so the methods used to tune on DB2 are comparatively indirect. There are three main steps involved in tuning on DB2:

1. Provide the optimizer with good statistics about the tables and indexes, so it can calculate the costs of alternatives accurately.

2. Choose the optimization level that DB2 applies to your query.

3. Modify the query to prevent execution plans that you do not want, mainly using the methods described earlier in "Universal Techniques for Controlling Plans."

## DB2 Optimization Prerequisites

Proving that a little knowledge is a dangerous thing, cost-based optimizers often do a terrible job if they do not have statistics on all the tables and indexes involved in a query. It is therefore imperative to maintain statistics on tables and indexes reliably; this includes regenerating statistics anytime table volumes change much or anytime tables or indexes are rebuilt. It is safest to regenerate statistics periodically, during times when load is relatively quiet, nightly or at least weekly. Edit a file *runstats_schema.sql* from the Unix prompt and type the following commands, replacing *<Schema_Name>* with the name of the schema that contains the objects you wish to run statistics on:

```
-- File called runstats_schema.sql
SELECT 'RUNSTATS ON TABLE <Schema_Name>.' || TABNAME || ' AND INDEXES ALL;'
FROM SYSCAT.TABLES
WHERE TABSCHEMA = '<Schema_Name>';
```

To use this script, log into *db2*, escape to the shell prompt with quit;, and run the following two commands from the Unix shell:

```
db2 +p -t < runstats_schema.sql > tmp_runstats.sql
grep RUNSTATS tmp_runstats.sql | db2 +p -t > tmp_anal.out
```

These commands can be scheduled to run automatically. Check *tmp_anal.out* in case any of the analyses fail.

Often, queries include conditions on highly skewed distributions, such as conditions on special types, codes, or flags, when these columns have only a few values. Normally, the CBO evaluates selectivity of a condition based on the assumption that all nonnull values of a column are equally selective. This assumption generally works well for foreign and primary keys that join business entities, but it breaks down when the columns have permanent special meanings and certain meanings apply much more rarely than others.

For example, in an Orders table, you might have a Status_Code column with three possible values: 'CL' for *closed* (i.e., fulfilled) orders, 'CA' for *cancelled* orders, and 'OP' for *open* orders. Most orders, by far, would be fulfilled; so, once the application has been running for a few months, you'd expect `'CL'` to point to a large and steadily increasing number of orders. A steady, significant fraction of orders would end up cancelled, so `'CA'` would also eventually point to a large list of orders. However, as long as the business keeps up with incoming orders, the number of open orders would remain moderate and steady, even as data accumulates for years. Quite early, a condition that specified `Status_Code='OP'` would be selective enough to justify indexed access, if you had an index with that leading column, and it is important to enable the optimizer to realize this fact, preferably without a lot of manual tuning. This requires two things:

- The SQL must mention the specific selective value, rather than use a bind variable. Use of bind variables is commonly attractive, since it makes SQL more general and easier to share between processes. However, this need to hardcode especially selective values is the exception to that rule. If you use `Status_Code= ?` instead of `Status_Code='OP'`, you will deny the CBO potential knowledge of the selectivity of the condition at parse time, when it does not yet know whether the bind variable ? will be assigned to a common or a rare `Status_Code`. Fortunately, in these cases, the usual reason to prefer using bind variables does not generally apply; since these special codes have special business meanings, it is unlikely that the SQL will ever require substituting a different value than the single selective value.

- You need to provide the CBO with special statistics that quantify how rare the uncommon code, type, or status values are, so it can know which values are highly selective.

DB2 stores special statistics on distribution, when you request them. To create distribution statistics for the example case, given an index named `Order_Stts_Code` and the schema owned by `ApplProd`, use the following command:

```
RUNSTATS ON TABLE ApplProd.Orders
  WITH DISTRIBUTION FOR INDEX ApplProd.Order_Stts_Code;
```

Anytime you have a column with a skewed distribution and an index that you wish to use when your condition on the column has a high degree of selectivity, be sure to create distribution statistics in the manner shown here.

## Choosing the Optimization Level

DB2 offers multiple optimization levels. An *optimization level* is basically a ceiling on how clever the optimizer attempts to be when it considers the range of possible execution plans. At optimization level 0, DB2 chooses the lowest cost plan within a subset of the plans it considers at level 1; at level 1, it considers just a subset of the plans it considers at level 2; and so on. Nominally, the highest optimization level should always yield the best plan, because it chooses the lowest cost plan from the widest possible range of alternatives. However, the plans enabled by the higher optimization levels tend to be less robust and often prove disappointing. In spite of the optimizer's calculations to the contrary, these less robust plans often run longer than the best robust plan that the lower-level optimization sees. Higher levels of optimization can also take longer to parse, since the optimizer has additional degrees of freedom to explore. Ideally, you parse every statement at the lowest level that is capable of finding the best execution plan for a given query.

DB2 offers seven levels of optimization: 0, 1, 2, 3, 5, 7, and 9.[*] Level 5 is normally the default, although database administration can override this default choice. I have never needed levels of optimization higher than 5; levels 7 and 9 appear mainly to enable relatively exotic query transformations that are rarely useful. However, I have frequently found excellent results with the lowest level of optimization, level 0, when level 5 produced a poor plan. Before executing a query (or checking an execution plan), set level 0 with the following SQL statement:

```
SET CURRENT QUERY OPTIMIZATION 0;
```

When you wish to return to level 5 for other queries that require it, use the same syntax, replacing 0 with 5. If you find a poor plan at level 5, I recommend trying level 0 after first verifying correct statistics on the tables and indexes involved. Level 0 frequently yields just the sort of robust plans that usually work best for real-world applications.

## Modifying the Query

Most manual tuning on DB2 uses the SQL changes described earlier in "Universal Techniques for Controlling Plans." However, one particular manual technique deserves special mention, because it proves useful more often on DB2 than on Oracle and SQL Server. DB2 stores index records even for null values of indexed columns, and it appears to treat null like just another indexed value.

When DB2 lacks special statistics on distribution (see "DB2 Optimization Prerequisites"), DB2 estimates the selectivity of Indexed_Column IS NULL to be just as high as Indexed_Column = 198487573 or any other nonnull value. Therefore, older DB2 versions often choose to drive to selective-looking IS NULL conditions on indexed columns. Occasionally, this works out fine. However, in my experience, IS NULL conditions are rarely anywhere near as selective as the average individual nonnull value, and indexed access driven by IS NULL conditions is almost always a mistake.

Therefore, when you find an IS NULL condition on an indexed column in a DB2 query, you often should prevent use of the index. The simplest equivalent condition that prevents index use is COALESCE(Indexed_Column, Indexed_Column) IS NULL. This version is perfectly equivalent to the original condition Indexed_Column IS NULL, but the COALESCE( ) function prevents index use.

---

[*] Levels 4, 6, and 8 are not available, presumably for historical reasons, although I have never found these reasons documented.

In addition to tuning techniques that can apply to any database, there are three useful techniques specific to DB2 that I describe in the following sections.

### Place inner joins first in your FROM clause

One sometimes useful technique is simply to list inner joins first in your FROM clause. This appears never to hurt, and on older versions of DB2 I have seen this simple technique produce greatly improved execution plans.

### Prevent too many outer joins from parsing at once

Older versions of DB2 can take minutes to parse queries with more than about 12 outer joins, and even then they might fail with errors. Fortunately, there is a workaround for this problem, using the following template for the SQL. The workaround uses DB2's nested-tables syntax, in which an outer query contains another query inside a FROM clause that is treated like a single table for purposes of the outer query:

```
SELECT ...
FROM (SELECT ...
        FROM (SELECT ... FROM <all inner joins and
                              ten outer joins>
                     WHERE <Conditions pertinent
                            to this innermost nested table>) T1
              LEFT OUTER JOIN <Joins for the 11th
                              through 20th outer join>
        WHERE <Conditions, if any, pertinent
               to this outermost nested table>) T2
        LEFT OUTER JOIN <The rest of the outer joins (at most 10)>
WHERE <Conditions, if any, pertinent to the outer query>
```

This template applies to a query with 21–30 outer-joined tables. With 11–20 outer-joined tables, you need only a single nested table. With more than 30 outer-joined tables, you need even deeper levels of nesting. In this syntax, DB2 effectively creates nested views on the fly, as defined by the queries inside parentheses in the FROM clauses. For purposes of handling outer joins, DB2 handles each of these smaller queries independently, sidestepping the problem of too many outer joins in a single query.

At my former employer, TenFold, we found this technique so useful that we enhanced the EnterpriseTenFold product to automatically generate this extraordinarily complex SQL when required. Admittedly, it is not an easy solution for manually written SQL, but it still might be the only technique that works if you run into slow or failed parses of many-way outer joins on DB2.

**Let DB2 know when to optimize the cost of reading just the first few rows**

Normally, DB2 calculates the cost of executing the entire query and chooses the plan it expects will run the fastest end to end. However, especially for online queries, you often care only about the first few rows and prefer to optimize to get the first rows soonest.

The technique to read the first rows fast, usually following nested loops, is to add the clause OPTIMIZE FOR <n> ROWS (or OPTIMIZE FOR 1 ROW), where <n> is the number of rows you actually need to see fast out of the larger rowset that the query might theoretically return. This clause goes at the very end of the query and instructs DB2 to optimize the cost of returning just those first <n> rows, without regard to the cost of the rest of the query execution. If you actually know how many rows you want and trust the optimizer to calculate the best plan, you can choose <n> on that basis. If you want to force a robust, nested-loops plan as strongly as possible, just use OPTIMIZE FOR 1 ROW.

In practice, this technique tends to dictate nested-loops joins, because they avoid reading whole rowsets before even beginning a join. However, it is possible for an explicit ORDER BY clause to defeat any attempt to reach the first rows fast. The ORDER BY clause usually requires a sort following the complete query, usually postponing return of the first row regardless of the execution plan. You can leave out a sort condition if you want to force nested-loops joins by this technique, performing the sort in your application if necessary. The OPTIMIZE FOR 1 ROW hint is the equivalent of the FIRST_ROWS hint on Oracle and the OPTION(FAST 1) hint on SQL Server.

Techniques to force precisely chosen execution plans on DB2 are sparse, in contrast to the extraordinary detail that DB2 reveals about the execution plan you already have and why DB2 chose it. However, in fairness, I should mention that the available techniques, in combination with DB2's fairly good optimizer, have proven sufficient in my own experience.

# Controlling Plans on SQL Server

There are three main steps involved in tuning on SQL Server:

1. Provide the optimizer with good statistics about the tables and indexes, so it can calculate the costs of alternatives accurately.

2. Modify the query to prevent execution plans that you do not want, mainly using methods specific to SQL Server.

3. Force a simple execution plan with FORCEPLAN when necessary.

# SQL Server Optimization Prerequisites

Proving that a little knowledge is a dangerous thing, cost-based optimizers often do a terrible job if they do not have statistics on all the tables and indexes involved in the query. It is therefore imperative to maintain statistics on tables and indexes reliably; this includes regenerating statistics anytime table volumes change much or anytime tables or indexes are rebuilt. It is safest to regenerate statistics periodically, during times when load is relatively quiet, nightly or at least weekly. Run the following from Query Analyzer, then cut and paste the resulting UPDATE STATISTICS commands into the query window and run them as well:

```
-- file called updateall.sql
-- update your whole database
SELECT 'UPDATE STATISTICS ', name
FROM sysobjects
WHERE type = 'U'
```

Often, queries include conditions on highly skewed distributions, such as conditions on special types, codes, or flags, when these columns have only a few values. SQL Server automatically maintains statistics on the distribution of indexed column values, enabling SQL Server to estimate selectivities automatically, even when indexed columns have skewed distributions.

Occasionally, it is useful to help the SQL Server estimate the selectivity of condition with a skewed distribution even when the distribution applies to a nonindexed column. In such a case, you need to specially request data on that column. For example, to request a statistics group named Eflag on the nonindexed column Exempt_Flag of the Employees table, run:

```
CREATE STATISTICS EFlag on Employees(Exempt_Flag)
```

As an example of a case in which such skewed distributions might apply, consider an Orders table in which you have a Status_Code column with three possible values: 'CL' for *closed* (i.e., fulfilled) orders, 'CA' for *cancelled* orders, and 'OP' for *open* orders. Most orders, by far, would be fulfilled once the application has been running for a few months, causing a steady rise in 'CL' values. A steady, significant fraction of orders would end up cancelled, so the value 'CA' would also eventually point to a large list of orders. However, as long as the business keeps up with incoming orders, the number of open orders would remain moderate and steady, even as data accumulates for years. Quite early, a condition that specified Status_Code='OP' would be selective enough to prefer joining to the corresponding table early, even if Status_Code is not indexed, and it is important to enable the optimizer to realize this fact, preferably without a lot of manual tuning. This requires that your SQL actually mention the specific value that applies to the condition, rather than use a generic stored procedure that only fills in the value of the constant after the parse, at execution time.

# Modifying the Query

You should usually tune SQL Server with hints. Hints generally go in either the `FROM` clause, when they apply to a specific table access, or in the SQL Server `OPTION( )` clause at the very end of a query. These are the most useful hints:

`WITH (INDEX(<Index_Name>))`

Immediately following a table alias in a `FROM` clause, this hint instructs SQL Server to use the specified index to access that table alias. The older alternative syntax `INDEX=<Index_Name>` is also supported, but it might be dropped in the future, so I don't recommend it. Even more obsolete and dangerous is the still-supported method of naming the internal object ID that corresponds to the desired index. Naming the index you want with the ID is horribly unreliable, because the index will get a new ID if anyone ever drops it and recreates it, or if the application moves to a new SQL Server database.

`WITH (INDEX(0))`

Immediately following a table alias in a `FROM` clause, this hint instructs SQL Server to use a full table scan to reach that table alias.

`WITH (NOLOCK)`

Immediately following a table alias in a `FROM` clause, this hint instructs SQL Server to read the specified table alias without requiring read locks or otherwise enforcing a consistent read. Read locks on SQL Server can create a bottleneck when combined with heavy update activity on a table. This hint avoids such a bottleneck, potentially at the cost of a consistent view of the data as of a single moment in time.

`LOOP` *and* `HASH`

These two different hints can each immediately precede the `JOIN` keyword in the `FROM` clause, instructing SQL Server to perform the specified join with the specified join method. These hints require the new-style join syntax with the `JOIN` keyword in the `FROM` clause. The presence of even a single hint of this type also forces all joins to take place in the same order the aliases are listed in the `FROM` clause.

`OPTION(LOOP JOIN)`

This hint goes at the end of a query and forces all joins to follow nested loops.

`OPTION(FORCE ORDER)`

This hint goes at the end of a query and forces all joins to take place in the same order the aliases are listed in the `FROM` clause.

`OPTION(FAST 1)`

This hint simply instructs SQL Server to attempt to reach the first returned rows as quickly as possible, which generally favors a nested-loops execution plan. Its effect is much like the `OPTION(LOOP JOIN)` hint, although in theory SQL Server might recognize that no execution plan could reach the first rows quickly in a query with an explicit `ORDER BY`, nullifying any effect from `OPTION(FAST 1)`. The

OPTION(FAST 1) hint is the equivalent of the FIRST_ROWS hint on Oracle and the OPTIMIZE FOR 1 ROW hint on DB2.

These hints can be combined. You can place multiple hints within a single WITH clause, separating them with commas—for example, WITH (INDEX(Employee_First_Name), NOLOCK). Multiple hints in a single OPTION clause also are separated by commas—for example, OPTION(LOOP JOIN, FORCE ORDER). Together, these hints give full control of the join order, the join methods, and the table access methods.

## Hint Examples

I'll demonstrate tuning with hints on a couple of queries. If you choose a robust all-nested-loops plan that drives from the employee last name to the other tables in optimum order, using the primary keys to reach the other tables, this query's hints force the desired plan:

```
SELECT E.First_Name, E.Last_Name, E.Salary, LE.Description,
       M.First_Name, M.Last_Name, LM.Description
FROM Employees E              WITH (INDEX(Employee_Last_Name))
    INNER JOIN Locations LE  WITH (INDEX(Location_PKey))
               ON E.Location_ID=LE.Location_ID
    INNER JOIN Employees M   WITH (INDEX(Employee_PKey))
               ON E.Manager_ID=M.Employee_ID
    INNER JOIN Locations LM  WITH (INDEX(Location_PKey))
               ON M.Location_ID=LM.Location_ID
WHERE E.Last_Name = 'Johnson'
  AND LE.Description='Dallas'
OPTION(LOOP JOIN, FORCE ORDER)
```

SET SHOWPLAN_TEXT ON (as described in Chapter 3) generates the following results when you run this query from SQL Server Query Analyzer:

```
StmtText
----------------------------------------------------------------
|--Bookmark Lookup(...(...[Locations] AS [LM]))
     |--Nested Loops(Inner Join)
          |--Bookmark Lookup(...(...[Employees] AS [M]))
          |    |--Nested Loops(Inner Join)
          |         |--Filter(WHERE:([LE].[Description]='Dallas'))
          |         |    |--Bookmark Lookup(...(...[Locations] AS [LE]))
          |         |         |--Nested Loops(Inner Join)
          |         |              |--Bookmark Lookup(...(...[Employees] AS [E]))
          |         |              |    |--Index Seek(...(...
(wrapped line) [Employees].[Employee_Last_Name]
(wrapped line) AS [E]), SEEK:([E].[Last_Name]='Johnson') ORDERED)
          |         |              |--Index Seek(...(...[Locations].[Location_PKey]
(wrapped line) AS [LE]), SEEK:([LE].[Location_ID]=[E].[Location_ID]) ORDERED)
          |         |--Index Seek(...(...[Employees].[Employee_PKey]
(wrapped line) AS [M]), SEEK:([M].[Employee_ID]=[E].[Manager_ID]) ORDERED)
          |--Index Seek(..(...[Locations].[Location_PKey]
(wrapped line) AS [LM]), SEEK:([LM].[Location_ID]=[M].[Location_ID]) ORDERED)

(12 row(s) affected)
```

If you don't want to specify all nested loops, you might need the join HASH and LOOP hints, as shown in the following alternative to the last query:

```
SELECT E.First_Name, E.Last_Name, E.Salary, LE.Description,
       M.First_Name, M.Last_Name, LM.Description
FROM Employees E                    WITH (INDEX(Employee_Last_Name))
    INNER HASH JOIN Locations LE  WITH (INDEX(Location_Description))
                ON E.Location_ID=LE.Location_ID
    INNER LOOP JOIN Employees M    WITH (INDEX(Employee_PKey))
                ON E.Manager_ID=M.Employee_ID
    INNER LOOP JOIN Locations LM   WITH (INDEX(Location_PKey))
                ON M.Location_ID=LM.Location_ID
WHERE E.Last_Name = 'Johnson'
  AND LE.Description='Dallas'
```

The preceding query delivers the following execution plan, triggered by SET SHOWPLAN_TEXT ON:

```
StmtText
------------------------------------------------------------
 |--Bookmark Lookup(...(...[Locations] AS [LM]))
      |--Nested Loops(Inner Join)
           |--Bookmark Lookup(...(...[Employees] AS [M]))
           |    |--Nested Loops(Inner Join)
           |    |    |--Hash Match(Inner Join...
(wrapped line) ([E].[Location_ID])=([LE].[Location_ID])...)
           |    |    |--Bookmark Lookup(...(...[Employees] AS [E]))
           |    |    |    |--Index Seek(...(...[Employees].[Employee_Last_Name]
(wrapped line) AS [E]), SEEK:([E].[Last_Name]='Johnson') ORDERED)
           |    |    |--Bookmark Lookup(...(...[Locations] AS [LE]))
           |    |    |    |--Index Seek(...(...[Locations].[Location_
Description]
(wrapped line) AS [LE]), SEEK:([LE].[Description]='Dallas') ORDERED)
           |         |--Index Seek(...(...[Employees].[Employee_PKey]
(wrapped line) AS [M]), SEEK:([M].[Employee_ID]=[E].[Manager_ID]) ORDERED)
           |--Index Seek(...(...[Locations].[Location_PKey]
(wrapped line) AS [LM]), SEEK:([LM].[Location_ID]=[M].[Location_ID]) ORDERED)

(11 row(s) affected)
```

There are two basic extremes involved in tuning with hints such as those in this example:

- Use as little direction as possible to get the execution plan you want, or at least to get close enough to the plan you want for reasonable performance. This approach reasons that SQL Server has more information than you have, and it should be left free to adapt to changing data distributions and take advantage of improvements in SQL Server with future releases. By leaving SQL Server the maximum degrees of freedom, you maximize its power to optimize well for you in the future. However, until you try, you won't know how much direction the SQL Server will need if it did not get the plan right in the first place, so this approach is likely to be iterative, involving adding one hint at a time until SQL Server delivers a good plan.

- If you did not get the plan you wanted from SQL Server automatically, assume the database has made bad assumptions that will propagate to distort all of its calculations. Therefore, leave it with very little freedom, specifying essentially the whole plan you want.

If you are confident in your chosen execution plan, as you should be if you apply the methods I describe later in this book, there is little reason to hold back from fully specifying that plan. I have yet to find a case in which a well-chosen, robust execution plan needed to evolve to handle new data distributions or new database features. On the other hand, it is easy for SQL with a partially restricting set of hints to go wrong, especially if some table or index loses its statistics. When SQL Server chooses incorrectly, the error that made the database choose incorrectly is likely to propagate over the entire plan. However, the OPTION(FAST 1) hint is the sort of instruction that can be useful even when SQL Server has perfect information, simply specifying that the time to reach the first row is more important than the time to reach the last row.

## Using FORCEPLAN

An older method to tune on both Microsoft SQL Server and Sybase is the FORCEPLAN option. You execute this option with a standalone SQL statement:

```
SET FORCEPLAN ON
```

This option affects all SQL for that connection until you execute this statement:

```
SET FORCEPLAN OFF
```

When FORCEPLAN is ON, the database is instructed to perform only the simplest optimization on the SQL it sees. It generally uses nested-loops execution plans that drive through indexes and join tables in the same order you list them in the FROM clause. When this is the sort of plan you want, SET FORCEPLAN can be ideal, not only forcing the plan simply, but even saving parse time that would otherwise be wasted considering a much wider range of plans, especially for joins of many tables. It is a blunt-edged sword, so to speak, so only use it when you know the FROM-clause join order is the correct join order and you want nested loops.

# CHAPTER 5
# Diagramming Simple SQL Queries

*Look ere ye leap.*
—John Heywood
   *Proverbs [1546], Pt. I, Ch. 2*

To convert the art of SQL tuning to a science requires a common language, a common *paradigm* for describing and solving SQL tuning problems. This book teaches, for the first time in print in any detail, a method that has served me well and served others I have taught over many years. I call this method the *query diagramming* method.

Like any new tool, the query diagramming method requires some up-front investment from the would-be tool user. However, mastery of this tool offers tremendous rewards, so I urge you to be patient; the method seems hard only for a while. Soon, it will lead you to answers you would never have found without the tool, with moderate effort, and in the end it can become so second-nature that (like the best tools) you forget you are using it.

## Why a New Method?

Since I am asking for your patience, I begin with a discussion of why this tool is needed. Why not use a tool you already know, like SQL, for solving performance problems? The biggest problem with using SQL for tuning is that it presents both too much and not enough information to solve the tuning problem. SQL exists to describe, functionally, which columns and rows an application needs from which tables, matched on which join conditions, returned in which order. However, most of this information is wholly irrelevant to tuning a query. On the other hand, information that is relevant, essential even, to tuning a query—information about the data distributions in the database—is wholly missing from SQL. SQL is much like the old word problems so notorious in grade-school math, except that SQL is more likely to be missing vital information. Which would you find easier to solve—this:

> While camping, Johnny cooked eight flapjacks, three sausages, one strip of bacon, and two eggs for himself and each of his friends, Jim, Mary, and Sue. The girls each gave one-third of their sausages, 25% of their flapjacks, and half their eggs to the boys. Jim dropped a flapjack and two sausages, and they were stolen by a raccoon. Johnny is allergic to maple syrup, and Mary had strawberries on half her flapjacks, but otherwise everyone used maple syrup on their flapjacks. How many flapjacks did the kids eat with maple syrup?

or this:

$$(8+(0.25 \times 8)-1)+(0.75 \times 8/2)+(0.75 \times 8)=?$$

The query diagram is the bare-bones synthesis of the tuning essentials of the SQL word problem and the key distribution data necessary to find the optimum execution plan. With the bare-bones synthesis, you lose distracting, irrelevant detail and gain focus on the core of the problem. The result is a far more compact language to use for both real-world problems and exercises. Problems that would take pages of SQL to describe (and, in the case of exercises, days to invent, for realistic problems that did not illegally expose proprietary code) distill to a simple, abstract, half-page diagram. Your learning rate accelerates enormously with this tool, partly because the similarities between tuning problems with functionally different queries become obvious; you recognize patterns and similarities that you would never notice at the SQL level and reuse your solutions with little effort.

No tool that I know of creates anything like the query diagram for you, just as no tool turns math word problems into simple arithmetic. Therefore, your first step in tuning SQL will be to translate the SQL problem into a query diagram problem. Just as translating word problems into arithmetic is usually the hardest step, you will likely find translating SQL tuning problems into query diagrams the hardest (or at least the most time-consuming) step in SQL tuning, especially at first. However, it is reassuring to consider that, although human languages grew up haphazardly to foster communication between complex human minds, SQL was designed with much more structure to communicate with computers. SQL tuning word problems occupy a much more restricted domain than natural-language word problems. With practice, translating SQL to its query diagram becomes fast and easy, even something you can do quickly in your head. Once you have the query diagram and even a novice-level understanding of the query-diagramming method, you will usually find the tuning problem trivial.

As an entirely unplanned bonus, query diagrams turn out to be a valuable aid in finding whole classes of subtle application-logic problems that are hard to uncover in testing because they affect mostly rare corner cases. In Chapter 7, I discuss in detail how to use these diagrams to help find and fix such application-logic problems.

In the following sections, I describe two styles of query diagrams: full and simplified. *Full* diagrams include all the data that is ever likely to be relevant to a tuning problem. *Simplified* diagrams are more qualitative and exclude data that is not usually necessary. I begin by describing full diagrams, because it is easier to understand simplified diagrams as full diagrams with details removed than to understand full diagrams as simplified diagrams with details added.

# Full Query Diagrams

Example 5-1 is a simple query that illustrates all the significant elements of a query diagram.

*Example 5-1. A simple query with one join*

```
SELECT D.Department_Name, E.Last_Name, E,First_Name
FROM Employees E, Departments D
WHERE E.Department_Id=D.Department_Id
  AND E.Exempt_Flag='Y'
  AND D.US_Based_Flag='Y';
```

This query translates to the query diagram in Figure 5-1.

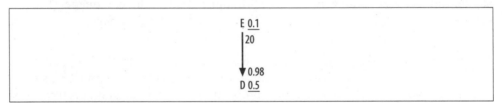

*Figure 5-1. A full query diagram for a simple query*

First, I'll describe the meaning of each of these elements, and then I'll explain how to produce the diagram, using the SQL as a starting point.

## Information Included in Query Diagrams

In mathematical terms, what you see in Figure 5-1 is a *directed graph*: a collection of nodes and links, where the links often have arrows indicating their directionality. The nodes in this diagram are represented by the letters E and D. Alongside both the nodes and the two ends of each link, numbers indicate further properties of the nodes and links. In terms of the query, you can interpret these diagram elements as follows.

### Nodes

Nodes represent tables or table aliases in the FROM clause—in this case, the aliases E and D. You can choose to abbreviate table or alias names as convenient, as long as doing so does not create confusion.

## Links

Links represent joins between tables, where an arrow on one end of the link means that the join is guaranteed to be unique on that end of the join. In this case, Department_ID is the primary (unique) key to the table Departments, so the link includes an arrow on the end pointing to the D node. Since Department_ID is not unique in the Employees table, the other end of the link does not have an arrow. Following my convention, always draw links with one arrow with the arrow pointing downward. Consistency is useful here. When you always draw arrows pointing downward, it becomes much easier to refer consistently to master tables as always being located below detail tables. In Chapters 6 and 7, I describe rules of thumb for finding optimum execution plans from a query diagram. Since the rules of thumb treat joins to master tables differently than joins to detail tables, the rules specifically refer to *downward* joins and *upward* joins as a shorthand means of distinguishing between the two types.

Although you might guess that Department_ID is the primary key of Departments, the SQL does not explicitly declare which side of each join is a primary key and which side is a foreign key. You need to check indexes or declared keys to be certain that Department_ID is guaranteed to be unique on Departments, so the arrow combines information about the nature of the database keys and information about which keys the SQL uses.

## Underlined numbers

Underlined numbers next to the nodes represent the fraction of rows in each table that will satisfy the filter conditions on that table, where filter conditions are nonjoin conditions in the diagrammed SQL that refer solely to that table. Figure 5-1 indicates that 10% of the rows in Employees have Exempt_Flag='Y' and 50% of the rows in Departments have US_Based_Flag='Y'. I call these the *filter ratios*.

Frequently, there are no filter conditions at all on one or more of the tables. In that case, use 1.0 for the filter ratio (*R*), since 100% of the rows meet the (nonexistent) filter conditions on that table. Also, in such cases, I normally leave the filter ratio off the diagram entirely; the number's absence implies *R*=1.0 for that table. A filter ratio cannot be greater than 1.0. You can often guess approximate filter ratios from knowledge of what the tables and columns represent (if you have such knowledge). It is best, when you have realistic production data distributions available, to find exact filter ratios by directly querying the data. Treat each filtered table, with just the filter clauses that apply to that table, as a single-table query, and find the selectivity of the filter conditions just as I describe in Chapter 2 under "Calculating Selectivity."

During the development phase of an application, you do not always know what filter ratio to expect when the application will run against production volumes. In that case, make your best estimate based on your knowledge of the application, not based on tiny, artificial data volumes on development databases.

### Nonunderlined numbers

Nonunderlined numbers next to the two ends of the link represent the average number of rows found in the table on that end of the join per matching row from the other end of the join. I call these the *join ratios*. The join ratio on the nonunique end of the join is the *detail join ratio*, while the join on the unique end (with the arrow) is the *master join ratio*.

Master join ratios are always less than or equal to 1.0, because the unique key ensures against finding multiple masters per detail. In the common case of a detail table with a mandatory foreign key and perfect referential integrity (guaranteeing a matching master row), the master join ratio is exactly 1.0.

Detail join ratios can be any nonnegative number. They can be less than 1.0, since some master-detail relationships allow zero, one, or many detail rows, with the one-to-zero case dominating the statistics. In the example, note that the average Employees row matches (joins to) a row in Departments 98% of the time, while the average Departments row matches (joins to) 20 Employees. Although you might guess approximate join ratios from knowledge of what the tables represent, query these values when possible from the real, full-volume data distributions. As with filter ratios, you might need to estimate join ratios during the development phase of an application.

## What Query Diagrams Leave Out

As important as what query diagrams include is what they do not include. The following sections describe several things that query diagrams omit, and explain why that is the case.

### Select lists

Query diagrams entirely exclude any reference to the list of columns and expressions that a query selects (everything between SELECT and FROM, that is). Query performance is almost entirely determined by which rows in the database you touch and how you reach them. What you do with those rows, which columns you return, and which expressions you calculate are almost irrelevant to performance. The main, but rare, exception to this rule is when you occasionally select so few columns from a table that it turns out the database can satisfy the query from data in an index, avoiding access to the base table altogether. Occasionally, this index-only access can lead to major savings, but it has little bearing on decisions you make about the rest of the execution plan. You should decide whether to try index-only access as a last step in the tuning process and only if the best execution plan without this strategy turns out to be too slow.

## Ordering and aggregation

The diagram excludes any indication of ordering (ORDER BY), grouping (GROUP BY), or post-grouping filtering (HAVING). These operations are almost never important. The sort step these generally imply is not free, but you can usually do little to affect its cost, and its cost is usually not the problem behind a badly performing query.

## Table names

Query diagrams usually abstract table names to table aliases. Once you have the necessary table statistics, most other details are immaterial to the tuning problem. For example, it makes no difference which tables a query reads or which physical entities the tables represent. In the end, you must be able to translate the result back to actions on the original SQL and on the database (actions such as creating a new index, for example). However, when you are solving the abstract tuning problem, the more abstract the node names, the better. Analogously, when your objective is to correctly add a series of numbers, it's no help to worry about whether you are dealing with items in an inventory or humans in a hospital. The more abstractly you view a problem, the clearer it is and the more clearly you notice analogies with similar, past problems that might have dealt with different entities.

## Detailed join conditions

The details of join conditions are lost when you abstract joins as simple arrows with a couple of numbers coming from outside of the SQL. As long as you know the statistics of the join, the details of the join columns and how they are compared do not matter.

## Absolute table sizes (as opposed to relative sizes)

The diagram does not represent table sizes. However, you can generally infer relative table sizes from the detail join ratio, by the upper end of the link. Given a query diagram, you need to know overall table sizes to estimate overall rows returned and runtime of the query, but it turns out that you do not need this information to estimate *relative* runtimes of the alternatives and therefore to find the best alternative. This is a helpful result, because you often must tune a query to run well not just on a single database instance, but also on a whole wide range of instances across many customers. Different customers frequently have different absolute table sizes, but the relative sizes of those tables tend not to vary so much, and join and filter ratios tend to vary far less; in fact, they tend to vary little enough that the differences can be ignored.

In my experience, it is a myth that one of the main advantages of cost-based optimizers is their ability to respond to varying table and index statistics with different plans for the same application's SQL. This theoretical possibility is cited as an argument against manual tuning of an application's SQL, since the result might (theoretically) hurt as many customers as it would help, by figuratively tying the optimizer's hands. On the contrary, I have yet to find a single query that didn't have an execution plan that worked fine on every data distribution I encountered or was likely to encounter. (These plans were not optimal for every distribution, but they were close enough to optimal so as not to matter.) As a result, careful manual tuning of a product's SQL need not harm one customer to help another.

### Filter condition details

The details of filter conditions are lost when you abstract them to simple numbers. You can choose an optimum path to the data without knowing anything about the details of how, or using which columns, the database excludes rows from a query result. You need only know how effective, numerically, each filter is for the purpose of excluding rows. Once you know that optimum abstract path, you need to return to the detailed conditions, in many cases, to deduce what to change. You can change indexes to enable that optimum path, or you can change the SQL to enable the database to exploit the indexes it already has, but this final step is simple once you know the optimum abstract path.

## When Query Diagrams Help the Most

Just as some word problems are too simple to really require abstraction (e.g., "If Johnny has five apples and eats two, how many apples does he have left?"), some queries, like the one in Example 5-1, are so simple that an abstracted representation of the problem might not seem necessary. If all queries were two-way joins, you could manage fine without query diagrams. However, in real-world applications, it is common to join 6 or more tables, and joining 20 or more is not as rare as you might think, especially among the queries you will tune, since these more complex queries are more likely to need manual tuning. (My personal record is a 115-way join, and I routinely tune joins with more than 40 tables.) The more fully normalized your database and the more sophisticated your user interface, the more likely it is that you will have many-way joins. It is a myth that current databases cannot handle 20-way joins, although it is no myth that databases (some more than others) are much more likely to require manual tuning to get decent performance for such complex queries, as compared to simple queries.

Apart from the obvious advantages of stripping away irrelevant detail and focusing attention on just the abstract essentials, query diagrams offer another, more subtle benefit: practice problems are much easier to generate! In this chapter, I begin each problem with realistic SQL, but I cannot use real examples from proprietary applications I have tuned. So, for good examples, I invent an application database design and imagine real business scenarios that might generate each SQL statement. Once I have thoroughly demonstrated the process of reducing a SQL statement to a query diagram, the rest of the book will have problems that *start* with the query diagrams. Similarly, most of a math text focuses on abstract math, not on word problems. Abstraction yields compact problems and efficient teaching, and abstraction further saves me the bother of inventing hundreds of realistic-sounding word problems that correspond to the mathematical concepts I need to teach. You might not worry much about how much bother this saves *me*, but it saves *you* time as well. To better learn SQL tuning, one of the best exercises you can do is to invent SQL tuning problems and solve them. If you start with realistic SQL, you will find this a slow and painful process, but if you just invent problems expressed through query diagrams, you will find you can crank out exercises by the hundreds.

## Conceptual Demonstration of Query Diagrams in Use

I have stated without proof that query diagrams abstract all the data needed to answer the most important questions about tuning. To avoid trying your patience and credulity too severely, I will demonstrate a way to use the query diagram in Figure 5-1 to tune its query in detail, especially to find the best join order. It turns out that the best access path, or execution plan, for most multitable queries involves indexed access to the first, driving table, followed by nested loops to the rest of the tables, where those nested loops follow indexes to their join keys, in some optimum join order.

 For small master tables, you sometimes can do slightly better by replacing the nested-loops joins to those small tables with hash joins, but the improvement is usually minor and likely not worth the bother or the robustness risk that comes with a hash join.

However, for many-way joins, the number of possible join orders can easily be in the high millions or billions. Therefore, the single most important result will be a fast method to find the best join order.

Before I demonstrate the complex process of optimizing join order for a many-way join using a query diagram, let's just see what the diagram in Figure 5-1 tells us about comparative costs of the two-way join in the underlying SQL query, if you were to try both possible join orders. To a surprisingly good approximation, the cost of all-indexed access, with nested loops, is proportional to the number of table rows the database accesses, so I will use rows touched as the proxy for query cost. If you begin with the detail node E, you cannot work out an absolute cost without assuming some rowcount for that table. However, the rowcount is missing from the diagram, so let it be $C$ and follow the consequences algebraically:

1. Using an index on the filter for E, the database must begin by touching $0.1 \times C$ rows in the driving table E.

2. Following nested loops to master table D, the master join ratio shows that the database will reach $0.1 \times C \times 0.98$ rows of D.

3. Adding the results of Steps 1 and 2, the total count of table rows touched is $(0.1 \times C) + (0.1 \times C \times 0.98)$.

4. The total rowcount the database will reach, then, factoring out $C$ and 0.1 from both terms, is $C \times (0.1 \times (1+0.98))$, or $0.198 \times C$.

Beginning with the other end of the join, let's still express the cost in terms of $C$, so first work out the size of D in terms of $C$. Given the size of D in terms of $C$, the cost of the query in terms of $C$ follows:

1. For every row in D, the database finds on average 20 rows in E, based on the detail join ratio. However, just 98% of the rows in E even match rows in D, so the total rowcount $C$ must be 20/0.98 times larger than the rowcount of D. Conversely, then, the rowcount of D is $C \times 0.98/20$.

2. Following an index to reach only the filter rows on D results in reaching half these rows for the driving table for this alternative, or $C \times 0.5 \times 0.98/20$.

3. Following the join to E, then, the database reaches 20 times as many rows in that table: $20 \times C \times 0.5 \times 0.98/20$, or $C \times 0.5 \times 0.98$.

4. Adding the two rowcounts and factoring out the common terms as before, find the total cost: $C \times (0.5 \times 0.98 \times ((1/20)+1))$, or $0.5145 \times C$.

The absolute cost is not really the question; the relative cost is, so you can choose the best plan and, whatever $C$ is, $0.198 \times C$ will surely be much lower than $0.5145 \times C$. The query diagram has all the information you need to know that the plan driving from E and joining to D will surely be much faster (about 2.6 times faster) than the plan driving from D and joining to E. If you found these alternatives to be much closer, you might worry whether the cost estimate based on simple rowcounts was not quite right, and I will deal with that issue later. The message here is that the query diagram answers the key questions that are relevant to optimizing a query; you just need an efficient way to use query diagrams for complex queries.

## Creating Query Diagrams

Now that you see what a query diagram means, here are the steps to create one from an SQL statement, including some steps that will not apply to the particular query shown earlier, but that you will use for later queries:

1. Begin with an arbitrary choice of table alias in the FROM clause, and place this in the middle of a blank page. For now, I will refer to this table as the *focus table*,

simply meaning that this table will be the current point from which to add further details to the query diagram. I will choose alias E as the starting point for the example, just because it is first in the query.

2. Search for join conditions that match up to a single value of the focus table's primary key. For each such join that you find, draw an arrow pointing down toward the focus table alias from above, labeling the other end of the arrow with the alias at the other end of the join. (You will usually find at most one join into a table from above, for reasons I will discuss later.) When the link represents an outer join, add an arrowhead halfway along the link and point the arrowhead toward the optional table.

   In the example, there is no join to the Employees table's primary key, presumed to be Employee_ID. If you want to be certain that Department_ID is not a poorly named primary key of Employees, you can check the table's declared keys and unique indexes. If you suspect that it might really be unique but that the database designer failed to declare or enforce that uniqueness with either a declared key or index, you can check for uniqueness with SELECT COUNT(*), COUNT(DISTINCT Department_ID) FROM Employees;. However, you might be surprised how rarely there is any doubt about where the unique end of the join lies, just from column and table naming. You can generally get by just fine with intelligent guesses, revisiting those guesses only if the answer you come up with performs worse than you expect or require.

3. Search for join conditions that go from a foreign key in the focus table to a primary key in another table, and draw arrows for those joins pointing down from the focus table, with aliases for the joined-to tables on the lower end of each arrow. When a link represents an outer join, add an arrowhead pointing to the optional table halfway along the link.

4. Shift focus to another, previously unvisited node in the diagram and repeat Steps 2 and 3 until you have nodes that represent every alias in the FROM clause and arrows that represent every join. (For example, I represent a multipart join as a single arrow from a multipart foreign key to a multipart primary key.) Usually, you will find just a single arrow pointing down into a node, so you will normally search for fresh downward-pointing joins from nodes already on the lower, arrow end of a join. This usually leads to an upside-down tree structure, descending from a single detail table at the top.

5. After completing all the nodes and links, fill in the numbers for filter ratios and join ratios based, if possible, on production-application table statistics. If you don't have production data, then estimate as best you can. It is not necessary to add join ratios alongside links that represent outer joins. You almost always find that the optional table in an outer join (on the (+) side of the join, in old Oracle notation, or following the LEFT OUTER keywords in the newer style) has no filter condition, leaving the filter ratio equal to 1.0, which you denote by omitting it from the diagram.

6. Place an asterisk next to the filter ratio for any filter that is guaranteed to return at most a single row. This is not a function just of the ratio and the rowcount of the table, since a condition might return an average of a single row without guaranteeing a maximum of a single row. To guarantee at most a single row, you should have a unique index or a well-understood application constraint that creates a true guarantee.

---

### Guaranteeing Uniqueness

Sometimes, a filter condition is so close to guaranteeing a unique match that it is tempting to treat it as unique. Usually, you can get away with this, but I find that it is useful to first try to make the guarantee complete, by filling in some missing condition or correcting the database design. For example, you might have a filter `Order_ID=:1` for an `Orders` table, with the primary key of `Orders` that consists of the `Order_ID` and `Company_ID` columns, but `Company_ID` is a single, dominant value 99.9% of the time. The most likely reason the developer left out any condition on `Company_ID` is simply that he forgot that it is sometimes not equal to the dominant value and that `Order_ID` does not always specify a unique order by itself. I have found that when filter conditions are close to unique, the intent is almost invariably to make them unique, and the missing condition or conditions should be added to achieve the original intended functionality.

Similar comments apply to almost-unique joins. When the join conditions imply a many–to–almost-always-one join, chances are high that the query or the database design should be corrected to guarantee a perfect many-to-one join.

---

If you have available production data, it is the ideal source of filter and join ratios. For Example 5-1, you would perform the following queries (Q1 through Q5) to determine these ratios rigorously:

```
Q1: SELECT COUNT(*) A1 FROM Employees
    WHERE Exempt_Flag='Y';
A1: 1,000

Q2: SELECT COUNT(*) A2 FROM Employees;
A2: 10,000

Q3: SELECT COUNT(*) A3 FROM Departments
    WHERE US_Based_Flag='Y';
A3: 245

Q4: SELECT COUNT(*) A4 FROM Departments;
A4: 490

Q5: SELECT COUNT(*) A5 FROM Employees E, Departments D
    WHERE E.Department_ID=D.Department_ID;
A5: 9,800
```

With A1 through A5 representing the results these queries return, respectively, do the following math:

- To find the filter ratio for the E node, find A1/A2.
- To find the filter ratio for the D node, find A3/A4.
- To find the detail join ratio, find A5/A4, the rowcount of the unfiltered join divided by the master-table rowcount.
- To find the master join ratio, find A5/A2, the rowcount of the unfiltered join divided by the detail-table rowcount.

For example, the results from queries Q1 through Q5—1,000, 10,000, 245, 490, and 9,800, respectively—would yield precisely the filter and join ratios in Figure 5-1, and if you multiplied all of these query results by the same constant, you would still get the same ratios.

## A More Complex Example

Now I illustrate the diagramming process for a query that is large enough to get interesting. I will diagram the query in Example 5-2, which expresses outer joins in the older Oracle style (try diagramming this query yourself first, if you feel ambitious).

*Example 5-2. A more complex query, with eight joined tables*

```
SELECT C.Phone_Number, C.Honorific, C.First_Name, C.Last_Name,
       C.Suffix, C.Address_ID, A.Address_ID, A.Street_Address_Line1,
       A.Street_Address_Line2, A.City_Name, A.State_Abbreviation,
       A.ZIP_Code, OD.Deferred_Shipment_Date, OD.Item_Count,
       ODT.Text, OT.Text, P.Product_Description, S.Shipment_Date
FROM Orders O, Order_Details OD, Products P, Customers C, Shipments S,
     Addresses A, Code_Translations ODT, Code_Translations OT
WHERE UPPER(C.Last_Name) LIKE :Last_Name||'%'
  AND UPPER(C.First_Name) LIKE :First_Name||'%'
  AND OD.Order_ID = O.Order_ID
  AND O.Customer_ID = C.Customer_ID
  AND OD.Product_ID = P.Product_ID(+)
  AND OD.Shipment_ID = S.Shipment_ID(+)
  AND S.Address_ID = A.Address_ID(+)
  AND O.Status_Code = OT.Code
  AND OT.Code_Type = 'ORDER_STATUS'
  AND OD.Status_Code = ODT.Code
  AND ODT.Code_Type = 'ORDER_DETAIL_STATUS'
  AND O.Order_Date > :Now - 366
ORDER BY C.Customer_ID, O.Order_ID DESC, S.Shipment_ID, OD.Order_Detail_ID;
```

As before, ignore all parts of the query except the FROM and WHERE clauses. All tables have intuitively named primary keys except Code_Translations, which has a two-part primary key: (Code_Type, Code).

Note that when you find a single-table equality condition on part of a primary key, such as in this query on Code_Translations, consider that condition to be part of the *join*, not a filter condition. When you treat a single-table condition as part of a join, you are normally looking at a physical table that has two or more logical subtables. I call these *apples-and-oranges tables*: tables that hold somewhat different, but related entity types within the same physical table. For purposes of optimizing a query on these subtables, you are really interested only in the statistics for the specific subtable the query references. Therefore, qualify all queries for table statistics with the added condition that specifies the subtable of interest, including the query for overall rowcount (SELECT COUNT(*) FROM *<Table>*), which becomes, for this example, a subtable rowcount (SELECT COUNT(*) FROM Code_Translations WHERE Code_Type='ORDER_STATUS').

If you wish to complete the skeleton of the query diagram yourself, as an exercise, follow the steps for creating a query diagram shown earlier up to Step 4, and skip ahead to Figure 5-4 to see if you got it right.

### Diagram joins to the first focus

For Step 1, place the alias O, arbitrarily, in the center of the diagram. For Step 2, search for any join to O's primary key, O.Order_ID. You should find the join from OD, which is represented in Figure 5-2 as a downward arrow from OD to O. To help remember that you have diagrammed this join, cross it out in the query.

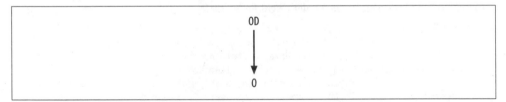

*Figure 5-2. Beginnings of the diagram for Example 5-2*

### Diagram joins from the first focus

Moving on to Step 3, search for other joins (not to Order_ID, but to foreign keys) to Orders, and add these as arrows pointing down from O to C and to OT, since these joins reach Customers and Code_Translations on their primary keys. At this point, the diagram matches Figure 5-3.

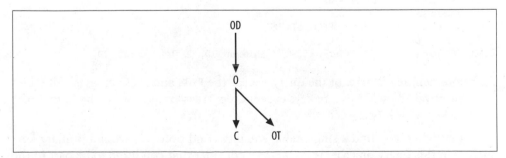

*Figure 5-3. After Step 3 for the second diagram*

## Change focus and repeat

This completes all joins that originate from alias O. To remember which part is complete, cross out the O in the FROM clause, and cross out the joins already diagrammed with links. Step 4 indicates you should repeat Steps 2 and 3 with a new focus, but it does not go into details about how to choose that focus. If you try every node as the focus once, you will complete the diagram correctly regardless of order, but you can save time with a couple of rules of thumb:

- Try to complete upper parts of the diagram first. Since you have not yet tried the top node OD as a focus, start there.

- Use undiagrammed joins to find a new focus that has at least some work remaining. Checking the list of joins that have not yet been crossed out would lead to the following list of potential candidates: OD, P, S, A, and ODT. However, out of this list, only OD is now on the diagram, so it is the only focus now available to extend the diagram. If you happened to notice that there are no further joins to C and OT, you could cross them out in the FROM clause as requiring no further work.

By following these rules of thumb you can complete the diagram faster. If at any stage you find the diagram getting crowded, you can redraw what you have to spread things out better. The spatial arrangement of the nodes is only for convenience; it carries no meaning beyond the meaning conveyed by the arrows. For example, I have drawn C to the left of OT, but you could switch these if it helps make the rest of the diagram fit the page.

The illustrators at O'Reilly have worked hard to make my example diagrams look nice, but you don't have to. In most cases, no one will see your diagrams except you, and you will probably find your own diagrams sufficiently clear with little bother about their appearance.

You find no joins to the primary key of Order_Details (to OD.Order_Detail_ID, that is), so all links to OD point downward to P, S, and ODT, which all join to OD with their primary keys. Since S and P are optional tables in outer joins, add downward-pointing arrowheads midway down these links. Cross out the joins from OD that these three new links represent. This leaves just one join left, an outer join from S to the primary key of A. Therefore, shift focus one last time to S and add one last arrow pointing downward to A, with a midpoint arrowhead indicating this outer join. Cross out the last join and you need not shift focus again, because all joins and all aliases are on the diagram.

You should quickly confirm that no alias is orphaned (i.e., has no join condition at all linking it to the rest of the diagram). This occasionally happens, most often unintentionally, when the query includes a Cartesian join.

At this stage, if you've been following along, your join diagram should match the connectivity shown in Figure 5-4, although the spatial arrangement is immaterial. I call this the *query skeleton* or *join skeleton*; once you complete it, you need only fill in the numbers to represent relevant data distributions that come from the database, as in Step 5 of the diagramming process.

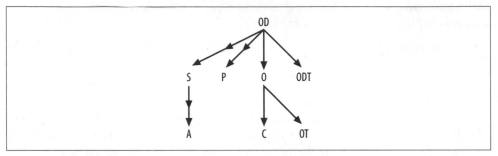

*Figure 5-4. The query skeleton*

### Compute filter and join ratios

There are no filter conditions on the optional tables in the outer joins, so you do not need statistics regarding those tables and joins. Also, recall that the apparent filter conditions OT.Code_Type = 'ORDER_STATUS' and ODT.Code_Type = 'ORDER_DETAIL_STATUS' are part of the joins to their respective tables, not true filter conditions, since they are part of the join keys to reach those tables. That leaves only the filter conditions on customer name and order date as true filter conditions. If you wish to practice the method for finding the join and filter ratios for the query diagram, try writing the queries to work out those numbers and the formulae for calculating the ratios before looking further ahead.

The selectivity of the conditions on first and last names depends on the lengths of the matching patterns. Work out an estimated selectivity, assuming that :Last_Name and :First_Name typically are bound to the first three letters of each name and that the end users search on common three-letter strings (as found in actual customer names) proportionally more often than uncommon strings. Since this is an Oracle example, use Oracle's expression SUBSTR(Char_Col, 1, 3) for an expression that returns the first three characters of each of these character columns.

Recall that for the apples-and-oranges table Code_Translations, you should gather statistics for specific types only, just as if each type was in its own, separate physical table. In other words, if your query uses order status codes in some join conditions, then query Code_Translations not for the total number of rows in that table, but rather for the number of order status rows. Only table rows for the types mentioned in the query turn out to significantly influence query costs. You may end up querying the same table twice, but for different subsets of the table. Example 5-3 queries Code_Translations once to count order status codes and again to count order detail status codes.

The queries in Example 5-3 yield all the data you need for the join and filter ratios.

*Example 5-3. Queries for query-tuning statistics*

```
Q1:  SELECT SUM(COUNT(*)*COUNT(*))/(SUM(COUNT(*))*SUM(COUNT(*))) A1
     FROM Customers
     GROUP BY UPPER(SUBSTR(First_Name, 1, 3)), UPPER(SUBSTR(Last_Name, 1, 3));
A1:  0.0002

Q2:  SELECT COUNT(*) A2 FROM Customers;
A2:  5,000,000

Q3:  SELECT COUNT(*) A3 FROM Orders
     WHERE Order_Date > SYSDATE - 366;
A3:  1,200,000

Q4:  SELECT COUNT(*) A4 FROM Orders;
A4:  4,000,000

Q5:  SELECT COUNT(*) A5 FROM Orders O, Customers C
     WHERE O.Customer_ID = C.Customer_ID;
A5:  4,000,000

Q6:  SELECT COUNT(*) A6 FROM Order Details;
A6:  12,000,000

Q7:  SELECT COUNT(*) A7 FROM Orders O, Order_Details OD
     WHERE OD.Order_ID = O.Order_ID;
A7:  12,000,000

Q8:  SELECT COUNT(*) A8 FROM Code_Translations
     WHERE Code_Type = 'ORDER_STATUS';
A8:  4

Q9:  SELECT COUNT(*) A9 FROM Orders O, Code_Translations OT
     WHERE O.Status_Code = OT.Code
       AND Code_Type = 'ORDER_STATUS';
A9:  4,000,000

Q10: SELECT COUNT(*) A10 FROM Code_Translations
     WHERE Code_Type = 'ORDER_DETAIL_STATUS';
A10: 3

Q11: SELECT COUNT(*) A11 FROM Order_Details OD, Code_Translations ODT
     WHERE OD.Status_Code = ODT.Code
       AND Code_Type = 'ORDER_DETAIL_STATUS';
A11: 12,000,000
```

Beginning with filter ratios, get the weighted-average filter ratio for the conditions on Customers' first and last name directly from A1. The result of that query is 0.0002. Find the filter ratio on Orders from A3/A4, which comes out to 0.3. Since no other alias has any filters, the filter ratios on the others are 1.0, which you imply just by leaving filter ratios off the query diagram for the other nodes.

Find the detail join ratios, to place alongside the upper end of each inner join arrow, by dividing the count on the lower table (the master table of that master-detail relationship) by the count on the join of the two tables. The ratios for the upper ends of the joins from OD to O and ODT are 3 (A7/A4) and 4,000,000 (A11/A10), respectively.

 To fit join ratios on the diagram, I will abbreviate millions as $m$ and thousands as $k$, so I will diagram the last result as $4m$.

The ratios for the upper ends of the joins from O to C and OT are 0.8 (from A5/A2) and 1,000,000 (or $1m$, from A9/A8), respectively.

Find the master join ratios for the lower ends of each inner-join arrow, by dividing the count for the join by the upper table count. When you have mandatory foreign keys and referential integrity (foreign keys that do not fail to point to existing primary-key values), you find master join ratios equal to exactly 1.0, as in every case in this example, from A7/A6, A11/A6, A5/A4, and A9/A4.

Check for any unique filter conditions that you would annotate with an asterisk (Step 6). In the case of this example, there are no such conditions.

Then, place all of these numbers onto the query diagram, as shown in Figure 5-5.

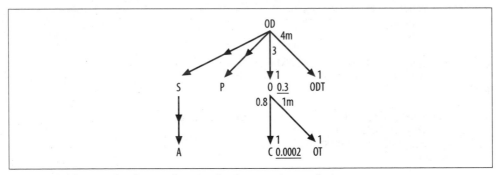

Figure 5-5. The completed query diagram for the second example

## Shortcuts

Although the full process of completing a detailed, complete query diagram for a many-way join looks and is time-consuming, you can employ many shortcuts that usually reduce the process to a few minutes or even less:

- You can usually guess from the names which columns are the primary keys.

- You can usually ignore ratios for the outer joins and the optional tables they reach. Often, you can leave outer joins off the diagram altogether, at least for a preliminary solution that shows how much room for improvement the query has.

# BUSINESS REPLY MAIL

FIRST CLASS MAIL   PERMIT NO. 80   SEBASTOPOL, CA

*Postage will be paid by addressee*

**O'Reilly & Associates, Inc.**
Book Registration
1005 Gravenstein Highway North
Sebastopol, CA 95472-9910

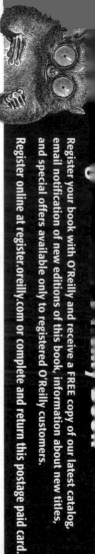

Register your book with O'Reilly and receive a FREE copy of our latest catalog, email notification of new editions of this book, information about new titles, and special offers available only to registered O'Reilly customers.

Register online at register.oreilly.com or complete and return this postage paid card.

**Which book(s) are you registering?** Please include title and ISBN # (above bar code on back cover)

| Title | ISBN # |
|---|---|
| Title | ISBN # |
| Title | ISBN # |
| Name | |
| Company/Organization | Job Title |
| Address | |
| City | State | Zip/Postal Code | Country |
| Telephone | Email address |

register.oreilly.com

Part #30031

- The master join ratio (on the primary-key end of a join) is almost always exactly 1.0, unless the foreign key is optional. Unless you have reason to suspect that the foreign key is frequently null or frequently points to no-longer-existing primary-key values, just leave it off, implying a value of 1.0. The master join ratio is never greater than 1.0.

- Some databases implement constraints that rigorously guarantee referential integrity. Even without such constraints, well-built applications maintain referential integrity, or at least near-integrity, in their tables. If you guarantee, or at least assume, referential integrity, you can assume that nonnull foreign keys always point to valid primary keys. In this case, you do not need to run the (comparatively slow) query for joined-table counts to find the join factors. Instead, you just need the percentage of rows that have a null foreign key and the two table counts. To compute those, begin by executing SQL similar to this:

```
SELECT COUNT(*) D, COUNT(<Foreign_Key_Column>) F FROM <Detail_Table>;
SELECT COUNT(*) M FROM <Master_Table>;
```

Letting D be the first count from the first query, F be the second count from the same query, and M be the count from the second query, the master join ratio is just F/D, while the detail join ratio is F/M.

Join ratios rarely matter; usually, you can just guess. The detail join ratio matters most in the unusual case when it is much less than 1.0, and it matters somewhat whether the detail join factor is close to 1.0 or much larger. You can usually guess closely enough to get in the right ballpark.

Informed guesses for join factors are sometimes best! Even if your current data shows surprising statistics for a specific master-detail relationship, you might not want to depend on those statistics for manual query tuning, since they might change with time or might not apply to other database instances that will execute the same SQL. (This last issue is especially true if you are tuning for a shared application product.)

- If you tune many queries from the same application, reuse join-ratio data as you encounter the same joins again and again.

- Filter ratios matter the most but usually vary by orders of magnitude, and, when filter ratios are not close, order-of-magnitude guesses suffice. You almost never need more precision than the first nonzero digit (one significant figure, if you remember the term from high school science) to tune a query well for any of the ratios, so round the numbers you show. (For example, 0.043 rounds to 0.04 with one significant figure, and 472 rounds to 500.)

Just as for join ratios, informed guesses for filter ratios are sometimes best. An informed guess will likely yield a result that works well across a range of customers and over a long time. Overdependence on measured values might lead to optimizations that are not robust between application instances or over time.

The key value of diagramming is its effect on your understanding of the tuning problem. With practice, you can often identify the best plan in your head, without physically drawing the query diagram at all!

## Interpreting Query Diagrams

Before I go further, take some time just to understand the content of the query diagram, so that you see more than just a confusing, abstract picture when you look at one. Given a few rules of thumb, interpreting a query diagram is simple. You might already be familiar with entity-relationship diagrams. There is a helpful, straightforward mapping between entity-relationship diagrams and the skeletons of query diagrams. Figure 5-6 shows the query skeleton for Example 5-1, alongside the corresponding subset of the entity-relationship diagram.

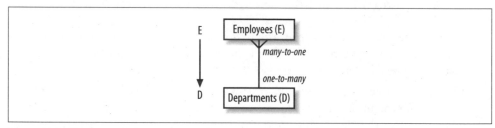

*Figure 5-6. The query skeleton compared to an entity-relationship diagram*

The entity-relationship diagram encodes the database design, which is independent of the query. Therefore, the query skeleton that encodes the same many-to-one relationship (with the arrow pointing to the *one*) also comes from the database design, not from the query. The query skeleton simply designates which subset of the database design is immediately relevant, so you restrict attention to just that subset encoded in the query skeleton. When the same table appears under multiple aliases, the query diagram also, in a sense, explodes the entity-relationship diagram, showing multiple joins to the same table as if they were joins to clones of that table; this clarifies the tuning problem these multiple joins involve.

With join ratios on the query skeleton, you encode quantitative data about the actual data, in place of the qualitative *many* indications in the entity-relationship diagram. With the join ratios, you say, on average, *how many* for many-to-one relationships (with the detail join ratio) and *how-often-zero* with the master join ratio, when you find many–to–zero-or-one relationships. This too is a function of the underlying data, though not of the database design, and it is independent of the query. These join ratios can vary across multiple database instances that run the same application with different detailed data, but within an instance, the join ratios are fixed across all queries that perform the same joins.

It is fortunate and true that the optimum plan is usually quite insensitive to the join ratios, because this almost always enables you to tune a query well for all customers of an application at once.

Only when you add filter ratios do you really pick up data that is specific to a given query (combined with data-distribution data), because filter conditions come from the query, not from the underlying data. This data shows the relative size of each subset of each table the query requires.

Query diagrams for correctly written queries (as I will show later) almost always have a single detail table at the top of the tree, with arrows pointing down to master (or *lookup*) tables below and further arrows (potentially) branching down from those. When you find this normal form for a query diagram, the query turns out to have a simple, natural interpretation:

> A query is a question asked about the detail entities that map to that top detail table, with one or more joins to master tables below to find further data about those entities stored elsewhere for correct normalization.

For example, a query joining Employees and Departments is really just a question about employees, where the database must go to the Departments table for employee information, like Department_Name, that you store in the Departments table for correct normalization.

Yes, I know, to a database designer, Department_Name is a property of the department, not of the employee, but I am speaking of the business question, not the formal database. In normal business semantics, you would certainly think of the department name (like other Departments properties) as a property of the employees, inherited from Departments.

Questions about business entities that are important enough to have tables are natural in a business application, and these questions frequently require several levels of joins to find inherited data stored in master tables. Questions about strange, unnatural combinations of entities are *not* natural to a business, and when you examine query diagrams that fail to match the normal form, you will frequently find that these return useless results, results other than what the application requires, in at least some corner cases.

Following are the rules for query diagrams that match the normal form. The queries behind these normal-form diagrams are easy to interpret as sensible business questions about a single set of entities that map to the top table:

- The query maps to one tree.
- The tree has one root, exactly one table with no join to its primary key. All nodes other than the root node have a single downward-pointing arrow linking

them to a detail node above, but any node can be at the top end of any number of downward-pointing arrows.

- All joins have downward-pointing arrows (joins that are unique on at least one end).

- Outer joins are unfiltered, pointing down, with only outer joins below outer joins.

- The question that the query answers is basically a question about the entity represented at the top (root) of the tree (or about aggregations of that entity).

- The other tables just provide reference data stored elsewhere for normalization.

## Simplified Query Diagrams

You will see that much of the detail on a full query diagram is unnecessary for all but the rarest problems. When you focus on the essential elements, you usually need only the skeleton of the diagram and the approximate filter ratios. You occasionally need join ratios, but usually only when either the detail join ratio is less than about 1.5 or the master join ratio is less than 0.9. Unless you have reason to suspect these uncommon values for the master-detail relationship, you can save yourself the trouble of even measuring these values. This, in turn, means that less data is required to produce the simplified join diagrams. You won't need table rowcounts for tables without filters. In practice, many-way joins usually have filters only on at most 3–5 tables, so this makes even the most complex query easy to diagram, without requiring many statistics-gathering queries.

Stripping away the usually unnecessary detail that I've just described, you can simplify Figure 5-5 to Figure 5-7.

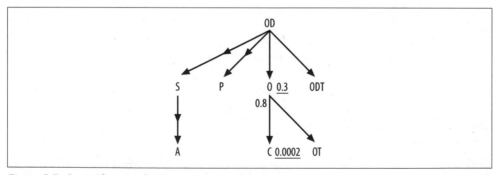

Figure 5-7. Query diagram for Figure 5-5, simplified

Note that the detail join ratio from C to O in Figure 5-5 is less than 1.5, so continue to show it even in the simplified diagram in Figure 5-7.

When it comes to filters, even approximate numbers are often unnecessary if you know which filter is best and if the other competing filters do not share the same parent detail node. In this case, you can simply indicate the best filter with a capital F and lesser filters with a lowercase f. Further simplify Figure 5-7 to Figure 5-8.

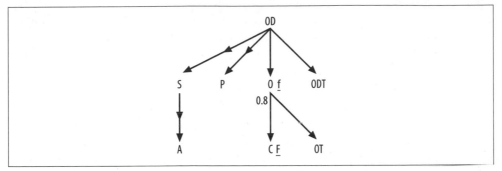

*Figure 5-8. Query diagram for Figure 5-7, fully simplified*

Note that the detail join ratio from C to O is less than 1.5, so continue to show it even in the fully simplified diagram in Figure 5-8.

Although I've removed the filter ratios from Figure 5-8, you should continue to place an asterisk next to any unique filters (filters guaranteed to return no more than one row). You should also indicate actual filter values for lesser filters that share the same parent detail node. For example, if you have lesser filters on nodes B and C in Figure 5-9, show their actual filter ratios, as illustrated, since they share the parent detail node A.

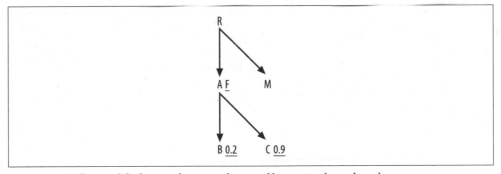

*Figure 5-9. Fully simplified query diagram, showing filter ratios for a shared parent*

In practice, you can usually start with a simplified query diagram and add detail only as necessary. If the execution plan (which I explain how to derive in Chapter 6) you find from the simplified problem is so fast that further improvement is pointless, you are finished. (You might be surprised how often this happens.) For example, a batch query that runs in just a few seconds a few times per day is fast enough that further improvement is pointless. Likewise, you need not further tune any online query that runs in under 100 milliseconds that the end user community, as a whole, runs fewer than 1,000 times per day. If after this first round of tuning you think further improvement would still be worth the trouble, you can quickly check the feasibility of more improvement by checking whether you missed important join ratios. The fastest way to do this is to ask whether the single best filter accounts for almost all of the overall reduction in rowcount versus a wholly unfiltered query of just the most detailed table. Assuming that the join diagram maps out as an upside-down tree, the default expectation is that the whole query, without filters, would return the same number of rows as the most detailed table at the root of the join tree (at the top, that is).

With filters, you expect that each filter reduces that rowcount returned from the most detailed table (at the root of the join tree) by the filter ratio. If the best filter ratio times the rowcount of the most detailed table accounts for close to the number of rows that the whole query returns, you know you have not missed any important filter, and the simplified diagram suffices. On the other hand, if the most detailed table's rowcount times the best filter (or what you *thought* was the best filter!) would yield far more rows than the actual query yields, then you might have missed an important source of row reduction and you should gather more statistics. If the product of all filter ratios (calculated or guessed) times the rowcount of the most detailed table does not come close to the whole-query rowcount, you should suspect that you need further information. In particular, you might have hidden *join filters*, which are join ratios that unexpectedly turn out to be much less than 1.0; recognizing these and using them for a better plan can yield important further gains.

## Exercises

1. Diagram the following query:

```
SELECT ...
FROM Customers C, ZIP_Codes Z, ZIP_Demographics D, Regions R
WHERE C.ZIP_Code=Z.ZIP_Code
  AND Z.Demographic_ID=D.Demographic_ID
  AND Z.Region_ID=R.Region_ID
  AND C.Active_Flag='Y'
  AND C.Profiled_Flag='N'
  AND R.Name='SOUTHWEST'
  AND D.Name IN ('YUPPIE', 'OLDMONEY');
```

Make the usual assumptions about primary-key names, except that the primary key of ZIP_Codes is simply ZIP_Code, and note that the Name columns of both REGIONS and ZIP_Demographics are also uniquely indexed. You have 5,000,000 rows in Customers, 250,000 rows in Zip_Codes, 20 rows in ZIP_Demographics, and 5 rows in Regions. Assume all foreign keys are never null and always point to valid primary keys. The following query returns 2,000,000 rows:

```
SELECT COUNT(*) FROM Customers C WHERE Active_Flag='Y' AND Profiled_Flag='N';
```

2. Diagram the following query:

```
SELECT ...
FROM Regions R, Zip_Codes Z, Customers C, Customer_Mailings CM,
     Mailings M, Catalogs Cat, Brands B
WHERE R.Region_ID(+)=Z.Region_ID
  AND Z.ZIP_Code(+)=C.ZIP_Code
  AND C.Customer_ID=CM.Customer_ID
  AND CM.Mailing_ID=M.Mailing_ID
  AND M.Catalog_ID=Cat.Catalog_ID
  AND Cat.Brand_ID=B.Brand_ID
  AND B.Name='OhSoGreen'
  AND M.Mailing_Date >= SYSDATE-365
GROUP BY... ORDER BY ...
```

Start with the same assumptions and statistics as in Exercise 1. Customer_Mailings contains 30,000,000 rows. Mailings contains 40,000 rows. Catalogs contains 200 rows. Brands contains 12 rows and has an alternate unique key on Name. The following query returns 16,000 rows:

```
SELECT COUNT(*) FROM Mailings M WHERE Mailing_Date >= SYSDATE-365;
```

3. Diagram the following query:

```
SELECT ...
FROM Code_Translations SPCT, Code_Translations TRCT, Code_Translations CTCT,
     Products P, Product_Lines PL, Inventory_Values IV, Brands B,
     Product_Locations Loc, Warehouses W, Regions R,
     Inventory_Taxing_Entities ITx, Inventory_Tax_Rates ITxR, Consignees C
WHERE W.Region_ID=R.Region_ID
  AND Loc.Warehouse_ID=W.Warehouse_ID
  AND W.Inventory_Taxing_Entity_ID=ITx.Inventory_Taxing_Entity_ID
  AND ITx.Inventory_Taxing_Entity_ID= ITxR.Inventory_Taxing_Entity_ID
  AND ITxR.Effective_Start_Date <= SYSDATE
  AND ITxR.Effective_End_Date > SYSDATE
  AND ITxR.Rate>0
  AND P.Product_ID=Loc.Product_ID
  AND Loc.Quantity>0
  AND P.Product_Line_ID=PL.Product_Line_ID(+)
  AND P.Product_ID=IV.Product_ID
  AND P.Taxable_Inventory_Flag='Y'
  AND P.Consignee_ID=C.Consignee_ID(+)
  AND P.Strategic_Product_Code=SPCT.Code
  AND SPCT.Code_Type='STRATEGIC_PRODUCT'
  AND P.Turnover_Rate_Code=TRCT.Code
  AND TRCT.Code_Type='TURNOVER_RATE'
  AND P.Consignment_Type_Code=CTCT.CODE
  AND CTCT.Code_Type='CONSIGNMENT_TYPE'
  AND IV.Effective_Start_Date <= SYSDATE
  AND IV.Effective_End_Date > SYSDATE
  AND IV.Unit_Value>0
  AND P.Brand_ID=B.Brand_ID
  AND B.Name='2Much$'
  AND ITX.Tax_Day_Of_Year='DEC31'
GROUP BY... ORDER BY ...
```

Start with the same assumptions and statistics as in Exercises 1 and 2, except that W.Inventory_Taxing_Entity_ID points to a valid taxing entity only when it is not null, which is just 5% of the time. The counts for table rows are as follows:

```
Products=8,500
Product_Lines=120
Inventory_Values=34,000
Brands=12
Product_Locations=176,000
Warehouses=80
Regions=5
Inventory_Taxing_Entities=4
Inventory_Tax_Rates=7
Consignees=14
```

Code_Translations has a two-part primary key: Code_Type, Code.

Inventory_Values and Inventory_Tax_Rates have a time-dependent primary key consisting of an ID and an effective date range, such that any given date falls in a single date range for any value of the key ID. Specifically, the join conditions to each of these tables are guaranteed to be unique by the Effective_Start_Date and Effective_End_Date conditions, which are part of the joins, not separate filters. (Unfortunately, there is no convenient way to enforce that uniqueness through an index; it is a condition created by the application.) The following queries return the rowcounts shown in the lines that follow each query:

```
Q1:  SELECT COUNT(*) A1 FROM Inventory_Taxing_Entities ITx
     WHERE ITx.Tax_Day_Of_Year='DEC31'
A1: 2

Q2:  SELECT COUNT(*) A2 FROM Inventory_Values IV
     WHERE IV.Unit_Value>0
       AND IV.Effective_Start_Date <= SYSDATE
       AND IV.Effective_End_Date > SYSDATE
A2: 7,400

Q3:  SELECT COUNT(*) A3 FROM Products P
     WHERE P.Taxable_Inventory_Flag='Y'
A3: 8,300

Q4:  SELECT COUNT(*) A4 FROM Product_Locations Loc
     WHERE Loc.Quantity>0
A4: 123,000

Q5:  SELECT COUNT(*) A5 FROM Inventory_Tax_Rates ITxR
     WHERE ITxR.RATE>0
       AND ITxR.Effective_Start_Date <= SYSDATE
       AND ITxR.Effective_End_Date > SYSDATE
A5: 4
```

```
Q6:   SELECT COUNT(*) A6 FROM Inventory_Values IV
         WHERE IV.Effective_Start_Date <= SYSDATE
            AND IV.Effective_End_Date > SYSDATE
A6: 8,500

Q7:   SELECT COUNT(*) A7 FROM INVENTORY_TAX_RATES ITxR
         WHERE ITxR.Effective_Start_Date <= SYSDATE
            AND ITxR.Effective_End_Date > SYSDATE
A7: 4

Q8:   SELECT COUNT(*) A8 FROM Code_Translations SPCT
         WHERE Code_Type = 'STRATEGIC_PRODUCT'
A8: 3

Q9:   SELECT COUNT(*) A9 FROM Code_Translations TRCT
         WHERE Code_Type = 'TURNOVER_RATE'
A9: 2

Q10: SELECT COUNT(*) A10 FROM CTCT
         WHERE Code_Type = 'CONSIGNMENT_TYPE'
A10: 3
```

4. Fully simplify the query diagram for Exercise 1. Try starting from the queries and the query statistics, rather than from the full query diagrams. Then, compare your result with what you get when you start from the full query diagrams that you already did.

5. Fully simplify the query diagram for Exercise 2, following the guidelines in Exercise 4.

6. Fully simplify the query diagram for Exercise 3, following the guidelines in Exercise 4.

# CHAPTER 6
# Deducing the Best Execution Plan

*For Tyme ylost may nought recovered be.*
—Geoffrey Chaucer
   *Troilus and Criseyde*

Just as reducing a word problem to abstract mathematics is usually the hardest part of solving the problem, you will usually find that producing the query diagram is harder than deducing the best execution plan from the query diagram. Now that you know the hard part, how to translate a query into a query diagram, I demonstrate the easy part. There are several questions you need to answer to fully describe the optimum execution plan for a query:

- How do you reach each table in the execution plan, with a full table scan or one or more indexes, and which indexes do you use, if any?
- How do you join the tables in the execution plan?
- In what order do you join the tables in the execution plan?

Out of these three questions, I make a case that the only hard question, and the main point of the query diagram, is the question of join order. If you begin by finding the optimum join order, which is nearly decoupled from the other questions, you will find that answers to the other two questions are usually obvious. In the worst cases, you might need to try experiments to answer the other two questions, but these will require at most one or two experiments per table. If you did not have a systematic way to answer the join-order question, you would require potentially billions of experiments to find the best plan.

## Robust Execution Plans

A subset of all possible execution plans can be described as *robust*. While such plans are not always quite optimum, they are almost always close to optimum in real-world queries, and they have desirable characteristics, such as predictability and low likelihood of errors during execution. (A nonrobust join can fail altogether, with an out-of-TEMP-space error if a hash or sort-merge join needs more space than is available.)

Robust plans tend to work well across a wide range of likely data distributions that might occur over time or between different database instances running the same application. Robust plans are also relatively forgiving of uncertainty and error; with a robust plan, a moderate error in the estimated selectivity of a filter might lead to a moderately suboptimal plan, but not to a disastrous plan. When you use robust execution plans, you can almost always solve a SQL tuning problem once, instead of solving it many times as you encounter different data distributions over time and at different customer sites.

 Uncertainty and error are inevitable in the inputs for an optimization problem. For example, even with perfect information at parse time (at the time the database generates the execution plan), a condition like Last_Name = :LName has uncertain selectivity, depending on the actual value that will be bound to :LName at execution time. The unavoidability of uncertainty and error makes robustness especially important.

Robust execution plans tend to have the following properties:

- Their execution cost is proportional to rows returned.
- They require almost no sort or hash space in memory.
- They need not change as all tables grow.
- They have moderate sensitivity to distributions and perform adequately across many instances running the same application, or across any given instance as data changes.
- They are particularly good when it turns out that a query returns fewer rows than you expect (when filters are more selective than they appear).

 In a sense, a robust plan is *optimistic*: it assumes that you have designed your application to process a manageably small number of rows, even when it is not obvious how the query narrows the rowset down to such a small number.

Robustness requirements imply that you should usually choose to:

- Drive to the first table on a selective index
- Drive to each subsequent table with a nested loop on the index of the full join key that points to a table that the database already read, following the links in the query diagram

 Nested loops on full join keys generally scale with the number of rows that match query conditions and avoid memory required to execute hash joins or sort-merge joins, for which memory use might turn out to be excessive. Such excessive memory use can even lead to out-of-temp-space errors if the cached rowsets turn out to be larger than you expect.

- Drive down to primary keys before you drive up to nonunique foreign keys

 Driving down before driving up avoids a potential explosion of rows earlier in the plan than you want when it turns out that the detail table has more details per master row than you expected.

If you consider only robust plans, robustness rules alone answer the first two questions of finding the best execution plan, leaving only the question of join order:

- You will reach every table with a single index, an index on the full filter condition for the first table, and an index on the join key for each of the other tables.
- You will join all tables by nested loops.

I later discuss when you can sometimes safely and profitably relax the robustness requirement for nested-loops joins, but for now I focus on the only remaining question for robust plans: the join order. I also later discuss what to do when the perfect execution plan is unavailable, usually because of missing indexes, but for now, assume you are looking for a truly optimum robust plan, unconstrained by missing indexes.

## Standard Heuristic Join Order

Here is the heuristic for finding the best robust execution plan, including join order:

1. Drive first to the table with the best (nearest to zero) filter ratio.
2. With nested loops—driving through the full, unique, primary-key indexes—drive down as long as possible, first to the best (nearest to zero) remaining filters.
3. Only when necessary, follow nested loops up diagram links (against the direction of the arrow) through full, nonunique, foreign-key indexes.

These steps might not be perfectly clear now. Don't worry. The rest of this chapter explains each of these steps in detail. The heuristic is almost easier to demonstrate than to describe.

When the driving table turns out to be several levels below the top detail table (the *root* table, so-called because it lies at the root of the join tree), you will have to return to Step 2 after every move up the tree in Step 3. I describe some rare refinements for special cases, but by and large, finding the optimum plan is that simple, once you have the query diagram!

After tuning thousands of queries from real-world applications that included tens of thousands of queries, I can state with high confidence that these rules are *just complex enough*. Any significant simplification of these rules will leave major, common classes of queries poorly tuned, and any addition of complexity will yield significant improvement only for relatively rare classes of queries.

Later in the book, I discuss these rarer cases and what to do with them, but you should first understand the basics as thoroughly as possible.

There is one subtlety to consider when Steps 2 and 3 mention following join links up or down: the tables reached in the plan so far are consolidated into a single virtual node, for purposes of choosing the next step in the plan. Alternatively, it might be easier to visualize the tables reached so far in the plan as one cloud of nodes. From the cloud of already-reached nodes, it makes no difference to the rest of the plan how already-reached table nodes are arranged within that cloud, or in what order you reached them. The answer to the question "Which table comes next?" is completely independent of the order or method you used to join any earlier tables. Which tables are in the cloud affects the boundaries of the cloud and matters, but how they got there is ancient history, so to speak, and no longer relevant to your next decision.

When you put together an execution plan following the rules, you might find yourself focused on the most-recently-joined table, but this is a mistake. Tables are equally joined upward or downward from the cloud if they are joined upward or downward from any member of the set of already-joined tables, not necessarily the most recently-joined table. You might even find it useful to draw the expanding boundaries of the cloud of so-far-reached tables as you proceed through the steps, to clarify in your mind which tables lie just outside the cloud. The relationship of remaining tables to the cloud clarifies whether they join to the cloud from above or from below, or do not even join to the cloud directly, being ineligible to join until you join further intermediate tables. I further illustrate this point later in the chapter.

## Simple Examples

Nothing illustrates the method better than examples, so I demonstrate the method using the query diagrams built in Chapter 5, beginning with the simplest case, the two-way join, shown again in Figure 6-1.

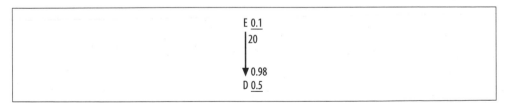

*Figure 6-1. A simple two-way join*

Applying Step 1 of the method, first ask which node offers the best (lowest) effective filter ratio. The answer is E, since E's filter ratio of 0.1 is less than D's ratio of 0.5. Driving from that node, apply Step 2 and find that the best (and only) downstream node is node D, so go to D next. You find no other tables, so that completes the join order. Following the rules for a robust execution plan, you would reach E with an index on its filter, on Exempt_Flag. Then, you would follow nested loops to the matching departments through the primary-key index on Department_ID for Departments. By brute force, in Chapter 5, I already showed the comforting result that this plan is in fact the best, at least in terms of minimizing the number of rows touched.

 The rules for robust plans and optimum robust plans take no account of what indexes you already have. Remember that this chapter addresses the question of which plan you *want*, and that question should not be confined by currently lacking indexes. I later address the question of settling for less than optimal plans when indexes are missing, but you must first find ideal plans before you can evaluate when to make compromises.

## Join Order for an Eight-Way Join

So far, so good, but two-way joins are too easy to need an elaborate new method, so let's continue with the next example, the eight-way join. Eight tables can, in theory, be joined in 8-factorial join orders (40,320 possibilities), enough to call for a systematic method. Figure 6-2 repeats the earlier problem from Chapter 5.

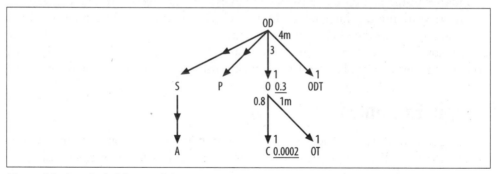

*Figure 6-2. A typical eight-way join*

Following the heuristics outlined earlier, you can determine the optimal join order for the query diagrammed in Figure 6-2 as follows:

1. Find the table with the lowest filter ratio. In this case, it's C, with a ratio of 0.0002, so C becomes the driving table.

2. From C, it is not possible to drive down to any table through a primary-key index. You must therefore move upward in the diagram.

3. The only way up from C is to O, so O becomes the second table to be joined.

4. After reaching O, you find that you can now drive downward to OT. Always drive downward when possible, and go up only when you've exhausted all downward paths. OT becomes the third table to be joined.

5. There's nothing below OT, so return to O and move upward to OD, which becomes the fourth table to be joined.

6. The rest of the joins are downward and are all unfiltered, so join to S, P, and ODT in any order.

7. Join to A at any point after it becomes eligible, after the join to S places it within reach.

 I will show that, when you consider join ratios, you will always place downward inner joins before outer joins. This is because such inner joins have at least the potential to discard rows, even in cases like this, when statistics indicate the join will have no effect on the running rowcount.

Therefore, you find the optimum join order to be C; O; OT; OD; S, P, and ODT in any order; and A at any point after S. This dictates 12 equally good join orders out of the original 40,320 possibilities. An exhaustive search of all possible join orders confirms that these 12 are equally good and are better than all other possible join orders, to minimize rows visited in robust execution plans.

This query diagram might strike you as too simple to represent a realistic problem, but I have found this is not at all the case. Most queries with even many joins have just one or two filters, and one of the filter ratios is usually obviously far better than any other.

For the most part, simply driving to that best filter first, following downward joins before upward joins, and perhaps picking up one or two minor filters along the way, preferably sooner rather than later, is all it takes to find an excellent execution plan. That plan is almost certainly the best or so close to the best that the difference does not matter. This is where the simplified query diagrams come in. The fully simplified query diagram, shown in Figure 6-3, with the best filter indicated by the capital F and the other filter by lowercase f, leads to the same result with only qualitative filter information.

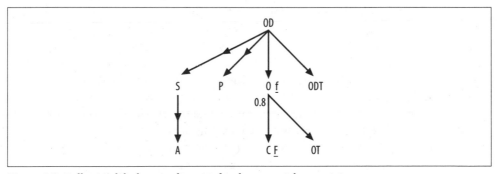

*Figure 6-3. Fully simplified query diagram for the same eight-way join*

I will return to this example later and show that you can slightly improve on this result by relaxing the requirement for a fully robust execution plan and using a hash join, but for now, I focus on teaching complete mastery of the skill of optimizing for the best robust plan. I already showed the 12 best join orders, and I need one of these for further illustration to complete the solution of the problem. I choose (C, O, OT, OD, ODT, P, S, A) as the join order to illustrate.

## Completing the Solution for an Eight-Way Join

The rest of the solution is to apply the robust-plan rules to get the desired join order in a robust plan. A robust plan calls for nested loops through indexes, beginning with the filter index on the driving table and followed by indexes on the join keys. Here is the best plan in detail (refer back to Chapter 5 for the original query and filter conditions):

1. Drive to Customers on an index on (Last_Name, First_Name), with a query somehow modified to make that index accessible and fully useful.

2. Join, with nested loops, to Orders on an index on the foreign key Customer_ID.

3. Join, with nested loops, to Code_Translations (OT) on its primary-key index (Code_Type, Code).

4. Join, with nested loops, to Order_Details on an index on the foreign key Order_ID.

5. Join, with nested loops, to Code_Translations (ODT) on its primary-key index (Code_Type, Code).

6. Outer join, with nested loops, to Products on its primary-key index Product_ID.

7. Outer join, with nested loops, to Shipments on its primary-key index Shipment_ID.

8. Outer join, with nested loops, to Addresses on its primary-key index Address_ID.

9. Sort the final result as necessary.

Any execution plan that failed to follow this join order, failed to use nested loops, or failed to use precisely the indexes shown would not be the optimal robust plan chosen here. Getting the driving table and index right is the key problem 90% of the time, and this example is no exception. The first obstacle to getting the right plan is to somehow gain access to the correct driving filter index for Step 1. In Oracle, you might use a functional index on the uppercase values of the Last_Name and First_Name columns, to avoid the dilemma of driving to an index with a complex expression. In other databases, you might recognize that the name values are, or should be, always stored in uppercase, or you might denormalize with new, indexed columns that repeat the names in uppercase, or you might change the application to require a case-sensitive search. There are several ways around this specific problem, but you would need to choose the right driving table to even discover the need.

Once you make it possible to get the driving table right, are your problems over? Almost certainly, you have indexes on the necessary primary keys, but good database design does not (and should not) guarantee that every foreign key has an index, so the next likely issue is to make sure you have foreign-key indexes `Orders(Customer_ID)` and `Order_Details(Order_ID)`. These enable the necessary nested-loops joins upward for a robust plan starting with `Customers`.

Another potential problem is that optimizers might choose a join method other than nested loops to one or more of the tables, and you might need hints or other techniques to avoid the use of methods other than nested loops. If they take this course, they will likely also choose a different access method for the tables being joined without nested loops, reaching all the rows that can join at once.

 However, I will show that sort-merge or hash joins to a small table like `Code_Translations` would be fine here, even slightly faster, and nearly as robust, since tables like this are unlikely to grow very large.

In this simple case, with just the filters shown, join order is likely the least of the problems, as long as you get the driving table right and have the necessary foreign-key indexes.

## A Complex 17-Way Join

Figure 6-4 shows a deliberately complex example to fully illustrate the method. I have left off the join ratios, making Figure 6-4 a partially simplified query diagram, since the join ratios do not affect the rules you have learned so far. I will step through the solution to this problem in careful detail, but you might want to try it yourself first, to see which parts of the method you already fully understand.

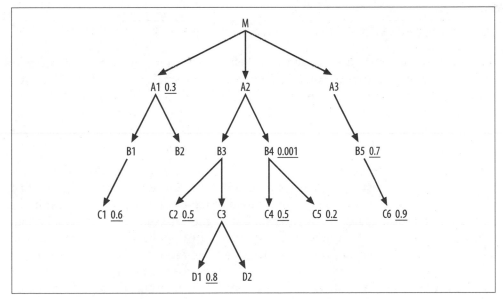

*Figure 6-4. A complex 17-way join*

For Step 1, you quickly find that B4 has the best filter ratio, at 0.001, so choose that as the driving table. It's best to reach such a selective filter through an index; so, in real life, if this were an important enough query, you might create a new index to use in driving to B4. For now though, we'll just worry about the join order. Step 2 dictates that you next examine the downward-joined nodes C4 and C5, with a preference to join to better-filtered nodes first. C5 has a filter ratio of 0.2, while C4 has a filter ratio of 0.5, so you join to C5 next. At this point, the beginning join order is (B4, C5), and the cloud around the so-far-joined tables looks like Figure 6-5.

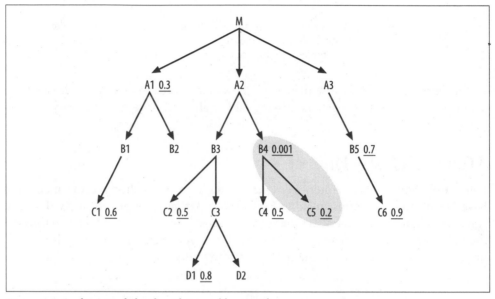

Figure 6-5. So-far-joined cloud, with two tables joined

If C5 had one or more nodes connected below, you would now have to compare them to C4, but since it does not, Step 2 offers only the single choice of C4. When you widen the cloud boundaries to include C4, you find no further nodes below the cloud, so you move on to Step 3, find the single node A2 joining the cloud from above, and add it to the building join order, which is now (B4, C5, C4, A2). The cloud around the so-far-joined tables now looks like Figure 6-6.

Note that I left in the original two-node cloud in gray. In practice, you need not erase the earlier clouds; just redraw new clouds around them. Returning to Step 2, find downstream of the current joined-tables cloud a single node, B3, so put it next in the join order without regard to any filter ratio it might have. Extend the cloud boundaries to include B3, so you now find nodes C2 and C3 applicable under Step 2, and choose C2 next in the join order, because its filter ratio of 0.5 is better than the implied filter ratio of 1.0 on unfiltered C3. The join order so far is now (B4, C5, C4, A2, B3, C2). Extend the cloud further around C2. This brings no new downstream nodes into play, so Step 2 now offers only C3 as an alternative. The join order so far is now (B4, C5, C4, A2, B3, C2, C3), and Figure 6-7 shows the current join cloud.

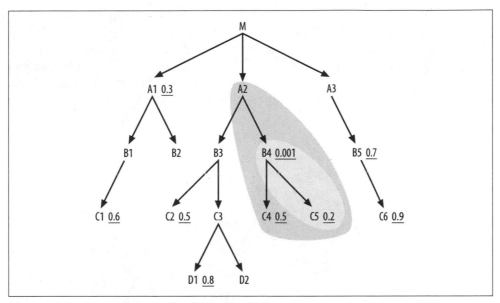

*Figure 6-6. So-far-joined cloud, after four tables joined*

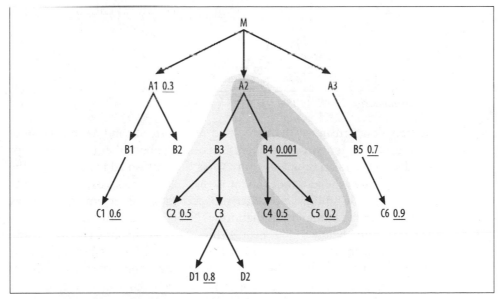

*Figure 6-7. So-far-joined cloud, with seven tables joined*

Step 2 now offers two new nodes below the current join cloud, D1 and D2, with D1 offering the better filter ratio. Since neither of these has nodes joined below, join to them in filter-ratio order and proceed to Step 3, with the join order so far now (B4, C5, C4, A2, B3, C2, C3, D1, D2). This completes the entire branch from A2 down, leaving only the upward link to M (the main table being queried) to reach the rest of the join tree, so Step 3 takes you next to M. Since you have reached the main table at the root of the join tree, Step 3 does not apply for the rest of the problem. Apply Step 2 until you have reached the rest of the tables. Immediately downstream of M (and of the whole join cloud so far), you find A1 and A3, with only A1 having a filter, so you join to A1 next. Now, the join order so far is (B4, C5, C4, A2, B3, C2, C3, D1, D2, M, A1), and Figure 6-8 shows the current join cloud.

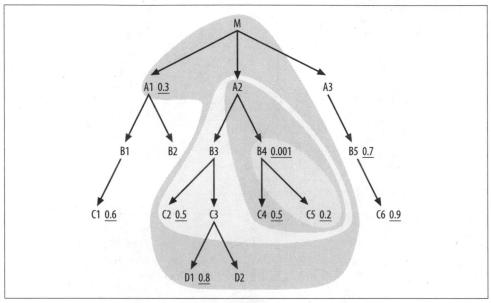

*Figure 6-8. So-far-joined cloud, with 11 tables joined*

Find immediately downstream of the join cloud nodes B1, B2, and A3, but none of these have filters, so look for two-away filters that offer the best filter ratios two steps away. You find such filters on C1 and B5, but C1 has the best, so add B1 and C1 to the running join order. Now, the join order so far is (B4, C5, C4, A2, B3, C2, C3, D1, D2, M, A1, B1, C1). You still find no better prospect than the remaining two-away filter on B5, so join next to A3 and B5, in that order. Now, the only two nodes remaining, B2 and C6, are both eligible to join next, being both directly attached to the join cloud. Choose C6 first, because it has a filter ratio of 0.9, which is better than the implied filter ratio of 1.0 for the unfiltered join to B2. This completes the join order: (B4, C5, C4, A2, B3, C2, C3, D1, D2, M, A1, B1, C1, A3, B5, C6, B2).

Apart from the join order, the rules specify that the database should reach table B4 on the index for its filter condition and the database should reach all the other tables in nested loops to the indexes on their join keys. These indexed join keys would be primary keys for downward joins to C5, C4, B3, C2, C3, D1, D2, A1, B1, C1, A3, B5, C6, and B2, and foreign keys for A2 (pointing to B4) and M (pointing to A2). Taken together, this fully specifies a single optimum robust plan out of the 17-factorial

(355,687,428,096,000) possible join orders and all possible join methods and indexes. However, this example is artificial in two respects:

- Real queries rarely have so many filtered nodes, so it is unlikely that a join of so many tables would have a single optimum join order. More commonly, there will be a whole range of equally good join orders, as I showed in the previous example.

- The later part of the join order matters little to the runtime, as long as you get the early join order right and reach all the later tables through their join keys. In this example, once the database reached node M, and perhaps A1, with the correct path, the path to the rest of the tables would affect the query runtime only slightly. In most queries, even fewer tables really matter to the join order, and often you will do fine with just the correct driving table and nested loops to the other tables following join keys in any order that the join tree permits.

 If you need to change a query anyway and have the chance to get the whole join order right, you might as well. However, if you already have a plan that is correct in the early join order, the improvement might not be worth the trouble of changing the query just to change the end of the join order.

# A Special Case

Usually, following the tuning-process steps without deviation works fine, but the problem shown in Figure 6-4 turns out to offer, potentially, one last trick you could apply, especially with Oracle.

 This section first describes an especially efficient trick that sometimes helps on Oracle. However, take heart if you need something like this outside of Oracle: at the end of the section, I describe a less efficient version of the trick for other databases.

## The Oracle Solution

Return to Figure 6-4 and consider a special case: all tables other than M are relatively small and well cached, but M is very large and therefore poorly cached and much more expensive to access than the other tables. Furthermore, M is a special *combinations* table to express a many-to-many relationship between A1 and A2. An example of such a combinations table would be a table of actor/movie combinations for a movie-history database, linking Movies and Actors, when the relationship between these is many-to-many. In such a combinations table, it is natural to use a two-part primary key made up of the IDs of the linked tables—in this case, Movie_ID and Actor_ID. As is commonly the case, this combinations table has an index on the combination of foreign keys pointing to the tables A2 and A1. For this example, assume the order of the keys within that index has the foreign key pointing to A2 first, followed by the foreign key pointing to A1 .

Consider the costs of accessing each table in the plan I found earlier as the original solution to Figure 6-4. You find low costs for the tables up to M, then a much higher cost for M because you get many more rows from that table than the previous tables and accessing those rows leads to physical I/O. Following M, the database joins to just as many rows in A1 (since M has no filter), but these are much cheaper per row, because they are fully cached. Then, the filter in A1 drops the rowcount back down to a much lower number for the remaining tables in the plan. Therefore, you find a cost almost wholly dominated by the cost of accessing M, and it would be useful to reduce that cost.

As it happens, in this unusual case, you find an opportunity to get from the foreign key in M pointing to A2 to the foreign key pointing to A1, stored in the same multicolumn index in M, without ever touching the table M! The database will later need to read rows from the table itself, to get the foreign key pointing to A3 and probably to get columns in the query SELECT list. However, you can postpone going to the table until after the database reaches filtered tables A1 and C1. Therefore, the database will need to go only to 18% as many rows in M ($0.3 \times 0.6$, picking up the filter ratios 0.3 on A1 and 0.6 on C1) as it would need to read if the database went to the table M as soon as it went to the index for M. This greatly reduces the query cost, since the cost of reading rows in table M, itself, dominates in this particular case.

No database makes it particularly easy to decouple index reads from table reads; a table read normally follows an index read immediately, automatically, even when this is not optimal. However, Oracle does allow for a trick that solves the problem, since Oracle SQL can explicitly reference rowids. In this case, the best join order is (B4, C5, C4, A2, B3, C2, C3, D1, D2, MI, A1, B1, C1, MT, A3, B5, C6, B2). Here, MI is the index on M(FkeyToA2,FkeyToA1), inserted into the join order where M was originally. MT is the table M, accessed later in the plan through the ROWID from MI and inserted into the join order after picking up the filters on A1 and C1. The trick is to refer to M twice in the FROM clause, once for the index-only access and once for a direct ROWID join, as follows, assuming that the name of the index on M(FkeyToA2,FkeyToA1) is M_DoubleKeyInd:

```
Select /*+ ORDERED INDEX(MI M_DoubleKeyInd) */ MT.Col1, MT.Col2,...
...
FROM B4, C5, C4, A2, B3, C2, C3, D1, D2,
M MI, A1, B1, C1, M MT, A3, B5, C6, B2
WHERE ...
AND A2.Pkey=MI.FKeyToA2
AND A1.Pkey=MI.FKeyToA1
AND MI.ROWID=MT.ROWID
AND...
```

So, two joins to M are really cheaper than one in this unusual case! Note the two hints in this version of the query:

ORDERED

Specifies that the tables are to be joined in the order they occur in the FROM clause

INDEX(MI M_DoubleKeyInd)

Guarantees use of the correct index at the point in the order where you want index-only access for MI

Other hints might be necessary to get the rest of the plan just right. Also note the unusual rowid-to-rowid join between MI and MT, and note that the only references to MI are in the FROM clause and in the WHERE clause conditions shown. These references require only data (the two foreign keys and the rowid) stored in the index. This is crucial: Oracle avoids going to the table M as soon as it reaches the index on the primary key to M only because MI refers solely to the indexed columns and the rowids that are also stored in the index. Columns in the SELECT clause and elsewhere in the WHERE-clause conditions (such as a join to A3, not shown) all come from MT. Because of all this, the optimizer finds that the only columns required for MI are already available from the index. It counts that join as index-only. The direct-ROWID join to MT occurs later in the join order, and any columns from the M table are selected from MT.

However, the technique I've just described is not usually needed, for several reasons:

- Combination indexes of the two foreign keys you need, in the right order you need, happen rarely.

- Usually, the root detail table does not add enough cost, in both relative and absolute terms, to justify the trouble.

- The benefits rarely justify creating a whole new multicolumn index if one is not already there.

## Solving the Special Case Outside of Oracle

If you cannot refer directly to rowids in your WHERE clause, can this trick still work in some form? The only part of the trick that depends on rowids is the join between MI and MT. You could also join those table aliases on the full primary key. The cost of the early join to MI would be unchanged, but the later join to MT would require looking up the very same index entry you already reached in the index-only join to MI for those rows that remain. This is not as efficient, but note that these redundant hits on the index will surely be cached, since the execution plan touches the same index entries moments before, leaving only the cost of the extra logical I/O. Since the database throws most of the rows out before it even reaches MT, this extra logical I/O is probably much less than the savings on access to the table itself.

# A Complex Example

Now, I demonstrate an example that delivers a less straightforward join order that requires more attention to the whole join cloud. You will find that the sequence of next-best tables can jump all over the query diagram in cases like the one I describe in this section. Consider the problem in Figure 6-9, and try it yourself before you read on.

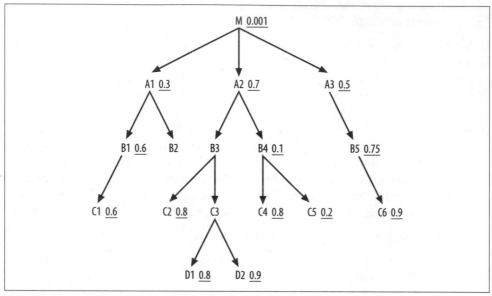

*Figure 6-9. Another problem with the same join skeleton*

Here, you see, as is quite common, that the best filter falls on the root detail table.

The best filter is often on the root detail table, because the entities of this table are the true focus of the query. It is common that the main filter references a direct property of those entities, rather than some inherited property in the joined tables.

Since you will drive from the root detail table, Step 3 will never apply; you have no nodes upstream of the starting point. The cloud of tables joined so far will grow downward from the top, but keep in mind that you can find the next-best node anywhere along the boundary of this cloud, not necessarily near the last table joined. Try to find the best join order yourself before you read on.

The first eligible nodes are A1, A2, and A3, and the best filter ratio lies on A1, so A1 falls second in the join order. After extending the join cloud to A1, add B1 and B2 to the eligible nodes, and A2 and A3 are still eligible. Between these four nodes, A3 has the best filter ratio, so join to it next. The join order, so far, is (M, A1, A3), and the join cloud now looks like Figure 6-10.

The list of eligible nodes attached to the join cloud is now B1, B2, A2, and B5. B1 has the best filter ratio among these, so join to it next, extending the cloud and adding C1 to the list of eligible nodes, which is now B2, A2, B5, and C1. Among these, C1 is the

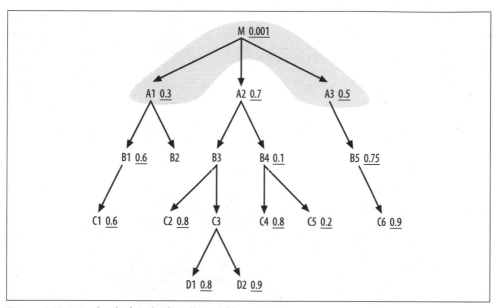

*Figure 6-10. Join cloud after the first three tables*

best, so join to it next and extend the cloud further. C1 has no downstream nodes, so proceed to the next-best node on the current list, A2, which adds B3 and B4 to the list of eligible nodes, which is now B2, B5, B3, and B4. The join order, so far, is (M, A1, A3, B1, C1, A2), and the join cloud now looks like Figure 6-11.

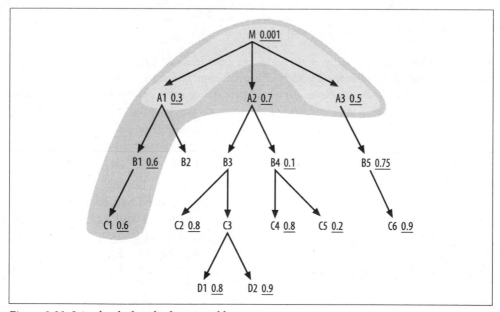

*Figure 6-11. Join cloud after the first six tables*

Among the eligible nodes, B4 has, by far, the best filter ratio, so it comes next. (It would have been great to join to it earlier, but it did not become eligible until the database reached A2.) The join order to B4 adds C4 and C5 to the eligible list, which now includes B2, B5, B3, C4, and C5. Of these, C5 is by far the best, so it comes next. The join order, so far, is (M, A1, A3, B1, C1, A2, B4, C5), and the join cloud now looks like Figure 6-12.

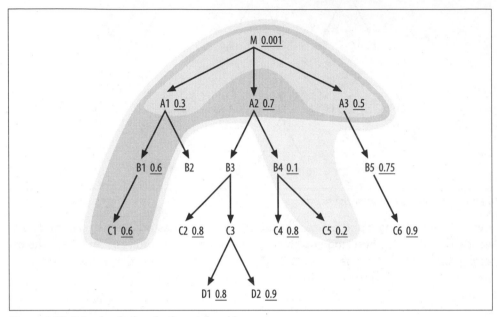

*Figure 6-12. Join cloud after the first eight tables*

Eligible nodes attached below the join cloud now include B2, B3, B5, and C4, and the best filter among these is B5. B5 adds C6 to the eligible list, and the next-best on the list is C4, which adds no new node to the list. C6 is the next-best node, but it also adds no new node to the eligible-nodes list, which is now just B2 and B3. Neither of these even has a filter, so you look for two-away filters and find that B3 at least gives access to the filter on C2, so you join to B3 next. The join order, so far, is (M, A1, A3, B1, C1, A2, B4, C5, B5, C4, C6, B3), and the join cloud now looks like Figure 6-13.

You now find eligible nodes B2, C2, and C3, and only C2 has a filter, so join to C2 next. It has no downstream node, so choose between B2 and C3 and again use the tie-breaker that C3 at least gives access to two-away filters on D1 and D2, so join C3 next. The join order, so far, is now (M, A1, A3, B1, C1, A2, B4, C5, B5, C4, C6, B3, C2, C3). The eligible downstream nodes are now B2, D1, and D2. At this point in the process, the eligible downstream nodes are the only nodes left, having no nodes further downstream. Just sort the nodes left by filter ratio, and complete the join order: (M,

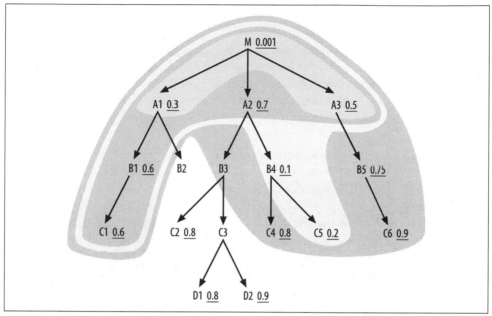

*Figure 6-13. Join cloud after the first 12 tables*

A1, A3, B1, C1, A2, B4, C5, B5, C4, C6, B3, C2, C3, D1, D2, B2). In real queries, you usually get to the point of just sorting immediately attached nodes sooner. In the common special case of a single detail table with only direct joins to master-table lookups (dimension tables, usually), called a *star join*, you sort master nodes right from the start.

Given the optimal order just derived, complete the specification of the execution plan by calling for access to the driving table M from an index for the filter condition on that table. Then join the other tables using nested loops joins that follow indexes on those tables' primary keys.

Driving from the root node of the join tree is particularly simple, since you can usually count on finding indexes already in place for the primary keys the database needs to join exclusively in the downward direction.

# Special Rules for Special Cases

The heuristic rules so far handle most cases well and nearly always generate excellent, robust plans. However, there are some assumptions behind the rationale for these rules, which are not always true. Surprisingly often, even when the assumptions are wrong, they are *right enough* to yield a plan that is at least close to optimum.

Here, I lay these assumptions out and examine more sophisticated rules to handle the rare cases in which deviations from the assumptions matter:

***Intermediate query results in the form of Cartesian products lead to poor performance.*** If you do not follow the joins when working out a join order, the result is a Cartesian product between the first set of rows and the rows from the leaped-to node. Occasionally, this is harmless, but even when it is faster than a join order following the links, it is usually dangerous and scales poorly as table volumes increase.

***Detail join ratios are large, much greater than 1.0.*** Since master join ratios (downward on the join tree) are never greater than 1.0, this makes it much safer to join downward as much as possible before joining upward, even when upward joins give access to more filters. (The filters on the higher nodes usually do not discard more rows than the database picks up going to the more detailed table.) Even when detail join ratios are small, the one-to-many nature of the join offers at least the possibility that they could be large in the future or at other sites running the same application. This tends to favor SQL that is robust for the case of a large detail join ratio, except when you have high confidence that the local, current statistics are relatively timeless and universal.

***The table at the root of the join tree is significantly larger than the other tables, which serve as master tables or lookup tables to it.*** This assumption follows from the previous assumption. Since larger tables have poorer hit ratios in cache and since the rowcount the database reads from this largest table is often much larger than most or all other rowcounts it reads, the highest imperative in tuning the query is to minimize the rowcount read from this root detail table.

***Master join ratios are either exactly 1.0 or close enough to 1.0 that the difference doesn't matter.*** This follows in the common case in which detail tables have non-null foreign keys with excellent referential integrity.

***When tables are big enough that efficiency matters, there will be one filter ratio that is much smaller than the others.*** Near-ties, two tables that have close to the same filter ratio, are rare. If the tables are large and the query result is relatively small, as useful query results almost always are, then the product of all filter ratios must be quite small. It is much easier to get this small result with one selective filter, sometimes combined with a small number of fairly unselective filters, than with a large number of comparable, semiselective filters. Coming up with a business rationale for lots of semiselective filters turns out to be difficult, and, empirically speaking, I could probably count on one hand the number of times I've seen such a case in over 10 years of SQL tuning. Given one filter that is much more selective than the rest, the way to guarantee reading the fewest rows from that most important root detail table is to drive the query from the table with that best filter.

*The rowcount that the query returns, even before any possible aggregation, will be small enough that, even for tiny master tables, there is little or no incentive to replace nested loops through join keys with independent table reads followed by hash joins.* Note that this assumption falls apart if you do the joins with a much higher rowcount than the query ultimately returns. However, the heuristics are designed to ensure that you almost never find a much higher rowcount at any intermediate point in the query plan than the database returns from the whole query.

The following sections add rules that handle rare special cases that go against these assumptions.

## Safe Cartesian Products

Consider the query diagrammed in Figure 6-14. Following the usual rules (and breaking ties by choosing the leftmost node, just for consistency), you drive into the filter on T1 and join to M following the index on the foreign key pointing to T1. You then follow the primary-key index into T2, discarding in the end the rows that fail to match the filter on T2. If you assume that T1 has 100 rows, based on the join ratios M must have 100,000 rows and T2 must have 100 rows.

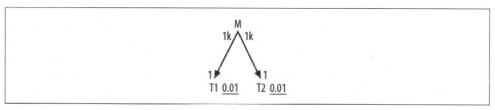

*Figure 6-14. A query with a potentially good Cartesian-product execution plan*

The plan just described would touch 1 row in T1, 1,000 rows in M (1% of the total), and 1,000 rows in T2 (each row in T2 10 times, on average), before discarding all but 10 rows from the result. Approximating query cost as the number of rows touched, the cost would be 2,001. However, if you broke the rules, you could get a plan that does not follow the join links. You could perform nested loops between T1 and T2, driving into their respective filter indexes. Because there is no join between T1 and T2 the result would be a Cartesian product of all rows that meet the filter condition on T1 and all rows that meet the filter condition on T2. For the table sizes given, the resulting execution plan would read just a single row from each of T1 and T2. Following the Cartesian join of T1 and T2, the database could follow an index on the foreign key that points to T1, into M, to read 1,000 rows from M. Finally, the database would discard the 990 rows that fail to meet the join condition that matches M and T2.

When you skip using a join condition at every step of the query, one of the joins ends up *left over*, so to speak, never having been used for the performance of a join. The database later discards rows that fail to match the leftover join condition, effectively treating that condition as a filter as soon as it reaches both tables the join references.

Using the Cartesian product, the plan costs just 1,002, using the rows-touched cost function.

What happens if the table sizes double? The original plan cost, following the join links, exactly doubles, to 4,002, in proportion to the number of rows the query will return, which also doubles. This is normal for robust plans, which have costs proportional to the number of rows returned. However, the Cartesian-product plan cost is less well behaved: the database reads 2 rows from T1; then, for each of those rows, reads the same 2 rows of T2 (4 rows in all); then, with a Cartesian product that has 4 rows, reads 4,000 rows from M. The query cost, 4,006, now is almost the same as the cost of the standard plan. Doubling table sizes once again, the standard plan costs 8,004, while the Cartesian-product plan costs 16,020. This demonstrates the lack of robustness in most Cartesian-product execution plans, which fail to scale well as tables grow. Even without table growth, Cartesian-product plans tend to behave less predictably than standard plans, because filter ratios are usually averages across the possible values. A filter that matches just one row on average might sometimes match 5 or 10 rows for some values of the variable. When a filter for a standard, robust plan is less selective than average, the cost will scale up proportionally with the number of rows the query returns. When a Cartesian-product plan runs into the same filter variability, its cost might scale up as the square of the filter variability, or worse.

Sometimes, though, you can have the occasional advantages of Cartesian products safely. You can create a Cartesian product of as many guaranteed-single-row sets as you like with perfect safety, with an inexpensive, one-row result. You can even combine a one-row set with a multirow set and be no worse off than if you read the multirow set in isolation from the driving table. The key advantage of robust plans is rigorous avoidance of execution plans that combine multiple multirow sets. You might recall that in Chapter 5 the rules required you to place an asterisk next to unique filter conditions (conditions guaranteed to match at most a single row). I haven't mentioned these asterisks since, but they finally come into play here.

Consider Figure 6-15. Note that you find two unique filters, on B2 and C3. Starting from the single row of C3 that matches its unique filter condition, you know it will join to a single row of D1 and D2, through their primary keys, based on the downward-pointing arrows to D1 and D2. Isolate this branch, treating it as a separate, single-row query. Now, query the single row of B2 that matches its unique filter condition, and combine these two independent queries by Cartesian product for a single-row combined set.

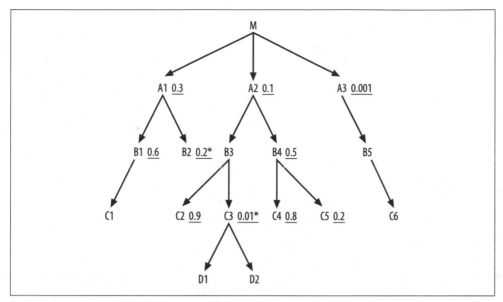

*Figure 6-15. A query with unique filter conditions*

Placing these single-row queries first, you find an initial join order of (C3, D1, D2, B2) (or (B2, C3, D1, D2); it makes no difference). If you think of this initial prequeried single-row result as an independent operation, you find that tables A1 and B3 acquire new filter conditions, because you can know the values of the foreign keys that point to B2 and C3 before you perform the rest of the query. The modified query now looks like Figure 6-16, in which the already-executed single-row queries are covered by a gray cloud, showing the boundaries of the already-read portion of the query.

Upward-pointing arrows show that the initial filter condition on A1 combines with a new filter condition on the foreign key into B2 to reach a combined selectivity of 0.06, while the initially unfiltered node B3 acquires a filter ratio of 0.01 from its foreign-key condition, pointing into C3.

 Normally, you can assume that any given fraction of a master table's rows will join to about the same fraction of a detail table's rows. For transaction tables, such as Orders and Order_Details, this is a good assumption. However, small tables often encode types or statuses, and the transaction tables usually do not have evenly distributed types or statuses. For example, with a five-row status table (such as B2 might be), a given status might match most of the transaction rows or almost none of them, depending on the status. You need to investigate the actual, skewed distribution in cases like this, when the master table encodes asymmetric meanings.

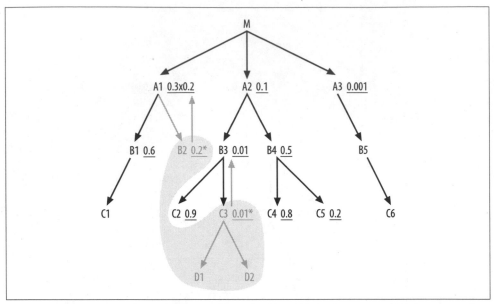

*Figure 6-16. A query with unique filter conditions, with single-row branches preread*

You can now optimize the remaining portion of the query, outside the cloud, exactly as if it stood alone, following the standard rules. You then find that A3 is the best driving table, having the best filter ratio. (It is immaterial that A3 does not join directly to B2 or C3, since a Cartesian product with the single-row set is safe.) From there, drive down to B5 and C6, then up to M. Since A1 acquired added selectivity from its inherited filter on the foreign key that points to B2, it now has a better filter ratio than A2, so join to A1 next. So far, the join order is (C3, D1, D2, B2, A3, B5, C6, M, A1), and the query, with a join cloud, looks like Figure 6-17.

Since you preread B2, the next eligible nodes are B1 and A2, and A2 has the better filter ratio. This adds B3 and B4 to the eligible list, and you find that the inherited filter on B3 makes it the best next choice in the join order. Completing the join order, following the normal rules, you reach B4, C5, B1, C4, C2, and C1, in that order, for a complete join order of (C3, D1, D2, B2, A3, B5, C6, M, A1, A2, B3, B4, C5, B1, C4, C2, C1).

Even if you have just a single unique filter condition, follow this process of prereading that single-row node or branch, passing the filter ratio upward to the detail table above and optimizing the resulting remainder of the diagram as if the remainder of the diagram stood alone. When the unique condition is on some transaction table, not some type or status table, that unique condition will also usually yield the best filter ratio in the query. In this case, the resulting join order will be the same order you would choose if you did not know that the filter condition was unique. However, when the best filter is not the unique filter, the best join order can *jump the join skeleton*, which is to say that it does not reach the second table through a join key that points to the first table.

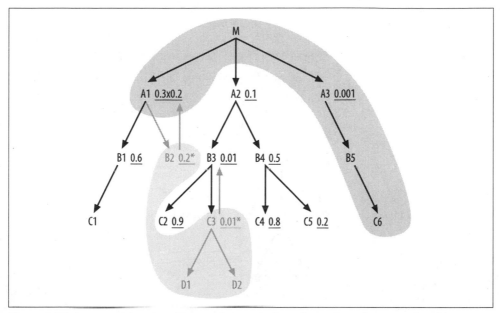

*Figure 6-17. A query with unique filter conditions, with single-row branches preread and a join cloud around the next five nodes read*

## Detail Join Ratios Close to 1.0

Treat upward joins like downward joins when the join ratio is close to 1.0 and when this allows access to useful filters (low filter ratios) earlier in the execution plan. When in doubt, you can try both alternatives. Figure 6-18 shows a case of two of the upward joins that are no worse than downward joins. Before you look at the solution, try working it out yourself.

As usual, drive to the best filter, on B4, with an index, and reach the rest of the tables with nested loops to the join-key indexes. Unlike previous cases, you need not complete all downward joins before considering to join upward with a join ratio equal to 1.0.

 These are evidently one-to-many joins that are nearly always one-to-one, or they are one-to-zero or one-to-many, and the one-to-zero cases cancel the row increase from the one-to-many cases. Either way, from an optimization perspective they are almost the same as one-to-one joins.

As usual, look for filters in the immediately adjacent nodes first, and find that the first two best join opportunities are C5 and then C4. Next, you have only the opportunity for the upward join to unfiltered node A2, which you would do next even if the detail join ratio were large. (The low join ratio to A2 turned out not to matter.) So far, the join order is (B4, C5, C4, A2).

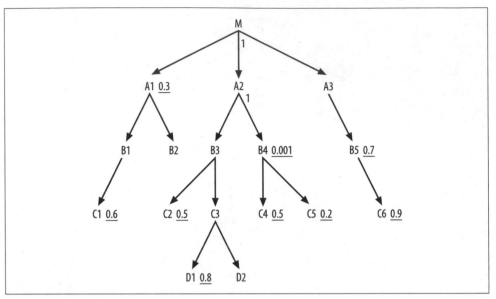

*Figure 6-18. A case with detail joins ratios equal to 1.0*

From the cloud around these nodes, find immediately adjacent nodes B3 (downward) and M (upward). Since the detail join ratio to M is 1.0, you need not prefer to join downward, if other factors favor M. Neither node has a filter, so look at filters on nodes adjacent to them to break the tie. The best filter ratio adjacent to M is 0.3 (on A1), while the best adjacent to B3 is 0.5 (on C2), favoring M, so join next to M and A1. The join order at this point is (B4, C5, C4, A2, M, A1). Now that the database has reached the root node, all joins are downward, so the usual rules apply for the rest of the optimization, considering immediately adjacent nodes first and considering nodes adjacent to those nodes to break ties. The complete optimum join order is (B4, C5, C4, A2, M, A1, B3, C2, B1, C1, A3, B5, C6, C3, D1, (D2, B2)).

Here, the notation (B2, D2) at the end of the join order signifies that the order of these last two does not matter.

Note that, even in this specially contrived case designed to show an exception to the earlier rule, you find only modest improvement for reaching A1 earlier than the simple heuristics would allow, since the improvement is relatively late in the join order.

## Join Ratios Less than 1.0

If either the detail join ratio or the master join ratio is less than 1.0, you have, in effect, a join that is, on average, [some number]-to-[less than 1.0]. Whether the less-than-1.0 side of that join is capable of being *to-many* is immaterial to the optimization problem, as long as you are confident that the current average is not likely to change much on other database instances or over time. If a downward join with a normal master join ratio of 1.0 is preferred over a to-many upward join, a join that follows a join ratio of less than 1.0 in any direction is preferred even more. These join ratios that are less than 1.0 are, in a sense, *hidden filters* that discard rows when you perform the joins just as effectively as explicit single-node filters discard rows, so they affect the optimal join order like filters.

### Rules for join ratios less than 1.0

You need three new rules to account for the effect of smaller-than-normal join ratios on choosing the optimum join order:

- When choosing a driving node, all nodes on the filtered side of a join inherit the extra benefit of the hidden join filter. Specifically, if the join ratio less than 1.0 is $J$ and the node filter ratio is $R$, use $J \times R$ when choosing the best node to drive the query. This has no effect when comparing nodes on the same side of a join filter, but it gives nodes on the filtered side of a join an advantage over nodes on the unfiltered side of the join.

- When choosing the next node in a sequence, treat all joins with a join ratio $J$ (a join ratio less than 1.0) like downward joins, and use $J \times R$ as the effective node filter ratio when comparing nodes, where $R$ is the single-node filter ratio of the node reached through that filtering join.

- However, for master join ratios less than 1.0, consider whether the hidden filter is better treated as an explicit foreign-key-is-not-null filter. Making the is-not-null filter explicit allows the detail table immediately above the filtering master join also to inherit the adjusted selectivity $J \times R$ for purposes of both choice of driving table and join order from above. See the following sections for more details on this rule.

### Detail join ratios less than 1.0

The meaning of the small join ratio turns out to be quite different depending on whether it is the master join ratio or the detail join ratio that is less than 1.0. A detail join ratio less than 1.0 denotes the possibility of multiple details, when it is more common to have no details of that particular type than to have more than one. For example, you might have an Employees table linked to a Loans table to track loans the company makes to a few top managers as part of their compensation. The database design must allow for some employees to have multiple loans, but far more employees have no loans from the company at all, so the detail join ratio would be nearly 0. For referential integrity, the Employee_ID column in Loans must point to a real employee; that is its only purpose, and all loans in this table are to employees. However, there is no necessity at all for an Employee_ID to correspond to any loan. The Employee_ID column of Employees exists (like any primary key) to point to its own row, not to point to rows in another table, and there is no surprise when the join fails to find a match in the upward direction, pointing from primary key to foreign key.

Since handling of detail join ratios less than 1.0 turns out to be simpler, though less common, I illustrate that case first. I'll elaborate the example of the previous paragraph to try to lend some plausibility to the new rules. Beginning with a query that joins Employees to Loans, add a join to Departments, with a filter that removes half the departments. The result is shown in Figure 6-19, with each node labeled by the initial of its table.

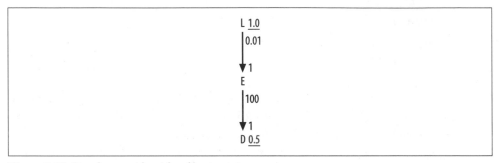

*Figure 6-19. Simple example with a filtering join*

Note that Figure 6-19 shows 1.0 as the filter ratio for L, meaning that L has no filter at all. Normally, you leave out filter ratios equal to 1.0. However, I include the filter ratio on L to make clear that the number 0.01 near the top of the link to L is the detail join ratio on the link from E to L, not the filter ratio on L.

Let there be 1,000 employees, 10 departments, and 10 loans to 8 of those employees. Let the only filter be the filter that discards half the departments. The detail join ratio to Loans must be 0.01, since after joining 1,000 employees to the Loans table, you would find only the 10 loans. The original rules would have you drive to the only filtered table, Departments, reading 5 rows, joining to half the employees, another 500 rows, then joining to roughly half the loans (from the roughly 4 employees in the chosen half of the departments). The database would then reach 5 loans, while performing 496 unsuccessful index range scans on the Employee_ID index for Loans using Employee_IDs of employees without loans.

On the other hand, if the Loans table inherits the benefit of the filtering join, you would choose to drive from Loans, reading all 10 of them, then go to the 10 matching rows in Employees (8 *different* rows, with repeats to bring the total to 10). Finally, join to Departments 10 times, when the database finally discards (on average) half. Although the usual objective is to minimize rows read from the top table, this example demonstrates that minimizing reads to the table on the upper end of a strongly filtering detail join is nowhere near as important as minimizing rows read in the much larger table below it.

How good would a filter on Employees have to be to bring the rows read from Employees down to the number read in the second plan? The filter would have to be exactly as good as the filtering join ratio, 0.01. Imagine that it were even better, 0.005, and lead to just 5 employees (say, a filter on Last_Name). In that case, what table should you join next? Again, the original rules would lead you to Departments, both because it is downward and because it has the better filter ratio. However, note that from 5 employees, the database will reach, on average, just 0.05 loans, so you are much better off joining to Loans before joining to Departments.

 In reality, the end user probably chose a last name of one of those loan-receiving employees, making these filters more dependent than usual. However, even in that case, you would probably get down to one or two loans and reduce the last join to Departments to a read of just one or two rows, instead of five.

### Optimizing detail join ratios less than 1.0 with the rules

Figure 6-20 illustrates another example with a detail join ratio under 1.0. Try working out the join order before you read on.

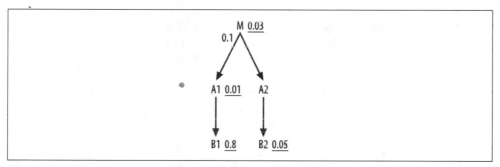

*Figure 6-20. Example with a detail join ratio less than 1.0*

First, examine the effect of the join ratio on the choice of driving table. In Figure 6-21, I show the adjustments to filter ratios from the perspective of choosing the driving table. After these adjustments, the effective filter of 0.003 on M is best, so drive from M. From this point, revert to the original filter ratios to choose the rest of the join order, because, when driving from any node (M, A2, or B2) on the detail side of that join, this join ratio no longer applies. In a more complex query, it might seem like a lot of work to calculate all these effective filter values for many nodes on one side of a filtering join. In practice, you just find the best filter ratio on each side (0.01 for A1 and 0.03 for M, in this case) and make a single adjustment to the best filter ratio on the filtered side of the join.

 If the join ratio has a single, constant effect throughout the query optimization, you can simply fold that effect into the filter ratios, but the effect changes as optimization proceeds, so you have to keep these numbers separate.

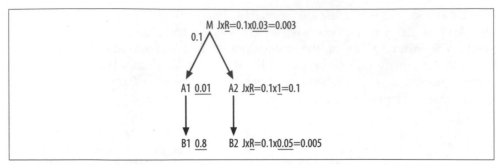

*Figure 6-21. Effective filters for choosing the driving table*

When choosing the rest of the join order, compare the original filter ratios on A1 and A2, and choose A1 next. Comparing B1 to A2, choose B1, and find the join order so far: (M, A1, B1). The rest of the join order is fully constrained by the join skeleton, for a complete join order of (M, A1, B1, A2, B2).

Figure 6-22 leads to precisely the same result. It makes no difference that this time the lowest initial filter ratio is not directly connected to the filtering join; all nodes on the filtered side of the join get the benefit of the join filter when choosing the driving table, and all nodes on the other side do not. Neither A1 nor A2 offers filters that drive from M, so choose A1 first for the better two-away filter on B1, and choose the same join order as in the last example.

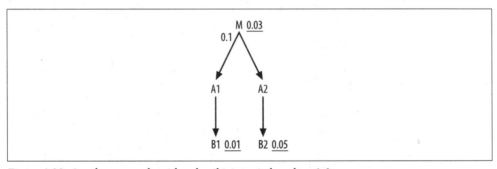

*Figure 6-22. Another example with a detail join ratio less than 1.0*

In Figure 6-23, M and B2 get the same benefit from the filtering join, so simply compare unadjusted filter ratios and choose B2. From there, the join order is fully constrained by the join skeleton: (B2, A2, M, A1, B1).

In Figure 6-24, again you compare only filtered nodes on the same side of the filtering join, but do you see an effect on later join order?

The benefit of the filtering join follows only if you follow the join in that direction. Since you drive from A2, join to M with an ordinary one-to-many join from A2, which you should postpone as long as possible. Therefore, join downward to B2 before joining upward to M, even though M has the better filter ratio. The join order is therefore (A2, B2, M, A1, B1).

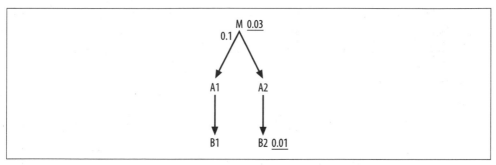

*Figure 6-23. An example comparing only filters on the same side of the filtering join*

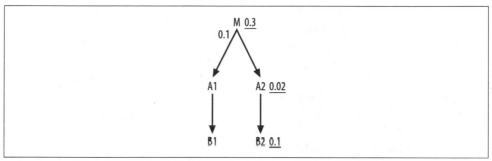

*Figure 6-24. Another example comparing only filters on the same side of the filtering join*

Try working out the complete join order for Figure 6-25 before you read on.

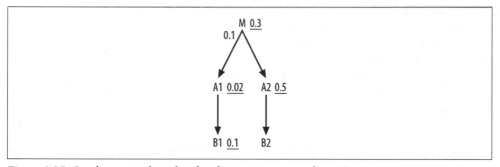

*Figure 6-25. One last example with a detail join ratio greater than 1.0*

Here, note that the adjustment to filter ratios when choosing the driving table is insufficient to favor the filtered side of the join; the best filter on A2 is still favored. Where do you go from there, though? Now, the filtering join does matter. This theoretically one-to-many join is really usually one-to-zero, so, even though it is upward on the diagram, you should favor it over an ordinary downward join with a normal join ratio (unshown, by convention) of 1.0. For purposes of choosing the next table, the effective filter on M is $R \times J$ ($0.3 \times 0.1 = 0.03$), better than the filter on B1, so join to

M next. However, when you compare A2 and B1, compare simple, unadjusted filter ratios, because you have, in a sense, already burned the benefit of the filtering join to M. The full join order, then, is (A1, M, B1, A2, B2).

### Master join ratios less than 1.0

Master join ratios less than 1.0 have two potential explanations:

- The relationship to the master does not apply (or is unknown) in some cases, where the foreign key to that master is null.

- The relationship to the master table is corrupt in some cases, where the nonnull foreign-key value fails to point to a legitimate master record. Since the only legitimate purpose of a foreign key is to point unambiguously to a matching master record, nonnull values of that key that fail to join to the master are failures of referential integrity. These referential-integrity failures happen in this imperfect world, but the ideal response is to fix them, either by deleting detail records that become obsolete when the application eliminates their master records, or by fixing the foreign key to point to a legitimate master or to be null. It is a mistake to change the SQL to work around a broken relationship that ought to be fixed soon, so you should generally ignore master join ratios that are less than 1.0 for such failed referential integrity.

The first case is common and legitimate for some tables. For example, if the company in the earlier Loans-table example happened to be a bank, they might want a single Loans table for all loans the bank makes, not just those to employees, and in such a Loans table Employee_ID would apply only rarely, nearly always being null. However, in this legitimate case, the database need not perform the join to pick up this valuable row-discarding hidden join filter. If the database has already reached the Loans table, it makes much more sense to make the filter explicit, with a condition Employee_ID IS NOT NULL in the query. This way, the execution engine will discard the unjoinable rows as soon as it reaches the Loans table. You can choose the next join to pick up another filter early in the execution plan, without waiting for a join to Employees.

 You might expect that database software could figure out for itself that an inner join implies a not-null condition on a nullable foreign key. Databases could apply that implied condition automatically at the earliest opportunity, but I have not seen any database do this.

In the following examples, assume that master join ratios less than 1.0 come only from sometimes-null foreign keys, not from failed referential integrity. Choose the driving table by following the rules of this section. If the driving table reaches the optional master table from above, make the is-not-null condition explicit in the query and migrate the selectivity of that condition into the detail node filter ratio. Consider the SQL diagram in Figure 6-26.

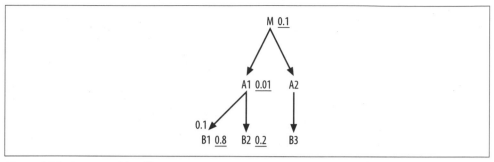

*Figure 6-26. A query with a filtering master join*

First, does the master join ratio affect the choice of driving table? Both sides of the join from A1 to B1 can see the benefit of this hidden join filter, and A1 has the better filter ratio to start with. Nodes attached below B1 would also benefit, but there are no nodes downstream of B1. No other node has a competitive filter ratio, so drive from A1 just as if there were no hidden filter. To see the best benefit of driving from A1, make explicit the is-not-null condition on A1's foreign key that points to B1, with an added clause:

```
A1.ForeignKeyToB1 IS NOT NULL
```

This explicit addition to the SQL enables the database to perform the first join to another table with just the fraction $(0.01 \times 0.1 = 0.001)$ of the rows in A1. If you had the column ForeignKeyToB1 in the driving index filter, the database could even avoid touching the unwanted rows in A1 at all. Where do you join next? Since the database has already picked up the hidden filter (made no longer hidden) from the now-explicit condition A1.ForeignKeyToB1 IS NOT NULL, you have burned that extra filter, so compare B1 and B2 as if there were no filtering join.

Effectively, there is no longer a filtering join after applying the is-not-null condition. The rows the database begins with before it does these joins will all join successfully to B1, since the database already discarded the rows with null foreign keys.

Comparing B1 and B2 for their simple filter ratios, choose B2 first, and choose the order (A1, B2, B1, M, A2, B3).

Now, consider the SQL diagram in Figure 6-27, and try to work it out yourself before reading further.

Again, the filtering join has no effect on the choice of driving table, since the filter ratio on M is so much better than even the adjusted filter ratios on A1 and B1. Where do you join next? When you join from the unfiltered side of the filtering master join, make the hidden filter explicit with an is-not-null condition on ForeignKeyToB1. When you make this filter explicit, the join of the remaining rows has an effective join ratio of just 1.0, like most master joins, and the adjusted SQL diagram looks like Figure 6-28.

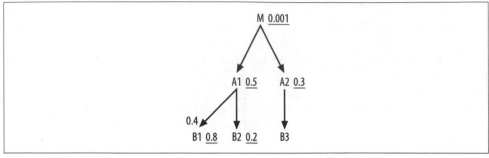

*Figure 6-27. Another query with a filtering master join*

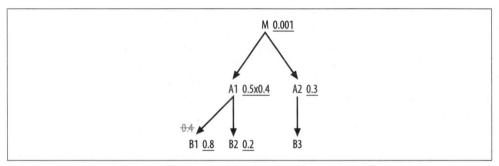

*Figure 6-28. Adjusting the SQL diagram to make the master-join filter explicit*

Now, it is clear that A1 offers a better filter than A2, so join to A1 first. After reaching A1, the database now has access to B1 or B2 as the next table to join. Comparing these to A2, you again find a better choice than A2. You join to B2 next, since you have already burned the benefit of the filtering join to B1. The complete optimum order, then, is (M, A1, B2, A2, B1, B3).

Next, consider the more complex problem represented by Figure 6-29, and try to solve it yourself before you read on.

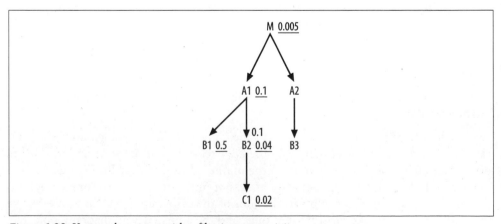

*Figure 6-29. Yet another query with a filtering master join*

Considering first the best effective driving filter, adjust the filter ratio on A1 and the filter ratios below the filtering master join and find C2 offers an effective filter of $0.1 \times 0.02=0.002$. You could make the filter explicit on A1 as before with an is-not-null condition on the foreign key that points to B2, but this does not add sufficient selectivity to A1 to make it better than C1. The other alternatives are unadjusted filter ratios on the other nodes, but the best of these, 0.005 on M, is not as good as the effective driving filter on C2, so choose C2 for the driving table. From there, the filtering master join is no longer relevant, because the database will not join in that direction, and you find the full join order to be (C1, B2, A1, B1, M, A2, B3).

How would this change if the filter ratio on A1 were 0.01? By making the implied is-not-null condition on ForeignKeyToB2 explicit in the SQL, as before, you can make the multiple-condition filter selectivity $0.1 \times 0.01=0.001$, better than the effective filter ratio on C1, making A1 the best choice for driving table. With the join filter burned, you then choose the rest of the join order based on the simple filter ratios, finding the best order: (A1, B2, C1, B1, M, A2, B3).

## Close Filter Ratios

Occasionally, you find filter ratios that fall close enough in size to consider relaxing the heuristic rules to take advantage of secondary considerations in the join order. This might sound like it ought to be a common, important case, but it rarely matters, for several reasons:

- When tables are big enough to matter, the application requires a lot of filtering to return a useful-sized (not too big) set of rows for a real-world application, especially if the query serves an online transaction. (End users do not find long lists of rows online or in reports to be useful.) This implies that the product of all filters is a small number when the query includes at least one large table.

- Useful queries rarely have many filters, usually just one to three.

- With few filters (but with the product of all filters being a small number), at least one filter must be quite small and selective. It is far easier to achieve sufficient selectivity reliably with one selective filter, potentially combined with a small number of at-best moderately selective filters, than with a group of almost equally selective filters.

- With one filter that is much more selective than the rest, usually much more selective than the rest put together, the choice of driving table is easy.

- Occasionally, you find near-ties on moderately selective filter ratios in choices of tables to join later in the execution plan. However, the order of later joins usually matters relatively little, as long as you start with the right table and use a robust plan that follows the join skeleton.

- My own experience tuning queries confirms that it is rarely necessary to examine these secondary considerations. I have had to do this less than once per year of intensive tuning in my own experience.

Nevertheless, if you have read this far, you might want to know when to at least consider relaxing the simple rules, so here are some rule refinements that have rare usefulness in the case of near-ties:

- Prefer to drive to smaller tables earlier. After you choose the driving table, the true benefit/cost ratio of joining to the next master table is $(1-R)/C$, where $R$ is the filter ratio and $C$ is the cost per row of reading that table through the primary key. Smaller tables are better cached and tend to have fewer index levels, making $C$ smaller and making the benefit/cost ratio tend to be better for smaller tables.

> In a full join diagram, the smaller tables lie at the low end of one or more joins (up to the root) that have large detail join ratios. You also often already know or can guess by the table names which tables are likely small.

- Prefer to drive to tables that allow you to reach other tables with even better filter ratios sooner in the execution plan. The general objective is to discard as many rows as early in the execution plan as possible. Good (low) filter ratios achieve this well at each step, but you might need to look ahead a bit to nearby filters to see the full benefit of reaching a node sooner.

- To compare nodes when choosing a driving table, compare the absolute values of the filter ratios directly; 0.01 and 0.001 are *not* close, but a factor of 10 apart, not a near-tie at all. Near-ties for the driving filter almost never happen, except when the application queries small tables either with no filters at all or with only moderately selective filters. In cases of queries that touch only small tables, you rarely need to tune the query; automated optimization easily produces a fast plan.

> Perhaps I should say that near-ties of the driving filter happen regularly, but only in queries against small tables that you will not need to tune! Automated optimizers have to tune these frequently, but you won't.

- To compare nodes when choosing later joins, compare $1-R$, where $R$ is each node's filter ratio. In this context, filter ratios of 0.1 and 0.0001 are close. Even though these $R$ values are a factor of 1,000 apart, the values of $1-R$ differ only by 10%, and the benefit/cost ratio (see the first rule in this list) would actually favor the less selective filter if that node were much smaller.

> If you had a filter ratio of 0.0001, you probably would have already used that node as your driving table, except in the unlikely event that you have two independent, super-selective conditions on the query.

Figure 6-30 shows the first example with a near-tie that could lead to a break with the original simple heuristic rules. Try to work it out yourself before moving on.

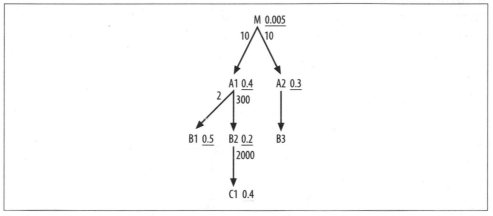

*Figure 6-30. A case to consider exceptions to the simple rules*

When choosing the driving node here, make no exception to the rules; M has far and away the best filter ratio from the perspective of choosing the driving table. The next choice is between A1 and A2, and you would normally prefer the lower filter ratio on A2. When you look at the detail join ratios from A1 to M and from A2 to M, you find that A1 and A2 are the same rowcount, so you have no reason on account of size to prefer either. However, when you look below these nearly tied nodes, note that A1 provides access to two nodes that look even better than A2. You should try to get to these earlier in the plan, so you would benefit moderately by choosing A1 first. After choosing A1 as the second table in the join order, the choice of third table is clear; B2 is both much smaller and better-filtered than A2.

 If some node below A1 were not clearly worth joining to before A2, then the nodes below A1 would not be relevant to the choice between A1 and A2!

The join order, so far, is (M, A1, B2). The choice of the next table is less obvious. C1 has a slightly worse filter ratio than A2 but is much smaller, by a factor of 300× 2,000, so its cost per row is surely low enough to justify putting it ahead of A2 as well. The join order, so far, is now (M, A1, B2, C1), and the next eligible nodes are B1 and A2. The values for these nodes (1–R) are 0.5 and 0.7, respectively, and B1 is half the size of A2, making its expected cost per row at least a bit lower. If B1 were right on the edge of needing a new level in its primary-key index, A2 would likely have that extra index level and B1 might be the better choice next. However, since each level of an index increases the capacity by about a factor of 300, it is unlikely that the index is so close to the edge that this factor of 2 makes the difference. Otherwise, it is unlikely that the moderate size difference matters enough to override the simple rule based on filter ratio. Even if B1 is better than A2, by this point in the execution plan it will not make enough difference to matter; all four tables joined so far have efficiently filtered rows to this point. Now, the cost of these last table joins will be tiny, regardless of the choice, compared to the costs of the earlier joins. Therefore, choose the full join order (M, A1, B2, C1, A2, B1, B3).

Now, consider the problem in Figure 6-31, and try your hand again before you read on.

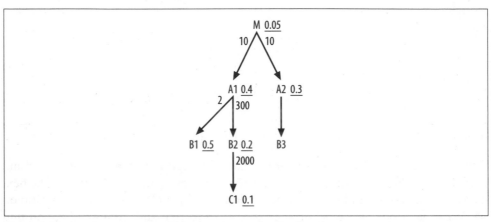

*Figure 6-31. Another case to consider exceptions to the simple rules*

This looks almost the same as the earlier case, but the filter on M is not so good, and the filters on the A1 branch are better, in total. The filter on M is twice as good as the filter on the next-best table, C1, but C1 has other benefits—much smaller size, by a factor of $2,000 \times 300 \times 10$, or 6,000,000, and it has proximity to other filters offering a net additional filter of $0.2 \times 0.4 \times 0.5 = 0.04$. When you combine all the filters on the A1 branch, you find a net filter ratio of $0.04 \times 0.1 = 0.004$, more than a factor of 10 better than the filter ratio on M.

The whole point of choosing a driving table, usually choosing the one with the lowest filter ratio, is particularly to avoid reading more than a tiny fraction of the biggest table (usually the root table), since costs of reading rows on the biggest table tend to dominate query costs. However, here you find the database will reach just 8% as many rows in M if it begins on the A1 branch, rather than driving directly to the filter on M, so C1 is the better driving table by a comfortable margin. From there, just follow the normal rules, and find the full join order (C1, B2, A1, B1, M, A2, B3).

All these exceptions to the rules sound somewhat fuzzy and difficult, I know, but don't let that put you off or discourage you. I add the exceptions to be complete and to handle some rare special cases, but you will see these only once in a blue moon. You will almost always do just fine, far better than most, if you just apply the simple rules at the beginning of this chapter. In rare cases, you might find that the result is not quite as good as you would like, and then you can consider, if the stakes are really high, whether any of these exceptions might apply.

## Cases to Consider Hash Joins

When a well-optimized query returns a modest number of rows, it is almost impossible for a hash join to yield a significant improvement over nested loops. However, occasionally, a large query can see significant benefit from hash joins, especially hash joins to small or well-filtered tables.

When you drive from the best-filtered table in a query, any join upward, from master table to detail table, inherits the selectivity of the driving filter and every other filter reached so far in the join order. For example, consider Figure 6-32. Following the usual rules, you drive from A1 with a filter ratio of 0.001 and reach two other filters of 0.3 and 0.5 on B1 and B2, respectively, on two downward joins. The next detail table join, to M, will normally reach that table, following the index on the foreign key that points to A1, on a fraction of rows equal to 0.00015 ($0.001 \times 0.3 \times 0.5$). If the detail table is large enough to matter and the query does not return an unreasonably large number of rows, this strategy almost guarantees that nested loops that follow foreign keys into detail tables win. Other join methods, such as a hash join that accesses the detail table independently, through its own filter, will read a larger fraction of that same table, since the best nested-loops alternative drives from the best filter ratio in the query.

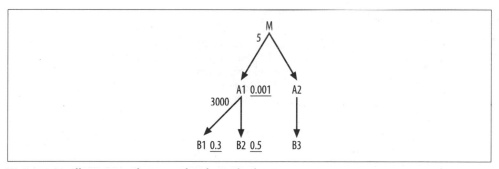

*Figure 6-32. Illustration of a query that favors hash joins*

 The one, uncommon case in which joining to the detail table by hash join pays off, at least a little, occurs when the cumulative filter product (the product of the already-reached filter ratios) before the detail join lies in the range where you might prefer a full table scan of the details. This case generally implies either a poorly filtered query that returns more rows than are useful, unless the tables are so small that optimization does not matter, or a rare query with many poor filters combined across different branches under the detail table.

On the other hand, when you join downward to a master table, you might be joining to a much smaller table, and the cost of reaching the rows through the primary key might be larger than the cost of reading the table independently for a hash join. From the statistics in Figure 6-32, you would find 3,000 times as many rows in A1 as in B1. Even discarding 999 out of 1,000 rows from A1, the database would join to each row in B1 an average of three times. Assume that A1 has 3,000,000 rows and B1 has 1,000 rows. After winnowing A1 down to 3,000 rows, using the driving filter, the database would join to rows in the 1,000-row table B1 3,000 times. If the database drove into B1 with B1's own filter, it would need to read just 300 ($0.3 \times 1,000$) rows, at roughly 1/10th the cost. Since the query reaches over 20% of the rows in B1, the database would find an even lower cost by simply performing a full table scan of B1 and filtering the result before doing the hash join. Therefore, while leaving the rest of the query cost unchanged, choosing a hash join to B1 would eliminate almost all the cost of the B1 table reads, compared to the standard robust plan that reads B1 through nested loops.

So, especially when you see large detail join ratios, hash joins to master tables can be fastest. How big is the improvement, though? In the example, the fractional improvement for this one table was high, over 90%, but the absolute improvement was quite modest, about 9,000 logical I/Os (6,000 in the two-level-deep key index and 3,000 on the table), which would take about 150 milliseconds. You would find no physical I/O at all to a table and index of this size. On the other hand, you would find the query reads about 2,250 ($3,000 \times 0.3 \times 0.5 \times 5$) rows from the 15,000,000-row table M with 3,600 logical I/Os.

 Nested loops drive 450 ($3,000 \times 0.3 \times 0.5$) range scans on the foreign-key index leading to M, and these range scans require 1,350 ($450 \times 3$) logical I/Os in the three-level-deep index. 2,250 logical I/Os to the table follow, to read the 2,250 rows in M. Thus, the total number of logical I/Os is 3,600 (1,350+2,250).

These 3,600 logical I/Os, especially the 2,250 to the table itself, will lead to hundreds of physical I/Os for such a large, hard-to-cache table. At 5–10 milliseconds per physical I/O, the reads to M could take seconds. This example is typical of cases in which hash joins perform best; these cases tend to deliver improvements only in logical I/Os to the smallest tables, and these improvements tend to be slight compared to the costs of the rest of the query.

A couple of rough formulae might help you choose the best join method:

$H=C \times R$
$L=C \times D \times F \times N$

The variables in these formulas are defined as follows:

$H$   The number of logical I/Os necessary to read the master table independently, for purposes of a hash join.

$C$   The rowcount of the master table.

$R$   The master table's filter ratio. Assume the database reaches the table independently, through an index range scan on that filter.

$L$   The number of logical I/Os to read the master table through nested loops on its primary key.

$D$   The detail join ratio for the link that leads up from the master table, which normally tells you how much smaller it is than the detail table above it.

$F$   The product of all filter ratios, including the driving filter ratio, reached before this join.

$N$   The number of logical I/Os required per row read through the primary-key index.

Since primary keys up to 300 rows normally fit in the root block, $N=2$ (1 for the index root block and 1 for the table) for $C$ up to 300. $N=3$ for $C$ between roughly 300 and 90,000. $N=4$ for $C$ between 90,000 and 27,000,000. Since you will normally drive from the best filter ratio, $F<R$, even if the plan picks up no additional filters after the driving-table filter.

$H$ is less than $L$, favoring the hash join for logical I/O costs, when $R<D \times F \times N$. $F<R$ when you drive from the node with the best filter ratio. $N$ is small, as shown, since B-trees branch heavily at each level. Therefore, to favor a hash join, either $F$ is close in magnitude to $R$, or $D$ is large, making this a join to a much smaller master table. This same calculation will sometimes show a logical-I/O savings when joining to a large master table, but use caution here. If the master table is too large to cache easily, physical I/O comes into play and tends to disfavor the hash join in two ways:

- Since table rows are much less well cached than index blocks, the hash-join cost advantage (if any) when physical I/O costs dominate mostly compares just the table-row counts, asking whether $R<D \times F$. Since I/O to the index is so much better cached than I/O to the table, costs dominated by physical I/O lose the $N$ factor for index-block reads. Without the $N$ factor, hash joins are less favored.

- If $C \times R$ is large, the hash join might have to write prehashed rows to disk and read them back, making the hash join much more expensive and potentially leading to out-of-disk errors for disk caching during query execution. This is the robustness risk of foregoing nested loops.

In all, it is difficult to find real queries that yield a hash-join savings over the best robust plan that are worth much bother. Almost the only cases of large savings for hash joins appear when the query starts with a poor driving filter and hits large tables, which almost inevitably means the whole query will usually return an unreasonably large rowset.

However, none of this implies that hash joins are a mistake; cost-based optimizers look for small improvements as well as large, and they are good at finding cases in which hash joins help a bit. While I almost never go out of my way to force a hash join, I usually do not attempt to override the optimizer's choice when it chooses one for me on a small table, as it often does, as long as the join order and index choices are still good. If in doubt, you can always experiment. First, find the best robust nested-loops plan.

 If you do not start with the best join order, replacing a nested-loops join with a hash join can easily lead to big savings, because then the early tables do not guarantee coming from the best filters (i.e., they do not guarantee $F<R$). Poorly optimized join orders can execute the join-key lookups an excessive number of times. If you find a query that showed dramatic improvement with a hash join, you should suspect that it had the wrong join order or failed to reach the joined table through the index on the full join key.

Then, replace nested loops to a master table with an optimized single-table access path to the same table and a hash join at the same point in the join order. This change will not affect costs to the other tables, decoupling the choice from the other optimization choices. Use whichever choice is fastest, keeping in mind that you must rerun tests or run tests far apart to avoid a caching bias against the first test.

The earlier example, in "Join Order for an Eight-Way Join," of the problem diagrammed in Figure 6-2 illustrates well a minor performance improvement available through hash joins. Notice that the detail join ratios above nodes OT and ODT are in the millions, indicating that these are joins to a tiny set of rows of the Code_Translations table. Since each set of eligible rows for the given values of Code_Type is so small, you will require less logical I/O to read the whole rowset once, probably through an index on the Code_Type column, then perform a hash join, rather than go to each row (more than once, probably) as you need it, though nested loops. Either alternative is cheap, though, and will make up just a small fraction of the overall query runtime, since the number of rows the query returns is modest and the physical index and table blocks of Code_Translations will be fully cached.

# Exercise

Here's an exercise that puts it all together with more filters and exceptions in a single query than you are likely to see in your life. Figure 6-33 is a more complex and difficult query diagram than I've ever encountered in a real-world tuning problem.

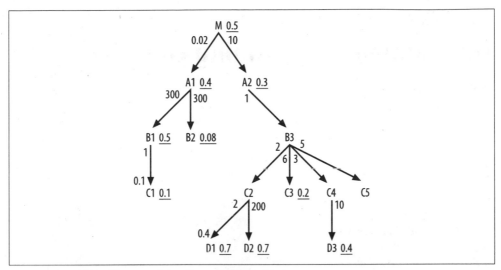

*Figure 6-33. A horribly, unrealistically complex problem*

If you can handle this, you can easily handle any query diagram you will ever find in real life, so give it a shot! (If you don't get it right the first time, come back and try again after more practice.) Find the best join order. Find the best join method for each join, assuming table A1 has 30,000,000 rows and assuming a full table scan is preferable for any table on which you will read at least 5% of the rows. Find the set of primary-key indexes needed, the set of foreign-key indexes needed, and any other indexes needed. Find any modifications to the SQL needed to pick up hidden filters soonest. Make the usual assumptions about referential integrity.

# CHAPTER 7

# Diagramming and Tuning Complex SQL Queries

*There is no royal road to geometry.*
—Euclid
   *Proclus's Commentary on Euclid, Prologue*

So far, you have seen how to diagram and tune queries of real tables when the diagram meets several expectations applicable to a normal business query:

- The query maps to one tree.
- The tree has one root, exactly one table with no join to its primary key. All nodes other than the root node have a single downward-pointing arrow linking them to a detail node above, but any node can be at the top end of any number of downward-pointing arrows.
- All joins have downward-pointing arrows (joins that are unique on one end).
- Outer joins are unfiltered, pointing down, with only outer joins below outer joins.
- The question that the query answers is basically a question about the entity represented at the top (root) of the tree or about aggregations of that entity.
- The other tables just provide reference data stored elsewhere for normalization.

I have called queries that meet these criteria *simple queries*, although, as you saw in Chapter 6, they can contain any number of joins and can be quite tricky to optimize in rare special cases of near-ties between filter ratios or when hidden join filters exist.

Queries do not always fit this standard, simple form. When they do not, I call such queries *complex*. As I will demonstrate in this chapter, some complex queries result from *mistakes*: errors in the database design, the application design, or in the implementation. Often, these types of mistakes make it easy to write incorrect queries. In this chapter, you'll learn about anomalies that you might see in query diagrams that can alert you to the strong possibility of an error in a query or in design. You will also see how to fix these functional or design defects, sometimes fixing performance as a side effect. These fixes usually convert the query to simple form, or at least to a form that is close enough to simple form to apply the methods shown earlier in this book.

Some complex queries go beyond any form I have yet explained how to diagram, using subqueries, views, or set operations such as UNION and UNION ALL. These complex queries are usually fine functionally and are fairly common, so you need a way to diagram and optimize them, which you can do by extending the earlier methods for simple queries.

# Abnormal Join Diagrams

If your query contains only simple tables (not views), no subqueries, and no set operations such as UNION, you can always produce some sort of query diagram by applying the methods of Chapter 5. However, sometimes a diagram has abnormal features that fail to match the usual join-tree template described earlier. I will describe these anomalies one by one and discuss how to handle each one.

To illustrate the anomalies, I will show partial query diagrams, in which the parts of the diagram that are not significant to the discussion are hidden behind gray clouds. This focuses attention on the part that matters, and makes clearer the generality of the example. As a convention, I will show links to parts of the join skeleton hidden behind the clouds in gray when they are not significant to the discussion. The number of gray links or even the existence of gray links is not significant to the examples, just illustrative of the potential existence of added joins in real cases. Occasionally, I will have black links to hidden parts of the query skeleton. The existence of the black links is significant to the discussion, but the hidden part of the query skeleton is not.

## Cyclic Join Graphs

How do you handle join skeletons that do not map to a simple tree but contain links that close a loop somewhere in the skeleton? There are several cases for which you might encounter such a diagram. In the following sections, I will discuss four cases with distinct solutions.

 *Graph theory* is the branch of mathematics that describes abstract entities, called *graphs*, that consist of links and nodes, such as the query diagrams this book uses. In graph theory, a *cyclic* graph has links that form a closed loop. In the following examples, up to Figure 7-8, note that a real or implied loop exists in the diagram, making these graphs cyclic.

## Case 1: Two one-to-one master tables share the same detail table

Figure 7-1 illustrates the first case, in which a single foreign key joins to primary keys in two different master tables.

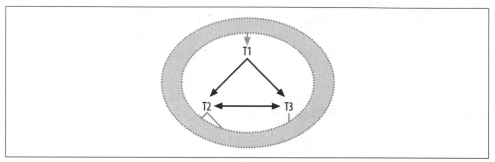

*Figure 7-1. Case 1 for a cyclic query diagram*

In this case, you can infer that the SQL itself looks something like this:

```
SELECT ...
FROM ...T1, ... T2, ... T3, ...
WHERE ... T1.FKey1=T2.PKey2
  AND T1.FKey1=T3.PKey3
  AND T2.PKey2=T3.PKey3 ...
```

Here, I have named the single foreign key that points to both tables from T1 FKey1, and I have named the primary keys of T2 and T3 PKey2 and PKey3, respectively. With all three of these joins explicit in the SQL, the cyclic links are obvious, but note that you could have left any one of these links out of the query, and transitivity (if *a=b* and *b=c*, then *a=c*) would imply the missing join condition. If one of these joins were left out, you might diagram the same query in any of the three forms shown in Figure 7-2.

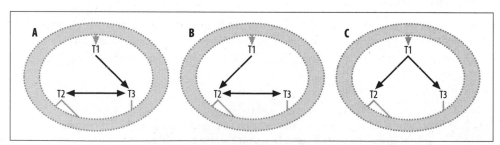

*Figure 7-2. The same cyclic query, missing one of the three transitive join conditions*

Note that in versions A and B of this query you can infer the missing arrow from the fact that the link between T2 and T3 has an arrowhead on both ends, and an arrow at both ends implies a one-to-one join. Version C, on the other hand, looks exactly like a plain-vanilla join tree, and you would not realize that it had cyclic joins unless you happened to notice that T1 used the same foreign key to join to both T2 and T3.

When you have one-to-one tables, cyclic joins like the one in Figure 7-1 are common. These are not a functional problem, though I will later describe issues to consider whenever you encounter a one-to-one join. Instead of being a problem, you can see such joins as an opportunity. If you have already reached T1, it is useful to have the choice of either T2 or T3 next, since either might have the better filter ratio or provide access to good filters lower down the tree. If you reach either T2 or T3 in the join order before you reach T1, it is also useful to have the option to join one-to-one to the other (from T2 to T3, or from T3 to T2). This enables you to reach any filter the other table might have, without joining to T1 first. Without the horizontal link, you could join from T2 to T3 or vice versa, only through T1, at likely higher cost.

Some optimizers are written cleverly enough to use transitivity to fill in a missing join condition even if it is left out and take advantage of the extra degrees of freedom that are provided in the join order. However, to be safe, it is best to make all three joins explicit if you notice that two joins imply a third by transitivity. At the least, you should make explicit in your SQL statement any join you need for the optimum plan you find.

There exists a special case in which the one-to-one tables shown as T2 and T3 are the same table! In this case, each row from T1 joins to the same row of T2 twice, a clear inefficiency. The obvious cause, having the same table name repeated twice in the FROM clause and aliased to both T2 and T3, is unlikely, precisely because it is too obvious to go unnoticed. However, a join to the same table twice can happen more subtly and be missed in code review. For example, it can happen if a synonym or simple view hides the true identity of the underlying table behind at least one of the aliases in the query. Either way, you are clearly better off eliminating the redundant table reference from the query and shifting all column references and further downward joins to the remaining alias.

### Case 2: Master-detail tables each hold copies of a foreign key that points to the same third table's primary key

Figure 7-3 shows the second major case with cyclic joins. Here, identical foreign keys in T1 and T2 point to the same primary key value in T3.

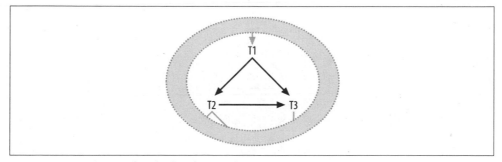

*Figure 7-3. A cyclic join that implies denormalization*

This time, the SQL looks like this:

```
SELECT ...
FROM ...T1, ... T2, ... T3, ...
WHERE ... T1.FKey1=T2.PKey2
  AND T1.FKey2=T3.PKey3
  AND T2.FKey2=T3.PKey3 ...
```

In this SQL statement, I name the foreign keys that point from T1 to T2 and T3 FKey1 and FKey2, respectively. By transitivity, the foreign-key column T2.FKey2 has the same value as T1.FKey, since both join to T3.PKey3. I name the primary keys of T2 and T3 PKey2 and PKey3, respectively. The most likely explanation for T1 and T2 joining to the same table, T3, on its full primary key is that T1 and T2 contain redundant foreign keys to that table. In this scenario, the FKey2 column in the detail table T1 has denormalized data from its master table T2. This data always matches the FKey2 value in the matching master row of T2.

 Alternatively, the FKey2 values are supposed to match but sometimes do not, since denormalized data is notoriously likely to get out of sync.

Chapter 10 covers the pros and cons of denormalization in cases like this. Briefly, if the normalization is justifiable, it is possible that the extra link in the query diagram will buy you access to a better execution plan. However, it is more likely that the denormalization is a mistake, with more cost and risk than benefit. Eliminating the denormalization would eliminate the foreign key FKey2 in T1, thus eliminating the link from T1 to T3 and making the query diagram a tree.

### Case 3: Two-node filter (nonunique on both ends) between nodes is already linked through normal joins

Figure 7-4 shows the third major case with cyclic joins. This time, you have normal downward arrows from T1 to T2 and T3, but you also have some third, unusual join condition between T2 and T3 that does not involve the primary key of either table.

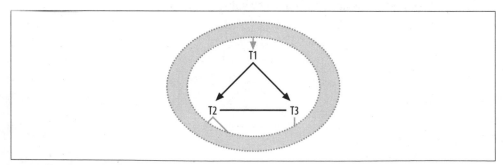

*Figure 7-4. A cyclic join with a two-node filter*

Since neither primary key is involved in the join between T2 and T3, the link between these two has no arrow on either end.

The SQL behind Figure 7-4 looks like this:

```
SELECT ...
FROM ...T1, ... T2, ... T3,...
WHERE ... T1.FKey1=T2.PKey2
  AND T1.FKey2=T3.PKey3
  AND T2.Col2<IsSomeHowComparedTo>T3.Col3 ...
```

For example, if T1 were on the Orders table, having joins to Customers, T2, and Salespersons, T3, a query might request orders in which customers are assigned to different regions than the salesperson responsible for the order:

```
SELECT ...
FROM Orders T1, Customers T2, Salespersons T3
WHERE T1.Customer_ID=T2.Customer_ID
  AND T1.Salesperson_ID=T3.Salesperson_ID
  AND T2.Region_ID!=T3.Region_ID
```

Here, the condition T2.Region_ID!=T3.Region_ID is technically a join, but it is better to view it as a filter condition that happens to require rows from two different tables before it can be applied. If you ignore the unusual, arrow-free link between T2 and T3, you will reach T1 before you can apply the two-node filter on Region_ID. The only allowed join orders, which avoid directly following the unusual join between T2 and T3, are:

(T1, T2, T3)
(T1, T3, T2)
(T2, T1, T3)
(T3, T1, T2)

Any join order other than these four (such as (T2, T3, T1)) would create a disastrous many-to-many explosion of rows after reaching the second table, almost a Cartesian product of the rows in T2 and T3. All of these join orders reach T1 by the first or second table, before you have both T2 and T3. These join orders therefore follow only the two ordinary many-to-one joins between the detail table T1 and its master tables T2 and T3.

The unusual, two-node filter acts like no filter at all when you reach the first of the two filtered tables, then it acts like an ordinary filter, discarding some fraction of rows, when you reach the second of the two tables. Viewed in this way, handling this case is fairly straightforward: consider the filter to be nonexistent (or at least not directly accessible) until you happen to join to one of the filtered tables as a matter of course. However, as soon as you have joined to either end of the two-node filter, the other node suddenly acquires a better filter ratio and becomes more attractive to join to next.

Figure 7-5 shows a specific example with a two-node filter, in which the fraction of rows from the ordinary joins from T1 to T2 and T3 that meet the additional two-node filter condition is 0.2. In this case, you would initially choose a join order independent of the existence of the two-node filter, following only ordinary join links. However, as soon as you happened to join to either T2 or T3, the other would have its former filter ratio (1.0 for T2 and 0.5 for T3) multiplied by 0.2, becoming much more attractive for future joins.

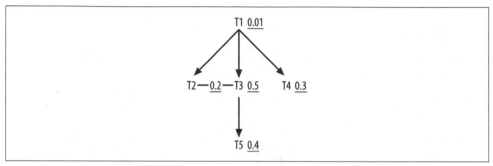

*Figure 7-5. A two-node filter with explicit two-node filter ratio*

Follow the normal procedure to tune Figure 7-5, ignoring the two-node filter between T2 and T3 until you reach one of those tables as a matter of course. The driving table is T1, followed by T4, the table with the best ordinary filter downstream of T1. T3 has the next best ordinary filter available, with the filter ratio 0.5, so it follows next in the join order. Now, you have a choice between T2 and T5 next in the join order, but T2 has at last seen the two-node filter activated, since you just reached T3, so it has a more effective filter ratio, at 0.2, than T5 has, and you join to T2 next. The final best join order is (T1, T4, T3, T2, T5).

> The join to T2 in the just-completed example is an ordinary join, following nested loops into the primary-key index on T2 from the foreign key pointing down from T1. Avoid nested loops into a table on the two-node filter. Referring back to the SQL just before Figure 7-5, you would be far better off reaching the Customers table on nested loops from the join T1.Customer_ID=T2.Customer_ID than on the two-node filter T2.Region_ID!=T3.Region_ID.

### Case 4: Multipart join from two foreign keys is spread over two tables to a multipart primary key

Finally, Figure 7-6 shows the fourth major case with cyclic joins. Here are two unusual joins to T3, neither using the whole primary key of that table nor the primary keys of the tables on the other ends of these joins. If such cases of failing to join to the whole primary key on at least one end of each join are "wrongs," then Case 4 is usually a case in which two wrongs make a right!

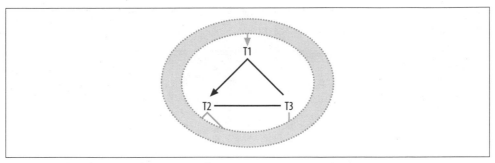

*Figure 7 6. A cyclic join with two unusual joins*

In a situation such as that shown in Figure 7-6, the SQL typically looks like this:

```
SELECT ...
FROM ...T1, ... T2, ... T3, ...
WHERE ... T1.FKey1=T2.PKey2
  AND T1.FKey2=T3.PKeyColumn1
  AND T2.FKey3=T3.PkeyColumn2 ...
```

Such SQL typically arises when you have a two-part primary key on T3 and the two-part foreign key is somehow distributed over two tables in a master-detail relationship.

A concrete example will clarify this case. Consider data-dictionary tables called Tables, Indexes, Table_Columns, and Index_Columns. You might choose a two-part primary key for Table_Columns of (Table_ID, Column_Number), where Column_Number designates the place that table column holds in the natural column order of the table—1 for the first column, 2 for the second, and so on. The Indexes table would have a foreign key to Tables on the Table_ID column, and the Index_Columns table would also have a two-part primary key, (Index_ID, Column_Number). The Column_Number value in the Index_Columns has the same meaning as Column_Number in Table_Columns: the place the column holds in the natural order of table columns (not its place in the index order, which is Index_Position). If you knew the name of an index and wished to know the list of column names that make up the index in order of Index_Position, you might query:

```
SELECT TC.Column_Name
FROM Indexes Ind, Index_Columns IC, Table_Columns TC
WHERE Ind.Index_Name='EMPLOYEES_X1'
  AND Ind.Index_ID=IC.Index_ID
  AND Ind.Table_ID=TC.Table_ID
  AND IC.Column_Number=TC.Column_Number
ORDER BY IC.Index_Position ASC
```

Try diagramming this query skeleton for yourself as a review before continuing.

If the condition on Index_Name had a filter ratio of 0.0002, the query diagram, leaving off the join ratios, would look like Figure 7-7.

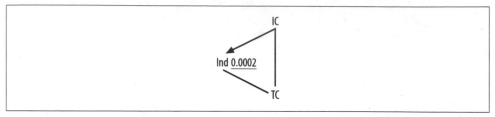

*Figure 7-7. A concrete example of the fourth type of cyclic join*

Here, two wrongs (i.e., two joins that fail to find a full primary key on either side) combine to make a right when you consider the joins to TC together, because combined they reach the full primary key of that table. You can transform the diagram of this uncommon case generically, as in Figure 7-8.

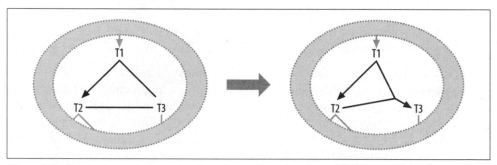

*Figure 7-8. Combining multipart joins from foreign keys distributed across two tables*

If you follow the rule of thumb to join either to or from full primary keys, the best join order for Figure 7-7 becomes clear. Drive from the filter on Ind and follow the upward link to IC. Only then, after reaching both parts of the primary key to TC, should you join to TC. This is, in fact, the best execution plan for the example. The rule of thumb in these cases is only to follow these unusual links into a multipart primary key once the database has reached all the upward nodes necessary to use the full primary key.

### Cyclic join summary

The following list summarizes the way in which you should treat each of the four cyclic join types just described:

*Case 1: Two one-to-one master tables share the same detail table*

   This is an opportunity for tuning, increasing the degrees of freedom in the join order, but you should consider options spelled out later in this chapter for handling one-to-one joins.

*Case 2: Master-detail tables each hold copies of a foreign key pointing to the same third table's primary key*

This too is an opportunity to increase the degrees of freedom in the join order, but the case implies denormalization, which is usually not justified. Remove the denormalization if you have the choice, unless the benefit to this or some other query justifies the denormalization. Chapter 10 describes further how to evaluate the trade offs involved in denormalization.

> Throughout this book, I recommend ideal actions under the assumption that you have complete power over the application, the database design, and the SQL. I've also tried to recommend compromise solutions that apply when you have more limited control. Sometimes, though, such as when you see unjustified denormalization in an already-released database design that you do not own or even influence, the only compromise is to do nothing.

*Case 3: Two-node filter (nonunique on both ends) between nodes is already linked through normal joins*

Treat this uncommon case as no filter at all until you reach one of the nodes. Then, treat the other node as having a better filter ratio for purposes of finding the rest of the join order.

*Case 4: Multipart join from two foreign keys is spread over two tables to a multipart primary key*

Perform this join into the primary key only when you have both parts of the key.

## Disconnected Query Diagrams

Figure 7-9 shows two cases of *disconnected query diagrams*: query skeletons that fail to link all the query tables into a single connected structure. In each of these cases, you are in a sense looking at two independent queries, each with a separate query diagram that you can optimize in isolation from the other query.

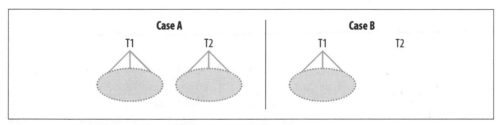

*Figure 7-9. Disconnected query diagrams*

In Case A, I show a query that consists of two independent-appearing queries that each have joins. In Case B, I show an otherwise ordinary-looking query that has one of its tables (table T2) disconnected from the join tree (i.e., not joined to any other table). Each of the two cases maps to two independent queries being run within a single query. What happens when you combine independent, disconnected queries into a single query? When two tables are combined in a single query without any join condition, the database returns a Cartesian product: every possible combination of the rows from the first table with the rows from the second table. In the case of disconnected query diagrams, think of the query result represented by each independent query skeleton (or isolated node) as being its own virtual table. From this point of view, you can see that the database will return all combinations of rows from the two independent queries. In short, you'll get a Cartesian product.

When confronted with a Cartesian product such as the one shown in Figure 7-9, you should investigate the reason behind it. Once you learn the reason, you can decide which of the following courses of action to take, depending on which of four cases of disconnected queries you have:

*Case 1: Query is missing a join that would connect the disconnected parts*
Add the missing join.

*Case 2: Query combines two independent queries, each returning multiple rows*
Eliminate this Cartesian product by running the independent queries separately.

*Case 3: One of the independent queries is a single-row query*
Consider separating the queries to save bandwidth from the database, especially if the multirow independent query returns many rows. Execute the single-row query first.

*Case 4: Both of the independent queries are single-row queries*
Keep the query combined, unless it is confusing or hard to maintain.

Before you turn a disconnected query into two separate queries, consider whether the developer might have inadvertently left a join out of the single query. Early in the development cycle, the most common cause of disconnected query diagrams is developers simply forgetting some join clause that links the disconnected subtrees. When this is the case, you should add in the missing join condition, after which you will no longer have a disconnected tree. Whenever one of the tables in one tree has a foreign key that points to the primary key of the root node of the other tree, that join was almost certainly left out accidentally.

If each independent query returns multiple rows, the number of combinations will exceed the number of rows you would get if you just ran the two queries separately. However, the set of combinations from the two contains no more information than you could get if you ran these separately, so the work of generating the redundant data in the combinations is just a waste of time, at least from the perspective of getting raw information. Thus, you might be better off running the two queries separately.

Rarely, there are reasons why generating the combinations in a Cartesian product is at least somewhat defensible, from the perspective of programming convenience.

However, you always have workarounds that avoid the redundant data if the cost is unjustified.

 If you were concerned only with physical I/O, the Cartesian product would likely be fine, since the redundant rereads of data from the repeated query would almost certainly be fully cached after the first read. I have actually heard people defend long running examples of queries like this based on the low physical I/O they saw! Queries like this are a great way to burn CPU and generate enormous logical I/O if you ever need to do so for some sort of stress test or other laboratory-type study, but they have no place in business applications.

If one of the independent queries returns just a single row, guaranteed, then at least the Cartesian product is safe and is guaranteed to return no more rows than the larger independent query would return. However, there is still potentially a small network cost in combining the queries, because the select list of the combined query might return the data from the smaller query many times over, once for each row that the multirow query returns, requiring more redundant bytes than if you broke up the queries. This bandwidth cost is countered somewhat with network-latency savings: the combined query saves you round trips to the database over the network, so the best choice depends on the details. If you do not break the up queries, the optimum plan is straightforward: just run the optimum plan for the single-row query first. Then, in a nested loop that executes only once, run the optimum plan for the multirow query. This combined execution plan costs the same as running the two queries separately. If, instead, you run the plan for the multirow query first, a nested-loops plan would require you to execute the plan for the single-row query repeatedly, once for every row of the other query.

Combining a single-row query with a multirow query is sometimes convenient and justified. There is a special case, matching the right half of Figure 7-9, in which the single-row query is simply a read of the only row of isolated table T2, which has no joins at all. A Cartesian product with an isolated table is sometimes useful to pick up site parameters stored in a single-row parameters table, especially when these parameters show up only in the WHERE clause, not in the SELECT list. When the query does not return data from the parameters table, it is actually cheaper to run the correctly combined query than to run separate queries.

An even rarer case guarantees that both isolated queries return a single row. It is fully justified and safe, from the performance perspective, to combine the queries in this case, which lacks any of the dangers of the other cases. However, from the programming and software-maintenance perspective, it might be confusing to combine queries like this, and the savings are generally slight.

## Query Diagrams with Multiple Roots

Figure 7-10 shows an example of a query diagram that violates the one-root expectation. This case is akin to the previous case (disconnected query diagrams). Here, for each row in the Master table shown that satisfies the query condition, the query will return all combinations of matching details from Root1 and Root2. Given the detail join ratios, you can expect all combinations of 5 Root1 details with 30 Root2 details, for 150 combination rows for each matching Master row. These 150 combination rows contain no more original data than the 5 Root1 details combined with the 30 Root2 details, so it is faster to read these 5 and 30 rows separately, avoiding the Cartesian product. While disconnected query diagrams generate a single large Cartesian product, multiple root nodes generate a whole series of smaller Cartesian products, one for each matching master row.

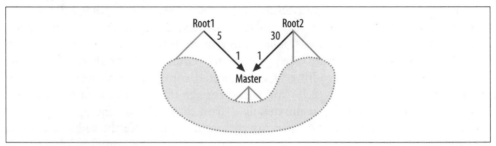

*Figure 7-10. Query diagram with multiple roots*

There are four possible causes of a query diagram with multiple roots. The following list details these causes, and describes their solutions:

*Case 1: Missing condition*
> The query is missing a condition that would convert one of the root detail tables into a master table, making a one-to-many join one-to-one.

> Solution: Add the missing join condition.

*Case 2: Many-to-many Cartesian product*
> The query represents a many-to-many Cartesian product per master-table row between detail tables that share a master table. This appears in the guise of detail join ratios greater than 1.0 from a single shared master to two different root detail tables.

> Solution: Eliminate this Cartesian product by separating the query into independent queries that read the two root detail tables separately.

*Case 3: Detail join ratio less than 1.0*
> One of the root detail tables joins to the shared master table with a detail join ratio less than 1.0.

> Solution: Although this is not a problem for performance, consider separating the query parts or turning one of the query parts into a subquery, for functional reasons.

*Case 4: Table used only for existence check*

One of the root detail tables supplies no data needed in the SELECT list and is included only as an existence check.

Solution: Convert the existence check to an explicit subquery.

## Case 1: Missing join conditions

Most often, the appearance of a second root node points to some missing join condition that would convert one of the root nodes to a master node. Figure 7-11 shows this transformation, where the join from Master to Root1 has been converted to a one-to-one join by the addition (or recognition) of some extra condition on Root1 (renamed R1) that ensures that the database will find at most one row in R1 for every row in Master. This is particularly likely when R1 contains time-interval detail data (such as a varying tax rate) that matches a master record (such as taxing entity) and the addition of a date condition (such as requesting the *current* tax rate) makes the join one-to-one.

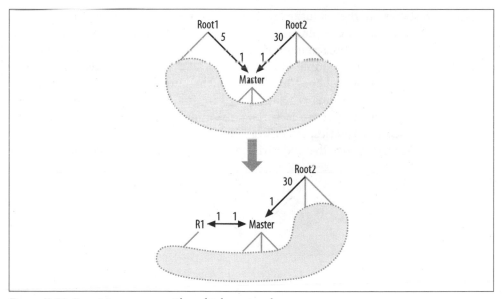

*Figure 7-11. Repairing a query with multiple root nodes*

Often, the condition that makes the join one-to-one is already there, and you find a combination of a many-to-one join and an apparent filter that just cancels the detail join ratio.

In the example, the filter ratio for such a filter would be 0.2, or 1/5, where the detail join ratio to Root1 was 5.

Alternatively, the condition that makes the join one-to-one might be missing from the query, especially if development happens in a test system where the one-to-many relationship is hidden.

 The previous example of a varying tax rate illustrates this. In a development environment, you might find records only for the current rate, obscuring the error of leaving out the date condition on the rates table.

Whether the condition that makes the join one-to-one was missing or was just not recognized as being connected with the join, you should include the condition and recognize it as part of the join, not as an independent filter condition. Such a missing join condition is particularly likely when you find that the foreign key for one of the root tables pointing downward to a shared master table is also part of the multipart primary key of that root table.

### Case 2: Breaking the Cartesian product into multiple queries

Figure 7-12 shows another solution to the multiroot-query-diagram problem. This solution is akin to running explicitly separate queries in the disconnected query diagram (discussed earlier), breaking up the Cartesian product and replacing it with the two separate sets. In the example, this replaces a query that would return 150 rows per Master row with two queries that, combined, return 35 rows per Master row. Whenever you have one-to-many relationships from a master table to two different detail root tables, you can get precisely the same underlying data, with far fewer rows read and with separate queries, as illustrated. Since the result takes an altered form, you will also need to change the underlying application logic to handle the new form.

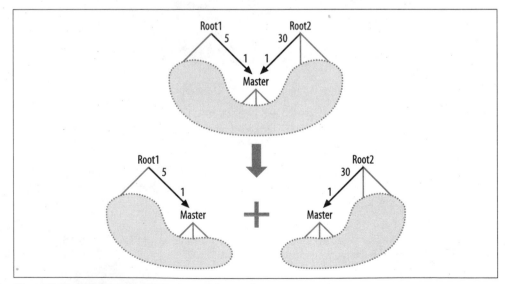

Figure 7-12. Resolving the Cartesian product with separate queries

## Case 3: Root detail tables that are usually no more than one-to-one

Figure 7-13 shows a case of multiple roots in which performance of the query, unaltered, is not a problem. Since the detail join ratio from Master to Root1 is 0.5, you see no Cartesian explosion of rows when you combine matching Root1 with Root2 records for the average matching Master record. You can treat Root1 as if it were a downward join, even favoring it as if it had a filter ratio enhanced by 0.5 for the filtering join, following the special-case rules in Chapter 6 for detail join ratios less than 1.0.

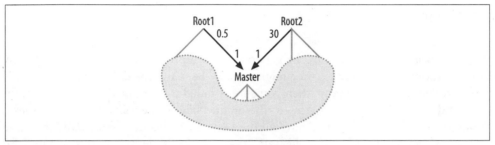

*Figure 7-13. A Cartesian product with a low detail join ratio*

Although this query is no problem for tuning, it might still be incorrect. The one-to-zero or one-to-many join from Master to Root1 evidently usually finds either the one-to-zero or the one-to-one case, leading to a well-behaved Cartesian product. However, as long as the join is ever one-to-many, you must consider that the result might return a Cartesian product with repeats for a given row of Root2. Since this case is rare, it is all too likely that the query was actually designed and tested to return results that map one-to-one with rows from Root2, and the application might not even work in the other rare case.

> The rarer the one-to-many case is, the more likely it is that this case has been neglected in the application design.

For example, if the application will alter Root2 data after reading it out with this query and attempt to post the alterations back to the database, the application must consider which copy of a repeated Root2 row should get posted back to the database. Should the application warn an end user that it attempted to post inconsistent copies? If the application aggregates Root2 data from the query, does it avoid adding data from repeated Root2 rows?

## Case 4: Converting an existence check to an explicit subquery

One solution to the functional problem that Figure 7-13 represents is already shown in Figure 7-12: just break up the query into two queries. Another solution, surprisingly often, is to isolate the branch to Root1 into a subquery, usually with an EXISTS condition. This solution works especially easily if the original query did not select columns from Root1 (or any of the tables joined below it through hidden gray links in Figure 7-13). In this relatively common special case, you are really interested only in whether a matching row in Root1 exists and perhaps matches some filter conditions, not in the contents of that row or the number of matches (beyond the first) that might exist. Later in this chapter, you will see how to diagram and tune queries with subqueries like this.

## Joins with No Primary Key

I use join links without arrows on either end to show joins that involve no primary key on either side of the join. In general, these represent unusual many-to-many joins, although in some cases they might usually be many-to-zero or many-to-one. If they are never many-to-many, then you simply failed to recognize the unique condition and you should add an arrow to the unique side of the join. If they are at least sometimes many-to-many, you have all the same problems (and essentially the same solutions) you have with query diagrams that have multiple root nodes. Figure 7-14 shows a many-to-many join between T1 and T2, where the detail join ratio on each end is greater than 1.0. (Master join ratios exist only on the unique end of a link, with an arrow, so this link has two detail join ratios.)

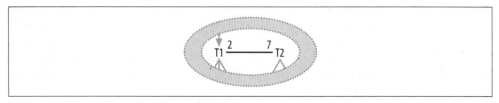

*Figure 7-14. A many-to-many join*

This case turns out to be much more common than the previous examples of abnormal join diagrams. Although it shares all the same possible problem sources and solutions as the case of multiple root nodes, the overwhelming majority of many-to-many joins are simply due to missing join conditions. Begin by checking whether filter conditions already in the query should be treated as part of the join, because they complete specification of the full primary key for one end of the join. Example 5-2 in Chapter 5 was potentially such a case, with the condition OT.Code_Type='ORDER_STATUS' needed to complete the unique join to alias OT. Had I treated that condition as merely a filter condition on alias OT, the join to OT would have looked many-to-many. Even if you do not find the missing part of the join among the query filter conditions, you should suspect that it was mistakenly left out of the query.

This case of missing join conditions is particularly common when the database design allows for multiple entity types or partitions within a table and the developer forgets to restrict the partition or type as part of the query. For example, the earlier example of a `Code_Translations` table has distinct types of translation entities for each `Code_Type`, and leaving off the condition on `Code_Type` would make the join to `Code_Translations` many-to-many. Often, testing fails to find this problem early, because even though the database design might allow for multiple types or partitions, the test environment might have just a single type or partition to begin with, a state of affairs developers might take for granted. Even when there are multiple types or partitions in the real data, the other, more selective part of the key might, by itself, be usually unique. This is both good and bad luck: while it prevents the missing join condition from causing much immediate trouble, it also makes the problem much harder to detect and correct, and lends a false sense that the application is correct. Finding and correcting the missing join condition might help performance only slightly, by making the join more selective, but it can be a huge service if it fixes a really pernicious hidden bug.

By direct analogy with query diagrams that have multiple root nodes, the solutions to many-to-many joins map to similar solutions to diagrams with multiple root nodes.

## One-to-One Joins

You have probably heard the joke about the old fellow who complains he had to walk five miles to school every morning *uphill both ways*. In a sense, one-to-one joins turn this mental picture on its head: for the heuristic rules of which table to join next, one-to-one joins are *downhill both ways*! As such, these joins create no problem for tuning at all, and these are the least troublesome of the unusual features possible in a query diagram. However, they do sometimes point to opportunities to improve database design, if you are at a point in the development cycle when database design is not yet set in stone. It is also useful to have a standard way to represent one-to-one joins on a query diagram, so I will describe ways to represent these cases.

### One-to-one join to a subset table

Figure 7-15 shows a typical one-to-one join embedded in a larger query. While many-to-many joins have detail join ratios on both ends, one-to-one joins have master join ratios on both ends. The master join ratios in the example show that the join between T1 and T2 is really one-to-zero or one-to-one; the one-to-zero case happens for 30% of the rows in T1.

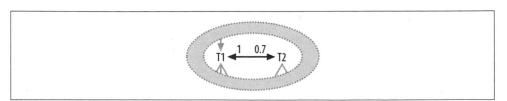

*Figure 7-15. A typical one-to-one join*

Since this is an inner join, the one-to-zero cases between T1 and T2 make up a hidden join filter, which you should handle as described at the end of Chapter 6. Also note that this might be a case of a hidden cyclic join, as often happens when a master table joins one-to-one with another table. If you have a detail table above T1, as implied by the gray link upward, and if that detail table joins to T1 by the same unique key as used for the join to T2, then you have, by transitivity, an implied join from the detail table to T2. Figure 7-16 shows this implied link in gray. Refer back to cyclic joins earlier in this chapter for how to handle this case.

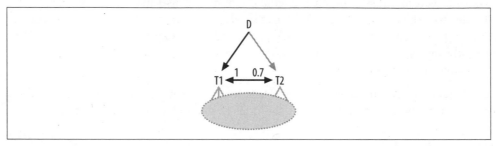

*Figure 7-16. An implied link making a cyclic join*

Whether or not you have a cyclic join, though, you might have an opportunity to improve the database design. The case in Figure 7-16 implies a set of entities that map one-to-one with T1 and a subset of those same entities that map one-to-one with T2, with T2 built out of T1's primary key and columns that apply only to that subset. In this case, there is no compelling need to have two tables at all; just add the extra columns to T1 and leave them null for members of the larger set that do not belong to the subset! Occasionally, there are good reasons why development prefers a two-table design for convenience in a situation like this. However, from the perspective of tuning, combining these two comparably sized tables is almost always helpful, so at least give it some thought if you have any chance to influence the database design.

### Exact one-to-one joins

Figure 7-17 shows an especially compelling case for combining the tables into a single table, when possible. Here, the master join ratios are each exactly 1.0, and the relationship between the tables is exactly one-to-one. Both tables, therefore, map to the same set of entities, and the join is just needless expense compared to using a combined table.

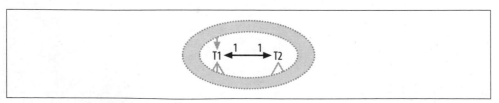

*Figure 7-17. A precise one-to-one join*

The only reason, from a performance perspective, to separate these tables is if queries almost always need just the data from one or the other and rarely need to do the join. The most common example of this is when one of the tables has rarely needed data, compared to the other. In that case, especially if the rarely needed data takes up a lot of space per row and the tables are large, you might find that the better compactness of the commonly queried table, resulting in a better cache-hit ratio, will (barely) justify the cost of the rarely needed joins. Even from a functional or development perspective, it is likely that the coding costs of adding and deleting rows for both tables at once—and, sometimes, updating both at once—are high. You might prefer to maintain a single, combined table. Usually, when you see an exact one-to-one join, it is a result of some bolted-on new functionality that requires new columns for existing entities, and some imagined or real development constraint prevented altering the original table. When possible, it is best to solve the problem by eliminating that constraint.

### One-to-one join to a much smaller subset

At the other end of the spectrum, you have the case shown in Figure 7-18, a one-to-zero or one-to-one join that is almost always one-to-zero. Here, the case for separating the tables is excellent. The tiny subset of entities represented by T2 might have different optimization needs than the superset represented by T1. Probably, T1 is usually queried without the join to T2, and, in these cases, it is useful that it excludes the inapplicable columns in T2 and has only the indexes that make sense for the common entities. Here, the hidden join filter represented by the small master join ratio on the T2 side of the join is excellent. It is so good, in fact, that you might choose to drive from an unfiltered full table scan of T2 and still find the best path to the rest of the data. Such an execution plan would be hard to approximate, without creating otherwise useless indexes, if you combined these tables into a single table.

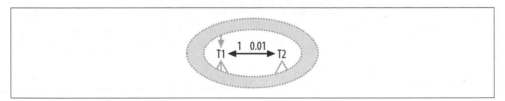

*Figure 7-18. A one-to-zero or one-to-one join between very different-sized tables*

Here, the key issue is not to neglect to take into account the hidden join filter from T1 to T2, either driving from the T2 side of the query or reaching it as soon as possible to pick up the hidden filter early.

### One-to-one joins with hidden join filters in both directions

Figure 7-19 shows a rare case of a [zero or one]-to-[zero or one] join, which filters in both directions. If one-to-one joins are downhill in both directions, then [zero or one]-to-[zero or one] joins are steeply downhill in both directions. However, unless data is corrupt (i.e., one of the tables is missing data), this rare case probably implies that yet a third table exists, or should exist, representing a superset of these two overlapping sets. If you find or create such a table, the same arguments as before apply for combining it with one or both of the subset tables.

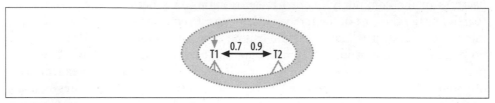

*Figure 7-19. A [zero or one]-to-[zero or one] join*

### Conventions to display one-to-one joins

It helps to have agreed-upon conventions for laying out query diagrams. Such conventions aid tuning intuition by presenting key information uniformly. Single-ended arrows always point down, by convention. Figure 7-20 shows two alternatives that work well for one-to-one joins that lie below the root detail table. The first alternative emphasizes the two-headed arrow, placing neither node above the other. The second alternative emphasizes the usual downward flow of reference links from the root detail table. Either alternative works well, as long as you remember that both directions of a one-to-one join are, in the usual sense, *downward*.

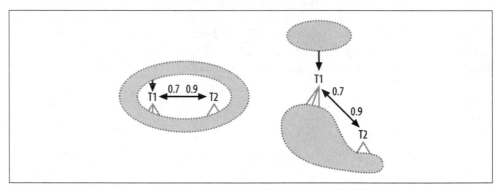

*Figure 7-20. Diagramming one-to-one joins lying under a root detail table*

For this case, in which both joined tables are below the root, keep in mind that if the one-to-one tables actually share a common primary key, then the link from above into T1 could probably just as easily be to T2, by transitivity, unless it is to some alternate unique key on T1 not shared by T2. This is the implied cyclic-join case illustrated with form B in Figure 7-2.

Figure 7-21 illustrates alternate diagrams for one-to-one joins of tables that both qualify as root detail tables (i.e., they have no joins from above), where at least one of the directions of the one-to-one join shows a master join ratio less than 1.0. Again, you can emphasize the one-to-one link with a horizontal layout, or you can emphasize which table is larger (and which direction of the join is "more downhill") by placing the node with the larger master join ratio higher. The node with the larger master join ratio represents a table with more rows in this [zero or one]-to-[zero or one] join.

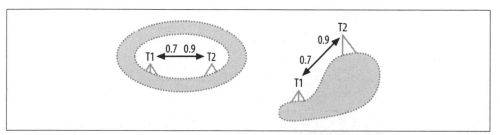

*Figure 7-21. Alternate diagram methods for [zero or one]-to-[zero or one] root detail tables*

Figure 7-22 illustrates a case similar to Figure 7-21, but with nodes that are perfectly one-to-one (tables that always join successfully). Again, you can emphasize the equal nature of the join directions by laying the nodes out horizontally. Alternatively, you can just choose a direction that makes a more balanced-looking tree, which fits better on the page, placing the node with deeper branches at the top. The choice in this case matters least, as long as you remember that both join directions are virtually downhill, regardless of how you lay out the diagram.

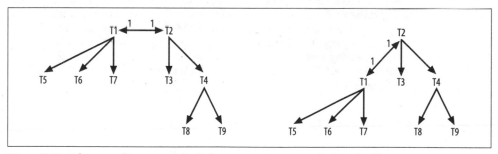

*Figure 7-22. Alternate diagram methods for exact one-to-one root detail tables*

## Outer Joins

Almost always, the sense and purpose of an outer join is that it prevents loss of desired information from the joined-from table, regardless of the contents of the outer-joined table. *Abnormal* outer joins, which I describe in the following sections, generally imply some contradiction of this reason behind the outer join.

## Filtered outer joins

Consider Figure 7-23, with an outer join to a table with a filter condition. In the outer case, the case where a T1 row has no matching T2 row, the database assigns null to every T2 column in the result. Therefore, except for T2.SomeColumn IS NULL, almost any filtering condition on T2 would specifically exclude a result row that comes from the outer case of the outer join.

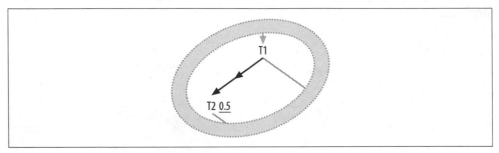

*Figure 7-23. Outer join to a filtered node*

Even conditions such as T2.Unpaid_Flag != 'Y' or NOT T2.Unpaid_Flag = 'Y', which you might expect to be true for the outer case, are not.

 Databases interpret nulls in a nonintuitive way, when it comes to conditions in the WHERE clause. If you think of the null as representing "unknown" with regard to a column of table, rather than the much more common "does-not-apply," you can begin to understand how databases treat nulls in conditions. Except for questions specifically about whether the column is null, almost anything you can ask about an unknown returns the answer "unknown," which is in fact the *truth value* of most conditions on nulls. From the perspective of rejecting rows for a query, the database treats the truth value "unknown" like FALSE, rejecting rows with unknown truth values in the WHERE clause. And, while NOT FALSE = TRUE, you'll find that NOT "unknown" = "unknown"!

Since most filters on the outer table discard the outer case of an outer join, and since the whole purpose of an outer join is to preserve such cases, you need to give careful attention to any filter on an outer table. One of the following scenarios applies, and you should take the time to determine which:

- The filter is one of the rare filters, such as SomeColumn IS NULL, that can return TRUE for null column values inserted in the outer case, and the filter is functionally correct.
- The developer did not intend to reject the outer case, and the filter condition must be removed.

- The filter condition was meant to reject the outer case, and the join might as well be an inner join. When this is the case, there is no functional difference between the query with the join expressed as an outer or as an inner join. However, by expressing it formally as an inner join, you give the database more degrees of freedom to create execution plans that might perform this join in either direction. When the best filter is on the same side of the join as the formerly-outer-joined table, the added degrees of freedom might enable a better execution plan. On the other hand, converting the join to an inner join might just enable the optimizer to make a mistake it would have avoided with an outer join. Outer joins are one way to constrain join orders when you consciously wish to do so, even when you do not need to preserve the outer case.

- The filter condition was intended, but it should be part of the join! With the filter condition made part of the join, you order the database: "For each detail-table row, provide the matching row from this table that fits this filter, if any; otherwise, match with an all-null pseudorow."

---

### Single-Table Outer Join Conditions

In the old-style Oracle notation, you make the filter condition part of the join by adding (+). For example, a two-part outer join to the Code_Translations table used in earlier examples would look like this:

```
WHERE ...
    AND O.Order_Type_Code=OTypeTrans.Code(+)
    AND OTypeTrans.Type(+)='ORDER_TYPE'
```

In the newer-style ANSI join notation, which is the only outer join notation allowed in DB2, the filter condition migrates into the FROM clause to become an explicit join condition:

```
FROM ... Orders O ...
LEFT OUTER JOIN Code_Translations OTypeTrans
        ON O.Order_Type_Code=OTypeTrans.Code
        AND OTypeTrans.Type='ORDER_TYPE'
```

In the original outer-join notation on SQL Server, the database simply *assumes* that the filter condition is part of the join:

```
WHERE ...
    AND O.Order_Type_Code*=OTypeTrans.Code
    AND OTypeTrans.Type='ORDER_TYPE'
```

Note that this makes the problem just discussed impossible for old-style SQL Server outer joins; the database has made the filter part of the join automatically. Also note that in the rare case in which the filter is truly a filter, you must either convert to a new-style outer join to get the desired result, or convert the join into an equivalent NOT EXISTS subquery, as I explain next.

---

Let's consider the first scenario in further depth. Consider the query:

```
SELECT ...
FROM Employees E
     LEFT OUTER JOIN Departments D
                 ON E.Department_ID=D.Department_ID
WHERE D.Dept_Manager_ID IS NULL
```

What is the query really asking the database in this case? Semantically, this requests two rather distinct rowsets: all employees that have no department at all and all employees that have leaderless departments. It is possible that the application actually calls for just two such distinct rowsets at once, but it is more likely that the developer did not notice that such a simple query had such a complex result, and did not intend to request one of those rowsets.

Consider a slightly different example:

```
SELECT ... FROM Employees E
         LEFT OUTER JOIN Departments D
                     ON E.Department_ID=D.Department_ID
WHERE D.Department_ID IS NULL
```

On the surface, this might seem to be a bizarre query, because the primary key (Department_ID) of Departments cannot be null. Even if the primary key could be null, such a null key value could never successfully join to another table with a join like this (because the conditional expression NULL = NULL returns the truth value "unknown"). However, since this is an outer join, there is a reasonable interpretation of this query: "Find the employees that fail to have matching departments." In the outer case of these outer joins, every column of Departments, including even mandatory nonnull columns, is replaced by a null, so the condition D.Department_ID IS NULL is true only in the outer case. There is a much more common and easier-to-read way to express this query:

```
SELECT ...
FROM Employees E
WHERE NOT EXISTS (SELECT *
                  FROM Departments D
                  WHERE E.Department_ID=D.Department_ID)
```

Although the NOT EXISTS form of this sort of query is more natural and easier to read and understand, the other form (preferably commented carefully with explanation) has its place in SQL tuning. The advantage of expressing the NOT EXISTS condition as an outer join followed by PrimaryKey IS NULL is that it allows more precise control of when in the execution plan the join happens and when you pick up the selectivity of that condition. Usually, NOT EXISTS conditions evaluate after all ordinary joins, at least on Oracle. This is the one example in which a filter (that is not part of the outer join) on an outer-joined table is really likely to have been deliberate and correct.

In the older-style SQL Server outer-join notation, the combination of outer join and is-null condition does not work. For example, adapting the example to SQL Server's notation, you might try this:

```
SELECT ...
FROM Employees E, Departments D
WHERE E.Department_ID*=D.Department_ID
  AND D.Department_ID IS NULL
```

However, the result will not be what you wanted! Recall that SQL Server interprets all filter conditions on the outer-joined table as part of the join. SQL Server will attempt to join to Departments that have null primary keys (i.e., null values of D.Department_ID). Even if such rows exist in violation of correct database design, they can never successfully join to Employees, because the equality join cannot succeed for null key values. Instead, the query will filter no rows, returning all employees, with all joins falling into the outer case.

## Outer joins leading to inner joins

Consider Figure 7-24, in which an outer join leads to an inner join.

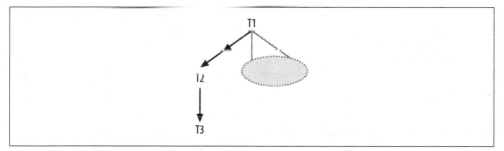

*Figure 7-24. An outer join leading to an inner join*

In old-style Oracle SQL, you express such a join as follows:

```
SELECT ...
FROM Table1 T1, Table2 T2, Table3 T3
WHERE T1.FKey2=T2.PKey2(+)
  AND T2.FKey3=T3.PKey3
```

In the outer case for the first join, the database will generate a pseudorow of T2 with all null column values, including the value of T2.FKey3. However, a null foreign key can never successfully join to another table, so that row representing the outer case will be discarded when the database attempts the inner join to T3. Therefore, the result of an outer join leading to an inner join is precisely the same result you would get with both joins being inner joins, but the result is more expensive, since the database discards the rows that fail to join later in the execution plan. This is always a mistake. If the intent is to keep the outer case, then replace the outer join to an inner join with an outer join leading to another outer join. Otherwise, use an inner join leading to an inner join.

## Outer joins pointing toward the detail table

Consider Figure 7-25, in which the midlink arrow shows the outer join that points toward the detail table.

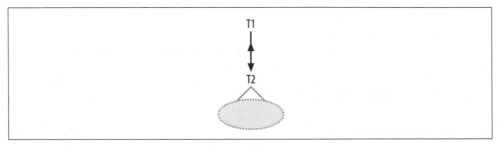

*Figure 7-25. An outer join toward a detail table*

In the new-style ANSI join notation, this might look like this:

```
SELECT ...
FROM Departments D
     LEFT OUTER JOIN Employees E
                ON D.Department_ID=E.Department_ID
```

Or, in older Oracle notation:

```
SELECT ...
FROM Departments D, Employees E
WHERE D.Department_ID=E.Department_ID(+)
```

Or, in older SQL Server notation:

```
SELECT ...
FROM Departments D, Employees E
WHERE D.Department_ID*=E.Department_ID
```

In any of these, what does this query semantically ask? It asks something like: "Give me all the employees that have departments (the inner case), together with their department data, and also include data for departments that don't happen to have employees (the outer case)." In the inner case, the result maps each row to a detail entity (an employee who belongs to a department), while in the outer case, the result maps each row to a master entity (a department that belongs to no employee). It is unlikely that such an incongruous mixture of entities would be useful and needed from a single query, so queries like this, with outer joins to detail tables, are rarely correct. The most common case of this mistake is a join to a detail table that usually offers zero or one detail per master, and that is only rarely many-to-one to the master table. Developers sometimes miss the implications of the rare many-to-one case, and it might not come up in testing.

## Outer joins to a detail table with a filter

Figure 7-26 shows an outer join to a detail table that also has a filter condition. Occasionally, two wrongs do make a right. An outer join to a detail table that also has a filter might be doubly broken, suffering from the problems described in the last two subsections. Sometimes, the filter cancels the effect of the problematic outer join, converting it functionally to an inner join. In such cases, you need to avoid removing the filter unless you also make the outer join inner.

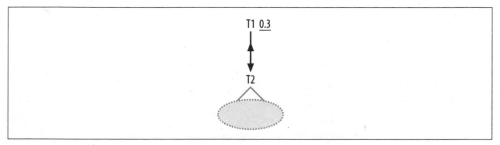

*Figure 7-26. An outer join to a filtered detail table*

The most interesting case Figure 7-26 can illustrate is the case in which the filter makes sense only in the context of the outer join. This is the case in which the filter condition on T1 is true only in the outer case—for example, T1.Fkey_ID IS NULL. (Here, T1.Fkey.ID is the foreign key pointing to T2.PKey_ID in the diagrammed join.) Like the earlier example of a join-key-value IS NULL condition (on the primary key, in the earlier case), this case is equivalent to a NOT EXISTS subquery. As in the earlier example, this unusual alternative expression for the NOT EXISTS condition sometimes offers a useful additional degree of control over when in the execution plan the database performs the join and discards the rows that do not meet the condition. Since all inner-joined rows are discarded by the IS NULL condition, it avoids the usual problem of outer joins to a detail table: the mixing of distinct entities behind rows from the inner and the outer cases of the join. Two wrongs make a right!

# Queries with Subqueries

Almost all real-world queries with subqueries impose a special kind of condition on the rows in the outer, main query; they must match or not match corresponding rows in a related query. For example, if you need data about departments that have employees, you might query:

```
SELECT ...
FROM Departments D
WHERE EXISTS (SELECT NULL
              FROM Employees E
              WHERE E.Department_ID=D.Department_ID)
```

Alternatively, you might query for data about departments that do not have employees:

```
SELECT ... FROM Departments D
WHERE NOT EXISTS (SELECT NULL
                      FROM Employees E
                      WHERE E.Department_ID=D.Department_ID)
```

The join E.Department_ID=D.Department_ID in each of these queries is the correlation join, which matches between tables in the outer query and the subquery. The EXISTS query has an alternate, equivalent form:

```
SELECT ...
FROM Departments D
WHERE D.Department_ID IN (SELECT E.Department_ID FROM Employees E)
```

Since these forms are functionally equivalent, and since the diagram should not convey a preconceived bias toward one form or another, both forms result in the same diagram. Only after evaluating the diagram to solve the tuning problem should you choose which form best solves the tuning problem and expresses the intended path to the data.

## Diagramming Queries with Subqueries

Ignoring the join that links the outer query with the subquery, you can already produce separate, independent query diagrams for each of the two queries. The only open question is how you should represent the relationship between these two diagrams, combining them into a single diagram. As the EXISTS form of the earlier query makes clear, the outer query links to the subquery through a join: the correlation join. This join has a special property: for each outer-query row, the first time the database succeeds in finding a match across the join, it stops looking for more matches, considers the EXISTS condition satisfied, and passes the outer-query row to the next step in the execution plan. When it finds a match for a NOT EXISTS correlated subquery, it stops with the NOT EXISTS condition that failed and immediately discards the outer-query row, without doing further work on that row. All this behavior suggests that a query diagram should answer four special questions about a correlation join, questions that do not apply to ordinary joins:

- Is it an ordinary join? (No, it is a correlation join to a subquery.)
- Which side of the join is the subquery, and which side is the outer query?
- Is it expressible as an EXISTS or as a NOT EXISTS query?
- How early in the execution plan should you execute the subquery?

When working with subqueries and considering these questions, remember that you still need to convey the properties you convey for any join: which end is the master table and how large are the join ratios.

## Diagramming EXISTS subqueries

Figure 7-27 shows my convention for diagramming a query with an EXISTS-type subquery (which might be expressed by the equivalent IN subquery). The figure is based on the earlier EXISTS subquery:

```
SELECT ... FROM Departments D
WHERE EXISTS (SELECT NULL
              FROM Employees E
              WHERE E.Department_ID=D.Department_ID)
```

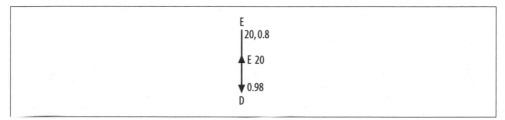

*Figure 7-27. A simple query with a subquery*

For the *correlation join* (known as a *semi-join* when applied to an EXISTS-type subquery) from Departments to Employees, the diagram begins with the same join statistics shown for Figure 5-1.

Like any join, the semi-join that links the inner query to the outer query is a link with an arrowhead on any end of the join that points toward a primary key. Like any join link, it has join ratios on each end, which represent the same statistical properties the same join would have in an ordinary query. I use a midpoint arrow to point from the outer-query correlated node to the subquery correlated node. I place an E beside the midpoint arrow to show that this is a semi-join for an EXISTS or IN subquery.

In this case, as in many cases with subqueries, the subquery part of the diagram is a single node, representing a subquery without joins of its own. Less frequently, also as in this case, the outer query is a single node, representing an outer query with no joins of its own. The syntax is essentially unlimited, with the potential for multiple subqueries linked to the outer query, for subqueries with complex join skeletons of their own, and even for subqueries that point to more deeply nested subqueries of their own.

The semi-join link also requires up to two new numbers to convey properties of the subquery for purposes of choosing the best plan. Figure 7-27 shows both potential extra values that you sometimes need to choose the optimum plan for handling a subquery.

The first value, next to the E (20 in Figure 7-27) is the *correlation preference ratio*. The correlation preference ratio is the ratio of $I/E$. $E$ is the estimated or measured runtime of the best plan that drives from the outer query to the subquery (following EXISTS logic). $I$ is the estimated or measured runtime of the best plan that drives from the inner query to the outer query (following IN logic). You can always measure this ratio directly by timing both forms, and doing so is usually not much trouble, unless you have many subqueries combined. Soon I will explain some rules of thumb to estimate *I/E* more or less accurately, and even a rough estimate is adequate to choose a plan when, as is common, the value is either much less than 1.0 or much greater than 1.0. When the correlation preference ratio is greater than 1.0, choose a correlated subquery with an EXISTS condition and a plan that drives from the outer query to the subquery.

The other new value is the *subquery adjusted filter ratio* (0.8 in Figure 7-27), next to the detail join ratio. This is an estimated value that helps you choose the best point in the join order to test the subquery condition. This applies only to queries that should begin with the outer query, so exclude it from any semi-join link (with a correlation preference ratio less than 1.0) that you convert to the driving query in the plan.

 If you have more than one semi-join with a correlation preference ratio less than 1.0, you will drive from the subquery with the lowest correlation preference ratio, and you still need adjusted filter ratios for the other subqueries.

Before I explain how to calculate the correlation preference ratio and the subquery adjusted filter ratios, let's consider when you even need them. Figure 7-28 shows a partial query diagram for an EXISTS-type subquery, with the root detail table of the subquery on the primary-key end of the semi-join.

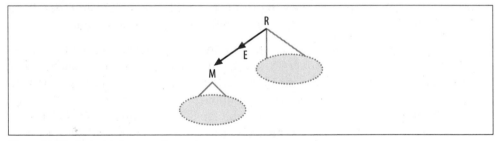

*Figure 7-28. A semi-join to a primary key*

Here, the semi-join is functionally no different than an ordinary join, because the query will never find more than a single match from table M for any given row from the outer query.

 I assume here that the whole subtree under M is *normal-form* (i.e., with all join links pointing downward toward primary keys), so the whole subquery maps one-to-one with rows from the root detail table M of the subtree.

Since the semi-join is functionally no different than an ordinary join, you can actually buy greater degrees of freedom in the execution plan by explicitly eliminating the EXISTS condition and merging the subquery into the outer query. For example, consider this query:

```
SELECT <Columns from outer query only>
FROM Order_Details OD, Products P, Shipments S,
    Addresses A, Code_Translations ODT
WHERE OD.Product_ID = P.Product_ID
  AND P.Unit_Cost > 100
  AND OD.Shipment_ID = S.Shipment_ID
  AND S.Address_ID = A.Address_ID(+)
  AND OD.Status_Code = ODT.Code
  AND ODT.Code_Type = 'Order_Detail_Status'
  AND S.Shipment_Date > :now - 1
  AND EXISTS (SELECT null
              FROM Orders O, Customers C, Code_Translations OT,
                  Customer_Types CT
              WHERE C.Customer_Type_ID = CT.Customer_Type_ID
                AND CT.Text = 'Government'
                AND OD.Order_ID = O.Order_ID
                AND O.Customer_ID = C.Customer_ID
                AND O.Status_Code = OT.Code
                AND O.Completed_Flag = 'N'
                AND OT.Code_Type = 'ORDER_STATUS'
                AND OT.Text != 'Canceled')
ORDER BY <Columns from outer query only>
```

Using the new semi-join notation, you can diagram this as shown in Figure 7-29.

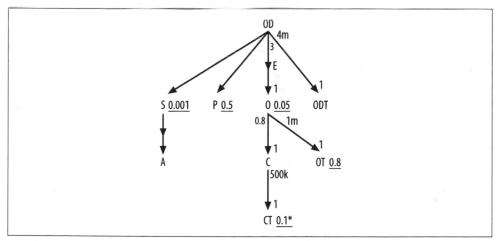

Figure 7-29. A complex example of a semi-join with a correlation to the primary key of the subquery root detail table

If you simply rewrite this query to move the table joins and conditions in the subquery into the outer query, you have a functionally identical query, since the semi-join is toward the primary key and the subquery is one-to-one with its root detail table:

```
SELECT <Columns from the original outer query only>
FROM Order_Details OD, Products P, Shipments S,
     Addresses A, Code_Translations ODT,
     Orders O, Customers C, Code_Translations OT, Customer_Types CT
WHERE OD.Product_Id = P.Product_Id
  AND P.Unit_Cost > 100
  AND OD.Shipment_Id = S.Shipment_Id
  AND S.Address_Id = A.Address_Id(+)
  AND OD.Status_Code = ODT.Code
  AND ODT.Code_Type = 'Order_Detail_Status'
  AND S.Shipment_Date > :now - 1
                AND C.Customer_Type_Id = CT.Customer_Type_Id
                AND CT.Text = 'Government'
                AND OD.Order_Id = O.Order_Id
                AND O.Customer_Id = C.Customer_Id
                AND O.Status_Code = OT.Code
                AND O.Completed_Flag = 'N'
                AND OT.Code_Type = 'ORDER_STATUS'
                AND OT.Text != 'Canceled'
ORDER BY <Columns from the original outer query only>
```

I have indented this version to make obvious the simple transformation from one to the other in this case. The query diagram is also almost identical, as shown in Figure 7-30.

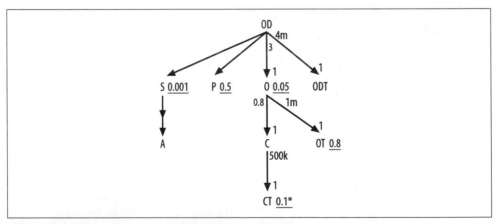

*Figure 7-30. The same query transformed to merge the subquery*

This new form has major additional degrees of freedom, allowing, for example, a plan joining to moderately filtered P after joining to highly filtered O but before joining to the almost unfiltered node OT. With the original form, the database would be forced to complete the whole subquery branch before it could consider joins to further nodes of the outer query. Since merging the subquery in cases like this can only help, and since this creates a query diagram you already know how to optimize, I will assume for the rest of this section that you will merge this type of subquery. I will only explain diagramming and optimizing other types.

In theory, you can adapt the same trick for merging EXISTS-type subqueries with the semi-join arrow pointing to the detail end of the join too, but it is harder and less likely to help the query performance. Consider the earlier query against departments with the EXISTS condition on Employees:

```
SELECT ...
FROM Departments D
WHERE EXISTS (SELECT NULL
              FROM Employees E
              WHERE E.Department_ID=D.Department_ID)
```

These are the problems with the trick in this direction:

- The original query returns at most one row per master table row per department. To get the same result from the transformed query, with an ordinary join to the detail table (Employees), you must include a unique key of the master table in the SELECT list and perform a DISTINCT operation on the resulting query rows. These steps discard duplicates that result when the same master record has multiple matching details.

- When there are several matching details per master row, it is often more expensive to find all the matches than to halt a semi-join after finding just the first match.

Therefore, you should rarely transform semi-joins to ordinary joins when the semi-join arrow points upward, except when the detail join ratio for the semi-join is near 1.0 or even less than 1.0.

To complete a diagram for an EXISTS-type subquery, you just need rules to estimate the correlation preference ratio and the subquery adjusted filter ratio. Use the following procedure to estimate the correlation preference ratio:

1. For the semi-join, let $D$ be the detail join ratio, and let $M$ be the master join ratio. Let $S$ be the best (smallest) filter ratio of all the nodes in the subquery, and let $R$ be the best (smallest) filter ratio of all the nodes in the outer query.

2. If $D \times S < M \times R$, set the correlation preference ratio to $(D \times S)/(M \times R)$.

3. Otherwise, if $S > R$, set the correlation preference ratio to $S/R$.

4. Otherwise, let $E$ be the measured runtime of the best plan that drives from the outer query to the subquery (following EXISTS logic). Let $I$ be the measured runtime of the best plan that drives from the inner query to the outer query (following IN logic). Set the correlation preference ratio to $I/E$. When Steps 2 or 3 find an estimate for the correlation preference ratio, you are fairly safe knowing which direction to drive the subquery without measuring actual runtimes.

The estimated value from Step 2 or Step 3 might not give the accurate runtime ratio you could measure. However, the estimate is adequate as long as it is conservative, avoiding a value that leads to an incorrect choice between driving from the outer query or the subquery. The rules in Steps 2 and 3 are specifically designed for cases in which such safe, conservative estimates are feasible.

When Steps 2 and 3 fail to produce an estimate, the safest and easiest value to use is what you actually measure. In this range, which you will rarely encounter, finding a safe calculated value would be more complex than is worth the trouble.

Once you have found the correlation preference ratio, check whether you need the subquery adjusted filter ratio and determine the subquery adjusted filter ratio when you need it:

1. If the correlation preference ratio is less than 1.0 and less than all other correlation preference ratios (in the event that you have multiple subqueries), stop. In this case, you do not need a subquery preference ratio, because it is helpful only when you're determining when you will drive from the outer query, which will not be your choice.

2. If the subquery is a single-table query with no filter condition, just the correlating join condition, measure $q$ (the rowcount with of the outer query with the subquery condition removed) and $t$ (the rowcount of the full query, including the subquery). Set the subquery adjusted filter ratio to $t/q$. (In this case, the EXISTS condition is particularly easy to check: the database just looks for the first match in the join index.)

3. Otherwise, for the semi-join, let $D$ be the detail join ratio. Let $s$ be the filter ratio of the correlating node (i.e., the node attached to the semi-join link) on the detail, subquery end.

4. If $D \leq 1$, set the subquery adjusted filter ratio equal to $s \times D$.

5. Otherwise, if $s \times D < 1$, set the subquery adjusted filter ratio equal to $(D-1+(s \times D))/D$.

6. Otherwise, set the subquery adjusted filter ratio equal to 0.99. Even the poorest-filtering EXISTS condition will avoid actually multiplying rows and will offer a better filtering power per unit cost than a downward join with no filter at all. This last rule covers these better-than-nothing (but not much better) cases.

Like other rules in this book, the rules for calculating the correlation preference ratio and the subquery adjusted filter ratio are heuristic. Because exact numbers are rarely necessary to choose the right execution plan, this carefully designed, robust heuristic leads to exactly the right decision at least 90% of the time and almost never leads to significantly suboptimal choices. As with many other parts of this book, a perfect calculation for a complex query would be well beyond the scope of a manual tuning method.

Try to see if you understand the rules to fill in the correlation preference ratio and the subquery adjusted filter ratio by completing Figure 7-31, which is missing these two numbers.

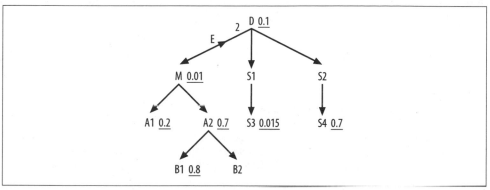

Figure 7-31. A complex query with missing values for the semi-join

Check your own work against this explanation. Calculate the correlation preference ratio:

1. Set $D=2$ and $M=1$ (implied by its absence from the diagram). Set $S=0.015$ (the best filter ratio of all those in the subquery, on the table S3, which is two levels below the subquery root detail table D). Then set $R=0.01$, which is the best filter for any node in the tree under and including the outer-query's root detail table M.

2. Find $D \times S = 0.03$ and $M \times R = 0.01$, so $D \times S > M \times R$. Move on to Step 3.

3. Since $S > R$, set the correlation preference ratio to $S/R$, which works out to 1.5.

To find the subquery adjusted filter ratio, follow these steps:

1. Note that the correlation preference ratio is greater than 1, so you must proceed to Step 2.

2. Note that the subquery involves multiple tables and contains filters, so proceed to Step 3.

3. Find $D=2$, and find the filter ratio on node D, $s=0.1$.

4. Note that $D>1$, so proceed to Step 5.

5. Calculate $s \times D = 0.2$, which is less than 1, so you estimate the subquery adjusted filter ratio as $(D-1+(s \times D))/D = (2-1+(0.1 \times 2))/2 = 0.6$.

In the following section on optimizing EXISTS subqueries, I will illustrate optimizing the completed diagram, shown in Figure 7-32.

### Diagramming NOT EXISTS subqueries

Subquery conditions that you can express with NOT EXISTS or NOT IN are simpler than EXISTS-type subqueries in one respect: you cannot drive from the subquery outward to the outer query. This eliminates the need for the correlation preference ratio. The *E* that indicates an EXISTS-type subquery condition is replaced by an *N* to indicate a NOT EXISTS–type subquery condition, and the correlation join is known as an *anti-join* rather than a semi-join, since it searches for the case when the join to rows from the subquery finds no match.

It turns out that it is almost always best to express NOT EXISTS–type subquery conditions with NOT EXISTS, rather than with NOT IN. Consider the following template for a NOT IN subquery:

```
SELECT ...
FROM ... Outer_Anti_Joined_Table Outer
WHERE...
  AND Outer.Some_Key NOT IN (SELECT Inner.Some_Key
                             FROM ... Subquery_Anti_Joined_Table Inner WHERE
                             <Conditions_And_Joins_On_Subquery_Tables_Only>)
  ...
```

You can and should rephrase this in the equivalent NOT EXISTS form:

```
SELECT ...
FROM ... Outer_Anti_Joined_Table Outer
WHERE...
  AND Outer.Some_Key IS NOT NULL
  AND NOT EXISTS (SELECT null
                  FROM ... Subquery_Anti_Joined_Table Inner WHERE
                  <Conditions_And_Joins_On_Subquery_Tables_Only>
                  AND Outer.Some_Key = Inner.Some_Key)
```

 To convert NOT IN to NOT EXISTS without changing functionality, you need to add a not-null condition on the correlation join key in the outer table. This is because the NOT IN condition amounts to a series of not-equal-to conditions joined by OR, but a database does not evaluate NULL!=<SomeValue> as true, so the NOT IN form rejects all outer-query rows with null correlation join keys. This fact is not widely known, so it is possible that the actual intent of such a query's developer was to include, in the query result, these rows that the NOT IN form subtly excludes. When you convert forms, you have a good opportunity to look for and repair this likely bug.

Both EXISTS-type and NOT EXISTS–type subquery conditions stop looking for matches after they find the first match, if one exists. NOT EXISTS subquery conditions are potentially more helpful early in the execution plan, because when they stop early with a found match, they discard the matching row, rather than retain it, making later steps in the plan faster. In contrast, to discard a row with an EXISTS condition, the database must examine every potentially matching row and rule them all out, a more expensive operation when there are many details per master across the semi-join. Remember the following rules, which compare EXISTS and NOT EXISTS conditions that point to detail tables from a master table in the outer query:

- An *unselective* EXISTS condition is inexpensive to check (since it finds a match easily, usually on the first semi-joined row it checks) but rejects few rows from the outer query. The more rows the subquery, isolated, would return, the less expensive and the less selective the EXISTS condition is to check. To be selective, an EXISTS condition will also likely be expensive to check, since it must rule out a match on every detail row.

- A *selective* NOT EXISTS condition is inexpensive to check (since it finds a match easily, usually on the first semi-joined row it checks) and rejects many rows from the outer query. The more rows the subquery, isolated, would return, the less expensive and the more selective the EXISTS condition is to check. On the other hand, unselective NOT EXISTS conditions are also expensive to check, since they must confirm that there is no match for every detail row.

Since it is generally both more difficult and less rewarding to convert NOT EXISTS subquery conditions to equivalent simple queries without subqueries, you will often use NOT EXISTS subqueries at either end of the anti-join: the master-table end or the detail-table end. You rarely need to search for alternate ways to express a NOT EXISTS condition.

Since selective NOT EXISTS conditions are inexpensive to check, it turns out to be fairly simple to estimate the subquery adjusted filter ratio:

1. Measure $q$ (the rowcount of the outer query with the NOT EXISTS subquery condition removed) and $t$ (the rowcount of the full query, including the subquery). Let $C$ be the number of tables in the subquery FROM clause (usually one, for NOT EXISTS conditions).

2. Set the subquery adjusted filter ratio to $(C-1+(t/q))/C$.

## Tuning Queries with Subqueries

As for simple queries, optimizing complex queries with subqueries turns out to be straightforward, once you have a correct query diagram. Here are the steps for optimizing complex queries, including subqueries, given a complete query diagram:

1. Convert any NOT IN condition into the equivalent NOT EXISTS condition, following the earlier template.

2. If the correlation join is an EXISTS-type join, and the subquery is on the master end of that join (i.e., the midpoint arrow points down), convert the complex query to a simple query as shown earlier, and tune it following the usual rules for simple queries.

3. Otherwise, if the correlation join is an EXISTS-type join, find the lowest correlation preference ratio of all the EXISTS-type subqueries (if there is more than one). If that lowest correlation preference ratio is less than 1.0, convert that subquery

condition to the equivalent IN condition and express any other EXISTS-type sub-query conditions using the EXISTS condition explicitly. Optimize the noncorre-lated IN subquery as if it were a standalone query; this is the beginning of the execution plan of the whole query. Upon completion of the noncorrelated sub-query, the database will perform a sort operation to discard duplicate correla-tion join keys from the list generated from the subquery. The next join after completing this first subquery is to the correlating key in the outer query, follow-ing the index on that join key, which should be indexed. From this point, treat the outer query as if the driving subquery did not exist and as if this first node were the driving table of the outer query.

4. If all correlation preference ratios are greater than or equal to 1.0, or if you have only NOT EXISTS–type subquery conditions, choose a driving table from the outer query as if that query had no subquery conditions, following the usual rules for simple queries.

5. As you reach nodes in the outer query that include semi-joins or anti-joins to not-yet-executed subqueries, treat each entire subquery as if it were a single, downward-hanging node (even if the correlation join is actually upward). Choose when to execute the remaining subqueries as if this virtual node had a filter ratio equal to the subquery adjusted filter ratio.

 Because correlated subqueries stop at the first row matched, if any, they avoid the row-multiplying risk of normal upward joins and can only reduce the running rowcount. However, since they must often examine many rows to have this filtering effect, the correct value of the subquery adjusted filter ratio often makes this virtual node equivalent to an almost unfiltered node in benefit/cost ratio.

6. Wherever you place the correlated join in the join order following Step 5, you then immediately perform the rest of that correlated subquery, optimizing the execution plan of that subquery with the correlating node as the driving node of that independent query. When finished with that subquery, return to the outer query and continue to optimize the rest of the join order.

As an example, consider Figure 7-32, which is Figure 7-31 with the correlation pref-erence ratio and the subquery adjusted filter ratio filled in.

Since the correlated join is EXISTS-type, Step 1 does not apply. Since the midpoint arrow of the semi-join points upward, Step 2 does not apply. The lowest (the only) correlation preference ratio is 1.5 (next to the *E*), so Step 3 does not apply. Applying Step 4, you find that the best driving node in the outer query is M. Applying Step 5, choose between downward joins to A1 and A2 with filter ratios of 0.2 and 0.7, respec-tively, or a virtual downward join to the virtual node representing the whole sub-query, with a virtual filter ratio of 0.6. A1 is the best of these three candidates, with

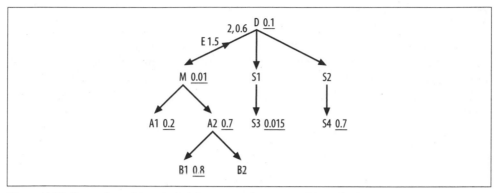

*Figure 7-32. Example problem optimizing a complex query with a subquery*

the best filter ratio, so join to it next. Finding nothing downstream of A1, you next find the subquery as the next-best choice in the join order (again applying Step 5), so perform the semi-join to D.

Applying Step 6, having begun the subquery, you must finish it, starting from D as the driving node. Following simple-query rules within that subquery, next join to S1, S3, S2, and S4, in that order. Returning to the outer query, applying the usual rules for simple queries, you find the remainder of the join order, A2, B1, B2. The whole optimum join order, including the semi-join, is then (M, A1, D, S1, S3, S2, S4, A2, B1, B2).

## Must You Worry About Subqueries?

The rules for subqueries are complex enough to be discouraging, so I'd like to offer a confession that might help your morale. For over 10 years, I've successfully tuned SQL with subqueries without using formal rules, following intuition and a general rule to choose between driving from the subquery or the outer query based on which had the most selective conditions. I don't usually worry much about when subqueries execute, except when they should actually drive the query, since this is usually hard to control and improvements versus the optimizers' automatic choices are usually minor.

I occasionally (less often than you might think, though) recognize borderline cases in which it makes sense to try multiple alternatives and choose the fastest. The same approach might work for you as well. If you mistrust intuition or want a basis for it that incorporates my own experience, you will find the formal rules useful. The formal rules of this section, which I worked out specifically for this book, handle the full range of realistic queries with a reasonable compromise between mathematical perfection and usability. Only massive brute-force calculation can handle the full complexity of the problem perfectly without trial and error, but these rules offer a sort of automated intuition, if you will, that is at least as good as my old seat-of-the-pants approach.

# Queries with Views

A view can make an arbitrarily complex query look like a simple table from the point of view of a person writing a query using the view. When multiple queries will share much underlying SQL, shared, reusable views can be a powerful mechanism to reduce complexity in application code. Unfortunately, simply hiding steps from the application developer does not reduce the underlying complexity of the steps to reach actual data. On the contrary, hiding complexity from the developer will more likely than not increase the difficulty of the tuning problem that the optimizer, whether automated or human, must overcome to find a fast execution plan. In this discussion, I refer to two types of queries important to the tuning problem:

*View-defining queries*

> These are the queries that underlie views (i.e., the queries used to create views with CREATE VIEW <*ViewName*> AS <*ViewDefiningQuery*>).

*View-using queries*

> These are queries you tune and that the database must actually execute. These queries reference views in their FROM clause (for example, SELECT ... FROM View1 V1, View2 V2,... WHERE ...).

> I am frequently asked to tune, or to estimate performance of, a view-defining query without having the list of view-using queries that use the defined view. I am also asked to tune view-using queries without knowing the view-defining query. Neither request is realistic: no view-defining query more complex than SELECT <*ListOfSimpleColumns*> FROM <*SingleTable*> will perform well in every possible view-using query, and no view-using query will perform well if the view-defining query interferes with an efficient path to the required data.
>
> For a given view, you must know and tune every view-using query to know that a view-defining query is completely correct in context. You must know the view-defining query of every view used to know that a view-using query is correct.

When you tune SQL, views tend to add complexity in three ways:

- You must translate a view-using query into an equivalent query against real tables to create and optimize a join diagram.

- Queries against views often contain unnecessary or redundant nodes in the query skeleton. Each view carries with it a whole view-defining query, complete with a subtree that includes all view-defining nodes and joins. Use of the view implies use of the entire subtree. However, the developer using the view often needs only a few of the view columns and could skip a number of the nodes and joins in the view-defining query if she wrote the equivalent query against simple tables. When the application requires all the nodes in the view, the view-using query still might be hitting those nodes redundantly, joining to the same rows of the same underlying tables in multiple hidden contexts. An example of this will follow in the section "Redundant reads in view-using queries."

- Sometimes, view-using queries cannot be expressed simply as equivalent queries against simple tables. Usually, the cases in which the view-using query returns different results from a simple table query are rare corner cases. However, the correct results in the corner cases are usually not the results the view-using query gets! When a view-using query does not decompose well into a simple, perfectly equivalent simple query against tables, performance almost always suffers, and the corner cases that define the view specific functional behavior are usually wrong. Nevertheless, to fix the performance with an almost equivalent simple query against tables does require at least a slight change in functionality, and you must exercise caution not to introduce a bug. (You will more often than not be fixing a bug, rather than creating one, but the new bugs will be noticed more!) An example of this will follow in the section "Outer joins to views."

## Diagramming View-Using Queries

Diagramming view-using queries is relatively straightforward, though sometimes tedious:

1. Create a diagram of each view-defining query as if it were a standalone query. Each query diagram that defines a view should be normal, in the sense that it has a single root detail table and has only downward-hanging many-to-one joins from that top node, in a tree structure. If a view-defining query does not map to a normal query skeleton, the queries that use the view will most likely perform badly and return incorrect results. Treat the primary key of the root detail table for the view-defining query as the virtual primary key of the whole view.

2. Create a query diagram of the view-using query as if each view were just a simple table. A join to a view should have an arrow on the view end (and you should place the view on the lower end of the link) only if the join is to the virtual primary key of the view. Show filter conditions on the view in the view-using query symbolically, as the letter $F$, without bothering to work out the filter ratio yet. Draw a dotted circle around each view node.

3. Expand the view-using query diagram of Step 2, replacing each node that represents a view with the entire view-defining query diagram from Step 1 with a dotted curve around the view-defining query subtree. Any join from above will attach to the view-defining subtree at its root detail node. Joins that reach downward from the view can attach to any node of the view, depending on which table of the view-defining query provided the foreign key (in the view-defining SELECT list) of the join. Any filter condition on the view becomes a filter condition on the appropriate node of the view-defining query, depending on which

node's column the filter condition restricts. Work out the actual filter ratio for each of these conditions in the usual way (expanding the symbolic *F* in the initial query diagram). As needed, combine filter ratios from the view-defining queries and from the view-using queries, when these two queries place distinct filters on the same nodes.

These rules probably strike you as abstract and complex, but an example should make the process much clearer. Consider these two view definitions:

```
CREATE VIEW Shipment_V AS
SELECT A.Address_ID Shipment_Address_ID, A.Street_Addr_Line1
       Shipment_Street_Address_Line1, A.Street_Addr_Line2
       Shipment_Street_Address_Line2, A.City_Name Shipment_City_Name,
       A.State_Abbreviation Shipment_State, A.ZIP_Code Shipment_ZIP,
       S.Shipment_Date, S.Shipment_ID
FROM Shipments S, Addresses A
WHERE S.Address_ID = A.Address_ID

CREATE VIEW Recent_Order_V AS
SELECT O.Order_ID, O.Order_Date, O.Customer_ID,
       C.Phone_Number Customer_Main_Phone, C.First_Name Customer_First_Name,
       C.Last_Name Customer_Last_Name,
       C.Address_ID Customer_Address_ID, OT.Text Order_Status
FROM Orders O, Customers C, Code_Translations OT
WHERE O.Customer_ID = C.Customer_ID
  AND O.Status_Code = OT.Code
  AND OT.Code_Type = 'ORDER_STATUS'
  AND O.Order_Date > SYSDATE - 366
```

Step 1 calls for query diagrams of these two view-defining queries, as shown in Figure 7-33. These query diagrams were created by following the method described in Chapter 5 and using the same filter ratio and join ratio statistics as for the related example shown in Figure 5-5.

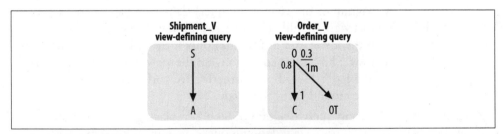

*Figure 7-33. Query diagrams for the example view-defining queries*

The view-using query, then, is:

```
SELECT OV.Customer_Main_Phone, C.Honorific, OV.Customer_First_Name,
       OV.Customer_Last_Name, C.Suffix, OV.Customer_Address_ID,
       SV.Shipment_Address_ID, SV.Shipment_Street_Address_Line1,
       SV.Shipment_Street_Address_Line2, SV.Shipment_City_Name,
       SV.Shipment_State, SV.Shipment_Zip, OD.Deferred_Shipment_Date,
       OD.Item_Count, ODT.Text, P.Product_Description, SV.Shipment_Date
```

```
    FROM Recent_Order_V OV, Order_Details OD, Products P, Shipment_V SV,
         Code_Translations ODT, Customers C
    WHERE UPPER(OV.Customer_Last_Name) LIKE :last_name||'%'
      AND UPPER(OV.Customer_First_Name) LIKE :first_name||'%'
      AND OD.Order_ID = OV.Order_ID
      AND OV.Customer_ID = C.Customer_ID
      AND OD.Product_ID = P.Product_ID(+)
      AND OD.Shipment_ID = SV.Shipment_ID(+)
      AND OD.Status_Code = ODT.Code
      AND ODT.Code_Type = 'ORDER_DETAIL_STATUS'
    ORDER BY OV.Customer_ID, OV.Order_ID Desc, SV.Shipment_ID, OD.Order_Detail_ID
```

Proceeding to Step 2, create the initial query diagram as if the views were simple tables, as shown in Figure 7-34.

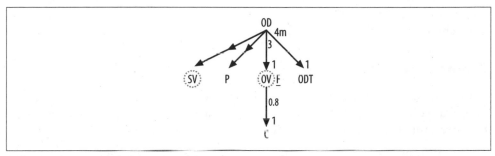

*Figure 7-34. Unexpanded diagram of the view-using query*

Replace each view node in Figure 7-34 with the earlier query diagrams for the view-defining queries in Figure 7-33, with each view-defining query skeleton surrounded by a dotted curve to show the boundaries of the view. Attach the view-defining query skeletons to the rest of the full query diagram at the appropriate table nodes, depending on which table in the view definition contains the joining key. Normally, any joins into the view from above will be to the root detail table of the view-defining query. However, master-table nodes that hang down from the view (for example, the node labeled C in Figure 7-34) can attach to any node of the view-defining skeleton, depending on which table contains the foreign key that points to that master node. Add explicit, numerical filter ratios to any nodes of the query skeleton that have filters either in the view-defining query or in the view-using query. In Figure 7-34, the filter ratio 0.3 next to node O comes from the filter in the view-defining query, while the filter ratio 0.0002 next to node C comes from the view-using query conditions on the customer's first and last names.

The result for the example should look like Figure 7-35, in which I have added an asterisk to the leftmost C node to clarify the distinction between the two otherwise identically labeled nodes. Again, I borrow the same statistics for the filter on customer name as in the similar example shown earlier in Figure 5-5, to arrive at the filter ratio of 0.0002 next to the C within the rightmost view skeleton.

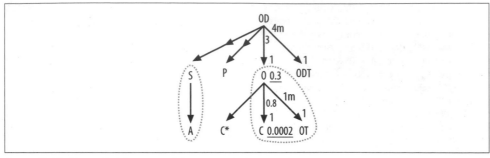

*Figure 7-35. Expanded diagram of the view-using query*

This completes the diagram you need to proceed to actual tuning of the view-using query, to determine whether either the view-defining query or the view-using query must change to enable the optimum plan.

## Tuning Queries with Views

Normally, the optimum execution plan for the view-using query is exactly the execution plan you would find for the corresponding query diagram against simple tables. However, there are four special problems you might have to resolve:

- Some joins to complex views are hard to express precisely as simple joins to simple tables. In particular, outer joins to views that have joins in the view-defining queries are complex to express with simple joins. This problem affects the example, and I will explain it in detail in the upcoming section "Outer joins to views."

- Some views reference precisely the same rows of the same table as another table in the view-using query, making redundant work for the database that you should eliminate. This happens for the nodes labeled C* and C in Figure 7-35, and I'll discuss this issue further too.

  The virtue of views, from the perspective of development simplicity, is hiding complexity, but this very virtue makes it all too easy to code redundant joins that would be obvious, and would actually require more work to code, if developers used only simple tables.

- Nodes within view-defining queries, and the joins to reach them, are often unnecessary to the required view-using query result.

- Using views limits your ability to fully control the execution plan. If you change a view-defining query to improve the execution plan of a view-using query, you might unintentionally harm performance of other queries that use the same view. You can always create a new view just for the use of a single query, but that defeats the code-sharing advantage of views. In general, SQL hints and other changes in the view-using query cannot control how the database accesses tables in the view-defining query. You sometimes must eliminate the use of views to get the execution plan you need.

## Outer joins to views

Returning to the earlier example, consider what it means to have an outer join to the view `Shipment_V`, which itself is an inner join between tables `Shipments` and `Addresses`. Since the database must behave as if there were a real table with precisely the rows the view would find, the join finds the inner case for `Shipment_ID`s that exist in `Shipments` and point to shipments that have an `Address_ID` that successfully joins to `Addresses`. When the database cannot successfully join to both `Shipments` and `Addresses`, the join to the view is entirely an outer join (to both tables), even if the initial join to `Shipments` could succeed. When searching for a nested-loops plan, the database cannot know whether the outer join finds the inner case until it joins successfully to both tables in the view-defining query.

Unfortunately, this is all too complex for most automated code to handle, so your database might simply give up on a nested-loops plan. Instead, the database code recognizes that no matter how complex the underlying logic might be, it cannot go wrong functionally if, in tricky cases like this, it gets every row from the view-defining query and treats the result like a real table. For the outer join to the view, the database normally performs a sort-merge join or a hash join to that temporarily created table. This is safe enough functionally, but it is usually a disaster for performance, unless the view-defining query is fast as a standalone query.

 As a general rule for performance, avoid outer joins into any view that is more complex than SELECT `<ListOfSimpleColumns>` FROM `<SingleTable>`.

Similar problems result for all sorts of joins into views that have UNIONs or GROUP BYs in the view-defining queries. However, joining *from* these views, when they contain the table you would choose as the driving table of the query, usually works fine.

Consider, again, the view-using query from the previous subsection. If you merge the view-defining query for `Shipment_V` into the view-using query, to resolve the performance problem with the outer join, you might expect this result:

```
SELECT OV.Customer_Main_Phone, C.Honorific, OV.Customer_First_Name,
       OV.Customer_Last_Name, C.Suffix, OV.Customer_Address_ID,
       A.Address_ID Shipment_Address_ID,
       A.Street_Addr_Line1 Shipment_Street_Address_Line1,
       A.Street_Addr_Line2 Shipment_Street_Address_Line2,
       A.City_Name Shipment_City_Name, A.State_Abbreviation Shipment_State,
       A.ZIP_Code Shipment_ZIP, OD.Deferred_Ship_Date, OD.Item_Count,
       ODT.Text, P.Prod_Description, S.Shipment_Date
FROM Recent_Order_V OV, Order_Details OD, Products P, Shipments S,
     Addresses A, Code_Translations ODT, Customers C
WHERE UPPER(OV.Customer_Last_Name) LIKE :last_name||'%'
  AND UPPER(OV.Customer_First_Name) LIKE :first_name||'%'
  AND OD.Order_ID = OV.Order_ID
  AND OV.Customer_ID = C.Customer_ID
```

```
      AND OD.Product_ID = P.Product_ID(+)
      AND OD.Shipment_ID = S.Shipment_ID(+)
      AND S.Address_ID = A.Address_ID(+)
      AND OD.Status_Code = ODT.Code
      AND ODT.Code_Type = 'ORDER_DETAIL_STATUS'
    ORDER BY OV.Customer_ID, OV.Order_ID Desc, S.Shipment_ID, OD.Order_Detail_ID
```

Unfortunately, this does not produce quite the same result as the original query, because of the peculiarity of the outer join to the view. Specifically, the original query returns a null Shipment_Date from the view whenever the entire view, including the join to Addresses, fails to join to Order_Details. Therefore, whenever the shipment does not have a valid, nonnull Address_ID, the original query returns null for Shipment_Date, even though the join to Shipments, by itself, is valid.

Almost certainly, this peculiar behavior is not what the developer intended and is not functionally necessary, so the form just shown will likely work fine, even better than the original in this corner case. However, any change in functionality, for a performance fix, is dangerous. Therefore, before making a change such as the one just described that merges the view-defining query into the main SQL statement, make certain the new corner-case behavior is correct and warn developers that the change might cause regression tests to return changed results. In the unlikely event that you really need the original behavior, or if you just want to play safe without investigating whether the original corner-case behavior was correct, you can perfectly emulate the original query functionality with this:

```
SELECT OV.Customer_Main_Phone, C.Honorific, OV.Customer_First_Name,
       OV.Customer_Last_Name, C.Suffix, OV.Customer_Address_ID,
       A.Address_ID Shipment_Address_ID,
       A.Street_Addr_Line1 Shipment_Street_Address_Line1,
       A.Street_Addr_Line2 Shipment_Street_Address_Line2,
       A.City_Name Shipment_City_Name, A.State_Abbreviation Shipment_State,
       A.ZIP_Code Shipment_ZIP, OD.Deferred_Ship_Date, OD.Item_Count,
       ODT.Text, P.Prod_Description,
       DECODE(A.Address_ID, NULL, TO_DATE(NULL),
                                 S.Shipment_Date) Shipment_Date
FROM Recent_Order_V OV, Order_Details OD, Products P, Shipments S,
     Addresses A, Code_Translations ODT, Customers C
WHERE UPPER(OV.Customer_Last_Name) LIKE :last_name||'%'
  AND UPPER(OV.Customer_First_Name) LIKE :first_name||'%'
  AND OD.Order_ID = OV.Order_ID
  AND OV.Customer_ID = C.Customer_ID
  AND OD.Product_ID = P.Product_ID(+)
  AND OD.Shipment_ID = S.Shipment_ID(+)
  AND S.Address_ID = A.Address_ID(+)
  AND OD.Status_Code = ODT.Code
  AND ODT.Code_Type = 'ORDER_DETAIL_STATUS'
ORDER BY OV.Customer_ID, OV.Order_ID Desc,
      DECODE(A.Address_ID, NULL, TO_NUMBER(NULL), S.Shipment_ID),
         OD.Order_Detail_ID
```

This query includes two changes that cause the query to return results as if the join to Shipments produced the outer case whenever the join to Addresses produced the outer case. Without the view, the query will treat the join to `Shipments` independently from the join to `Addresses`. However, the `DECODE` expressions in both the end of the `SELECT` list and the middle of the `ORDER BY` list cause the inner case of the first join to emulate the outer case of the join (producing `NULL` in place of `Shipment_Date` and `Shipment_ID`) whenever the join to `Addresses` finds the outer case.

Occasionally, you will have some functional need to use a view in place of simple tables. The most common reason for this is to work around limitations in autogenerated SQL. Functionally, you might require some bit of complex SQL syntax that the SQL generator cannot handle. The common workaround is to bury that complexity in a view-defining query that you create manually and have the SQL generator simply treat the view as if it were a simple table, hiding the complexity from the SQL-generator code. In these cases, you might not be able to eliminate use of a view, such as I suggest in the earlier solutions. Your alternate approach is to extend use of the view, burying more of the SQL in the view definition. For example, since the previous problem involved an outer join to a view, you could solve the problem by pulling the outer join into the view-defining query. With this solution, you would replace use of `Shipment_V` with `OrderDetail_V`, using this view-defining query:

```
CREATE VIEW Order_Detail_V AS
SELECT A.Address_ID Shipment_Address_ID,
       A.Street_Addr_Line1 Shipment_Street_Address_Line1,
       A.Street_Addr_Line2 Shipment_Street_Address_Line2,
       A.City_Name Shipment_City_Name, A.State_Abbreviation Shipment_State,
       A.ZIP_Code Shipment_ZIP,  S.Shipment_Date, S.Shipment_ID,
       OD.Deferred_Ship_Date, OD.Item_Count, OD.Order_ID,
       OD.Order_Detail_ID, OD.Product_ID, OD.Status_Code
FROM Shipments S, Addresses A, Order_Details OD
WHERE OD.Shipment_ID = S.Shipment_ID(+)
  AND S.Address_ID = A.Address_ID(+)
```

The view-using query, using the extended view, then becomes:

```
SELECT OV.Customer_Main_Phone, C.Honorific, OV.Customer_First_Name,
       OV.Customer_Last_Name, C.Suffix, OV.Customer_Address_ID,
       ODV.Shipment_Address_ID, ODV.Shipment_Street_Address_Line1,
       ODV.Shipment_Street_Address_Line2, ODV.Shipment_City_Name,
       ODV.Shipment_State, ODV.Shipment_Zip, ODV.Deferred_Ship_Date,
       ODV.Item_Count, ODT.Text, P.Prod_Description, ODV.Shipment_Date
FROM Recent_Order_V OV, Order_Detail_V ODV, Products P,
     Code_Translations ODT, Customers C
WHERE UPPER(OV.Customer_Last_Name) LIKE :last_name||'%'
  AND UPPER(OV.Customer_First_Name) LIKE :first_name||'%'
  AND ODV.Order_ID = OV.Order_ID
  AND OV.Customer_ID = C.Customer_ID
  AND ODV.Product_ID = P.Product_ID(+)
  AND ODV.Status_Code = ODT.Code
  AND ODT.Code_Type = 'ORDER_DETAIL_STATUS'
ORDER BY OV.Customer_ID, OV.Order_ID Desc, ODV.Shipment_ID, ODV.Order_Detail_ID
```

## Redundant reads in view-using queries

Now, consider the case of the joins in Figure 7-35 to nodes labeled C* and C. These nodes represent the same table, with identical join clauses, so any execution plan that hits both nodes is redundant, reading the same table rows and probably the same index entries twice. The second, redundant read in every case should avoid physical I/O, because the first read, likely less than a millisecond earlier, should place the table or index block safely at the head of the shared cache. If the execution plan is highly filtered before it reaches the second, redundant node, the excess logical I/Os might be negligible, but for large queries or queries that filter most rows only after such redundant reads, the costs of the extra logical I/Os are important.

If the developer wrote the query originally against simple tables, this sort of error would be unlikely; he would have to go out of his way to include the redundant join, and the redundancy would be obvious in code review. With views, however, these errors are easy to make and are well hidden.

How do you fix the redundant join to Customers? You have three options:

- Add new columns as needed to the SELECT list of the view-defining query and use them in place of the column references to the redundant table in the view-using query. This is safe for other queries that use the same view, since it only adds columns and does not change the view-defining query diagram.

- Eliminate the redundant join from the view-defining query and use only the columns from the simple table node in the view-using query. However, this is dangerous if there are other view-using queries that might require the view columns you eliminated.

- Eliminate the use of the view from the view-using query, replacing it with equivalent, nonredundant joins to simple tables.

## Unnecessary nodes and joins

Consider the join to node OT in the recent view-using query. The original view-defining query appears to include that join to support queries of the order status, but the view-using query does not even refer to the order status, so you might question whether this node is necessary. If you did not happen to notice the seemingly unused node, you could diagnose the unused node if you noticed a join, in the execution plan, to the primary-key index of this table with no read of the table itself. Such index-only reads of primary-key indexes usually point to unnecessary joins.

Safely eliminating these unnecessary joins is not simple, because they sometimes have functional side effects. Since this is an inner join, it is at least possible that, even with no filter on the node, the join itself eliminates rows the query should not return. This can result either by eliminating rows where Orders.Status_Code IS NULL or where Status_Code points to invalid status codes that fail to find a match in the

Code_Translations table. The latter possibility is unlikely or should be eliminated by repairing referential integrity. However, null foreign keys are common, and if the column can be null, you should consider adding an explicit Status_Code IS NOT NULL condition before eliminating the join, to emulate the implicit filtering function of the inner join. More likely, the developer using the view did not even think about the implicit filtering function of the view, and the implicit filter was entirely unintentional and undesirable. Therefore, before emulating the old behavior in a base-table-only query that eliminates the unneeded join, check whether the old behavior was even correct. If your change will subtly change behavior, even for the better, warn testers that regression test results might change for this corner case.

## Queries with Set Operations

Occasionally, you must tune multipart queries that use set operations like UNION, UNION ALL, INTERSECT, and EXCEPT to combine results of two or more simple queries. The extension of the SQL-diagramming tuning method to these multipart queries is usually straightforward: diagram and tune each part independently, as if it were a standalone query. When the parts are fast, combining the results with set operations generally works well.

 EXCEPT is the keyword specified by the ANSI SQL standard for the set operation to find the difference between two sets. DB2 and SQL Server follow the standard by supporting EXCEPT. Oracle, however, uses MINUS for the same operation, most likely because it supported the operation before the standard existed.

However, some of these set operations deserve a little extra discussion. The UNION operation, in addition to combining the parts, also must sort them and discard duplicates. This last step is often unnecessary, especially if you design the parts to avoid duplicates in the first place. In Oracle, you can replace the UNION operation with UNION ALL when you determine that duplicates are either impossible or need not be discarded. In databases that do not support UNION ALL, you can skip the duplicate-eliminating step by replacing the single UNION query with two or more simple queries, combining the results in the application layer, rather than in the database.

The INTERSECT operation can generally be profitably replaced with an EXISTS-type subquery that looks for the matching row that the second part would produce. For example, if you had two Employees tables, you might look for shared employee records with this:

```
SELECT Employee_ID FROM Employees1
INTERSECT
SELECT Employee_ID FROM Employees2
```

You could always replace this INTERSECT query with this:

```
SELECT DISTINCT Employee_ID
FROM Employees1 E1
WHERE EXISTS (SELECT null
              FROM Employees2 E2
              WHERE E1.Employee_ID=E2.Employee_ID)
```

Using the methods of the section "Queries with Views," you would then determine whether this EXISTS subquery should be expressed in the EXISTS or IN form, or converted to a simple join. Note that the correlating join conditions become numerous if the SELECT list contains many items. Also note that INTERSECT will match column lists with nulls, but a correlation join will not, unless you use join conditions designed for that purpose. For example, if the positive-valued foreign key Manager_ID is allowed to be null (but Employee_ID is not), the Oracle equivalent of this query:

```
SELECT Employee_ID, Manager_ID FROM Employees1
INTERSECT
SELECT Employee_ID, Manager_ID FROM Employees2
```

is this query:

```
SELECT DISTINCT Employee_ID, Manager_ID
FROM Employees1 E1
WHERE EXISTS (SELECT null
              FROM Employees2 E2
              WHERE E1.Employee_ID=E2.Employee_ID
              AND NVL(E1.Manager_ID,-1)=NVL(E2.Manager_ID,-1))
```

The expression NVL(...,-1) in the second correlation join condition converts null values on the nullable column so that they join successfully when null is matched with null.

The EXCEPT (or MINUS) operation can generally be profitably replaced with a NOT EXISTS–type subquery. Searching for employee records in the first table but not in the second table, you might have used this:

```
SELECT Employee_ID FROM Employees1
MINUS
SELECT Employee_ID FROM Employees2
```

You could always replace that with this:

```
SELECT DISTINCT Employee_ID
FROM Employees1 E1
WHERE NOT EXISTS (SELECT null
                  FROM Employees2 E2
                  WHERE E1.Employee_ID=E2.Employee_ID)
```

You would then solve this query using the methods described in the earlier section, "Queries with Subqueries."

# Exercise

Here is an unrealistically complex query to thoroughly test your understanding of tuning queries with subqueries. Figure 7-36 is a more complex and difficult query diagram than you will likely find in a year of intensive SQL tuning. If you can handle this, you will easily handle any subquery scenario you will ever find in real life, so give it a shot!

If you don't get it right the first time, come back and try again after more practice and review.

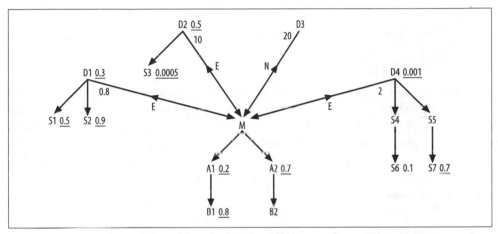

*Figure 7-36. A complex problem with multiple subqueries*

Fill in the missing ratios for the correlated joins. Assume that $t=5$ (the rowcount of the whole query, including the NOT EXISTS subquery), while $q=50$ (the rowcount of the query with the NOT EXISTS condition removed). Find the best join order, including all the tables in the subqueries and in the outer query.

# CHAPTER 8

# Why the Diagramming Method Works

*It is well to moor your bark with two anchors.*

—Publilius Syrus (a.k.a. Publius)
   *Maxim 119*

Chapters 5–7 covered how to tune SQL with the diagramming method but did not discuss why the method leads to well-tuned SQL. With a lot of faith and good memory, you could likely get by without knowing why the method works. However, even with unbounded, blind faith in the method, you will likely have to explain your SQL changes occasionally. Furthermore, the method is complex enough that an understanding of why it works will help you remember its details better than blind memorization ever could.

## The Case for Nested Loops

Throughout this book, I have asserted that nested-loops joins on the join keys offer more robust execution plans than hash or sort-merge joins. Let's examine why. Consider a two-table query diagram, as shown in Figure 8-1.

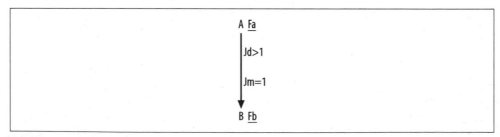

*Figure 8-1. A prototype two-table query*

Sight-unseen, it is possible to say a surprising amount about this query, to a high probability, if you already know that it is a functionally useful business query that has come to you for tuning:

228

- The top table, at least, is large or expected to grow large. Because $Jd$, the detail join ratio, is greater than 1.0 (as is usual), the bottom table is smaller than the top table by some factor, but that factor could be moderate or large. Queries that read only small tables are common enough, but they rarely become a tuning concern; the native optimizer produces fast execution plans without help when every table is small.

- Large tables are likely to grow larger with time. They usually became large in the first place through steady growth, and that growth rarely stops or slows down.

- The query should return a moderate number of rows, a small fraction of the number in the detail table. Certainly, queries can return large rowsets, but such queries are usually not useful to a real application, because end users cannot effectively use that much data at once. Online queries for a real application should generally return fewer than 100 rows, while even batch queries should usually return no more than a few thousand.

- While tables grow with time, the inability of end users to digest too much data does not change. This often means that the query conditions must point to an ever-decreasing fraction of the rows in the larger table. Usually, this is achieved by some condition that tends to point to recent data, since this tends to be more interesting from a business perspective. Although a table might contain an ever-lengthening history of a business's data, the set of recent data will grow much more slowly or not at all.

- The number of rows the query returns is $Ca \times Fa \times Fb$, where $Ca$ is the rowcount of table A.

These assertions lead to the conclusion that the product of the two filter ratios ($Fa \times Fb$) must be quite small and will likely grow smaller with time. Therefore, at least one of $Fa$ and $Fb$ must also be quite small. In practice, this is almost always achieved with one of the filter ratios being much smaller than the other; the smaller filter ratio is almost always the one that grows steadily smaller with time. Generally, the smallest of these filter ratios justifies indexed access in preference to a full table scan.

If the best (smallest) filter ratio is $Fb$ and it is low enough to justify indexed access to table B, then nested loops from B will generally point to the same fraction ($Fb$) of rows in table A. (A given fraction of master records will point to the same fraction of details.) This fraction will also be low enough to justify indexed access (through the foreign key, in this case) to table A, with lower cost than a full table scan. Since $Fb<Fa$ under this assumption, nested loops will minimize the number of rows touched and therefore minimize the number of physical and logical I/Os to table A, compared to an execution plan that drives directly through the index for the filter on A. Either a hash or a sort-merge join to table A would require a more expensive full table scan or index range scan on the less selective filter for table A. Since index blocks for the join are better cached than the large table A, they are inexpensive to read, by comparison to table blocks. Therefore, when the best filter ratio is $Fb$, nested loops minimize the cost of the read to table A.

When the best filter is on the detail table (table A, in this case), the same argument holds at the limit where $Jd=1$. When $Jd>1$, larger values of $Jd$ tend to favor hash joins. However, unless $Jd$ is quite large, this factor does not usually overcome the usually strong advantage of driving to every table from the most selective filter. When $Jd$ is large, this implies that the master table B is much smaller than the detail table A and will be consequently much better cached and less expensive to reach, regardless of the join method. I already discussed this case at length in the section "Cases to Consider Hash Joins" in Chapter 6, and I won't repeat it all here. The key point is that, even in the cases in which hash joins improve a given join cost the most, they usually reduce only a comparatively minor component of the query cost—the cost of reaching a much smaller, better-cached master table. To achieve even this small benefit, the database must place the joined-to rowset in memory or, worse, store the hashed set temporarily on disk.

# Choosing the Driving Table

The most important choice you make when putting together an execution plan is your choice of the driving table. You will rarely find a good execution plan without driving from the single best choice, and the best choice of driving table usually ensures at worst a pretty good plan, even if you pick the remainder of the join order quite haphazardly. I've stated that the rule for choosing the best driving table is simple: just drive from the table with the lowest filter ratio. Here, I make the case that such a simple rule almost always works and is really the only possible rule that is both simple and usually right.

The dilemma for all optimizers, human or otherwise, is how to choose the best driving table without iterating through every join order or even a significant fraction of the join orders. Any fast method for choosing the driving table must depend on *localized* information—information that does not reflect the entire complexity of the query. To demonstrate the reasoning behind the simple rule to drive from the table with the lowest filter ratio, I discuss a problem with deliberately hidden details, hiding the full complexity of the query. Consider the partially obscured query diagram of Figure 8-2.

What does such a diagram convey, even in the absence of the join links? Without the join links or join ratios, you can still say, with fair confidence:

- M is the root detail table, likely the largest and least-well-cached table in the query. Call the rowcount of this table C.
- A1, A2, and A3 are master tables that join directly to M.
- All the other tables are also master tables and appear to be joined indirectly to M, through intermediate joins.

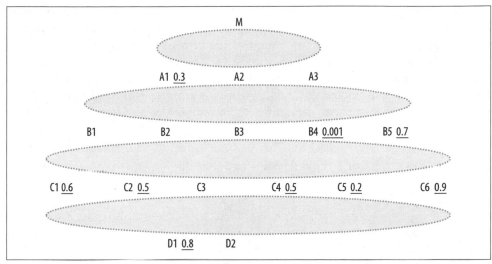

*Figure 8-2. A partially hidden query diagram*

Even with this sparse information, you can deduce a key property of the cost of reading that largest and least-well-cached root detail table M:

> The number of rows read from the root detail table will be no more than that table's rowcount (C) times the driving table's filter ratio.

For example, even if table B4 holds the only filter you can reach before you join to M, driving from B4 with nested loops ensures that you read just one-thousandth of the rows in M. Figure 8-3 illustrates this case.

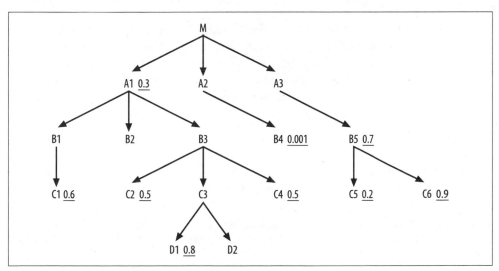

*Figure 8-3. The query diagram with possible join links uncovered*

Of course, if B4 connects directly to more nodes with filters before it must join to M, you can do even better. However, as long as you choose nested-loops joins, you know immediately that the upper bound of the cost of the read of the root detail table is $C \times Fd$, where $Fd$ is the filter ratio for the chosen driving table. This explains the driving-table rule, which chooses the node with the lowest filter factor as the driving table. To drive home this point, Figure 8-4 rearranges the links in Figure 8-3 to make a new diagram that maximizes the advantage of an alternative to driving from B4.

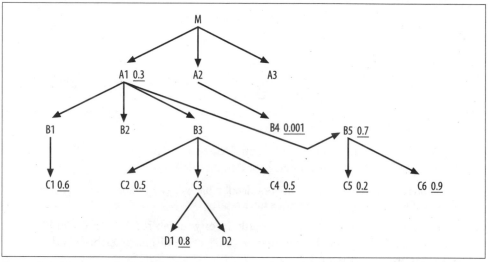

*Figure 8-4. The query diagram modified to minimize the disadvantage of driving from table A1*

Now, if you drive from A1 or any node connected below it, you can pick up every filter except the filter on B4 before reaching M. The result is that you reach a number of rows in M equal to $C \times 0.0045$ ($C \times 0.3 \times 0.7 \times 0.6 \times 0.5 \times 0.5 \times 0.2 \times 0.9 \times 0.8$), which is over four times worse than the cost of driving from B4. Furthermore, with a poor initial driving filter, the other early-table access costs will also likely be high, unless all those tables turn out to be small.

You might wonder whether this example is contrived to make the best driving filter look especially good, but the contrary is true: most real queries favor driving from the lowest filter ratio even more dramatically! Most queries have far fewer filters to combine, and those filters are more spread out across different branches under the root detail table than they are in this example. If you had two almost equally good filters, you could build a plausible-looking case for driving from the second-best filter if it had more near-neighbor nodes with helpful filters as well, such as in Figure 8-5.

In this contrived case, B3 would likely make a better driving node than B4, since B3 receives so much help from its neighboring nodes before you would join to M. This might sound like a plausible case, and I don't doubt it can occur, but empirically it is

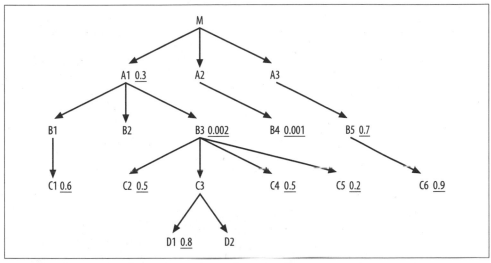

*Figure 8-5. A query diagram with competitive driving nodes*

rare. I haven't seen a case such as this in 10 years of tuning, mainly because it is so rare to find two very selective filters with roughly the same magnitude of selectivity in the same query. It is much more common that most of the selectivity of a query comes from a single highly selective condition.

## Choosing the Next Table to Join

After you choose the driving table, the rest of the decisions for a robust execution plan consist of a series of choices amounting to "What's next?" When you ask this question, you have, effectively, a single cloud of already-joined nodes that you chose earlier in the join order and a series of nodes linked to that cloud that are eligible for the next join. If the query diagram is a typical tree structure, at most one node will be upward from the current cloud, and any number of nodes can be reachable downward. Figure 8-6 illustrates this typical case.

Consider the question "What's next?" for this point in the join order. The database has reached some number of rows, which I will call $N$. Joins to tables downward of the current join cloud will multiply the running rowcount by some fraction: the filter ratio times the master join ratio. Let $F=R \times M$, where $R$ is the filter ratio and $M$ is the master join ratio (which is 1.0, unless shown otherwise). The larger the reduction in rows, which is $1-F$, the lower the cost of the future joins, so nodes with high values of $1-F$ have high value to optimizing the rest of the query, when joined early. That reduction in rowcount has a cost too, based on the cost per row driving into the join, which I will call $C$. The benefit-to-cost ratio of a downward join under consideration is then $(1-F)/C$. If you assume a uniform cost per row read for all tables downward of the already-joined nodes, choosing the downstream node with the maximum value of $(1-F)/C$ is the same as choosing the node with the minimum value of $F$.

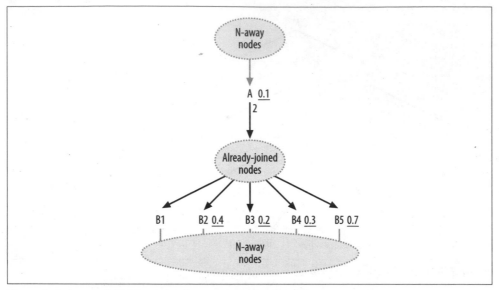

*Figure 8-6. A typical decision point during join-order optimization*

How could this optimization be refined further? There are three opportunities for improvements, all reflected in the "Special Rules for Special Cases" section in Chapter 6:

1. Not all downstream nodes have equal cost per row joined, so *C* really does vary between nodes.

2. The full payoff for a join is sometimes not immediate, but comes after joining to nodes further downstream made accessible through that intermediate join.

3. Sometimes, the upstream node actually offers the best benefit-to-cost ratio, even while downstream nodes remain.

I will discuss these improvement opportunities one at a time to illustrate how they create the special rules that occasionally override the simpler rules of thumb.

## Accounting for Unequal Per-Row Costs

Downstream nodes are nearly guaranteed to be smaller than the largest table already reached in the execution plan. As such, they are generally better cached and unlikely to have deeper indexes than the largest table already reached, so their impact on overall cost is typically minor. Even when the costs of reading downstream nodes vary considerably, the performance cost of assuming uniform costs for these nodes usually is minor compared to the overall costs of the query. Nevertheless, the possibility of significant join cost differences justifies the exception already mentioned in Chapter 6:

Prefer to drive to smaller tables earlier, in near-ties. After you choose the driving table, the true benefit-to-cost ratio of joining to the next master table is $(1-F)/C$. Smaller tables are better cached and tend to have fewer index levels, making $C$ smaller and making the benefit-to-cost ratio tend to be better for smaller tables.

## Accounting for Benefits from Later Joins

Occasionally, especially when nodes have no filter at all, the greatest benefit of a join is that it provides access to a further-downstream node that has a good filter. This gives rise to another exception described in Chapter 6:

> In the case of near-ties, prefer to drive to tables earlier that allow you to reach other tables with even better filter ratios sooner in the execution plan. The general objective is to discard as many rows as soon in the execution plan as possible. Good (low) filter ratios achieve this well at each step, but you might need to look ahead a bit to nearby filters to see the full benefit of reaching a given node sooner.

A perfect account of these distributed effects of filters spread across nodes is beyond the scope of this book and beyond any optimization method meant for manual implementation. Fortunately, this limitation turns out to be minor; I have never seen a case when such a perfect account was necessary. Almost always, the preceding rough rule delivers a first solution that is optimum or close enough to optimum not to matter. Rarely, a little trial and error is worth trying when a case is right on the borderline. Such rarely needed trial and error is far easier and more accurate than the most elaborate calculations.

## When to Choose Early Joins to Upstream Nodes

Upstream nodes can potentially offer the most effective benefit-to-cost ratio. For upstream nodes, you calculate $F = R \times D$, where $R$ is the node's filter ratio, as before, and $D$ is the detail join ratio. However, unlike the master join ratio, which must be less than or equal to 1.0, the detail join ratio can be any positive number and is usually greater than 1.0. When it is large, $F$ is typically greater than 1.0 and the benefit-to-cost ratio, $(1-F)/C$, is actually negative, making the upward join less attractive than even a completely unfiltered downward join (where $1-F$ is 0). When $F$ is greater than 1.0, the choice is obvious: postpone the upward join until downward joins are exhausted. Even when the detail join ratio $(D)$ is small enough that $F$ is less than 1.0, an early upward join carries a risk: the detail join ratio might be much larger for other customers who will run the same application, or for the same customer at a later time. The early upward join that helps this one customer today might later, and at other sites, do more harm than good. Upward joins are not robust to changes in the data distribution.

Large detail join ratios carry another, more subtle effect: they point to large tables that will require the database to read multiple rows per joined-from row, making $C$ higher by at least the detail join ratio, just to account for the higher rowcount read. If these upstream tables are particularly large, they will also have much larger values for $C$ (compared to the downstream joins), owing to poorer caching and deeper indexes. Together, these effects usually make $C$ large enough that the benefit-to-cost ratio of an upstream join is poor, even with very low detail-table filter ratios.

In Figure 8-6, the factor ($F$) for A is 0.2 ($0.1 \times 2$), the same as the best downstream node, B3, but the cost ($C$) would be at least twice as high as for any downstream node, since the database must read two rows in A for every joined-from row from the already-joined nodes. Setting $Cd$ (the detail-table per-row cost) equal to $2 \times Cm$ (the worst-case per-row cost of a master-table join) gives you $(1-0.2)/(2 \times Cm) = (1-Fe)/Cm$, where $Fe$ is the filter ratio a worst-case downstream join would have if it had a benefit-to-cost ratio equal to the upstream join to A. Solving for $Fe$, you find $1-Fe=0.8/2$, or $Fe=0.6$. Based on this calculation, you would certainly choose the joins to B3, B4, and B2 before the join to A. Even the join to B5 would likely be best before the join to A, since B5 would likely be better cached and have fewer index levels than A. Only the join to B1 would be safely postponed until after the join to A, if you had confidence that the $F$ factor for A would never exceed 1.0 and you had no further filters available in nodes downstream of B1. By the time you reach a point where the upward join might precede a downward join, it often hardly matters, because by that point there are so few rows left after the earlier filters that the savings are miniscule compared with the costs of the rest of the query. In conclusion, the need even to consider upward joins early, with any detail join ratio of 2 or more, is slight.

However, detail join ratios are sometimes reliably less than 1.0, leading to the simplest exception to the rule that you should not consider upward joins early:

> When choosing the next node in a sequence, treat all joins with a join ratio $D$ less than 1.0 like downward joins. And, when comparing nodes, use $D \times R$ as the effective node filter ratio, where $R$ is the single-node filter ratio.

When detail join ratios are near 1.0 but not less than 1.0, the case is more ambiguous:

> Treat upward joins like downward joins when the join ratio is close to 1.0 and when this allows access to useful filters (low filter ratios) earlier in the execution plan. When in doubt, you can try both alternatives.

The key in this last case is how confident you are in the detail join ratio being close to 1.0. If it might be large later, or at another site, it is best to push the upward join later in the plan, following the simplest heuristic rule that postpones the upward joins until downward joins are complete. (Important exceptions to this rule are surprisingly rare.)

## Summary

Short of a brute-force analysis of huge numbers of execution plans, perfect optimization of queries with many tables is beyond the state-of-the-art. Even with advances in the art, perfect optimization is likely to remain beyond the scope of manual tuning methods. If you make your living tuning SQL, this is actually good news: you are not about to be put out of business! The problem of SQL tuning is complex enough that this result is not surprising. What is surprising, perhaps, is that by focusing on robust execution plans and a few fairly simple rules, you can come close to perfect optimization for the overwhelming majority of queries. Local information about the nodes in a join diagram—in particular, their filter ratios—turns out to be enough to choose an efficient, robust execution plan, without considering the problem in its full combinatorial complexity.

# CHAPTER 9

# Special Cases

*Defer no time; delays have dangerous ends.*
—William Shakespeare
  *King Henry the Sixth, Part I*

This chapter covers a collection of special cases that occasionally arise. Chapters 6 and 7 cover standard solutions to standard classes of the problem "What execution plan do I want?" Here, I extend those solutions to handle several special cases better.

## Outer Joins

In one sense, this section belongs in Chapter 6 or Chapter 7, because in many applications outer joins are as common as inner joins. Indeed, those chapters already cover some of the issues surrounding outer joins. However, some of the questions about outer joins are logically removed from the rest of the tuning problem, and the answers to these questions are clearer if you understand the arguments of Chapter 8. Therefore, I complete the discussion of outer joins here.

Outer joins are notorious for creating performance problems, but they do not have to be a problem when handled correctly. For the most part, the perceived performance problems with outer joins are simply myths, based on either misunderstanding or problems that were fixed long ago. Properly implemented, outer joins are essentially as efficient to execute as inner joins. What's more, in manual optimization problems, they are actually easier to handle than inner joins.

I already discussed several special issues with outer joins in Chapter 7, under sections named accordingly:

- Filtered outer joins
- Outer joins leading to inner joins
- Outer joins pointing toward the detail table
- Outer joins to views

## Justification of Outer Joins

I often hear discussions of outer joins that follow lines like this: "Justify making this join an outer join: prove that the expense of an outer join is necessary, here."

Since I find no expense in correctly implemented outer joins, I tend to ask the opposite: "Why use an inner join when the outer case of the outer join might be useful?"

Specifically, when I find unfiltered leaf nodes in a query diagram, I suspect that the join ought to be an outer join. Whole branches of join trees should often be outer-joined to the rest of the query diagram when those branches lack filters. As I mention in Chapter 7, filtered nodes generally exclude the outer case of an outer join. By making these effectively inner joins explicitly inner, you increase the degrees of freedom in the join order, which can give the optimizer access to a better execution plan. Inner joins to nodes without filters can also serve a subtle filtering role, when the master join ratio to those nodes is even slightly less than 1.0. When this filtering effect is functionally necessary, the inner join is essential. However, it is far more common that this subtle filtering effect was the farthest thing from the developer's mind when she was writing the SQL. More commonly, the filtering effect of an inner join to a node without filters is unintentional and undesirable.

Even when the foreign key is nonnull and the join will produce the outer case only when referential integrity fails, ask yourself "Would it be better to show the rows with failed referential integrity, or to hide them?" Failed referential integrity is a problem whether you see it or not, so I argue for using outer joins to reveal such a failure to the end user and give developers or DBAs a chance to learn of the defect, as the first step to repairing it.

These cases all require special measures already described in Chapter 7. Here, I extend the rules given in Chapter 7 to further optimize the simplest, most common case: simple, unfiltered, downward outer joins to tables, either nodes that are leaf nodes of the query diagram or nodes that lead to further outer joins. Figure 9-1 illustrates this case with 16 outer joins.

I call these unfiltered, downward outer joins to simple tables *normal* outer joins. Normal outer joins have a special and useful property, from the point of view of optimization:

> The number of rows after performing a normal outer join is equal to the number of rows just before performing that join.

This property makes consideration of normal outer joins especially simple; normal outer joins have no effect at all on the *running rowcount* (the number of rows reached at any point in the join order). Therefore, they are irrelevant to the optimization of the rest of the query. The main justification for performing downward joins before upward joins does not apply; normal outer joins, unlike inner joins, cannot reduce

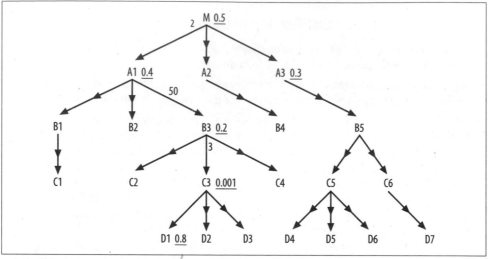

*Figure 9-1. A query with 16 unfiltered outer joins*

the rowcount going into later, more expensive upward joins. Since they have no effect on the rest of the optimization problem, you should simply choose a point in the join order where the cost of the normal outer join itself is minimum. This turns out to be the point where the running rowcount is minimum, after the first point where the outer-joined table is reachable through the join tree.

## Steps for Normal Outer Join Order Optimization

The properties of normal outer joins lead to a new set of steps specific to optimizing queries with these joins:

1. Isolate the portion of the join diagram that excludes all normal outer joins. Call this the inner query diagram.

2. Optimize the inner query diagram as if the normal outer joins did not exist.

3. Divide normal outer-joined nodes into subsets according to how high in the inner query diagram they attach. Call a subset that attaches at or below the driving table $s\_0$; call the subset that can be reached only after a single upward join from the driving table $s\_1$; call the subset that can be reached only after two upward joins from the driving table $s\_2$; and so on.

4. Work out a relative running rowcount for each point in the join order just before the next upward join and for the end of the join order.

> By *relative* running rowcount, I mean that you can choose any *starting* rowcount you like, purely for arithmetic convenience, as long as the calculations after that point are consistent.

Call the relative running rowcount just before the first upward join $r\_0$; call the relative running rowcount just before the second upward join $r\_1$; and so on. Call the final relative rowcount $r\_j$, where $j$ is the number of upward joins from the driving table to the root detail table.

5. For each subset $s\_n$, find the minimum value $r\_m$ (such that $m \geq n$) and join all the nodes in that subset, from the top down, at the point in the join order where the relative rowcount equals that minimum. Join the last subset, which hangs from the root detail table, at the end of the join order after all inner joins, since that is the only eligible minimum for that subset.

## Example

These steps require some elaboration. To apply Steps 1 and 2 to Figure 9-1, consider Figure 9-2.

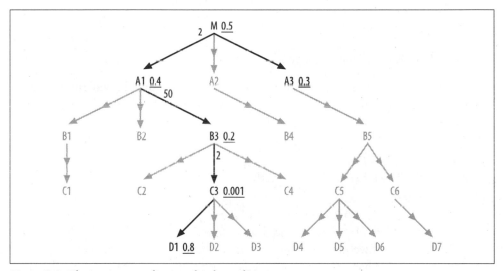

*Figure 9-2. The inner query diagram for the earlier query*

The initially complex-looking 22-way join is reduced in the inner query diagram in black to a simple 6-way join, and it's an easy optimization problem to find the best inner-join order of (C3, D1, B3, A1, M, A3).

Now, consider Step 3. The driving table is C3, so the subset $s\_0$ contains any normal outer-joined tables reachable strictly through downward joins hanging below C3, which would be the set {D2, D3}. The first upward join is to B3, so $s\_1$ is {C2, C4}, the set of nodes (excluding $s\_0$ nodes) reachable through downward joins from B3. The second upward join is to A1, so $s\_2$ is {B1, B2, C1}. The final upward join is to M, so $s\_3$ holds the rest of the normal outer-joined tables: {A2, B4, B5, C5, C6, D4, D5, D6, D7}. Figure 9-3 shows this division of the outer-joined tables into subsets.

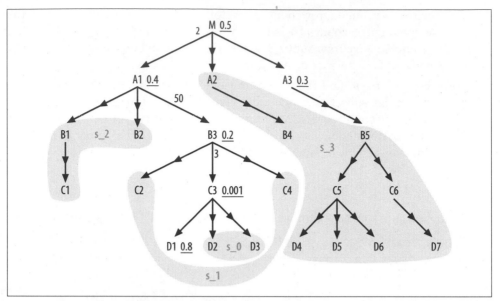

*Figure 9-3. The outer-joined-table subsets for the earlier query*

Now, consider Step 4. Since you need only comparative (or relative) running row-counts, let the initial number of rows in C3 be whatever it would need to be to make $r\_0$ a convenient round number—say, 10. From there, work out the list of values for $r\_n$:

*$r\_0$: 10*

Arbitrary, chosen to simplify the math.

*$r\_1$: 6 ($r\_0 \times 3 \times 0.2$)*

The numbers 3 and 0.2 come from the detail join ratio for the join into B3 and the product of all filter ratios picked up before the next upward join. You would also adjust the rowcounts by master join ratios less than 1.0, if there were any, but the example has only the usual master join ratios assumed to be 1.0. (Since there are no filtered nodes below B3 reached after the join to B3, the only applicable filter is the filter on B3 itself, with a filter ratio of 0.2.)

*$r\_2$: 120 ($r\_1 \times 50 \times 0.4$)*

The numbers 50 and 0.4 come from the detail join ratio for the join into A1 and the product of all filter ratios picked up before the next upward join. (Since there are no filtered nodes below A1 reached after the join to A1, the only applicable filter is the filter on A1 itself, with a filter ratio of 0.4.)

*$r\_3$: 36 ($r\_2 \times 2 \times 0.15$)*

The numbers 2 and 0.15 come from the detail join ratio for the join into M and the product of all remaining filter ratios. (Since there is one filtered node reached after the join to M, A3, the *product of all remaining filter ratios* is the product of the filter ratio on M (0.5) and the filter ratio on A3 (0.3): $0.5 \times 0.3 = 0.15$.)

Finally, apply Step 5. The minimum for all relative rowcounts is $r\_1$, so the subsets $s\_0$ and $s\_1$, which are eligible to join before the query reaches A1, should both join at that point in the join order just before the join to A1. The minimum after that point is $r\_3$, so the subsets $s\_2$ and $s\_3$ should both join at the end of the join order. The only further restriction is that the subsets join from the top down, so that lower tables are reached through the join tree. For example, you cannot join to C1 before you join to B1, nor to D7 before joining to both B5 and C6. Since I have labeled master tables by level, Ds below Cs, Cs below Bs, Bs below As, you can assure top-down joins by just putting each subset in alphabetical order. For example, a complete join order, consistent with the requirements, would be: (C3, D1, B3, {D2, D3}, {C2, C4}, A1, M, A3, {B1, B2, C1}, {A2, B4, B5, C5, C6, D4, D5, D6, D7}), where curly brackets are left in place to show the subsets.

# Merged Join and Filter Indexes

The method I've explained so far points you to the best join order for a robust execution plan that assumes you can reach rows in the driving table efficiently and that you have all the indexes you need on the join keys. Occasionally, you can improve on even this nominal best execution plan with an index that combines a join key and one or more filter columns. The problem in Figure 9-4 illustrates the case in which this opportunity arises.

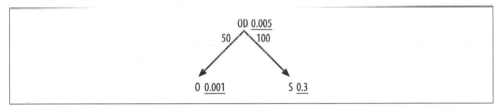

*Figure 9-4. A simple three-way join*

The standard robust plan, following the heuristics of Chapter 6, drives from O with nested loops to the index on OD's foreign key that points to O. After reaching the table OD, the database discards 99.5% of the rows because they fail to meet the highly selective filter on OD. Then, the database drives to S on its primary-key index and discards 70% of the remaining rows, after reading the table S, because they fail to meet the filter condition on S. In all, this is not a bad execution plan, and it might easily be fast enough if the rowcount of OD and the performance requirements are not too high.

However, it turns out that you can do still better if you enable indexes that are perfect for this query. To make the problem more concrete, assume that Figure 9-4 comes from the following query:

```
SELECT ... FROM Shipments S, Order_Details OD, Orders O
WHERE O.Order_ID=OD.Order_ID
  AND OD.Shipment_ID=S.Shipment_ID
```

```
AND O.Customer_ID=:1
AND OD.Product_ID=:2
AND S.Shipment_Date>:3
```

Assuming around 1,000 customers, 200 products, and a date for :3 about 30% of the way back to the beginning of the shipment records, the filter ratios shown in the diagram follow. To make the problem even more concrete, assume that the rowcount of Order_Details is 10,000,000. Given the detail join ratio from Orders to Order_Details, the rowcount of Orders must be 200,000, so you would expect to read 200 Orders rows, which would join to 10,000 Order_Details rows. After discarding Order_Details with the wrong Product_IDs, 50 rows would remain in the running rowcount. These would join to 50 rows of Shipments, and 15 rows would remain after discarding the earlier shipments.

Where is the big cost in this execution plan? Clearly, the costs on Orders and Shipments and their indexes are minor, with so few rows read from these tables. The reads to the index on Order_Details(Order_ID) would be 200 range scans, each covering 50 rows. Each of these range scans would walk down a three-deep index and usually touch one leaf block for each range scan for about three logical I/Os per range scan. In all, this would represent about 600 fairly well-cached logical I/Os to the index. Only the Order_Details table itself sees many logical I/Os, 10,000 in all, and that table is large enough that many of those reads will likely also trigger physical I/O. How can you do better?

The trick is to pick up the filter condition on Order_Details before you even reach the table, while still in the index. If you replace the index on Order_Details(Order_ID) with a new index on Order_Details(Order_ID, Product_ID), the 200 range scans of 50 rows each become 200 range scans of an average of just a half row each.

 The reverse column order for this index would work well for this query, too. It would even show better self-caching, since the required index entries would all clump together at the same Product_ID.

With this new index, you would read only the 50 Order_Details rows that you actually need, a 200-fold savings on physical and logical I/O related to that table. Because Order_Details was the only object in the query to see a significant volume of I/O, this change that I've just described would yield roughly a 50-fold improvement in performance of the whole query, assuming much better caching on the other, smaller objects.

So, why did I wait until Chapter 9 to describe such a seemingly huge optimization opportunity? Through most of this book, I have implied the objective of finding the best execution plan, a priori, regardless of what indexes the database has at the time. However, behind this idealization, reality looms: many indexes that are customized to optimize individual, uncommon queries will cost more than they help. While an index that covers both a foreign key and a filter condition will speed the example query, it will slow every insert and delete and many updates when they change the indexed columns. The effect of a single new index on any given insert is minor. However, spread across all inserts and added to the effects of many other custom indexes, a proliferation of indexes can easily do more harm than good.

Consider yet another optimization for the same query. Node S, like OD, is reached through a join key and also has a filter condition. What if you created an index on `Shipments(Shipment_ID, Shipment_Date)` to avoid unnecessary reads to the `Shipments` table? Reads to that table would drop 70%, but that is only a savings of 35 logical I/Os and perhaps one or two physical I/Os, which would quite likely not be enough to even notice. In real-world queries, such miniscule improvements with custom indexes that combine join keys and filter conditions are far more common than opportunities for major improvement.

 I deliberately contrived the example to maximize the improvement offered with the first index customization. Such large improvements in overall query performance from combining join and filter columns in a single index are rare.

When you find that an index is missing on some foreign key that is necessary to enable a robust plan with the best join order, it is fair to guess that the same foreign-key index will be useful to a whole family of queries. However, combinations of foreign keys and filter conditions are much more likely to be unique to a single query, and the extra benefit of the added filter column is often minor, even within that query.

Consider both the execution frequency of the query you are tuning and the magnitude of the tuning opportunity. If the summed savings in runtime, across the whole application, is an hour or more per day, don't hesitate to introduce a custom index that might benefit only that single query. If the savings in runtime is less, consider whether the savings affect online performance or just batch load, and consider whether a custom index will do more harm than good. The cases in which it is most likely to do good look most like my contrived example:

- Queries with few nodes are most likely to concentrate runtime on access to a single table.

- The most important table for runtime tends to be the root detail table, and that importance is roughly proportional to the detail join ratio to that table from the driving table.

- With both a large detail join ratio and a small filter ratio (which is not so small that it becomes the driving filter), the savings for a combined key/filter index to the root detail table are maximized.

When you find a large opportunity for savings on a query that is responsible for much of the database load, these combined key/filter indexes are a valuable tool; just use the tool with caution.

# Missing Indexes

The approach this book has taken so far is to find optimum robust plans as if all driving-table filter conditions and all necessary join keys were already indexed. The implication is that, whenever you find that these optimum plans require an index you don't already have, you should create it and generate statistics for it so that the optimizer knows its selectivity. If you are tuning only the most important SQL—SQL that contributes (or will contribute) significantly to the load and the perceived performance (from the perspective of the end user) of a real production system—any index you create by following this method will likely be well justified. Cary Millsap's book *Optimizing Oracle Performance* (O'Reilly), which I heartily recommend, provides a method for finding the most important SQL to tune.

Unfortunately, you must often tune SQL without much knowledge of its significance to overall production performance and load, especially early in the development process, when you have only tiny data volumes to experiment with and do not yet know the future end users' patterns of use.

To estimate how important a SQL statement will be to overall load and performance, ask the following questions:

- Is it used online or only in batch? Waiting a few minutes for a batch job is usually no great hardship; end users can continue productive work while waiting for a printout or an electronic report. Online tasks should run in less than a second if they are at all frequent for a significant community of end users.

- How many end users are affected by the application delay caused by the long-running SQL?

- How often are the end users affected by the application delay per week?

- Is there an alternate way the end user can accomplish the same task without a new index? For example, end users who are looking up employee data might have both Social Security numbers and names available to search on, and they need not have indexed paths to both if they have the freedom and information available to search on either. Some performance problems are best solved by training end users to follow the fast paths to the data that already exist.

- Compare the runtimes of the best execution plan under the current indexes with the best plan under ideal indexes. How much slower is the best constrained plan that requires no (or fewer) new indexes? A nonideal index to the driving table, or even a full table scan, might be almost as fast as the ideal index, especially if the driving table is not the most expensive part of the query. A missing join-key index can force a plan that drives from a second-best-filtered or even worse driving node, where the alternate node has access to the whole join tree through current indexes. How much worse is that? The only way to know for sure is to try your query both ways. Alternatively, try hash joins when join-key indexes are missing, and see whether the improvement is enough to obviate the need for new indexes.

Estimate weekly lost productivity for online delays by using the length of each delay times the frequency of the task per end user times the number of end users. Summed delays of days per week add up to serious lost money. Summed delays of a couple of minutes per week amount to less than you might save by buying an extra coffee maker to save employees steps during coffee breaks; don't get carried away going after the little stuff!

Consider overriding external effects too. For example, online delays for a live customer-support application that cause customers to find a new vendor can be disproportionately expensive! Similarly, batch delays that trigger penalties for missed deadlines might carry huge costs. When SQL delays are costly and the improvement for adding a new index is significant, don't hesitate to add the index. Otherwise, consider the trade offs.

 It is far easier to add indexes than to get rid of them! Once an index is in production use for any length of time, the perceived risk of dropping it is high. It is next to impossible to ensure in advance that an index can be safely dropped. After an index is in production, the initial justification for the index is soon forgotten, and new code might become dependent on the index without anyone realizing it. The time to say "No" to a poor index is before it becomes an established part of the production environment that end users depend on.

# Unfiltered Joins

The method so far generally assumes that you are tuning queries against large tables, since these dominate the set of SQL that needs tuning. For such queries, especially when they are online queries, you can generally count on finding at least one selective filter that leads to an attractive driving table. Occasionally, especially for large batch queries and online queries of small tables, you will tune unfiltered joins—joins of whole tables without restriction. For example, consider Figure 9-5.

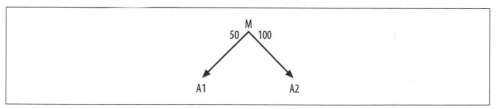

*Figure 9-5. An unfiltered three-way join*

How do you optimize such a query, with no guidance based on filter selectivities? For nested-loops plans, it hardly matters which join order you choose, as long as you follow the join tree. However, these are precisely the queries that most reward hash joins, or sort-merge joins when hash joins are unavailable. Assuming hash joins are available, the database should read all three tables with full table scans and should hash the smaller tables, A1 and A2, caching these hashed tables in memory if possible. Then, during the single pass through the largest table, M, each hashed row is rapidly matched with the in-memory matching hashed rows of A1 and A2. The cost of the query, ideally, is roughly the cost of the three full table scans. The database can't do better than that, even theoretically, given that you need all the rows from all three tables. Cost-based optimizers are generally good at finding optimum plans for queries such as these, without manual help.

When either A1 or A2 is too large to cache in memory, consider the more robust nested-loops plan driving from table M, and check how much slower it turns out to be. Indexed lookups, one row at a time, will likely be much slower, but they will eventually succeed, while the hash join runs the risk of exhausting temporary disk space if A1 or A2 is too big to hold in memory.

# Unsolvable Problems

So far, I've described strategies for solving what I would call *pure* SQL tuning problems, where the text of a slow query constitutes essentially the whole problem statement and where you can tune that query out of context with the rest of the application. The following narrowly defined performance problem statement illustrates the boundaries of the problem I've attacked so far:

> Alter a given SQL statement to deliver precisely the same rows it already delivers (thus requiring no change to the rest of the application) faster than some predefined target runtime.

Assuming the predefined target runtime is set rationally according to real business needs, there are four basic ways that this problem can be unsolvable:

- The query runs so many times that the target runtime must be set very low. This is particularly true of queries that the application repeats hundreds of times or more to resolve a single, online, end-user request.

- The query must return too many table rows (taking into account the number of tables) to have any hope of meeting the target, even with excellent caching in the database.

- The query must aggregate too many table rows (taking into account the number of tables) to have any hope of meeting the target, even with excellent caching in the database.

- The layout of the data provides no potential execution plan that avoids high running rowcounts at some point in the execution plan, even while the final returned rowcount is moderate.

In this section, I describe how to recognize each type of problem. In Chapter 10, I will discuss solving these "unsolvable" problems by stepping outside the box that the too-narrow problem statement imposes.

The first problem type is self-explanatory: the target is way lower than an end user should care about. The explanation turns out to be that a given end-user action or batch process requires the query to run hundreds or even millions of times to perform what, to the end user, is a single task.

The second and third problem types are easy to recognize in a query diagram. Like Figure 9-5, the query, which reads at least one large table, turns out to have no filters or only a couple of weakly selective filters. If you have no aggregation (no GROUP BY, for example), you have the second problem. When you test the best nested-loops plan you can find, with any row-ordering steps removed so you can see rows before sorting, you discover that the query returns rows at a very high rate but returns so many rows that it runs interminably. The third problem, with a GROUP BY or other aggregation, looks just like the second problem type, but with the addition of aggregation.

The fourth problem type is the subtlest. A query diagram with at least one large table has several semiselective filters spread throughout a query diagram, often with subqueries, in such a way that large fractions of one or more large tables must be read before you can reach enough filters to reduce the rowcount to something moderate. This case might sound like it should be quite common, but it actually turns out to be rare; I've run into it probably less than once a year, on average.

# CHAPTER 10

# Outside-the-Box Solutions to Seemingly Unsolvable Problems

*It is not every question that deserves an answer.*
—Publilius Syrus (a.k.a. Publius)
  *Maxim 581*

Computers are fast enough that they never have to be the bottleneck in a business process. When they turn out to be a bottleneck, solutions always exist. However, the solutions do not always take the form of answers to the question "How do I make this query return the same rows faster?" So far, this book has focused on answering that single question, and Chapter 9 described a few circumstances in which satisfactory answers to that question do not exist. This chapter takes the performance problem out of that self-imposed box and considers how to solve the rare query runtime problems that cannot be solved just by tuning a given statement.

## When Very Fast Is Not Fast Enough

Online steps in a business process that run in less than a second are unlikely to significantly slow the end user who is performing the process. Even steps that take well over a second can often be made convenient to the end user if those parts of the process are taken offline and made into batch processes. The only business-driven need for queries to run very fast—under a half a second, for example—comes about when a single step in a business process requires queries to run repeatedly. Some application designs repeat a query hundreds of times for a single online event, or up to millions of times for a single batch process. In these cases, clearly, a query would have to run in a few milliseconds or less to meet an end user's needs, and most queries are not that fast, even after perfect tuning. When you run into this problem, the real issue is the need for so many queries, not the runtime of each query. There are three basic solutions to the need for repeated queries:

- Cache everything the repeated queries might need, once, in application memory, and subsequently get data as needed from the application cache.

- Consolidate the repeated queries into a new, single query.

- Merge the repeated queries into joins that are added to a single query the application already runs.

Before I discuss these three solutions, consider a typical repeated query, which retrieves the pricing history for a given product:

```
SELECT Product_Price FROM Price_List
WHERE Product_ID = :1
AND Effective_Date <= :today
ORDER BY Effective_Date DESC;
```

To find the best solution to such a repeated query, you need to consider several questions:

- How many times must the application run the query sequentially to perform a task?
- What is the source of the values of :1 and :today that drive the query?
- How many rows would you need to preread and cache for the cache to supply all the data the application might need? How much future use could you get from that cache?
- What is the rowcount range and average for the query? How many of those rows does the application actually use?

The next few sections describe three possible solutions and show how the answers to these questions can lead to one of those solutions.

## Caching to Avoid Repeated Queries

If the set of possible Product_IDs is small compared to the number of times the example query repeats, you have a good case to cache the whole set. For example, we might have 10 Product_IDs while repeating the query 1,000 times, so it makes more sense to precache results across the whole set and read from the cache in place of repeated queries to the database. For example, you could issue this query:

```
SELECT Product_Price FROM Price_List
WHERE Effective_Date <= :today
ORDER BY Product_ID ASC, Effective_Date DESC;
```

The cache could then hold these results—for example, in a structure in application memory using hash buckets or a binary tree that gives rapid (microseconds) access to the results for a particular Product_ID. Since individual reads from the first approach outnumber the Product_IDs, this approach offers two advantages in terms of the cost of database access:

- The database reads fewer rows, with fewer logical I/Os. In the original approach, the database read each row more than once, on average, since it hit the average Product_ID more than once. These reads were likely less efficient in terms of logical I/Os per row as well, because they likely drove through an index read that required more than one logical I/O per row read. The precaching approach, in contrast, likely drives from a full table scan that reads several rows per logical I/O.

- The database gets the data in a single query, likely with a single round trip over the network. Even with reuse of a preparsed query, the repeated-query approach requires at least one round trip to the database per repeat of the query, with considerable overhead.

In the current example, the repeated query likely returns multiple rows for each Product_ID, but it is quite likely that only the row with the highest Effective_Date returned (the first one in the sort order) is relevant to the application. An ideal caching algorithm would take this into account and simply discard the other rows, saving memory and other costs to fill the cache.

Therefore, even if such a cache is used one set of times, to perform a single business task for a single end user, it can cost less than the repeated queries it makes unnecessary. If the cache continues to be useful for future tasks by the same end user, the benefit increases, even justifying a cache that is initially more expensive to populate than the repeated queries for a single task. If the cache resides in shared memory that is accessible to multiple end users, assuming its contents are useful to the whole community of end users, the benefits multiply still further.

---

### Caching in the Application Versus Caching in the Database

The database already caches frequently used database blocks in its own shared memory, so why have a redundant application cache holding data the database is probably caching already? The answer is certainly not to reduce physical I/O; both approaches to caching work well at eliminating physical I/O. The application cache does have advantages, though:

- It is physically local, requiring no network traffic for the application to access.
- It can be custom designed to reach precisely the data that the application needs most frequently with as little CPU time as possible, without the overhead, such as locking and read-concurrency, that a database engine must pay.

The price paid for a fast application cache is increased application complexity. A few simple, static caches for repeatedly read rowsets are easy enough, but if you get carried away, you will have reinvented the database software functionality in your own application. At the extreme, you will be using Oracle, SQL Server, or DB2 as nothing more than a glorified fileserver, and your own application will be responsible for all the real work of a database, with orders of magnitude less development behind it than behind those databases.

---

## Consolidated Queries

A blind query to read every row that a repeated query might potentially touch can be too expensive, and the result set might be too large to cache. However, that does not prevent the application from consolidating the multiple queries into a single query with one of two forms. In the current example, each pass through the loop would

---

find a `Product_ID` to drive the initial repeated query. You could run through the loops without querying and simply compile a list of IDs to use in a single consolidated query. For the example, these forms would look like this:

```
SELECT Product_Price FROM Price_List
WHERE Product_ID in (<long list of IDs>)
AND Effective_Date <= :today
ORDER BY Product_ID ASC, Effective_Date DESC;
```

or this:

```
SELECT Product_Price FROM Price_List
WHERE Product_ID in (<subquery that returns the list of IDs>)
AND Effective_Date <= :today
ORDER BY Product_ID ASC, Effective_Date DESC;
```

This still has the advantages of eliminating the overhead of handling multiple queries, and it handles a case in which caching the set of all possible query results would not work, but it produces a result that yields far less row reuse. In all, this query-consolidation approach resolves a broad class of repeated-query performance problems.

## Merging Repeated Queries into a Preexisting Query

Usually, the source of the variables in repeated queries is an earlier query. In the current example, :today surely comes from the clock/calendar, but :1 almost certainly comes from an earlier query that returned a long list of Product_IDs. The most likely reason behind the repeated query is to fill in a current (with the most recent Effective_Date) product price for each of the rows the earlier query returned, based on the first row that the query returns each time it runs. Since the goal of the query is to find a matching price row for each of the earlier query's rows, this is functionally like a join, though not nearly so efficient.

The technique in these cases is to convert these to actual joins. When these repeated queries are just simple single-row queries on a primary key, the conversion to a join is obvious. In cases like the current example, the solution is subtler. The query returned a price history sorted by Effective_Date to place the currently effective price at the top. This currently effective price record is the only record you actually want. To consolidate this repeated query with the query that provides the list of Product_IDs, you have to find a way to join with the first row a sorted query returns without reading the other rows.

There are several approaches that resolve this requirement, and I will describe two. Each approach begins with a new column, Current_Price_Flag, which equals 'Y' if and only if the price is the price currently in effect:

- If rows are never created with future Effective_Dates, create a trigger that sets the newly obsolete price's Current_Price_Flag to 'N' and that creates new prices with Current_Price_Flag set to 'Y'.

- If not-yet-effective price records are sometimes created, run a nightly batch process that looks for future effective price records that just became current at midnight, and have that process update those records to have `Current_Price_Flag` equal to `'Y'`, while updating `Current_Price_Flag` of newly obsolete prices to `'N'`. This nightly batch process will probably supplement trigger-driven updates from new price records that are current at creation time.

Given such a properly maintained `Current_Price_Flag` column, the join is simple. If the initial query looked like this:

```
SELECT ... OD.Product_ID, ...
FROM ... Order_Details OD, ...
WHERE ...
```

the new query that incorporates the join would be:

```
SELECT ... OD.Product_ID, ..., PL.Product_Price
FROM ... Order_Details OD, ..., Price_List PL
WHERE ...
AND OD.Product_ID=PL.Product_ID
AND PL.Current_Price_Flag='Y'
```

Not all procedural code is replaced by a join as easily as in this last example. However, SQL incorporates powerful logic expressions, such as `CASE`, that enable virtually any procedural data-lookup function to be converted to some series of joins combined with complex (often nested) SQL expressions.

# Queries that Return Data from Too Many Rows

There are four main contexts in which queries cover too many rows, resulting in long-running queries even when per-row costs are as low as they can be:

*Online queries that return hundreds or more rows*
> These queries are invariably excessive from the point of view of end users; such large result sets are inconvenient or impossible to use online. The most likely response of an end user is simply to repeat such a query with some further refinement to the conditions to try to reduce the results to a manageable size.

*Batch reports that return tens of thousands or more rows*
> These queries are invariably excessive from the point of view of end users; such large result sets are inconvenient to read, even in a report. Certainly, a large, well-ordered report does not have to be read from cover to cover, but if the intent is just to provide a way to look up selected facts, why not use a well-designed online transaction for the purpose? A well-designed application on a relational database is a better way to look up selected facts than the output of a huge flat report.

*Aggregations*

> Queries sometimes *aggregate* (i.e., summarize) large rowsets into results that are small enough for end users to digest. This can happen online or in batch.

*Middleware*

> Batch processes sometimes function as *middleware*—software that moves data around within a system or systems without sending that data to the end users. Since end users aren't part of the picture and computers have plenty of patience for large data volumes, these batch processes sometimes legitimately need to handle data volumes that are too large for human consumption.

Let's examine ways to fix each of these types of excessive reads, in turn.

## Large Online Queries

In the long run, large online queries tend to take care of themselves. Every time end users deliberately or accidentally trigger a query with insufficiently selective filter criteria, they receive negative feedback in the form of a long wait and a returned result that is inconveniently large for online viewing. The returned result has too much chaff (unneeded data) mixed in with the wheat (the data the end users really want) for convenient use. Over time, end users learn which query criteria will likely deliver punishingly large result sets, and they learn to avoid those query criteria. End-user education can help this learning process along, but the problem is somewhat self-repairing even without formal effort.

Unfortunately, there are two key times in the short run when this sort of automated behavior modification doesn't prevent serious trouble:

*During test usage*

> End users and developers often try out online forms in scenarios in which any value will suffice. In real use, an end user knows the name, or at least most of the name, before looking it up, and he knows to type at least a partial name to avoid having to scroll through a pick list of thousands of entries to find the right name. However, in a test scenario, the tester might be perfectly happy querying every name (such a query is called a *blind query*) and picking, for convenience, "Aaron, Abigail" from the top of the huge alphabetic list.

> Blind queries such as this are much more common when end users are just surfing a test system, to test a preproduction application, than when they have production work to do. Blind queries like this can even find their way into hurriedly compiled, automated benchmark load tests, horribly distorting benchmark results. Unfortunately, it is exactly during such testing that you will likely be searching for performance problems, so these blind queries distort the problem picture and deliver a poor first impression of the application performance.

*Early in end users' learning process*

Novice end users do not yet know to avoid blind and insufficiently selective (i.e., *semiblind*) queries even in production use. When they execute such long-running queries, they form a poor, often costly first impression of the application performance. In early production use, and even later if end-user turnover is high, the system-wide load from these mistakes can be high, hurting everyone, even end users who avoid the mistakes.

Blind and semiblind queries in the most frequently used transactions are worth preventing in the application layer. When possible, the application should simply refuse to perform a potentially large query that does not have at least one known-to-be-selective search criteria specified at query time. This requires a little extra effort to discover in advance which selective search criteria will be available to end users in production use. These selective search criteria will map to a list of table columns that must drive efficient queries. However, you need to ask just these questions to make sure that you have indexed paths from those columns to the rest of the data; otherwise, you end up tuning queries, with otherwise harmful indexes, that will never come up in real application use. When end users query without reasonable search criteria, it is better to return immediate error messages that suggest more selective search criteria than to tie up their windows with long-running, useless queries.

Sometimes, you cannot guess in advance how selective a search will be until it runs; the selectivity depends on the application data. For example, the application might return far more matches to a last name of "Smith" than "Kmetec," but you would not want to hardcode a list of name frequencies into the application. In these cases, you need a way to see that a list is too long, without the expense of reading the whole list. The solution has several steps:

1. Determine the maximum-length list you want to return without error. For purposes of discussion, let's say the maximum length is 500.

2. In the call to the database, request one more row than that maximum length (501 rows for this discussion).

3. Arrange in advance that the query execution plan is robust, following nested loops to return rows without having to prehash, sort, or otherwise store whole large rowsets before returning the first 501 rows.

4. Request that the query result from the database be unsorted, so the database does not need to read all the rows before returning the first rows.

5. Sort the result as needed in the application layer if the result does not trigger an error by hitting the error threshold (501 rows for this discussion).

6. Cancel the query and return an error that suggests a more selective search if the rowcount hits the maximum length (501 rows for this discussion).

In my former performance-tuning position at TenFold Corporation, this technique proved so useful that we made it the automatic behavior of the EnterpriseTenFold application platform, with an adjustable maximum rowcount.

In summary, prevent large online queries with a three-pronged approach:

- Train end users to specify narrow enough searches that they don't get more data than is useful or efficient to read.
- Return error messages when end users attempt obviously unselective queries, especially blind queries based on large root detail tables.
- Run potentially large queries in such a way that you get the first rows quickly, and return an error as soon as the number of returned rows is excessive.

# Large Batch Reports

Slow online events are punishing enough that they don't go uncorrected. The affected end users either modify their behavior or complain loudly enough that the problem is corrected. Batch load can be more subtly dangerous in the end, since batch performance problems sometimes go unnoticed, creating enormous load and preventing adequate system throughput without being an obvious problem. When overall load is too high, all parts of an application slow down, but the villains, the batch processes that consume too much of the system resources, might be performing well enough to go unnoticed, especially when they are low-priority processes that no one is awaiting. Automatically prescheduled, periodic batch processes are especially dangerous: they might run much more frequently than needed, without anyone noticing. They might cease to be needed as often as they once were, or cease to be needed at all, but go right on tying up your system unnoticed.

Conceptually, there are several questions regarding a large batch report that are relevant to choosing a performance solution:

- What is the reason for the report?
- How is the report triggered?
- Why is performance of the report a concern?
- What sort of information does the reader extract from the report?

The answers to these questions all affect the best answer to the final question: how do you fix the report performance?

## Reasons for large reports

Beginning with the assumption that no one person will ever read a huge application report from cover to cover, why should applications ever need huge report queries?

Common reasons for huge report queries, and performance strategies for each reason, include:

***A report has many readers, each of whom is interested in a different subset of the data.*** No one reads the report from cover to cover, but any given part of it might be interesting to at least one reader. The needs filled by such all-inclusive reports are often better served by multiple smaller reports. These can run in parallel, when needed, making it easier for the system to reach all the necessary data quickly enough. They also can each run just as often as their readers need, rather than read everyone's data as often as the most demanding readers require.

***All details of a report are potentially interesting at the time the report is requested, but end users will read only a small part of the report, based on which questions happen to arise that the end users must answer.*** The need to answer such ad hoc questions as they arise is far better met by online application queries to the database. A flat report structure in a huge report can never offer a path to data as convenient as a well-built application. When you use reports for ad hoc data access in place of online applications, you are bypassing all the advantages of a relational database. Since the ad hoc online queries that replace the entire huge report will touch only a small subset of the data the report must read, the online solution requires far less logical and physical I/O.

***Only a subset of the query data is ever used.*** Here, the solution is obvious and overwhelmingly beneficial: eliminate from the query and the report those rows that are never used. Where the report lists fewer rows than the query returns, add filters to match just the rows the report needs. If you trim the report itself, add filters to the queries that serve the trimmed report and tune the queries so they never touch the unused data. A special case in which only a subset of the data is required occurs when the end user needs only the summary information (the aggregations) in a report that includes both details and aggregations. In this case, eliminate the details from both the report and the database queries, and see the section "Aggregations of Many Details" to consider further solutions.

***A report is required only for legal reasons, not because anyone will ever read it.*** Such a justification for a report invites several questions. Is it still legally mandated, or did that requirement vanish and you're just producing the report out of habit? Is it really required as often as you are producing it? Rare huge reports are not likely to be a performance or throughput problem, so the essential point is to run them rarely if you cannot get rid of them. Does the law really require the data in the form of that report, or is it enough just to have access to the data in some form? Often, requirements for data retention do not specify the form of the retained data. The database itself, or its backups, might satisfy the requirements without an application report. If the report is required only for legal reasons, it can likely run during off hours, when load is less of an issue.

I once heard a thirdhand tale of a report produced for legal reasons that had been broken from the beginning; it filled many pages with a system dump every time it ran. Since no one actually used the report, no one noticed that it didn't work. However, each paper printout of the system dump was dutifully filed away, and the filer checked off a box in a form stating that the legal requirement to run and file the report was met. When the system was reengineered, the report was finally recognized as broken and was eliminated. The reengineering team concluded the report had never really been necessary after all. However, even when told that the report didn't work and never had, the person in charge of checking off the ran and filed box in the old form wanted the report put back in its original, broken form.

## Ways reports are triggered

There are two basic ways reports get triggered:

*Ad hoc requests*

When a report is specifically, manually requested, chances are high that at least the requestor knows a genuine need for at least part of the report. It is also likely that the requestor cares how long she will have to wait for the report output, and a long report runtime might cost the business. When the requestor needs the report soon, it should get high priority, potentially even running parallel processes that consume much of the system's resources to meet the deadline. Otherwise, it is helpful to ensure that the queries avoid running in parallel, thus avoiding harm to higher-priority process performance. Furthermore, low-priority reports should automatically be relegated to run during low-load periods, which is often enough to eliminate any performance impact from these reports.

*Automatic requests*

Much of the batch load on most business systems is automatic, in the form of reports that were long ago scheduled to run automatically every day or week, or on some other periodic basis. These periodic batch processes are a particularly insidious load source, because they are so easy to forget and to ignore. Most addressees of reports receive far more material than they could ever read, even if you count only material produced by humans, setting aside monster automated reports with vast collections of uninteresting numbers. Somehow, most business people also feel vaguely embarrassed by their inability to read and digest the vast amount of information that comes their way. Therefore, rather than complain that they never read some monster of a report that they receive daily or weekly and argue that it is a waste of resources, they will keep meekly quiet about their embarrassing inability to accomplish the impossible. (I know *I've* done this; haven't you?) If you want to reduce the frequency of huge reports or eliminate them altogether, don't wait for the addressees to complain that the reports aren't needed!

One strategy to eliminate reports is to ask a leading question: "We suspect this report is no longer useful; what do you think?" Another strategy is to state, "We're going to eliminate this report, which we suspect is no longer useful, unless one of you lets us know you still need it. If you still need it, do you still need it on the same frequency, or can we produce it less often?" My favorite strategy is to eliminate everyone except yourself from the addressee list and just see if anyone complains. If they complain, send them your copy and keep the report, adding them back to the addressee list. If no one complains, drop the scheduled report after a safe interval. (Of course, I wouldn't suggest doing this without authority.) For *pull* reports—reports that the reader must navigate to, rather than receiving them by email or on paper (these are called *push* reports)—you can get the same result by making the file inaccessible and waiting for complaints.

## Reasons batch performance is a concern

If a long-running batch job does not create an overloaded system or otherwise cost the business money, don't worry about it. Otherwise, there are several reasons to address performance of the process, with different solutions for each:

*End users await results*
> When a process requires an end user to request a report and the next important task the end user can do requires the output of that report, then report runtime is the main concern. Parallelizing the report process is one solution, allowing several processors to attack the problem at once. You can accomplish this in the database layer with parallel execution plans (which I have never found necessary in my own experience) or in the application layer, spawning multiple application processes that attack the problem at once and consolidate results in the end. However, much more often the solution lies in eliminating all or part of the report with the strategies described earlier under "Reasons for large reports." This is especially true because a bottleneck process like this rarely requires the reader to digest enormous amounts of data; chances are that only a few lines of the report are really required by the end user.

*Report fails to fit a processing time-window*
> Many recurring processes take place in time-windows that are preassigned for the work, often in the middle of the night or over weekends. The rest of this chapter has strategies to reduce runtimes, making it easier to meet any given time-window. However, often the simplest strategy is to relax the time-window constraints. When you step back and examine the fundamental needs of the business, time-window constraints usually turn out to be more flexible than they appear. Usually, the window of a process exists within a larger window for a whole collection of processes. That larger window might be smaller than it needs to be. Even if it is not, you can almost always rearrange the processes within the collection to allow enough time for any given process, if the other processes are reasonably tuned.

*Report overloads the system*

The runtime of the report might not directly be a problem at all; no one needs the results right away. This is usually the easiest problem to solve: just make sure the report ties up only moderate amounts of scarce resources during its run. Avoid running parallel processes to hurry a low-priority report at the expense of higher-priority work. Almost always, you can find a way to push such low-priority processes to off hours, when system resources are not scarce and when the effect on the performance of other processes is negligible.

## Report information types

Behind every report is (or should be) one or more business needs that the report addresses. If a report never influences the behavior of its addressees, it is a waste of resources. In a perfect world, a report would simply say, "Do the following: ...," and would be so well designed that you could follow that advice with perfect confidence. Since the recommended action would never take long to describe, long reports would be nonexistent. In the real world, the report helps some human to reach the same conclusion by following human reasoning about the information the report provides. However, it is still the case that, when the report is much longer than the description of the decision it supports, it is probably not distilling the data as well as it should. By discovering how to distill the data to a reasonable volume in the report queries, you not only make the queries inherently faster, you also produce a more usable report, helping to find the forest for the trees, so to speak.

Consider different ways a manager might use a long report, on the assumption that thousands of lines of numbers cannot each, individually, be relevant to business decision-making:

***Only the totals, averages, and other aggregations are interesting, and the detail lines are useless.*** When this is the case, eliminate the detail lines and report only the aggregations. Refer to the strategies under the following section, "Aggregations of Many Details," to further tune the resulting queries.

***The aggregations are what really matter, at least as approximations, but they're not even in the report.*** Instead, the poor manager must scan the details to do her own "eyeball" averages or sums, a miserable waste of human effort and an unreliable way to do arithmetic. If the addressees find themselves doing such eyeball arithmetic, it is a sure sign that the report is poorly designed and that it should report the aggregations directly.

***Exceptions are what matter.*** The vast majority of report rows are useless, but the manager scans the report for special cases that call for action. In the manager's head are criteria for the conditions that call for action, or at least for closer consideration. The answer in this case is clear: define the exception criteria and report only the exceptions. When the exception criteria are fuzzy, at least figure out what defines a clear nonexception and filter those out. The result is almost certain to run much faster and to be a much more usable report.

*The top (or bottom) n (for some nice, round n) are what really matter.* This is really a special case of exceptions, but it is somewhat harder to define the exception criteria without first examining all the details from a sort. The key to handling this case is to realize that there is nothing magic about a nice, round *n*. It is probably just as good to produce a sorted list of records that meet a preset exception criteria. For example, you might choose to reward your top 10 salespersons. However, would you really want to reward the 10th-best if the 10th-best sold less than last year's average salesperson? On the flip side, would you want to bypass rewarding the 11th-best, who missed being 10th-best by $15? The point is that, compared to a top-*n* list, it is probably at least as useful to report a sorted list of exceptions—for example, salespersons who exceeded half a million dollars in sales in the quarter. By defining good exception criteria, which can change as the business evolves, you save the database the work of finding every row to perform a complete sort when almost all of the data is unexceptional and has no real chance to reach the top of the sort. You also provide added information, such as how close the 11th-best was to the 10th-best and how many salespersons exceeded the threshold, compared to the last time you read the report.

*A subset of the data is what matters.* Discard the rest of the set.

## Solutions

For any particular large report, at least one of the earlier sets of questions should lead to a solution to your performance problem. Sometimes, a combination of questions will lead to a multipart solution or will just reinforce the set of reasons for a single solution. In summary, these are the techniques that resolve performance problems:

- Eliminate unused subsets of the reported data. Make sure these unused subsets are not only not reported, but are not even queried from the database. Special cases of this include:
  - Eliminate details, in favor of aggregations only, and see the next section, "Aggregations of Many Details," for how to report aggregations of many details quickly.
  - Report exceptions only, eliminating nonexceptional rows.
  - Replace top-*n* reporting with sorted lists of exceptions.
- Replace large reports with several smaller reports that each cover just the needs of a subset of the addressees.
- Eliminate large reports in favor of online functionality that helps the end users find the information they need as they decide they need it, instead of having them search a report for that information.
- Eliminate reporting driven by data-retention requirements in favor of just maintaining access to the same data in the database or its backups.
- Parallelize processing of high-priority reports that are needed quickly.

- Serialize processing of low-priority reports, and push processing to off hours and lower frequency. Often, the correct frequency for low-priority reports is *never*.

- Rearrange load during processing time-windows to relax time-window-driven constraints.

Admittedly, use of these techniques is more art than science, but take heart: I have never found a case in which no reasonable solution existed.

## Aggregations of Many Details

It never makes sense to show an end user a million rows of data, either online or in a report. However, it makes perfect sense that an end user would want to know something about an aggregation of a million or more rows, such as "What was last quarter's revenue?," where that revenue summarizes a million or more order details. Unfortunately, it is no easier for the database to read a million rows for purposes of aggregation than for purposes of detail reporting. As a result, these large aggregations are often the ultimate in thorny performance problems: perfectly reasonable queries, from a functional perspective, that are inherently expensive to run, even with perfect tuning. These problems often call for a two-pronged attack:

***Examine the query as if it were a query of many details, using the methods of the earlier sections, and apply techniques for large detail queries when possible.*** In particular, consider eliminating details that do not contribute to the aggregations. For example, when summarizing order details for revenue, you might find many order details, such as advertising inserts included for free, that have no cost to the customer. The aggregations are unaffected by these, so the developer might not have bothered to exclude them from the query. But if you exclude them explicitly, the query handles fewer rows without changing the result.

***When necessary, preaggregate data in the database and report the summaries without touching the details.*** This is the most commonly justified form of redundant data stored in a database. It might be possible, for example, to deduce an account balance from the sum of all transactions to that account in its history. However, account balances are needed so commonly that it makes much more sense to store the running balance directly and make very sure that it is rigorously synchronized with the sum of all past transactions. Much of the complexity, error, and redundancy in applications originates from just such synchronization demands. Today, much of this need can be met, with careful design, through database triggers that automatically increment or decrement running sums and counts every time a detail record is inserted, updated, or deleted. With a trigger-based approach, the application frontend need not handle the synchronization needs at all, and many different sources of detail change can all propagate to a summary through a single trigger in the background. This guarantees, far better than the application code can, clean, rigorous synchronization of the redundant data.

## Middleware Processes Handling Too Many Rows

When the destination for collected data is a system (either the same system, when creating redundant data, or another system, when propagating data) rather than a human, larger data volumes often make sense. Nevertheless, the techniques to reduce middleware data volumes look much like the techniques for reducing data volume in reports, substituting a machine addressee for a human one. These are the techniques most reminiscent of report-load-reduction techniques:

- Eliminate unused subsets of the transferred data. Make sure these unused subsets are not only not transferred, but are not even queried from the database. Special cases of this include:

  — Eliminate details, in favor of aggregations only, and see the previous section, "Aggregations of Many Details," for how to collect aggregations of many details quickly.

  — Transfer exceptions only, eliminating nonexceptional rows.

- Parallelize processing of high-priority system interfaces that must move data quickly.

- Serialize processing of low-priority system interfaces, and push processing to off hours and lower frequency. Often, the correct frequency for low-priority system interfaces is *never*.

- Rearrange load during processing time-windows to relax time-window-driven constraints.

In addition to these familiar-looking techniques, there are several techniques specific to middleware:

***Transfer only changed data, not data that hasn't changed since the last run.*** This is, by far, the most powerful technique to reduce middleware data volumes, since changes to data involve much lower volumes than fresh collections of all data. However, middleware commonly takes the slower path to all data, because it is harder, functionally, to keep data in sync through propagating changes to data rather than through complete data refreshes. Just as for preaggregation, which is after all just a special case of data transfer, the safest strategies for propagating only data changes depend on well-designed database triggers. With triggers, any data change, from any cause, will automatically fire the trigger and record the necessary changes whenever the source data is changed.

***Eliminate the interface.*** When applications share a database instance, you can often eliminate interfaces, allowing applications to read each other's data instead of copying data from one application to another.

***Move the dividing line between applications.*** For example, you might have one application that is responsible for Order Entry, and another for Order Fulfillment and Accounts Receivable, combined. The interface between Order Entry and Order Fulfillment would likely involve almost complete duplication of data. If you rearranged the systems to combine Order Entry and Order Fulfillment, you would find a much thinner interface, moving less data, to Accounts Receivable.

*Make the interface faster.* If you must move high data volumes between applications, at least arrange that those high volumes can move fast. The fastest interface simply moves data between tables within a database instance. The next-fastest interface moves data between instances on the same hardware. The next-fastest moves data across a local area network between instances on different machines. The slowest interface alternative transfers data across low-bandwidth, wide-area network links, potentially over intercontinental distances.

# Tuned Queries that Return Few Rows, Slowly

Rarely, a fully tuned query that returns few rows, even without aggregation, runs slowly. Since tuned queries drive from the best filter, this implies that such a query must reach many rows at some point in the execution plan before later filters reduce the rowcount to something moderate. The rules of thumb this book describes are designed to make this a rare event; in my own experience, it has happened just once or twice per year of tuning, on average.

## Why Queries Sometimes Read Many Rows to Return Few

Modest-rowcount queries that are slow even after tuning can be traced to important filters that cannot all be reached before at least one large table is reached. Consider, for example, Figure 10-1. If the root detail table, M, has 50,000,000 rows, then the detail join ratios show that A1 and A2 have 10,000,000 rows each, and B1 and B2 have 100,000 rows each. Robust, index-driven execution plans with join order (B1, A1, M, A2, B2) or (B2, A2, M, A1, B1) are equally attractive, by symmetry. For concreteness, consider just the first join order. In that plan, you reach 100 rows in B1, 10,000 rows in A1, and 50,000 rows in M, A2, and B2 before you discard all but 50 rows for failing to meet the filter condition on B2.

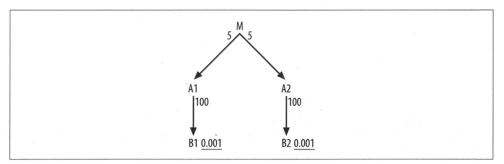

*Figure 10-1. A slow query that returns few rows*

If you relax the robustness requirement, you can preread the 100 rows that meet the filter in B2 and join those to the earlier-reached rows by a hash join. You could even prejoin those 100 rows to A2 with nested loops and perform a hash join between rows reached with nested loops to (B1, A1, M) and rows reached with nested loops that join the combination (B2, A2) (assuming you could get your optimizer to produce such an exotic plan). This would reduce the rowcount you would need to reach A2 to 10,000, while keeping the rowcount to reach B2 at 100. However, none of these strategies eliminates the need to read 50,000 rows from the largest, least well-cached table, M, and that will surely take longer than you would like for a query that returns just 50 rows.

The root of this problem is a join diagram that has selective filters distributed across two or more branches under some large table. The result is that the ultimate level of filtration (a net filter ratio equal to the product of the individual filter ratios) cannot even be approached until after the database has already reached the large table. The highly selective combination of filters is reached too late in the execution plan to avoid excessive reads.

## Optimizing Queries with Distributed Filters

To make optimum use of distributed filters, you need to somehow bring them closer together in the query diagram, preferably into a single table. Consider Figure 10-1 again. Assume that each of the filters on B1 and B2 is an equality condition on some column of that filter's table. A normalized database design places the filter column for B1 where it is because it encodes a property that you need to specify only once per B1 entity. Furthermore, this is a property that you could not infer from knowledge of entities for any master tables that join one-to-many to B1. If you placed this column in A1, that would be a *denormalization*, defined as a property you could infer from knowledge of A1's matching master entity stored in B1. Such a denormalization would require redundant data to be stored in the A1 table, since all 100 A1 entities (on average) that join to any particular B1 row must have the same value for this inherited column. However, in principle, all properties of master-table entities are inherited properties of the detail entities that match those master table entities.

 The form of denormalization I describe is not the only form of denormalization there is. Whole books are written on the subject of normalizing databases, but this simplest form of denormalization is the only form pertinent to this discussion.

For example, if Customer_ID is a property of Orders, it is also an inherited property of the Order_Details that match those orders. With denormalization, you can always push properties up the join tree to nodes above the nodes that own the properties under normalized design. Such inheritance of filter properties need not stop at the first level. For example, `Customer_Name`, a normalized property of `Customers`, could be inherited up two levels, through `Orders`, all the way to `Order_Details`.

This possibility of pushing filter columns up the join tree as high as you wish points to the ultimate solution to performance problems of distributed filters. To avoid distributed-filter problems, keep pushing the most selective filter conditions upward until they come together in a single node, which will inherit a combined filter that has the product of the original filter selectivities. In the extreme case, all filters rise all the way to the root detail node, and the query will read only the few rows it ultimately returns from that table and join downward to the same number of rows from the downstream master tables. In the problem shown in Figure 10-1, table `M` acquires two denormalized columns, from `B1` and `B2`, respectively. The combined filter on these two columns has a selectivity of 0.000001 (0.001×0.001), or one row out of 1,000,000, as shown in Figure 10-2. The optimum execution plan for that query diagram reads 50 rows from `M` and does nested loops, through primary-key indexes, to the 50 rows from each of the other tables, `A1`, `A2`, `B1`, and `B2`. This is a very fast plan.

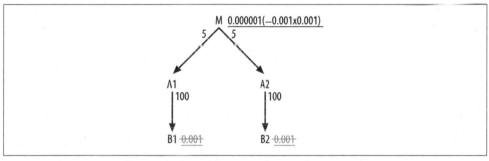

*Figure 10-2. Promoting filters to higher tables, using denormalization*

It might seem odd to mention this powerful technique for combining filters so late in the book. Many texts assume that denormalization is a ubiquitous necessity, but I have not found this to be the case at all. On most applications I have tuned, I have not needed to add a single denormalization for tuning purposes, and tuning purposes are the only good reason for denormalization. If you follow the techniques of the rest of this book, you too should have to use denormalization only rarely, only when you identify a specific important query that cannot otherwise be made fast enough.

Many queries can be made faster through denormalization, but that is not the point. The point is that, even without denormalization, almost all queries can be made fast enough, with correct tuning. An improvement of a few milliseconds does not justify the costs of denormalization. Most performance-driven denormalizations deliver little more than a tiny improvement versus the best optimization possible without denormalization.

If done perfectly, with rigorously designed database triggers that automatically keep the denormalized data perfectly in sync, denormalization can be functionally safe. However, it is not free; it takes up disk space and slows inserts, updates, and deletes that must fire the triggers that keep the data in sync. Given the unavoidable costs of denormalization, I recommend it only when you find a specific, high-priority SQL statement that cannot be made fast enough by other means, which is a very rare case.

> *Time goes, you say? Ah no!*
> *Alas, Time stays, we go.*
> —Henry Austin Dobson
> *The Paradox of Time*

# Exercise Solutions

*When I rest, I rust [Rast'ich, so rost ich].*
—Anonymous
*German proverb*

This appendix contains solutions to the exercises in Chapters 5 through 7.

## Chapter 5 Solutions

Following are the solutions to the exercises in Chapter 5.

### Exercise 1

Figure A-1 shows the solution to Exercise 1.

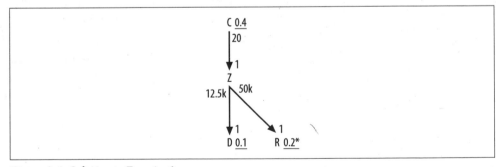

*Figure A-1. Solution to Exercise 1*

The subtlest aspect of this exercise is that you need to notice that you do not need queries (other than the total table rowcounts) to find the filter ratios for the R and D nodes. From the exact matches on uniquely indexed names for each of these, a single match for R and an IN list for D, you can deduce the ratios. You just need to calculate $1/R$ and $2/D$, where $D$ and $R$ are the respective rowcounts of those tables, to find their filter ratios. Did you remember to add the * to the filter ratio on R to indicate that it turns out to be a unique condition? (This turns out to be important for optimizing some queries!) You would add an asterisk for the condition on D, as well, if the match were with a single name instead of a list of names.

The other trick to notice is that, by the assumption of never-null foreign keys with perfect referential integrity, the rowcounts of the joins would simply equal the rowcounts of the detail tables. Therefore, the detail join ratios are simply $d/m$, where $d$ is the rowcount of the upper detail table and $m$ is the rowcount of the lower master table. The master join ratios under the same assumptions are exactly 1.0, and you simply leave them off.

## Exercise 2

Figure A-2 shows the solution to Exercise 2.

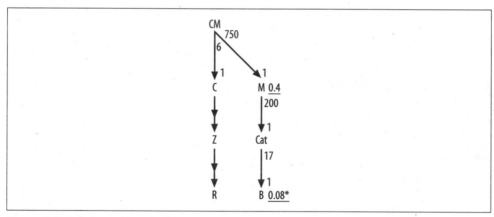

*Figure A-2. Solution to Exercise 2*

In this problem, you need the same shortcuts as for Exercise 1, for join ratios and for the filter ratio to B. Did you remember to add the * for the unique filter on B? Did you remember to indicate the direction of the outer joins to Z and R with the midpoint arrows on those join links?

## Exercise 3

Figure A-3 shows the solution to Exercise 3.

In this problem, you need the same tricks as for Exercise 1, for join ratios and for the filter ratio to B. Did you remember to add the * for the unique filter on B? Did you remember to indicate the direction of the outer joins to C and PL with the midpoint arrows on those join links?

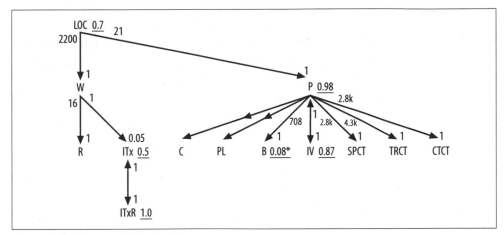

*Figure A-3. Solution to Exercise 3*

The joins to ITxR and IV from ITx and P, respectively, are special one-to-one joins that you indicate with arrows on both ends of the join links. The filter ratios on both ends of these one-to-one joins are exactly 1.0. These are a special class of detail table that frequently comes up in real-world applications: time-dependent details that have one row per master row corresponding to any given effective date. For example, even though you might have multiple inventory tax rates for a given taxing entity, only one of those rates will be in effect at any given moment, so the date ranges defined by Effective_Start_Date and Effective_End_Date will be nonoverlapping. Even though the combination of ID and date-range condition do not constitute equality conditions on a full unique key, the underlying valid data will guarantee that the join is unique when it includes the date-range conditions.

Since you count the date range defined by Effective_Start_Date and Effective_End_Date as part of the join, do not count it as a filter, and consider only the subtable that meets the date-range condition as effective for the query diagram. Thus, you find P and IV to have identical effective rowcounts of 8,500, and you find identical row-counts of 4 for ITx and ITxR. This confirms the one-to-one nature of these joins and the join ratios of 1.0 on each end of the links.

As for the example in Figure 5-4, you should use only subtable rowcounts for the joins to SPCT, TRCT, and CTCT, because Code_Translations is one of those apples-and-oranges tables that join only a specific subtable at a time.

> I have relaxed my own rule about showing just a single significant fig-
> ure in the join and filter ratios. This is largely just to help you see that
> you really have made the right calculations; you haven't just hit the
> right number for the wrong reason.

## Exercise 4

Figure A-4 shows the solution to Exercise 4, the fully simplified solution to Exercise 1.

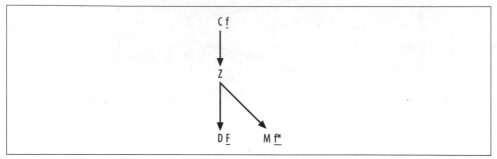

*Figure A-4. Solution to Exercise 4*

Since this problem involves only large detail join ratios and master join ratios equal to 1.0, you just add a capital *F* to the most highly filtered node and add a lowercase *f* to the other filtered nodes, with an asterisk for the unique filter on node R. (Did you remember the asterisk?)

## Exercise 5

Figure A-5 shows the solution to Exercise 5, the fully simplified solution to Exercise 2.

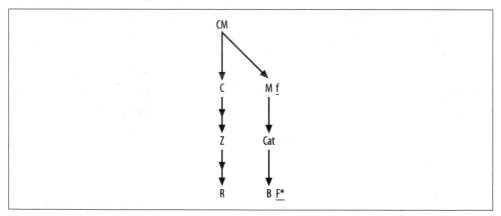

*Figure A-5. Solution to Exercise 5*

Since this problem involves only large detail join ratios, and master join ratios equal to 1.0, you just add a capital *F* to the most highly filtered node and add a lowercase *f* to the other filtered node, with an asterisk for the unique filter on node B. (Did you remember the asterisk?)

## Exercise 6

Figure A-6 shows the solution to Exercise 6, the fully simplified solution to Exercise 3.

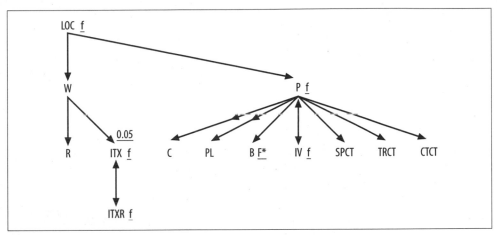

*Figure A-6. Solution to Exercise 6*

Since this problem involves only large detail join ratios, you can leave those out. However, note that it does include one master join ratio well under 1.0, in the join down into ITx, so you leave that one in. Otherwise, you just add a capital *F* to the most highly filtered node and add a lowercase *f* to the other filtered nodes, with an asterisk for the unique filter on node B. (Did you remember the asterisk?)

# Chapter 6 Solution

Chapter 6 included only one, outrageously complicated problem. This section details the step-by-step solution to that problem.

Figure A-7 shows how to adjust effective filters to take account of join factors less than 1.0, which occur in three places in Figure 6-33.

You adjust effective filters immediately on either side of the master join ratios, since you can migrate those filters upward with explicit IS NOT NULL conditions on the foreign keys. This adjusts filters on B1, C1, C2, and D1, and you cross out the master join ratios to show that you took them into account. Note the detail join ratio of 0.02 between M and A1 for even bigger adjustments on every filter from M down through the A2 branch.

> If there were other branches, you would adjust them as well. Only the A1 branch, attached through that filtering join, does not see the adjustment.

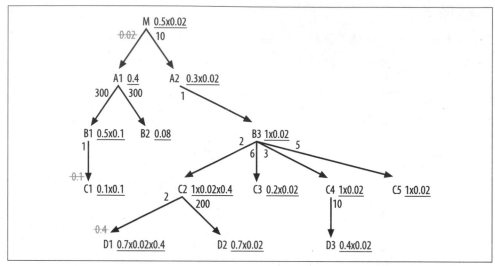

*Figure A-7. Effective filters taking account of join factors, to choose the driving table*

Note that you adjust the effective join ratio for C2 and D1 twice, since two filtering joins affect these. Working through the numbers, you find the best effective filter, 0.004 (0.2×0.02), lies on C3, so that is the driving table.

After choosing the driving table, you need a whole new set of adjustments to take account of the two low master join ratios before choosing the rest of the join order. Note that you no longer need to take account of the detail join ratio, since the database is coming from the side of the join that does not discard rows through the join. This happens whenever you choose a driving table with an effective filter adjusted by the detail join ratio. In a sense, you burn the filter at the beginning, coming from smaller tables that point to only a subset of the master table (A1 in this case) on the other side of that join.

It is best to get the benefit of the hidden join filters that point to C1 and D1 as early in the join order as possible. Therefore, make explicit the is-not-null filters on the foreign keys (in B1 and C2) that point to these filtering joins, as shown in Figure A-8. By making these filters explicit (and assuming referential integrity), you no longer see filtering in the joins themselves, so you cross out those join ratios.

From C3, you can join only to B3, so it is next in the join order. From these two, you can join to C2, C4, C5 (below), or A2 (above). Normally, you would consider joining only next to the tables below, but notice that the detail join ratio to A2 is 1.0, so it is eligible early and, in fact, it turns out to have the best effective filter of the choices, so you join to it next. This adds M to the list of nodes now in reach, but the detail join ratio to M is high, so postpone that join as long as possible. The only eligible node below with a filter is now C2, thanks to the now-explicit not-null condition on the foreign key that points to D1, so join to C2 next. The join order, so far, is (C3, B3, A2, C2).

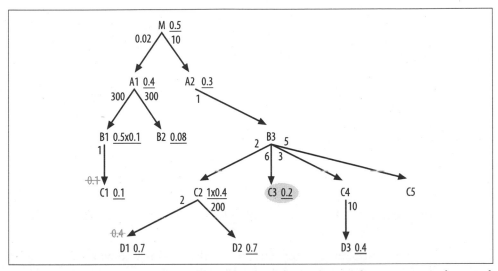

*Figure A-8. Adjusting to make is-not-null conditions on foreign keys explicit, to optimize the rest of the join order*

The join to C2 adds D1 and D2 to the list of eligible nodes downward from the joined tables so far, and these are the only eligible tables in that direction with filters, so choose one of them next. The filter ratios are identical, so look at other considerations to break the tie and note that D2 must be smaller, since the detail join ratio above it is much larger. Therefore, following the smaller-table-first tiebreaker, join to D2 before D1. The join order, so far, is (C3, B3, A2, C2, D2, D1).

Between C4 and C5, you also have a tie on filter ratios (unshown) equal to 1.0, but you break the tie with the filter-proximity rule that favors C4 for the path it provides to the filter on D3. After reaching C4, go to D3 for that filter and finally join to the unfiltered C5. The join order, so far, is (C3, B3, A2, C2, D2, D1, C4, D3, C5).

From here, there is no choice in the next node, the upward join to M. After reaching M, there is again no choice; A1 is the only node attached. At this point, you could join to either B1 or B2. Their filter ratios are nearly a tie for purposes of later joins, but their detail join ratios are the same, so they should be the same size, leaving table size out of the picture. You can also leave proximity out of the picture, because the filter on C1 is no better than the filter on B1. With no reason to override going to the best filter, on B1, you choose to join to it next. This leaves the join order, so far, of (C3, B3, A2, C2, D2, D1, C4, D3, C5, M, A1, B1). The only two nodes left, B2 and C1, are both eligible now. B2 has the better filter, and the combination of master join ratio and detail join ratio to C1 shows it to be 1/10th the size of B1. B1, in turn, was the same size as B2, so B2 and C1 are different in size by a factor of 10, probably enough for the smaller-table-first tiebreaker rule to favor C1 in the near-tie between B2 and C1. Therefore, go with C1 first, leaving the complete join order of (C3, B3, A2, C2, D2, D1, C4, D3, C5, M, A1, B1, C1, B2).

These last few joins actually will affect the query cost very little, since the query will be down to a few rows by this point.

To reach the root table from C3, for a robust nested-loops plan, the database needs foreign-key indexes (from M to A2, from A2 to B3, and from B3 to C3) on M, A2, and B3. You probably need no index at all on C3, since the 20% filter on that table is not selective enough to make an index outperform a full table scan. (This is probably a small table, based on the join factors.) All other tables require indexes on their primary keys to enable a robust plan.

To make the hidden join filters to C1 and D1 explicit and apply them earlier in the plan, add the conditions C2.FkeyToD1 IS NOT NULL AND B1.FkeyToC1 IS NOT NULL to the query.

Now, relax the robust-plan requirement, and work out which joins should be hash joins and which access path should be used for the hash-joined tables. Recall that table A1 has 30,000,000 rows. From the detail join ratios, B1 and B2 have 1/300th as many rows: 100,000 each. From the combination of master join ratio and detail join ratio, C1 has 1/10th as many rows as B1: 10,000. Going up from A1 to M, M has far fewer (0.02 times as many) rows as A1: 600,000. Coming down from M, using detail join ratios, calculate 60,000 for A2 and B3, 30,000 for C2, 10,000 for C3, 20,000 for C4, and 12,000 for C5. Using both master and detail join ratios from C2 to D1, calculate 6,000 (30,000×0.4/2) rows for D1. From detail join ratios, find 150 rows in D2 and 2,000 rows in D3.

Any part of the plan that reads more rows from a table than the database would read using the filter on that table tends to favor accessing that table through the filter index and using a hash join at the same point in the original execution plan. Any part of the plan that reads at least 5% of the rows in a table tends to favor a full table scan of that table with a hash join. When both sorts of hash-join access are favored over nested loops (i.e., for a hash join with an indexed read of the filter or with a full table scan), favor the full table scan if the filter matches at least 5% of the table.

As discussed in Chapter 2, the actual cutoff for indexed access can be anywhere between 0.5% and 20%, but this exercise stated 5% as the assumed cutoff, to make the problem concrete.

In summary, Table A-1 shows the table sizes and full-table-scan cutoffs, arranged in join order.

Table A-1. Table sizes and full-table-scan cutoffs for the Chapter 6 exercise solution

| Table | Rowcount | Full-table-scan cutoff |
|-------|----------|------------------------|
| C3 | 10,000 | 500 |
| B3 | 60,000 | 3,000 |
| A2 | 60,000 | 3,000 |
| C2 | 30,000 | 1,500 |
| D2 | 150 | 8 |
| D1 | 6,000 | 300 |
| C4 | 20,000 | 1,000 |
| D3 | 2,000 | 100 |
| C5 | 12,000 | 600 |
| M | 600,000 | 30,000 |
| A1 | 30,000,000 | 1,500,000 |
| B1 | 100,000 | 5,000 |
| C1 | 10,000 | 500 |
| B2 | 100,000 | 5,000 |

Now, working out the rowcounts at each stage of the query, you find that, after the full table scan to C3, the filter on C3 drops the rowcount to 2,000 rows. Joining upward with nested loops to B1 touches 12,000 rows of that table, since the detail join ratio is 6. B3 has no filter, so following the one-to-one (on average) join to A2 also reaches 12,000 rows, after which the filter on A2 leaves 30% (3,600 rows) for the next join to C2. With an implied master join ratio of 1.0, nested loops would touch 3,600 rows of C2. The filters on C2 (including the now-explicit is-not-null filter on the foreign key to D1) reduce that rowcount to 1,440 before the join to D2. Nested loops to D2 read 1,440 rows of that table, after which the filter leaves 1,008 rows. Nested loops to D2 read 1,008 rows of that table (since by this point all rows have nonnull foreign keys that point to D1), after which the filter leaves 706 rows (rounding, as I will for the rest of the calculation).

Nested loops to C4 read 706 rows of that table, which are unfiltered, leaving 706. Nested loops to D3 read 706 rows of that table, after which the filter leaves 282. Nested loops to C5 read 282 rows of that table, which are unfiltered, leaving 282. With the detail join ratio of 10, the join upward into M reaches 2,820 rows of that table, after which the filter leaves 1,410. With the implied master join ratio of 1.0, nested loops reach 1,410 rows of the biggest table, A1, after which the filter leaves 564. Nested loops to B1 read 564 rows of that table, after which the filters (including the now-explicit foreign-key-is-not-null condition on the key on B1 that points to C1) leave 28. Nested loops to C1 read 28 rows of that table (since by this point all rows have nonnull foreign keys that point to C1), after which the filter leaves 3. Nested loops to B2 read 3 rows of that table, after which the final filter leaves 0 or 1 row in the final result.

If you compare these counts of rows reached by nested loops with the full-table-scan cutoffs, you see that hash joins to full table scans reduce cost for several of the tables. Since none of the filters in this query were selective enough to prefer single-table indexed access to full table scans (by the assumed 5% cutoff), you would choose hash joins to rowsets read by full table scans, when you choose hash joins at all. This example shows an unusually favorable case for hash joins. More common examples, with queries of large tables that have at least one selective filter, show fractionally much smaller improvements for hash joins to the smallest tables only.

Table A-2 shows the rowcounts calculated for the best robust plan, alongside the cutoff rowcounts that would result in a hash join to a full table scan being faster. The rightmost column, labeled *Method/Join*, shows the optimum table access and join methods that result for each table in the leftmost column.

*Table A-2. Best access/join methods for the example*

| Table | Rowcount | Full-table-scan cutoff | Robust-plan rows reached | Method/Join |
|---|---|---|---|---|
| C3 | 10,000 | 500 | 2,000 | Full scan/Driving |
| B3 | 60,000 | 3,000 | 12,000 | Full scan/Hash |
| A2 | 60,000 | 3,000 | 12,000 | Full scan/Hash |
| C2 | 30,000 | 1,500 | 3,600 | Full scan/Hash |
| D2 | 150 | 8 | 1,440 | Full scan/Hash |
| D1 | 6,000 | 300 | 1,008 | Full scan/Hash |
| C4 | 20,000 | 1,000 | 706 | Index/Nested loop |
| D3 | 2,000 | 100 | 706 | Full scan/Hash |
| C5 | 12,000 | 600 | 282 | Index/Nested loop |
| M | 600,000 | 30,000 | 2,820 | Index/Nested loop |
| A1 | 30,000,000 | 1,500,000 | 1,410 | Index/Nested loop |
| B1 | 100,000 | 5,000 | 564 | Index/Nested loop |
| C1 | 10,000 | 500 | 28 | Index/Nested loop |
| B2 | 100,000 | 5,000 | 3 | Index/Nested loop |

Note that replacing nested-loops joins with hash joins as shown eliminates the need (for this query, at least) for the foreign-key indexes on B3 and A2 and the primary-key indexes on C2, D2, D1, and D3.

# Chapter 7 Solution

Chapter 7 included only one problem, which was deliberately very complex to exercise most of the subquery rules. This section details the step-by-step solution to that problem. Figure A-9 shows the missing ratios for the three semi-joins and the anti-join.

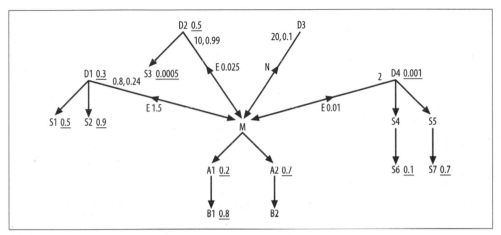

I'll begin by reviewing the calculation of the missing ratios shown in Figure A-9. To find the correlation preference ratio for the semi-join to D1, follow the rules stated in Chapter 7, in the section "Diagramming EXISTS subqueries." In Step 1, you find that the detail join ratio for D1 from Figure 7-36 is $D$=0.8. This is an uncommon case of a many-to-one join that averages less than one detail per master row. Assume $M$=1, the usual master join ratio when it is not explicitly shown on the diagram. The best filter ratio among the nodes of this subquery (D1, S1, and S2) is 0.3 on D1, so $S$=0.3. The best filter ratio among the nodes of the outer query (M, A1, A2, B1, and B2) is 0.2 for A1, so $R$=0.2. For Step 2 of the rules, find $D \times S$=0.24 and $M \times R$=0.2, so $D \times S > M \times R$. Therefore, proceed to Step 3. You find $S > R$, so you set the correlation preference ratio to $S/R$=1.5, next to the semi-join indicator $E$ from M to D1.

To find the correlation preference ratio for the semi-join to D2, repeat the process. In Step 1, you find the detail join ratio from Figure 7-36 ($D$=10). Assume $M$=1, the usual master join ratio when it is not explicitly shown on the diagram. The best filter ratio between D2 and S3 is 0.0005 on S3, so $S$=0.0005. The best filter ratio among the nodes of the outer query, as before, is $R$=0.2. For Step 2 of the rules, find $D \times S$=0.005 and $M \times R$=0.2, so $D \times S < M \times R$. Therefore, Step 2 completes the calculation, and you set the correlation preference ratio to $(D \times S)/(M \times R)$=0.025, next to the semi-join indicator $E$ from M to D2.

To find the correlation preference ratio for the semi-join to D4, repeat the process. In Step 1, you find that the detail join ratio from Figure 7-36 is $D=2$. Assume $M=1$, the usual master join ratio when it is not explicitly shown on the diagram. The best filter ratio among D4, S4, S5, S6, and S7 is 0.001 on D4, so $S=0.001$. The best filter ratio among the nodes of the outer query, as before, is $R=0.2$. For Step 2 of the rules, find $D \times S=0.002$ and $M \times R=0.2$, so $D \times S < M \times R$. Therefore, Step 2 completes the calculation, and you set the correlation preference ratio to $(D \times S)/(M \times R)=0.01$, next to the semi-join indicator $E$ from M to D4.

Now, shift to the next set of rules, to find the subquery adjusted filter ratios. Step 1 dictates that you do not need a subquery adjusted filter ratio for D4, because its correlation preference ratio is both less than 1.0 and less than any other correlation preference ratio. Proceed to Step 2 for both D1 (which has a correlation preference ratio greater than 1.0) and D2 (which has a correlation preference ratio greater than D4's correlation preference ratio). The subqueries under both D1 and D2 have filters, so proceed to Step 3 for both. For D1, find $D=0.8$ and $s=0.3$, the filter ratio on D1 itself. At Step 4, note that $D<1$, so you set the subquery adjusted filter ratio equal to $s \times D=0.24$, placed next to the 0.8 on the upper end of the semi-join link to D1.

At Step 3 for D2, find $D=10$ and $s=0.5$, the filter ratio on D2 itself. At Step 4, note that $D>1$, so proceed to Step 5. Note that $s \times D=5$, which is greater than 1.0, so proceed to Step 6. Set the subquery adjusted filter ratio equal to 0.99, placed next to the 10 on the upper end of the semi-join link to D2.

The only missing ratio now is the subquery adjusted filter ratio for the anti-join to D3. Following the rules for anti-joins, for Step 1, find $t=5$ and $q=50$ from the problem statement. In Step 2, note that there is (as with many NOT EXISTS conditions) just a single node in this subquery, so $C=1$, and calculate $(C-1+(t/q))/C=(1-1+(5/50))/1=0.1$.

Now, proceed to the rules for tuning subqueries, with the completed query diagram. Following Step 1, ensure that the anti-join to D3 is expressed as a NOT EXISTS correlated subquery, not as a noncorrelated NOT IN subquery. Step 2 does not apply, because you have no semi-joins (EXISTS conditions) with midpoint arrows that point downward. Following Step 3, find the lowest correlation preference ratio, 0.01, for the semi-join to D4, so express that condition with a noncorrelated IN subquery and ensure that the other EXISTS-type conditions are expressed as explicit EXISTS conditions on correlated subqueries. Optimizing the subquery under D4 as if it were a standalone query, you find, following rules for simple queries, the initial join order of (D4, S4, S6, S5, S7). Following this start, the database will perform a sort-unique operation on the foreign key of D4 that points to M across the semi-join. Nested loops follow to M, following the index on the primary key of M. Optimize from M as if the subquery condition on D4 did not exist.

Step 4 does not apply, since you chose to drive from a subquery IN condition. Step 5 applies, because at node M you find all three remaining subquery joins immediately available. The semi-join to D1 acts like a downward-hanging node with filter ratio of 0.24, not as good as A1, but better than A2. The semi-join to D2 acts like a downward-hanging node with a filter ratio of 0.99, just better than a downward join to an unfiltered node, but not as good as A1 or A2. The anti-join to D3 is best of all, like many selective anti-joins, acting like a downward-hanging node with a filter ratio of 0.1, better than any other.

Therefore, perform the NOT EXISTS condition to D3 next, and find a running join order of (D4, S4, S6, S5, S7, M, D3). Since the subquery to D3 is single-table, return to the outer query and find the next-best downward-hanging node (or virtual downward-hanging node) at A1. This makes B1 eligible to join, but B1 is less attractive than the best remaining choice, D1, with its subquery adjusted filter ratio of 0.24, so D1 is next. Having begun that subquery, you must finish it, following the usual rules for optimizing a simple query, beginning with D1 as the driving node. Therefore, the next joins are S1 and S2, in that order, for a running join order of (D4, S4, S6, S5, S7, M, D3, A1, D1, S1, S2).

Now, you find eligible nodes A2, B1, and D2, which are preferred in that order, based on their filter ratios or (for D2) their subquery adjusted filter ratio. When you join to A2, you find a new eligible node, B2, but it has a filter ratio of 1.0, which is not as attractive as the others. Therefore, join to A2, B1, and D2, in that order, for a running join order of (D4, S4, S6, S5, S7, M, D3, A1, D1, S1, S2, A2, B1, D2). Having reached D2, you must complete that subquery with the join to S3, and that leaves only the remaining node B2, so the complete join order is (D4, S4, S6, S5, S7, M, D3, A1, D1, S1, S2, A2, B1, D2, S3, B2).

# The Full Process, End to End

*Do not delay,*
*Do not delay: the golden moments fly!*
—Henry Wadsworth Longfellow
  *Masque of Pandora (Pt. VII)*

Throughout the book, there are examples that illustrate each step of the process in detail, but I have not yet followed a single example through the entire process. If you like seeing whole processes from end to end and working from those examples, this appendix is for you.

The example in this appendix follows a query that is just complex enough to illustrate the main points that come up repeatedly, while having something wrong that needs fixing. Imagine that the following query were proposed for an application designed to run well on Oracle, DB2, and SQL Server, and you were asked to pass judgement regarding its optimality on those databases and to propose changes to tune it as needed:

```
SELECT C.Phone_Number, C.Honorific, C.First_Name, C.Last_Name, C.Suffix,
C.Address_ID, A.Address_ID, A.Street_Addr_Line1, A.Street_Addr_Line2,
A.City_Name, A.State_Abbreviation, A.ZIP_Code, OD.Deferred_Ship_Date,
OD.Item_Count, P.Prod_Description, S.Shipment_Date
FROM Orders O, Order_Details OD, Products P, Customers C, Shipments S,
Addresses A
WHERE OD.Order_ID = O.Order_ID
AND O.Customer_ID = C.Customer_ID
AND OD.Product_ID = P.Product_ID
AND OD.Shipment_ID = S.Shipment_ID
AND S.Address_ID = A.Address_ID
AND C.Phone_Number = 6505551212
AND O.Business_Unit_ID = 10
ORDER BY C.Customer_ID, O.Order_ID Desc, S.Shipment_ID, OD.Order_Detail_ID;
```

# Reducing the Query to a Query Diagram

For the first step in the process, create a query diagram. Start with a query skeleton, and then add detail to complete the diagram. The next few subsections walk you through the process of creating the diagram for the example query.

## Creating the Query Skeleton

As a starting point, place a random alias in the center of the diagram under construction. For illustration purposes, I'll begin with the node O. Draw arrows downward from that node to any nodes that join to O through their primary key (named, for all these tables, by the same name as the table, with the s at the end replaced by _ID). Draw a downward-pointing arrow from any alias to O for any join that joins to O on the Orders table's primary key, Order_ID. The beginning of the query skeleton should look like Figure B-1.

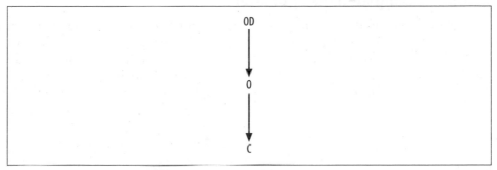

Figure B-1. The beginning of the query skeleton

Now, shift focus to OD. Find joins from that node, and add those links to the join skeleton. The result is shown in Figure B-2.

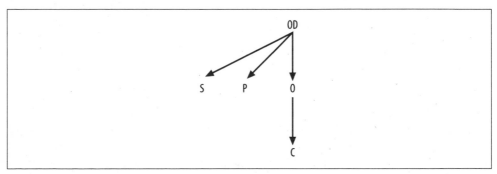

Figure B-2. An intermediate stage of the query skeleton

Find undiagramed join conditions. The only one left is S.Address_ID = A.Address_ID, so add a link for that join to complete the query skeleton, as shown in Figure B-3.

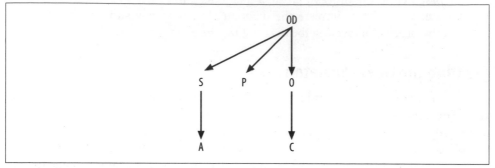

*Figure B-3. The completed query skeleton*

## Creating a Simplified Query Diagram

To build the simplified query diagram, find the most selective filter and identify it with an underlined *F* next to the filtered node. The condition on the customer's phone number is almost certainly the most selective filter. Add a small underlined *f* for the only other filter, the much less selective condition on Business_Unit_ID for Orders. The result, shown in Figure B-4, is the simplified query diagram.

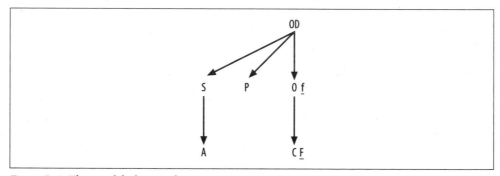

*Figure B-4. The simplified query diagram*

## Creating a Full Query Diagram

The simplified query diagram is sufficient to tune this particular query. However, for purposes of illustration, I will show the creation of a full query diagram, with all the details. Use the following queries to gather statistics necessary for a full query diagram. The results I'm using for this example are shown following each query. As an exercise, you might wish to work out the filter and join ratios for yourself.

```
Q1:  SELECT SUM(COUNT(Phone_Number)*COUNT(Phone_Number))/
            (SUM(COUNT(Phone_Number))*SUM(COUNT(*))) A1
     FROM Customers
     GROUP BY Phone_Number;
A1:  0.000003

Q2:  SELECT COUNT(*) A2 FROM Customers;
A2:  500,000

Q3:  SELECT SUM(COUNT(Business_Unit_ID)*COUNT(Business_Unit_ID))/
            (SUM(COUNT(Business_Unit_ID))*SUM(COUNT(*))) A3
     FROM Orders
     GROUP BY Business_Unit_ID;
A3:  0.2

Q4:  SELECT COUNT(*) A4 FROM Orders;
A4:  400,000

Q5:  SELECT COUNT(*) A5
     FROM Orders O, Customers C
     WHERE O.Customer_ID = C.Customer_ID;
A5:  400,000

Q6:  SELECT COUNT(*) A6 FROM Order_Details;
A6:  1,200,000

Q7:  SELECT COUNT(*) A7
     FROM Orders O, Order_Details OD
     WHERE OD.Order_ID = O.Order_ID;
A7:  1,2000,000

Q8:  SELECT COUNT(*) A8 FROM Shipments;
A8:  540,000

Q9:  SELECT COUNT(*) A9
     FROM Shipments S, Order_Details OD
     WHERE OD.Shipment_ID = S.Shipment_ID;
A9:  1,080,000

Q10: SELECT COUNT(*) A10 FROM Products;
A10: 12,000

Q11: SELECT COUNT(*) A11
     FROM Products P, Order_Details OD
     WHERE OD.Product_ID = P.Product_ID;
A11: 1,200,000

Q12: SELECT COUNT(*) A12 FROM Addresses;
A12: 135,000

Q13: SELECT COUNT(*) A13
     FROM Addresses A, Shipments S
     WHERE S.Address_ID = A.Address_ID;
A13: 540,000
```

I downsized the tables in this example so that I could provide practical data-generation scripts to test the execution plans that cost-based optimizers will generate for these tables. If you want to follow along with the example, you can download these scripts from the O'Reilly catalog page for this book: *http://www.oreilly.com/catalog/sqltuning/*. (However, I cannot guarantee identical results, since results depend on your database version number, parameters set by your DBA, and the data.) The larger tables in this example would likely be around 10 times bigger in a production environment.

Beginning with filter ratios, get the weighted-average filter ratio for the condition on Customers Phone_Number directly from A1, which is the result from query Q1 (0.000003). Find the filter ratio on Orders the same way, from Q3, which returns the result of 0.2 for A3.

Since no other alias has any filters, the filter ratios on the other four are 1.0, which you imply by just leaving filter ratios off the query diagram for the other nodes.

For each join, find the detail join ratio, to place alongside the upper end of each join arrow, by dividing the count on the join of the two tables by the count on the lower table (the master table of that master-detail relationship). The ratios for the upper ends of the joins from OD to S, O, and P are 2 (A9/A8), 3 (A7/A4), and 100 (A11/A10), respectively. The ratio for the upper end of the join from S to A is 4 (A13/A12). The ratio for the upper ends of the join from O to C is 0.8 (A5/A2).

Find the master join ratios, to place alongside the lower end of each join arrow, by dividing the count on the join of the two tables by the count on each upper table (the detail table of a master-detail relationship). The ratio for the lower end of the join from OD to S is 0.9 (A9/A6). All the other master join ratios turn out to be 1.0, so leave these off the diagram.

Add filter ratios and join ratios to the query skeleton (see Figure B-3) to create the full query diagram, as shown in Figure B-5.

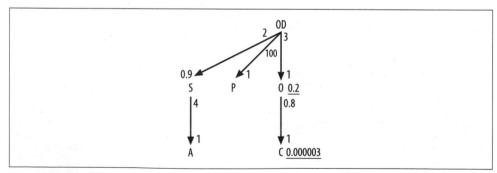

*Figure B-5. The full query diagram*

# Solving the Query Diagram

After you've reduced the detail-filled query to an abstract join diagram, you are 80% of the way to finding the best execution plan, just as math word problems usually become trivial once you convert them to symbolic form. However, you still must solve the symbolic problem. Using the methods of Chapter 6, solve the problem abstracted in Figure B-5:

1. Choose the best driving table. By far, the best (closest to 0) filter ratio is on C, so choose C as the driving table.

2. From C, you find no downward joins, so you choose the only upward join, to 0, placing 0 second in the join order.

 Even if there were downward joins available from C, you would still consider joining to 0 early, since the detail join ratio to 0 is less than 1.0 and since 0 has a good filter itself.

3. From 0, you find no unused downward joins, so you choose the only upward join, to OD, placing OD third in the join order.

4. From OD, you find two unused downward joins, to S and to P. There are no more simple filters on the remaining nodes, but there is a hidden join filter in the join to S, since the master join ratio on that join is less than 1.0. Therefore, join to S next, placing S fourth in the join order.

 If there were a filter on node P, you would make the implicit filter OD.Shipment_ID IS NOT NULL (which is implied by the master join ratio to S being less than 1.0) explicit, so you could pick up that filter early without joining to S and reach the filter on P after getting the benefit of that NOT NULL filter, without paying the added price of joining to S before P.

5. The remaining nodes, A and P, are both unfiltered, are reachable directly with joins from tables already reached, and have master join ratios equal to 1.0, so it makes no difference which order you join to these last two nodes. Just to make the rest of the problem concrete, arbitrarily choose A as the fifth in the join order and then choose P as the last. This leads you to the optimum join order of (C, 0, OD, S, A, P).

6. Given the join order, specify the full execution plan, following the rules for robust execution plans, in the optimum join order:

   a. Drive to the first table, Customers, on an index on the filter column, Phone_Number, with a query modified if necessary to make that index accessible and fully useful.

   b. With nested loops, join to Orders on an index on the foreign key Customer_ID.

c. With nested loops, join to Order_Details on an index on the foreign key Order_ID.

d. With nested loops, join to Shipments on its primary-key index on Shipment_ID.

e. With nested loops, join to Addresses on its primary-key index on Address_ID.

f. With nested loops, join to Products on its primary-key index on Product_ID.

This completes the second step in the tuning process: finding the execution plan that you want. Next, you need to see which execution plan you actually get, on all three databases, since this example illustrates SQL that is designed to run on any of the three.

# Checking the Execution Plans

For this exercise, imagine that the base development is performed on Oracle, with later testing to check that the same SQL functions correctly and performs well on DB2 and SQL Server. You learned of this SQL because it performed more slowly than expected on Oracle, so you already suspect it leads to a poor execution plan on at least that database. You will need to check execution plans on the other databases, which have not yet been tested.

## Getting the Oracle Execution Plan

Place the SQL in a file named *tmp.sql* and run the script *ex.sql*, as described in Chapter 3. The result is as follows:

```
PLAN
--------------------------------------------------------------------------------
SELECT STATEMENT
  SORT ORDER BY
    NESTED LOOPS
      NESTED LOOPS
        NESTED LOOPS
          NESTED LOOPS
            NESTED LOOPS
              TABLE ACCESS FULL 4*CUSTOMERS
              TABLE ACCESS BY INDEX ROWID 1*ORDERS
                INDEX RANGE SCAN ORDER_CUSTOMER_ID
            TABLE ACCESS BY INDEX ROWID 2*ORDER_DETAILS
              INDEX RANGE SCAN ORDER_DETAIL_ORDER_ID
          TABLE ACCESS BY INDEX ROWID 5*SHIPMENTS
            INDEX UNIQUE SCAN SHIPMENT_PKEY
        TABLE ACCESS BY INDEX ROWID 6*ADDRESSES
          INDEX UNIQUE SCAN ADDRESS_PKEY
      TABLE ACCESS BY INDEX ROWID 3*PRODUCTS
        INDEX UNIQUE SCAN PRODUCT_PKEY
```

You notice that your database is set up to use the rule-based optimizer, so you switch to cost-based optimization, check that you have statistics on the tables and indexes, and check the plan again, finding a new result:

```
PLAN
----------------------------------------------------------------------------
SELECT STATEMENT
  SORT ORDER BY
    HASH JOIN
      TABLE ACCESS FULL 3*PRODUCTS
      HASH JOIN
        HASH JOIN
          HASH JOIN
            HASH JOIN
              TABLE ACCESS FULL 4*CUSTOMERS
              TABLE ACCESS FULL 1*ORDERS
            TABLE ACCESS FULL 2*ORDER_DETAILS
          TABLE ACCESS FULL 5*SHIPMENTS
        TABLE ACCESS FULL 6*ADDRESSES
```

Neither execution plan is close to the optimum plan. Instead, both the rule-based and the cost-based optimization plans drive from full table scans of large tables. The database ought to reach the driving table on a highly selective index, so you know that an improvement is certainly both necessary and possible.

## Getting the DB2 Execution Plan

Place the SQL in *tmp.sql* and run the following command according to the process described in Chapter 3:

```
cat head.sql tmp.sql tail.sql | db2 +c +p -t
```

The result is an error; DB2 complains that it sees inconsistent column types in the condition on Phone_Number. You discover that the Phone_Number column is of the VARCHAR type, which is incompatible with the number type of the constant 6505551212.

Unlike Oracle, DB2 does not implicitly convert character-type columns to numbers when SQL compares inconsistent datatypes. This is just as well, in this case, since such a conversion might deactivate an index on Phone_Number, if there is one. You might even suspect, already, that this is precisely what has caused poor performance in the Oracle baseline development environment.

You fix the problem in the most obvious way, placing quotes around the phone number constant to make it a character type:

```
SELECT C.Phone_Number, C.Honorific, C.First_Name, C.Last_Name, C.Suffix,
C.Address_ID, A.Address_ID, A.Street_Addr_Line1, A.Street_Addr_Line2,
A.City_Name, A.State_Abbreviation, A.ZIP_Code, OD.Deferred_Ship_Date,
OD.Item_Count, P.Prod_Description, S.Shipment_Date
FROM Orders O, Order_Details OD, Products P, Customers C, Shipments S,
Addresses A
```

```
WHERE OD.Order_ID = O.Order_ID
AND O.Customer_ID = C.Customer_ID
AND OD.Product_ID = P.Product_ID
AND OD.Shipment_ID = S.Shipment_ID
AND S.Address_ID = A.Address_ID
AND C.Phone_Number = '6505551212'
AND O.Business_Unit_ID = 10
ORDER BY C.Customer_ID, O.Order_ID Desc, S.Shipment_ID, OD.Order_Detail_ID;
```

Placing this new version of the SQL in *tmp.sql*, you again attempt to get the execution plan:

```
$ cat head.sql tmp.sql tail.sql | db2 +c +p -t
DB20000I  The SQL command completed successfully.
DB20000I  The SQL command completed successfully.
```

| OPERATOR_ID | TARGET_ID | OPERATOR_TYPE | OBJECT_NAME | COST |
|---|---|---|---|---|
| 1 | - | RETURN | - | 260 |
| 2 | 1 | NLJOIN | - | 260 |
| 3 | 2 | NLJOIN | - | 235 |
| 4 | 3 | NLJOIN | - | 210 |
| 5 | 4 | TBSCAN | - | 185 |
| 6 | 5 | SORT | - | 185 |
| 7 | 6 | NLJOIN | - | 185 |
| 8 | 7 | NLJOIN | - | 135 |
| 9 | 8 | FETCH | CUSTOMERS | 75 |
| 10 | 9 | IXSCAN | CUST_PH_NUMBER | 50 |
| 11 | 8 | FETCH | ORDERS | 70 |
| 12 | 11 | IXSCAN | ORDER_CUST_ID | 50 |
| 13 | 7 | FETCH | ORDER_DETAILS | 75 |
| 14 | 13 | IXSCAN | ORDER_DTL_ORD_ID | 50 |
| 15 | 4 | FETCH | PRODUCTS | 50 |
| 16 | 15 | IXSCAN | PRODUCT_PKEY | 25 |
| 17 | 3 | FETCH | SHIPMENTS | 75 |
| 18 | 17 | IXSCAN | SHIPMENT_PKEY | 50 |
| 19 | 2 | FETCH | ADDRESSES | 75 |
| 20 | 19 | IXSCAN | ADDRESS_PKEY | 50 |

```
  20 record(s) selected.

DB20000I  The SQL command completed successfully.
$
```

That's more like it, just the execution plan you chose when you analyzed the SQL top-down, except for the minor issue of reaching Products before Shipments, which will have virtually no effect on the runtime. Since the type inconsistency involving Phone_Number might require correcting on SQL Server and Oracle, you need to try this modified version immediately on the other databases.

# Getting the SQL Server Execution Plan

Suspecting that you already have the solution to slow performance for this query, you fire up SQL Server's Query Analyzer and use set showplan_text on to see a concise view of the execution plan of the statement modified with C.Phone_Number = '6505551212' to correct the type inconsistency. A click on the Query Analyzer's Execute-Query button results in the following output:

```
StmtText
----------------------------------------------------------------------------
 |--Bookmark Lookup(...(...[Products] AS [P]))
      |--Nested Loops(Inner Join)
           |--Bookmark Lookup(...(...[Addresses] AS [A]))
           |    |--Nested Loops(Inner Join)
           |         |--Sort(ORDER BY:([O].[Customer_ID] ASC, [O].[Order_ID] DESC,
(wrapped line) [OD].[Shipment_ID] ASC, [OD].[Order_Detail_ID] ASC))
           |         |    |--Bookmark Lookup(...(...[Shipments] AS [S]))
           |         |         |--Nested Loops(Inner Join)
           |         |              |--Bookmark Lookup(...(...[Order_Details] AS
[OD]))
           |         |              |    |--Nested Loops(Inner Join)
           |         |              |         |--Filter(WHERE:([O].[Business_Unit_
ID]=10))
           |         |              |         |    |--Bookmark Lookup(    (
[Orders] AS [O]))
           |         |              |         |         |--Nested Loops(Inner Join)
           |         |              |         |              |--Bookmark Lookup(...
(...
(wrapped line) [Customers] AS [C]))
           |         |              |         |              |    |--Index Seek(...
(...
(wrapped line) [Customers].[Customer_Phone_Number]
(wrapped line) AS [C]), SEEK:([C].[Phone_Number]='6505551212') ORDERED)
           |         |              |         |              |--Index Seek(...(...
(wrapped line) [Orders].[Order_Customer_ID] AS [O]),
(wrapped line) SEEK:([O].[Customer_ID]=[C].[Customer_ID]) ORDERED)
           |         |              |         |--Index Seek(...(...
(wrapped line) [Order_Details].[Order_Detail_Order_ID]
(wrapped line) AS [OD]), SEEK:([OD].[Order_ID]=[O].[Order_ID]) ORDERED)
           |         |              |--Index Seek(...(...[Shipments].[Shipment_PKey]
(wrapped line) AS [S]), SEEK:([S].[Shipment_ID]=[OD].[Shipment_ID]) ORDERED)
           |         |--Index Seek(...(...[Addresses].[Address_PKey]
(wrapped line) AS [A]), SEEK:([A].[Address_ID]=[S].[Address_ID]) ORDERED)
           |--Index Seek(...(...[Products].[Product_PKey]
(wrapped line) AS [P]), SEEK:([P].[Product_ID]=[OD].[Product_ID]) ORDERED)

(19 row(s) affected)
```

Good news! The corrected SQL leads to exactly the optimum plan here. Just out of curiosity, you check the execution plan for the original SQL, and you find the same result! Evidently, SQL Server is doing the data conversion on the constant, avoiding disabling the index.

# Altering the Database to Enable the Best Plan

The earlier results on DB2 and SQL Server have already demonstrated that the database design has the necessary indexes to enable the execution plan that you need, unless the Oracle database is missing indexes that you have on the other databases. Therefore, you could skip this step. However, if you did not already know that they existed, you would check for indexes on Customers(Phone_Number), Orders(Customer_ID), and Order_Details(Order_ID) using the methods of Chapter 3. You can generally take for granted that the primary-key indexes that you need already exist. Look for missing primary-key indexes only when more likely reasons for an incorrect execution plan do not solve the problem and lead you to check for unusual sources of trouble.

# Altering the SQL to Enable the Best Plan

You already suspect that the solution to getting a good plan on Oracle is to eliminate the type inconsistency on that platform. After all, the other databases avoided the type conversion on the indexed column and delivered a good plan. Therefore, immediately try the query again on Oracle, but with the corrected comparison C.Phone_Number = '6505551212' to avoid the implicit datatype conversion. Use the original setting for rule-based optimization to check the execution plan:

```
PLAN
-------------------------------------------------------------------------------
SELECT STATEMENT
  SORT ORDER BY
    NESTED LOOPS
      NESTED LOOPS
        NESTED LOOPS
          NESTED LOOPS
            NESTED LOOPS
              TABLE ACCESS BY INDEX ROWID 4*CUSTOMERS
                INDEX RANGE SCAN CUSTOMER_PHONE_NUMBER
              TABLE ACCESS BY INDEX ROWID 1*ORDERS
                INDEX RANGE SCAN ORDER_CUSTOMER_ID
            TABLE ACCESS BY INDEX ROWID 2*ORDER_DETAILS
              INDEX RANGE SCAN ORDER_DETAIL_ORDER_ID
          TABLE ACCESS BY INDEX ROWID 5*SHIPMENTS
            INDEX UNIQUE SCAN SHIPMENT_PKEY
        TABLE ACCESS BY INDEX ROWID 3*PRODUCTS
          INDEX UNIQUE SCAN PRODUCT_PKEY
      TABLE ACCESS BY INDEX ROWID 6*ADDRESSES
        INDEX UNIQUE SCAN ADDRESS_PKEY
```

This is precisely the execution plan you want. Suspecting that the application will soon switch to cost-based optimization, you check the cost-based execution plan, and it turns out to be the same.

Both Oracle optimizers now return the optimal plan, so you should be done! To verify this, you run the SQL with the *sqlplus* option set timing on and find that Oracle returns the result in just 40 milliseconds, compared to the earlier performance of 2.4 seconds for the original rule-based execution plan and 8.7 seconds for the original cost-based execution plan

## Altering the Application

As is most commonly the case, the only change the application needs, in this example, is the slight change to the SQL itself. This is always the most favorable result, since such SQL-only changes have the lowest risk and are the easiest to make. This query will return just a few rows, since the best filter, alone, is so selective. If the query returned excessively many rows, or if the query ran excessively often just to perform a single application task, you would explore changes to the application to narrow the query or to run it less often.

## Putting the Example in Perspective

Most queries are just this easy to tune, once you master the method this book describes. Usually, a missing index or some trivial problem in the SQL is the only thing obstructing the optimizer from delivering the optimum execution plan you choose, or a plan so close to optimum as not to matter. You rarely need the elaborate special techniques covered at the end of Chapter 6 and throughout Chapter 7.

 However, when you do need the special-case techniques, you *really* need them!

The primary value of the method is that it leads you quickly to a single answer you can be completely confident in, without any nagging worries that long trial and error might just lead you to something better. When the method leads you to a super-fast query, you find little argument. When the method leads to a slower result than you'd like (usually for a query that returns thousands of rows), you need to know that the slower result really is the best you can do without stepping outside the SQL-tuning box. The outside-the-box solutions for these slower queries tend to be inconvenient. It's invaluable to know with complete confidence when these inconvenient solutions are truly necessary. You need to justify this confidence without endless, futile attempts to tune the original SQL by trial and error, and with solid arguments to make your case for more difficult solutions when needed.

# Glossary

*Proper words in proper places,*
*make the true definition of a style.*
—Jonathan Swift
*Letter to a Young Clergyman*

**Aggregation**

The summarization of details into a smaller number of summary datapoints (sums, counts, and averages, usually), usually using GROUP BY.

**Anti-join**

A *correlation join* applied to a NOT EXISTS–type subquery.

**Apples-and-oranges tables**

Tables that hold somewhat different, but related entity types within the same physical table.

**B-tree index**

A balanced, branched, sorted structure that allows the database to rapidly locate a row or set of rows that match conditions of the indexed column or columns.

**Block**

The smallest unit of physical storage or cached storage in a database. Blocks are usually just a few kilobytes in size and most often contain from less than one hundred rows to at most a few hundred rows.

**Block buffer cache**

The cache that stores recently used table and index blocks in shared memory for logical I/O, avoiding the need for physical I/O of the cached blocks. Any user's SQL can read blocks into the block buffer cache, and any other user's SQL automatically takes advantage of these cached blocks. See *LRU caching*.

**Branch block**

An index block that the database reaches from a root block or a higher branch block. The branch block, in turn, points to leaf blocks or lower branch blocks that contain entries in the desired range. See *root block* and *leaf block*.

**Cache-hit ratio**

The fraction of logical I/Os that avoid physical I/Os.

**Cartesian join**

A join between two tables or two combinations of tables in which the SQL fails to specify any condition or combination of conditions that relate the joined tables to each other.

**Cartesian product**

The set of all possible combinations of rows from two or more rowsets. A Cartesian product results when SQL contains a *Cartesian join*.

**Cold**

A database block is said to be *cold* when it is rarely accessed. A block might be cold in the context of a particular type of I/O.

For example, a block that is hot with respect to logical I/O might be so well cached that it is cold with respect to physical I/O.

## Complex query

A multitable query that is not a simple query. See *simple query*.

## Correlation joins

The joins in subqueries that correlate the subquery rows to values from the outer query.

## Correlation preference ratio

The ratio of the runtime of the IN form (which drives from the subquery out) of a query with an EXISTS-type subquery divided by the runtime of the EXISTS form (which drives from the outer query to the subquery) of the same query. A correlation preference ratio greater than 1.0 implies that the best execution plan drives from the outer query to the subquery, since the alternative takes longer.

## CPU

Central Processing Unit. The computer component where in-memory software instructions execute. CPU operations are fast compared to physical I/O to and from the database, but databases can nonetheless spend long intervals simply consuming CPU (these intervals are called *CPU time*) to service inefficient queries against well-cached data. Logical I/O requires CPU time, while physical I/O consumes time in the disk subsystem.

## Cyclic join graph

A query diagram that has links that form a closed loop.

## Denormalization

Storage of *denormalized data* in one or more tables.

## Denormalized data

Data that is redundant with other data already available in the database. For example, storing Customer_ID in Order_ Lines would be denormalized data if a join from Order_Lines to Orders would yield the same Customer_ID stored as a column in Orders.

## Detail join ratio

The join ratio on the nonunique end of the join. See *join ratio*.

## Detail table

A table that potentially has more than one matching row for any given row in a another table (usually a *master table*) that joins to it. A table might be a master table to one table and a detail table to another, so the term *detail table* describes a table's position in a relationship with another table with respect to a particular join.

## Distributed filters

*Filter conditions* spread across multiple tables that are cumulatively more selective than the filter conditions of any one of the individual tables.

## Driving table

The first table reached as the database executes a query. The database must find a path into the driving table that does not depend on having data from any other table.

## Execution plan

The path that the database will follow to reach the data the query requires. The execution plan consists mainly of table-access methods for each table queried; a join order, beginning with the driving table; and join methods for each table joined, following the driving table.

## EXISTS-type subquery

A subquery related to the outer query with an EXISTS condition or with an IN condition capable of being converted to an EXISTS condition.

## Filter condition

A condition in the WHERE clause that can be evaluated as true or false with data from only a single table, used to narrow a query to a subset of the rows of that table. Selective filter conditions are key to efficient *execution plans*.

## Filter independence

The assumption, usually true, that you can calculate multiple-condition selectivity as the simple product of individual-condition filter ratios. For example, a condition on a person's first name and a condition on a person's Zip Code are logically independent. You can assume that the fraction of rows that have both the correct first name and the correct Zip Code will be roughly the product of the fraction of rows that have the correct name and the fraction that have the correct Zip Code. For example, if 1/100th of the rows contain the desired first name and 1/500th of the rows contain the desired Zip Code, then the multiple-condition filter selectivity is 1/50,000 $((1/100) \times (1/500))$.

## Filter ratio

The fraction of rows of a table for which a set of *filter conditions* on that single table is true. Mathematically, this is the *rowcount* from the table with the filter conditions applied divided by the complete table rowcount.

## Filter redundancy

A relationship between filters wherein the truth of one condition guarantees the truth of another (the opposite of *filter independence*). For example, a condition on a Zip Code likely guarantees a single value for telephone area code, so the selectivity of conditions on both would be no better than the selectivity of the Zip Code alone. You can always test for complete or partial filter redundancy by calculating the multicondition filter selectivity based on filter independence and seeing if it yields the actual selectivity of the combination of the conditions.

## Focus table

The table that is the current point from which to add further details to the query diagram, as you build the query diagram. When a query diagram has no missing elements around the current focus table, you choose a new focus table.

## Foreign key

A value or *tuple* stored in a table row that matches a unique key in some other table row, which is identified by the matching *primary key*.

## Full index scan

The operation of reading every index entry across all *leaf blocks*.

## Full table scan

The operation of reading an entire table directly, without first obtaining table *rowids* from an index.

## Hash join

A join method wherein the two *rowsets* being joined are reached independently, once, and matched according to the output of a randomizing hash function applied to the join columns. The smaller rowset (or at least the rowset the database expects will be smaller) is generally presorted into hash buckets in memory. Then, the database calculates the hash function on the fly while reading the larger rowset and matches rows from the larger rowset to the hashed rows in memory from the smaller rowset.

## High-water mark

The block address in a table that shows the highest block that has contained table rows since the table was created or since it was last truncated. *Full table scans* must read from the beginning of a table up to the high-water mark, including every block in the table extents between those two points, even when deletes have emptied most of those blocks.

## Hot

A database block is said to be *hot* when it is frequently accessed. A block might be hot in the context of a particular type of I/O. For example, a block that is hot with respect to logical I/O might be so well cached that it is cold with respect to physical I/O.

## I/O

Input/output. Usually refers to *physical I/O*, but it can also refer to *logical I/O*.

## Index

A database structure that helps the database efficiently reach just a desired subset of the table rows without having to read the whole table. See *B-tree index* (the most common type, by far).

### Index range scan

The operation of reading (usually with *logical I/O* from cache) an *index range* (a set that might include pointers to multiple rows) over as many *leaf blocks* as necessary.

### Individual-condition filter selectivity

The fraction of table rows that satisfy a single condition on that table.

### Inner join

An operation that matches rows between two data sources, usually tables, and returns combinations that satisfy one or more join conditions that relate the data sources. Rows are returned only in combination. Any given source row that does not have a match in the joined table is discarded.

### Join

An operation that matches rows between two data sources, usually tables. See *inner join* and *outer join*.

### Join condition

A condition in the WHERE clause that requires values from two (or, rarely, more) tables for the condition to be evaluated as true or false. Conditions in a WHERE clause that are not *filter conditions* are join conditions. Join conditions typically provide an efficient path to other tables, once you reach rows from the best possible *driving table*.

### Join filter

A *join ratio* that turns out to be less than 1.0, resulting in a loss of rows when performing the join itself. Only *inner joins* can have join filters.

### Join ratio

For a join between table A and table B, the *join ratio* on the A end of the join is the *rowcount* of the join of A and B divided by the rowcount of B. If A is a *detail table* to *master table* B, the join ratio on the A end (the *detail join ratio*) conveys "how many" details A contains in its many-to-zero or many-to-one relationship to B. On the B end of the same join, the *master join ratio* conveys "how often it is one" on the zero-to-one end of the same many-to-zero or many-to-one relationship.

### Join skeleton

Same as *query skeleton*, that part of the query diagram that shows how the tables join but does not include filter ratios or join ratios.

### Leaf block

A lowest-level index block that the database reaches from a *root block* or a *branch block*. Leaf blocks do not point to lower-level index blocks. Instead, they point to table blocks that hold the indexed rows. A leaf block contains *tuples* of indexed column values and *rowids* that point to rows that contain those column values.

### Logical I/O

Any read or write of a database block from or to the shared cache during the execution of SQL, even if the database must first read the block from disk to place it in the shared cache.

### LRU caching

The usual form of caching a database uses to keep blocks in the shared cache. In LRU caching, the database overwrites the least recently used (LRU) cached block (at the *tail* of the cached list of blocks) whenever the database needs to read a new block off disk into cache. Subsequently, logical I/O to a cache moves blocks to the *head* of the list, where the most recently used blocks reside. Databases sometimes treat I/O for large *full table scans* as a special case, leaving blocks from full table scans at the tail of the LRU cache to avoid pushing more useful blocks off the cache.

### Many-to-one join

A join from a *detail table* to a *master table*.

### Master join ratio

The join ratio on the unique end of the join. See *join ratio*.

### Master table

A table that has at most one matching row for every row in another table (usually a *detail table*) that joins to it. A table might be a master table to one table and a detail table to another, so the term *master table* describes a table's position in a relationship with another table with respect to a particular join.

## Middleware

Software that moves data around within a system or systems, without sending that data to the end users. Since end users aren't part of the picture and computers have plenty of patience for large data volumes, these batch processes sometimes legitimately need to handle data volumes that are too large for human consumption.

## Multiple-condition filter selectivity

The fraction of table rows that satisfy the combination of conditions that refer exclusively to that table.

## Nested-loops join

A join method that uses each row of the query result reached so far to drive into the joined-to table, usually through an index on the join key.

## Normalized data

Wholly nonredundant data (data that lacks denormalized data). See *denormalized data*.

## NOT EXISTS–type subquery

A subquery related to the outer query with a NOT EXISTS condition, or a NOT IN condition capable of being converted to a NOT EXISTS condition.

## Outer join

An operation that combines rows between two data sources, usually tables. An outer join returns rows that satisfy either the inner case of the outer join or the outer case of the outer join. Rows that satisfy the inner case of the outer join are identical to the result the database would return if the outer join were replaced by an inner join. In the outer case of the outer join, the database finds no matching row in the joined-to table but returns a row that appends columns from the joined-from row to artificial all-null columns wherever the SQL references the joined-to table.

## Physical I/O

The subset (usually small) of logical I/O that fails to find the necessary block cached, resulting in a call for a physical read or write. Although the database views any call to the access disk as physical I/O, the operating system and the disk subsystem normally maintain caches of their own and often rapidly satisfy disk-access calls without true physical I/O that requires slow physical disk reads.

## Post-read filter

A *filter condition* that can be evaluated for truth only after the database reads a table row in a given execution plan. The index used to reach the table does not contain the data necessary to evaluate the truth of the post-read filter condition, so the database must first read the table row to find columns that the post-read filter references.

## Primary key

A value or *tuple* stored in a table row that uniquely identifies a row in a table. *Foreign keys* point to primary keys. In a one-to-one relationship, a primary key can also serve as a foreign key.

## Query diagram

A diagram in the form of nodes and links, with associated numerical values, such as *filter ratios* and *join ratios*. The query diagram concisely conveys the mathematical essentials of a query tuning problem. Chapter 5 describes how to create a query diagram from a SQL query, and Chapter 7 adds some refinements for complex queries.

## Query skeleton

Same as *join skeleton*, that part of the query diagram that shows how the tables join but does not include filter ratios or join ratios.

## Referential integrity

A property of a *foreign key* such that every row in the table has a foreign-key value that points to a matching *primary key* for a row in the corresponding *master table*. When foreign keys fail to have referential integrity, you can usually infer a defect in the application or database design, since foreign keys become meaningless when they fail to point to primary keys that are still in existence.

## Robust execution plan

An *execution plan* that reaches the *driving table* efficiently, usually through an indexed read, and that reaches the rest of the tables through nested loops to the join-key indexes.

## Root detail table

A table in a query diagram that joins to other tables only through *foreign keys*, lying at the detail end of every join it takes part in. Most query diagrams take the form of a tree, with a single root detail table at the top. Rows returned from such a query map one-to-one with rows that the query returns from the root detail table. The root detail table is usually the largest table in the query.

## Root block

The first block read for an *index range scan* or unique scan on a *B-tree index*. The root block contains pointers to the subranges covered by each index block at the level below, when the index does not fit into a single block. Occasionally (usually when the index covers fewer than 300 rows), the entire index fits within the root block. Root blocks of useful indexes are almost invariably cached, since they require logical I/O too frequently to reach the tail end of the LRU cache.

## Rowid

The internal address of a physical table row, consisting of a block address that points to the table block that contains the row and a row address within the block, leading directly to the actual row.

## Rowcount

The count of rows in a *rowset*.

## Rowset

Any set of rows—either table rows or result rows from a complete or partial query. During execution of a query, the database builds return rowsets as it joins queried tables, discarding rows along the way when inner joins fail to find matches or when joined table rows fail to meet query conditions, finally returning rows that satisfy all conditions of the query.

## Self-caching

Most queries find most of the blocks they need already cached by earlier queries, usually from other sessions. *Self-caching* happens when a query performs repeated logical I/O to the same database blocks that might not have been cached before the query started. The initial I/O to each of these blocks might be physical, but the tendency of queries to reuse the same blocks provides self-caching, in which the query itself ensures that the cache becomes loaded with blocks that are needed repeatedly by that query. The effectiveness of self-caching depends on how well-clustered the queried rows are (i.e., how closely they reside in the physical tables and indexes). Self-caching is especially effective for index blocks, especially higher-level index blocks.

## Semi-join

A *correlation join* applied to an EXISTS-type subquery.

## Simple query

A query that meets the following conditions: (1) The query maps to one tree. (2) The tree has exactly one root (one table with no join to its *primary key*). All nodes other than the root node have a single downward-pointing arrow that links them to a detail node above, but any node can be at the top end of any number of downward-pointing arrows. (3) All joins have downward-pointing arrows (joins that are unique on one end). (4) *Outer joins* are unfiltered, pointing down, with only outer joins below outer joins. (5) The question that the query answers is basically a question about the entity represented at the top (root) of the tree or about aggregations of that entity. (6) The other tables just provide reference data that is stored elsewhere for normalization.

## Sort-merge join

A join method in which the two *rowsets* being joined are reached independently, once, sorted, and matched by a coordinated merge of the rowsets sorted on the join keys.

**Subquery adjusted filter ratio**

An estimated value that helps you choose the best point in the join order to test the subquery condition.

**Subquery root detail table**

The *root detail table* of the query diagram of the subquery, isolated from the outer query.

**Tuple**

An ordered grouping of a fixed number of values, especially column values or expressions. For example, two-column primary keys consist of two-value tuples that map to unique table rows.

**View-defining query**

The query that defines a database view— the result you get if you perform SELECT * FROM <View_Name>.

**View-using query**

Any query that references a database view.

# Index

<> (angle brackets), surrounding missing
portions of SQL statement, xvii
( ) (parentheses)
in FROM clause for DB2, 101
surrounding ordered list of items, xvii
+ (plus sign)
in comment, 92
in join clause, 199

## A

aggregation, 295
not included in query diagrams, 113
queries aggregating too many rows, 248,
255, 263
in reports, 261
(see also grouping; post group filtering)
ALL_ROWS hint, 94
AND-EQUAL MERGE operation, 36
angle brackets (<>), surrounding missing
portions of SQL statement, xvii
anti-join, 212, 295
apples-and-oranges tables, 295
application
altering, determining necessity of, 7, 248,
250, 254, 265
altering, example of, 292, 293
caching in, 251, 252
data volume produced by, 2, 250,
254–263
transferring data between
applications, 264
(see also queries)
arithmetic expressions, indexes disabled
when using, 74

arrow
absence of, at ends of link, 181
at end of link, 111
at midpoint of link, 121, 205
audience for this book, xiv
author, contact information for, xviii

## B

batch reports, large, 257–263
Beaulieu, Alan (Mastering Oracle SQL), xiv
benefit-to-cost ratio, 233, 235
bind variable peeking, 91
bit-mapped indexes, 21
blind queries, 255
block buffer cache, 9, 295
blocks, 13, 295
branch, 16, 295
cold, 10, 295
hot, 10, 297
caching of, 10, 11
choosing for performance, 12
hot data grouped in, 11
indexed access and, 25
physical I/O on, 11
query causing, 11
leaf, 16, 298
LRU (least recently used), 10
MRU (most recently used), 10
root, 16, 300
books
about Oracle Performance, 246
about Oracle SQL, xiv
branch blocks, 16, 295
B-tree indexes, 15, 295

We'd like to hear your suggestions for improving our indexes. Send email to *index@oreilly.com*.

## C

cache-hit ratio, 13, 295
caching, 9–12
    in application, 251, 252
    block buffer cache, 295
    B-tree indexes and, 17
    continuous growth pattern and, 13
    full table scans and, 23
    indexed table access and, 25
    LRU caching, 10, 298
    performance effects of, 11
    purge eldest pattern and, 14
    purge, not by age pattern and, 14
    self-caching, 11, 300
calcuations (see benefit-to-cost ratio;
        cache-hit ratio; correlation
        preference ratio; join ratio; filter
        ratio)
capitalized text used in this book, xvii
Cartesian join, 37, 295
Cartesian product, 295
    optimizing execution plan for, 152,
        153–156
    resulting from absence of join, 186–187
    resulting from query with multiple
        roots, 188, 190
CBO (see cost-based optimizer)
Central Processing Unit (see CPU)
cloud of nodes, 137
COALESCE() function, 77
cold blocks, 10, 295
columns
    relevance to SQL tuning, 112
    statistics for, used by cost-based
        optimizer, 83
comments about this book, sending, xviii
complete purge and regrowth pattern, 14
complex queries, 176, 296
    abnormal outer joins in, 197–203
    cyclic joins in, 177–185
    disconnected queries, 185–187
    joins with no primary key in, 192
    multiple roots in, 188–192
    one-to-one joins in, 193–197
    set operations in, 225
    subqueries in, 203
    views in, 216–225
conditions (see filters; joins; selectivity)
contact information for this book, xviii
continuous growth pattern, 13
conventions used in this book, xvi

corner-case problems, 6
    abnormal query diagrams indicating, 127
    changing functionality for, 222
    view-using queries causing, 217
correlated subqueries, forcing evaluation
        of, 96
correlation joins, 82, 296
    anti-join, 212, 295
    in query diagrams, 204
    semi-join, 205–209, 300
correlation preference ratio, 205, 209, 296
cost-based optimizer, 84, 85
    choosing, 86–89
    controlling execution plans with, 90–97
    response to varying table and index
        sizes, 114
    rule-based optimizer used with, 89
    statistics affecting, 83
CPU (Central Processing Unit), 296
cyclic join graphs, 177–185, 296

## D

data
    amount produced by application, 2, 250,
        254–263
    denormalized, 296
    normalized, 299
    path to (see data access; execution plans)
    transferring between applications, 264
data access
    caching and, 9–12
    indexes and, 15–18, 21
    joins and, 36–42
    reasons to understand, 8
    selectivity, 27–36
    single-table access paths, 22–27
    tables and, 12–14, 18, 20
data type conversions, indexes enabled and
        disabled by, 31, 74
database
    adding merged join and filter indexes
        to, 243–245
    adding missing indexes to, 246
    adding table to, for joins with hidden join
        filters, 195
    altering, example of, 292
    combining tables in
        for exact one-to-one joins, 194
        for joins with hidden join filters, 195
    separating tables in, for one-to-one join to
        small subset, 195
    (see also caching; indexes; tables)

## G

graph theory, 177
graphs, 177
    (see also cyclic join graphs; query
        diagrams)
GROUP BY clause (see aggregation;
        grouping)
grouping, not included in query
        diagram, 113

## H

hash bucket, 41
HASH hint, 104
hash joins, 40, 297
    forcing use of, 97, 104
    in Oracle execution plan, 52
    in SQL Server execution plan, 70
    when to use, 115, 141, 171–174, 230, 247
HAVING clause (see post-group filtering)
hidden join filters, 130, 159, 195
high-water mark, 13, 14, 297
hints
    in Oracle, 92–97
    in SQL Server, 104–107
hot blocks, 10, 297
    caching of, 10, 11
    choosing for performance, 12
    hot data grouped in, 11
    indexed access and, 25
    physical I/O on, 11
    query causing, 11
    (see also self-caching)

## I

icons used in this book, xvii
IN condition, execution order when
        using, 81
index blocks, 16, 295, 298, 300
INDEX() hint, 94
index range scan, 16, 298
index range-condition selectivity, 30–33
INDEX_DESC() hint, 94
indexed table access, 23–25
    in DB2 execution plan, 61
    in Oracle execution plan, 49
    in SQL Server execution plan, 68
    when to use, 25–27
indexes, 15–18, 23–25, 297
    adding, effects on performance, 17
    adding for specific queries, 243–245

bit-mapped indexes, 21
B-tree indexes, 15, 295
combining, 35
date-type columns in, 32
disabling use of, 77
dropping, risks of, 247
enabling use of, 74–76
forcing use in descending order, 94
forcing use of specific index, 94, 104
full index scan, 33, 297
function-based, 30
with merged join key and filter
        columns, 243–245
missing, 138, 140, 246
rowids used by, 16
satisfying query without accessing
        database, 112
selectivity on rows reached from, 33 35
size of
    caching and, 11
    cost-based optimizer's response
        to, 114
    statistics for, used by cost-based
        optimizer, 83
    updating, performance effects of, 18
index-organized tables, 18
individual-condition filter selectivity, 28, 298
inequality condition, index ranges with, 33
inner joins, 37, 101, 298
Input/Output (see I/O)
inserts into index, performance effects of, 17
INTERSECT operation (see set operations)
I/O (Input/Output), 297
    logical, 9, 11, 35, 298
    physical, 9, 10, 299
italic font used in this book, xvi, xvii

## J

join execution methods, 38–42
    hash joins, 40
        forcing use of, 97, 104
        in Oracle execution plan, 52
        in SQL Server execution plan, 70
        when to use, 115, 141, 171–174, 230,
          247
    nested-loops joins, 39
        in DB2 execution plan, 60
        forcing use of, 97, 104
        in Oracle execution plan, 48
        in SQL Server execution plan, 68
        when to use, 135, 228–230

join execution methods (*continued*)
  sort-merge joins, 41
    in DB2 execution plan, 63
    in Oracle execution plan, 52
    when to use, 141, 247
join filters, 130, 159, 195, 298
join key, merged with filter column in
    index, 243–245
join order
  calculating cost of, 116
  choosing, 136–145, 147–151, 233–236
  controlling, 95, 145
  disabling undesired join orders, 79–81
  enabling desired join order, 78
  for outer joins, 240–243
  (see also execution plans)
join ratio, 112, 298
  calculating, 122–124
  information about actual data provided
    by, 126
  less than 1.0, 158–167
    (see also join filters)
  in query diagrams, 112, 128
  referential integrity, effect on, 125
  shortcuts for, 124, 125
  (see also detail join ratio; master join
    ratio)
join skeleton (query skeleton), 298
joins, 36–38, 298
  anti-join, 212, 295
  Cartesian join, 37, 295
  condition for, 298
    missing, 188, 189, 192
    not included in query diagrams, 113
  correlation join, 82, 204, 296
  cyclic, 177–185, 296
  forcing order of, 89, 104
  hash join (see hash joins)
  inner joins, 37, 101, 298
  many-to-one, 298
  missing, 186
  multipart join, 182–184
  nested-loops join (see nested-loops joins)
  one-to-many, unintended, 191
  one-to-one, 178–179, 193–197
  order of (see join order)
  outer joins (see outer joins)
  in query diagrams, 111, 120–122
  redundant joins, 78
  semi-join, 205–209, 300
  sort-merge join (see sort-merge joins)

unfiltered, 247
unnecessary, in queries with views, 224
without primary key, 192

## K

keys
  foreign key, 297, 299
  join key, merged with filter columns in
    index, 243–245
  primary key, 111, 192, 299

## L

LEADING hint, 95
leaf blocks, 16, 298
least recently used blocks (see LRU blocks)
least recently used caching (see LRU caching)
links in query diagrams, 111
logic errors, 7
  (see also problem cases)
logical I/O, 298
  performance of, 11, 35
  pure, caching used for, 9
LOOP hint, 104
LRU (least recently used) blocks, 10
LRU (least recently used) caching, 10, 298

## M

many-to-one join, 298
master join ratio, 112, 298
  equal to 1.0, affecting optimum execution
    plan, 152
  example of, 286
  less than 1.0, affecting optimum execution
    plan, 159, 164–167
  shortcuts for, 125
master table, 298
Mastering Oracle SQL (Mishra;
    Beaulieu), xiv
memory-only data access (see pure logical
    I/O)
merge joins (see sort-merge joins)
merged join and filter indexes, 243–245
Microsoft SQL Server (see SQL Server)
middleware, 2, 264, 299
Millsap, Cary (Optimizing Oracle
    Performance), 246
MINUS operation (see set operations)
Mishra, Sanjay (Mastering Oracle SQL), xiv
most recently used blocks (see MRU blocks)

partitioned tables, 20

path to data (see data access; execution
  plans)

performance
  adding indexes affecting, 17
  caching scheme affecting, 11
  calculations performed on data
    affecting, 2
  compared to throughput, 3
  database operations affecting, 2
  logical I/Os and, 35
  physical layout of table rows and, 12
  SQL as factor in, xiii
  (see also SQL tuning)

physical I/O, 299
  caching used to minimize, 9
  performance of, 10

PLAN_TABLE table, 44

plus sign (+)
  in comment, 92
  in join clause, 199

post-group filtering, not included in query
    diagram, 113

post-read filter, 52, 62, 299

primary keys, 299
  indicated by arrows in query
    diagrams, 111
  missing from join, 192

problem cases
  abnormal outer joins, 197–203
  all tables relatively small except
    one, 145–147
  Cartesian products between first set of
    rows, 153–156
  corner-case problems, 6, 127, 217, 222
  cyclic join graphs, 177–185
  detail join ratios close to 1.0, 157–158
  detail join ratios less than 1.0, 159–164,
    188
  disconnected query diagrams, 185–187
  filter ratios close to each other, 167–171
  join ratios less than 1.0, 158–167
  joining to the same table twice, 179
  joins with no primary key, 192
  large detail join ratios, 172
  large rowcount returned by query, 171
  master join ratios less than 1.0, 159,
    164–167
  middleware processes handling too many
    rows, 264
  one-to-one joins, 178–179, 193–197
  outer joins to views, 221–223

performance and throughput problems, 3

queries aggregating too many rows, 248,
  255, 263

queries repeated a large number of
  times, 248, 250–254

queries returning too many rows, 248,
  254–263

queries running slowly even when
  returning few rows, 248, 265–268

queries with set operations, 225

queries with subqueries, 203, 213–215

queries with views, 216, 220–225

query diagrams with multiple
  roots, 188–192

redundant reads in view-using
  queries, 224

unfiltered joins, 247

unnecessary nodes and joins, 224
  (see also exercises; SQL tuning)

programmers, tuning their own SQL, 3

pure logical I/O, caching used for, 9

purge eldest pattern, 14

purge, not by age pattern, 14

PUSH_SUBQ hint, 96

# Q

queries
  aggregating too many rows, 248, 255, 263
  altering to enable optimum execution
    plan, 292
  for batch reports, large, 257–263
  blind, 255
  choosing indexed access or full table scan
    for, 26
  complex queries, 176
    abnormal outer joins in, 197–203
    cyclic joins in, 177–185
    disconnected, 185–187
    joins with no primary keys in, 192
    multiple roots in, 188–192
    one-to-one joins in, 193–197
    set operations in, 225
    subqueries in, 203
    views in, 216–225
  distributed filters in, 265–268
  errors in (see problem cases)
  middleware processes handling too many
    rows in, 264
  modifying with DB2, 100–102
  modifying with Oracle, 92–97
  modifying with SQL Server, 104–107

subquery adjusted filter ratio, 206, 210, 301
subquery root detail table, 301
Sybase
    execution plans for, 66
    FORCEPLAN option, 107
    (see also SQL Server)

## T

tables, 12–14
    adding, for joins with hidden join
        filters, 195
    aliases of, in query diagrams, 110
    apples-and-oranges tables, 295
    combining
        for exact one-to-one joins, 194
        for tables with hidden join filters, 195
    complete purge and regrowth pattern
        for, 14
    conditions on (see filters; joins; selectivity)
    continuous growth pattern for, 13
    detail table, 296
    driving, 39, 95, 136, 153–156, 230–233,
        296
    focus table, 297
    full table scan, 22, 25–27, 94, 104, 297
    growth patterns for, 12–14
    high-water mark of, 13, 14, 297
    indexed access of, 23–27, 49, 61, 68
    index-organized, 18
    large
        affecting caching, 12, 23
        affecting indexed read
            performance, 25, 27
        affecting optimum execution
            plan, 145–147, 152
        nested loops for, 229
    master table, 298
    multitable clusters, 20
    multitable queries, 36–42
    names of, not included in query
        diagram, 113
    nodes representing (see nodes)
    partitioned, 20
    physical layout of, affecting
        performance, 12
    purge eldest pattern for, 14
    purge, not by age pattern for, 14
    root detail table, 300
    selectivity on rows reached from
        index, 33–35

separating, for one-to-one join to small
    subset, 195
single-table access paths, 22–27
single-table clusters, 20
single-table queries, 22–27
size of
    cost-based optimizer's response
        to, 114
    indicating necessity of index, 23
    represented in query diagrams, 113
    small, affecting caching, 11
    statistics for, used by cost-based
        optimizer, 83
throughput, 3
    (see also performance)
TOAD software tool, 43
transitivity, implying missing join conditions
    with, 178
TRUNCATE command, 14
tuning (see SQL tuning)
tuple, 301
two node filter, 180–182, 185
type conversions, indexes enabled and
    disabled by, 31, 74

## U

underlined numbers in query diagrams, 111
unfiltered joins, 247
UNION ALL operation (see set operations)
UNION operation (see set operations)
unique indexes, performance effects of, 18
unique keys (see primary keys)
updates in index, performance effects of, 18
uppercase text used in this book, xvii
upstream nodes, when to choose, 235
USE_HASH hint, 97
USE_NL hint, 97

## V

vendors, database
    SQL tuning and, xiii, 1
    tools for execution plans provided by, 43
view-defining queries, 216, 301
views, 216–225
    nested, created by DB2, 101
    outer joins to, 221–223
    tuning queries with, 216, 220–225
view-using queries, 216, 217–220, 224, 301
Visual Explain tool, 54

# W

web sites
    author's, xviii
    O'Reilly & Associates, Inc., xviii
    O'Reilly catalog page for this book, xviii,
       286
WHERE clause (see filters; joins)
WITH (INDEX( )) hint, 104
WITH (NOLOCK) hint, 104

## About the Author

**Dan Tow** is an independent consultant, operating under the banner *Singing*SQL (*www.singingsql.com*). His experience solving Oracle-related performance problems goes all the way back to his 1989 hire by Oracle Corporation. During most of his tenure at Oracle, Dan focused on the performance of Oracle Applications, managing the performance group for that division. In this role, he found a fertile testing ground for his SQL tuning method applied to the huge set of complex SQL contained in those applications, including both online SQL and diverse batch processes. In 1998, Dan left Oracle to lead performance for TenFold Corporation, where he applied the same methods to tuning questions on DB2, SQL Server, and Sybase, as well as on Oracle.

In 2002, Dan started his own business, *Singing*SQL, through which he offers diverse database-related tuning services, including SQL tuning and systematically analyzing load to learn which SQL should be tuned. He has introduced his SQL tuning method to over 1,000 people in short lectures, and he now offers in-depth courses in the material, using this book as his textbook.

Dan lives in Palo Alto, California, and can be reached at *dantow@singingsql.com*.

## Colophon

Our look is the result of reader comments, our own experimentation, and feedback from distribution channels. Distinctive covers complement our distinctive approach to technical topics, breathing personality and life into potentially dry subjects.

The animal on the cover of *SQL Tuning* is a salamander. Though mature salamanders bear a superficial resemblance to small lizards, salamanders are not reptiles; rather, they are amphibians that retain their tails as adults. Like all amphibians, a salamander begins life underwater as a gelatinous egg and develops through a series of stages. Newly hatched salamander larvae resemble tadpoles (the larval form of toads and frogs) and breathe through gills. As they mature, salamanders develop legs and lungs, which allow them to leave the water and breathe air. But they remain in or around streams, rivers, ponds, lakes, or moist woodlands throughout their lives. They must return to a freshwater source to lay their eggs.

The most immediately recognizable difference between adult salamanders and lizards is the former's lack of scales; a salamander's skin is smooth and porous and is used to absorb moisture. Salamanders' skin can be any of a variety of colors—from brown or black to yellow or red—and is often covered with dark spots, bars, or stripes. As they grow, salamanders molt their skin, usually every few days or every few weeks. Salamanders also have the ability to shed and regrow their tails and other parts of their body that become severed or damaged. Unlike other amphibians, salamanders are carnivorous at every stage of their life cycle (tadpoles are herbivorous), and their diet consists of worms, insects, snails, and small fish.

Mature salamanders are usually about 4 to 8 inches long, though they can be as short as 2 inches and as long as 70 inches. Most have four legs, though some have only two forelegs. Their front feet each have four clawless toes, while hind feet, when present, have five toes. Salamanders are nocturnal and usually divide their time between the land and water, though some live exclusively in the water and a few are purely land-dwelling. When they swim, they make little use of their limbs. Instead, they use their laterally compressed (i.e., taller than it is wide) tail and muscle contraction to propel themselves through the water, as eels do. Some tree-dwelling salamanders have prehensile tails, which they can use to grasp branches.

The name *salamander* (from the Greek *salamandra*) originally applied to a legendary creature that could live in and extinguish fire. Aristotle is largely responsible for perpetuating this myth; in his *History of Animals*, he supports the story that the salamander "not only walks through the fire but puts it out in doing so." The application of the name *salamander* to an actual amphibian was first recorded in 1611, at which time the supernatural characteristics of the mythological animal became attributed to the actual animal. The common belief (mistaken, of course) that salamanders can endure fire persisted well into the 19th century.

Brian Sawyer was the production editor and copyeditor for *SQL Tuning*. Matt Hutchinson was the proofreader. Darren Kelly and Claire Cloutier provided quality control. Angela Howard wrote the index.

Ellie Volckhausen designed the cover of this book, based on a series design by Edie Freedman. The cover image is a 19th-century engraving from the Dover Pictorial Archive. Emma Colby produced the cover layout with QuarkXPress 4.1 using Adobe's ITC Garamond font.

Melanie Wang designed the interior layout, based on a series design by David Futato. This book was converted by Julie Hawks to FrameMaker 5.5.6 with a format conversion tool created by Erik Ray, Jason McIntosh, Neil Walls, and Mike Sierra that uses Perl and XML technologies. The text font is Linotype Birka; the heading font is Adobe Myriad Condensed; and the code font is LucasFont's TheSans Mono Condensed. The illustrations that appear in the book were produced by Robert Romano and Jessamyn Read using Macromedia FreeHand 9 and Adobe Photoshop 6. The tip and warning icons were drawn by Christopher Bing. This colophon was written by Brian Sawyer.